Are there [illegible] sh-
bucklers [illegible] usi-
ness deci[illegible] ves
is there r[illegible] ar?
It wasn't [illegible] en-
hauer tha[illegible] ese
questions.

Both Ike and his former employer, Robert Vesco, are rugged individualists and the stuff of which great narrative is made. When Ike recounted his experiences to me as commander of international corporate buccaneer Robert Vesco's Boeing 707 jet aircraft, I knew this story had to be told. In a year of political sex exposés and kick-back scandals what could be more timely than the inside story of a man like Robert Lee Vesco? Ike Eisenhauer, the man who flew Vesco around the world, provides the astonishing, true tale of an incredible—and successful—quest for power and riches. Possibly one of the biggest investment capers of all time! Ike's book proves the old adage; money is freely convertible to power and visa versa.

This book is all Ike's, his impressions, his special turn of a phrase. He's not only a helluva pilot, he's a born storyteller . . . with an unerringly vivid memory. My function was to direct this ribald, rollicking, sometimes shocking, and always revealing epic of the global skyways and get it published. Day-by-day writing and rewriting assistance came from our esteemed colleague, Bob Flood.

I am confident that the reader will find this book as fascinating to read as I found it to be. They don't make 'em like Ike anymore, I'm afraid. And one doesn't often see the likes of a Vesco, either . . . not even in fiction. Somehow I get the feeling we'll be hearing from each of these characters again!

—Robin Moore
Westport, Conn.
June 1976

The Flying Carpetbagger

by Captain A. L. "Ike" Eisenhauer
with Robert J. Flood & Robin Moore

PINNACLE BOOKS NEW YORK CITY

Dedication

To Dottie and to Lou—my right and left hands—and the rest of the world's finest crew; to the martyrs in all aviation who don't know the sky isn't blue; to Howard, to Marvin, to Vito, and Chuck; to Al, Ned, Pete, Ron, and friend Bruce; to slaves of the flying machine anywhere . . . don't unchain; move around; and stay loose.

And to Barry Farber.

THE FLYING CARPETBAGGER

Photo Credits: The photographs in this book are published with permission as indicated here, on a page by page basis, from top to bottom, left to right, according to layout: Page One: UPI. Page Two: Wide World, Wide World, courtesy of author. Page Three: both courtesy of Wide World. Page Four: Wide World, UPI. Page Five: Wide World, UPI. Pages Six, Seven, Eight, Nine, Ten, and Eleven: all courtesy of the author. Page Twelve: UPI. Page Thirteen: Keystone. Pages Fourteen and Fifteen: all courtesy of Wide World. Page Sixteen: UPI.

An original Pinnacle Books edition, published for the first time anywhere.

ISBN: 0-523-00985-2

First printing, September 1976
Cover photo courtesy of A. L. Eisenhauer

Printed in the United States of America

PINNACLE BOOKS, INC.
275 Madison Avenue
New York, N. Y. 10016

The Flying Carpetbagger

1

May 9, 1974 Tocumen—Newark

"Panama, this is Niner-Niner Whiskey Tango ready to take it on the roll."

"Boeing Niner-Niner Whiskey Tango, you are cleared for takeoff. Contact departure control airborne and have a nice trip."

"Thank you gentlemen. Keep the faith—be seeing you." In a pig's ass, we would! This was a one-way trip—out!

The Silver Phyllis lumbered onto the runway from the taxi strip. I took one look down that long stretch of concrete and made a decision. I stopped the airplane. My crew looked at me and, although they wouldn't say, I knew they were wondering what I was up to. If the guys in the tower were watching—and I knew they were—they were wondering too. I had called for a rolling takeoff, then, for no apparent reason, I had stopped the plane.

"Takeoff power—all four!" With the brakes locked, the crew now knew what was going on. A rolling takeoff would, for my purposes, use up too much runway. I wanted to be off the ground—now! It was like my carrier days, when the engines had to be at full power before starting takeoff. When the brakes were released you felt like you were being kicked in the ass by an elephant.

The engineer gave me what I asked for; full, roaring power. Silver Phyllis bucked under the force of more than 70,000 pounds of thrust. She literally skipped forward. But I held her back.

Silver Phyllis shook like a dog shitting peach pits. But I wouldn't let her go.

"You've got it, Captain. Across the board!" my engineer yelled. But I still held back. I had to *feel* it. I had to *hear* it. I knew something they didn't know. I had to get Silver Phyllis off the ground in 4,000 feet. There was an X factor and a Y factor operating that I didn't have time to explain. The X factor was Robert L. Vesco. The Y factor was a taxiway that intersected the runway at the 4,000-foot mark.

I was taking Robert L. Vesco's pride and joy, Silver Phyllis, the symbol of his success, out of the one place he thought it was secure. The Boeing was in Panama by design. An arrangement had been worked out by Vesco, using the close friendship between ex-President Don Pepe of Costa Rica and Brigadier General Omar Torrijos Herrera, president of Panama, to hide the Boeing. My action would have to embarrass Herrera.

I had worked for Vesco for five years. I knew him intimately. I knew what this airplane meant to him. That's why he had stashed it in Panama, to keep it safe from the very thing I was about to do—repossess it for his creditors. I knew from experience that the man had the balls of a burglar and the coldness of a Mafia hit man. To take from Vesco was to invite an almost insane retaliation. What I did not know was whether Vesco had any idea of what I was doing and, if he did, what he would do to prevent it. I would find out very soon.

I released the brakes. The Boeing sprang ahead like a quarter horse coming out of the chute. Z factor!

Z factor had nothing to do with airplanes. It had to do with the possibility of some asshole Panamanian guard, hired by Vesco and associates, hiding God-knows where in that airport, bunging off a 30.06

toward the space between my eyebrows. I was sweating blood.

"Eighty knots!" the First Officer called out. I put the Panamanian asshole out of my mind with great effort. The world, the universe, existed now only in the center line of the runway for me and for my First Officer in the airspeed indicator. I wished fervently that I had the vision of a fly. I had a morbid need to know where disaster was coming from. That four-thousand-foot point was coming up fast. I wanted to look to see if anything—a truck, a bus, a jeep load of Panamanian militia, or a guy riding a jackass with a bag full of rocks—was trying to beat me to the intersection. Anything on that runway short of my lift-off point would stop my takeoff as effectively as the entire Mormon Tabernacle Choir playing volleyball. But, like a guy driving a runaway truck through a nudist camp, I had to keep my eyes on the road. I was so uptight that even flyshit on the windshield looked ominous.

At eighty knots I had rudder pressure, the first indicator that the airplane was functioning normally. I did not have to rely on the nosewheel steering to maintain direction.

"Vee-One!" We were committed. That point of no return. We either take off or we crash. Simple as that.

"Vee-R!" the First Officer called out. I pulled back on the wheel to put the airplane into a flight attitude. Thump! The nosewheel came off the ground. The taxiway was coming up fast. But I couldn't look. All I could do was pucker.

Thump! Thump! I felt the main gear struts extend. The wheels were clear of the ground. We were airborne! We cleared that intersection by twenty feet give or take a nose hair.

"Vee-Two! Positive rate of climb!" the First Officer said. Everything was tickety-poo—except for the landing gear. Would it come up and lock? If it didn't there was only one question—where should we send the bodies?

"Gear up!" I called. The First Officer raised the lever. We both watched. The red light came on. We sweated for eight seconds. That's how long it takes for the "gear-up" sequence to be completed. All the appropriate lights went out and the familiar noises stopped, which meant that we had cleared that hurdle.

"Four hundred feet!" I began to breathe. I called for flaps "twenty" and rated power. Things were looking good. The airspeed continued to build up. At the proper time and proper speed I called for flaps up. One thousand feet, still climbing. I made a beeline for the Canal Zone, United States territory. In the unlikely event I was shot down, forced down, or ordered down, it would not be in the Republic of Panama. I had no intention of getting my ass slung in a Panamanian slammer.

"Takeoff checklist complete," my First officer said. We were at 1500 feet, less than two minutes from the time I had released the brakes. Normal procedure would have been simply to switch over to departure control frequency and continue on my nail-biting way. But my imagination was working on all twelve cylinders. I had to know if anything was boiling back at Tocumen. It wouldn't have surprised me if everybody at the airport, considering what *I* had just done, suddenly realized what *they* had just allowed to happen. I could visualize a bunch of Panamanians pointing their fingers at each other, passing the buck. What I wanted to find out was, if somebody knew what had happened, was anybody doing something about it? There was only one way to find out. I contacted Tocumen tower.

"Tocumen, Niner-Niner Whiskey Tango switching over to departure control," I said with the utmost nonchalance I could muster. As far from the fan as I was, if the shit was flying, I would be hit.

"Roger," was all I heard. Ho! Ho! Ho! I switched over to departure control. Everything was cool. I might just as well have been over Muncie, Indiana. They assigned me a heading to fly and told me to check as I passed through 18,000 feet.

Robert Lee Vesco is a mean man. He is a devious man. He is a street guy. After five years with him, through all the bullshit, I knew what the bottom line was with him. And the bottom line was: "What's mine is mine." There is something of the dog in the manger about him as well. If he couldn't have that airplane, nobody else would.

Back in Panama I had considered the probability that Vesco had had people, armed people, watching the airplane. As a matter of fact, I had actually euchred one of them into running an errand for me. I had even considered the possibility of sabotage, a missing part, an explosive device, etc., that would detonate at engine start, for example. The crew and I had even conducted a cursory search of the airplane. But it's a very big airplane and we were looking for something obvious. I did not tell the crew that I was worried about the not-so-obvious.

There are explosive devices, no bigger than a cigarette pack, that are activated by changes in air pressure. The explosion does not have to be massive. In fact, in the right place, the explosion might not even be heard. The only sounds you hear on the flight deck besides conversation, are the rush of air over the fuselage and the roar of the engines at low level. You could, of course, hear a firecracker in the cockpit, but a Boeing 707 is half the length of a football field. A small explosive charge, for example, a glob of *plastique* with a pressure-activated detonator about the size of a square of ravioli and placed in the tail section, would destroy the cable run to the elevator control and cripple the airplane in flight—all without making a hell of a lot of noise. Something as large as a deck of cards could blow the entire tail off the airplane and cause it to plummet to earth like a streamlined brick. Vesco is the kind of guy who would prefer the latter.

I didn't know if I had split the Canal Zone down the middle. At the time I didn't really care. Plan A was to go along with the flow of the game. Plan B was, if trouble developed, to ignore any instructions that would bring me within the jurisdiction of the Panamanians and to set the Silver Phyllis down in the U.S.-controlled Canal Zone. Since nobody had raised a stink, I made my turn as instructed by Departure Control and set my course for Florida. Thank God for small favors. Now I could concentrate on discovering if Vesco had taken any other preventive measures.

There are three ways you can blow up an airplane—aside from direct military action. You can set a charge with a fuse while the plane is on the ground and watch it blow. You can set a charge with a timing device and wait for it to blow while you're off having a cool drink in a hot bar. Or you can set a charge with a pressure-activated detonator and let it sit there for months. This third possibility was what I was worried about.

Vesco knew, as probably any experienced air traveler knows, that the cabin pressure of a jet seldom goes above eight thousand feet. The odds were that anybody acting for Vesco would place an explosive device within the pressurized area of the airplane, because there it would do the most damage. It would take somebody with a fairly sophisticated knowledge of aircraft construction to seek out a more exotic and fatal location. Of course I knew that Vesco had such a man on his payroll. He was a former crew member. A bastard by anybody's standards. But a knowledgeable bastard and one who could be bought. However, even *he* would probably take the easy road. I was gambling on that with the full realization that I could be wrong.

"Bring the cabin altitude up to 9,000 feet," I told the engineer. Shit, if you're going to die, do it in a hurry. Bravado? You bet your ass it was.

In jet aircraft, pressurization keeps the altitude of the cabin considerably lower than the actual altitude of the aircraft for passenger comfort. This means that at 40,000 feet the inside of the aircraft is at a much lower level, perhaps 8,000 feet. However, the rate of pressurization change is controlled from the cockpit and lags considerably behind the rate of climb of the airplane. If you want to find out if there is anything on the airplane in the pressurized area that will go *boom!* you simply throw procedure out the window, pull the plug, and go for broke. At our altitude, we had a better chance of survival if something blew. At 10,000 feet, the force of an explosion would be considerably less than at 39,000 feet, when the interior pressure of the aircraft would be many times the pressure outside the aircraft.

"Cabin's at nine, Captain," the engineer said. I

glades. Then they told me to "hold." This meant "taking a station" and flying in fucking circles until they could get me down. I wanted to tell them to "send me up a fucking fuel truck and I'll hold all night." Instead I advised them of my fuel state and they directed me to Fort Lauderdale.

I called ahead to Bruce Bottoms, Eastern Aircraft Service, to arrange for ground handling, Customs, and a place to sleep for a few hours. We needed the rest. The whole purpose of this venture was to repossess Silver Phyllis on behalf of Vesco's creditors in the United States of which, in my book, I was *numero uno*. To that end I had arranged through my New York attorney, Howard A. Singer, to obtain a writ against the aircraft through a Florida lawyer. The first person I intended to call when I finished with Customs and Immigration at Fort Lauderdale was the local lawyer. I didn't think I was going to need him to fight the United States government over Vesco's booze.

The United States Customs Service is a necessary service with a bunch of fine, intelligent, compassionate, sensible people, for the most part. But, there also exists a smattering of bureaucratic dunderheads. I, unfortunately, got at least one of these dunderheads when I landed at Fort Lauderdale. I'll admit I was not Cheerful Charlie when I got out of the goddamned airplane. I was ready for surly mechanics. I was ready for an entire battalion of fatheads. I was in that kind of a mood. After that flight all I wanted was the most boring kind of routine. If Billy Graham had come up to bless me I would have bit him on his dimpled chin. Enter the United States Customs Service.

Vesco enjoyed his booze and he kept a great deal of it aboard the Silver Phyllis. The best booze in the world costs about two cents per ounce to make. I like the stuff. It fizzes up the blood. It makes life nice. But I would not go out of my way to rescue a barrel of the finest booze in the world from spilling down a sewer. I am perfectly willing to pay for my share, an ounce and a quarter at a time, at any price the management cares to charge.

At any international airport a Customs official must

invade an arriving aircraft and survey its contents. If something he sees offends him he waxes officious. Invariably, the item or items that offend him are subject to duty and the proprietor thereof pays the duty and that's the end of it. Under present Customs regulations a returning citizen may import into this republic a certain amount of ardent waters. However, in my case the only thing I was importing into this country was a Boeing 707. And that was fucking all. Aboard said 707 was a quantity of booze of varying types. I took special pains to point this out to the particular representative of the Customs Service of the U.S. of A. I pointed out to him that the indicated beverages had been purchased outside the United States of America. That they did not have tax stamps and that, as far as I was concerned, they were proper booty for my country 'tis of thee. In short, I told him to confiscate the stuff. I didn't want it. I didn't need it. I wasn't about to pay for it, even if I had the money.

A discussion ensued. Reduced to its simplest terms the alternatives were:

1. I don't want the stuff.
2. They have no place to put it.
3. Eastern Aircraft Service has a place to put it and keep it until they dispose of it.

They conferred with Bruce. I think that they like the idea of moving the booze to E.A.S. and locking it up. I start to taxi the airplane to E.A.S. where the booze can be unloaded and locked up. I am told that if I move the airplane, I will be locked up instead of the booze. I don't like that idea. I come back to the ramp, to where the Customs people are. They are standing very firm, four of them, looking very grim, their arms folded across their chests. They look at me like I am a perpetrator of a terrible crime. I don't like that idea either.

"What, ho," I said, or words to that effect. They didn't like that idea. They didn't say anything. Bruce got into the act again. He tried to ensure that neither of us lost face. The airport manager was screaming at me to get my fucking airplane out of the way because he had another airplane that he had to put in the same place mine was. I didn't want to stay where I was. I wanted to climb into a goddamned sack and go beddy-bye. But the four horsemen of the Apocalypse stood firm.

"You'll have to pay for it," one said.

"I don't want it," I said. "You can have it." I had about eight cases of booze aboard the airplane. It would have taken three strong girls and a young boy to carry it from the airplane, but these clowns acted as if they all had double hernias. There was only one thing to do. I picked up a case of the juice—some of it thirty dollars a bottle—and dropped it fifteen feet to the concrete below. It made a beautiful sound. But it shocked the bejeezus out of those four stalwarts. Now it was their turn to be baffled. I think it finally got through to them that I would break every fucking bottle on that airplane.

Whether out of religious zeal—after all this was sacred stuff—or because of a convulsion of reason, they hollered, "Stop!"

They formed a human chain and rescued the remaining soup from wanton wastage. I have no idea what happened to all that busthead. Frankly, I don't give a shit. Some of it was very good brandy that gives you the shits. Good luck, Customs!

Bruce had told me the night before that the press in Miami had gotten word of the repossession of Vesco's Boeing. He understood better than I did the impact of what I had done. I didn't realize until much later how much of a service he had done me. For example, he had registered me at one motel and booked me at another under a false name—precisely to screen me from the media. He had cooperated in providing an armed guard for the airplane, which made sense to me at the time. The following day he arranged for an escort for me and my crew from the motel directly to the aircraft. I was in total ignorance of the furor I had generated. It never occurred to me that what I had done was important to anybody except the receivers and Vesco's creditors.

We took off shortly before noon. I made a stop at Wilmington, Delaware, because of weather. When I shut off the engines at Newark International Airport at 3:15 on the afternoon of May 10, 1974, I found that I had become more than a celebrity. I had become notorious.

2

Late November, 1968

I was out of a job—for the first time in my life. This particular morning, about seven A.M., I was sitting at a kitchen table in my in-laws' home in York, Nebraska. I was up to my belly button in crumbled efforts at writing a résumé. I was on my tenth cup of coffee and pissed off enough to bite through an iron bar. The telephone rang. Who in the name of sweet Jesus would make a telephone call at that time of the morning in York, Nebraska? They probably wanted the fire department. But the call was for me. It was from Ken Spinney, an executive with Atlantic Aviation, Wilmington, Delaware. I had called him two days before. He wasn't in so I left a message. Frankly, the most I expected was a polite note saying, "Got your message. Will keep my ears open." But Kenny called back with a job lead he thought I would be interested in.

A guy named Robert L. Vesco, who ran something called International Controls Corporation in New Jersey, God forbid, was looking for someone to build a corporate aviation operation for him from ground zero.

"Who the hell is Robert L. Vesco?" I asked him.

"Beats the hound-dog shit out of me," Ken said. "I

got this call from a guy named Jack Clarey who runs something called Fairfield Aviation."

"Never heard of it," I said.

"Me too," Ken said, "but apparently it's part of this International Controls operation. We checked into ICC and they look good. They have money in the bank, and they pay their bills."

"Sounds interesting," I said. "What do I do?"

"Just wait," Ken said. "I sent your name in to them and gave them your phone number. If they mean what they say, they need someone with your experience. Besides, Vesco's a young guy about 35 and doesn't want some grizzled old veteran." I thanked Ken for his endorsement. He told me that Clarey would probably call me in a couple of days.

"Hey, buddy," he went on. "Don't forget, we sell airplanes. If you score, don't forget where it all started."

I hung up the phone thinking to myself that this was probably a way-out chance. I really wasn't too impressed with the possibilities.

Jobs—the good ones—in the corporate-aviation field come by personal contact or referral. Some jobs are filled through agencies specializing in aviation. But a company looking for a director of aviation, which is analogous to an airline chief of operations, usually pirates one already working for someone else. A man planning a move or retirement might refer a friend on his own or even be asked by his company to find a replacement.

As I said, there aren't many people in my profession and most of us are pretty well known around the country. I was surprised and a little curious as to why Ken had been asked to find a director of aviation for Vesco. It didn't say much for ICC's knowledge of the industry. An operation like the one Ken mentioned meant heavy money. But . . . hell, Ken didn't even know what kind of business ICC was in.

Clarey called me the very same day.

At that point, Clarey's relationship with Vesco was none of my business, but he explained anyway. He told me that he once owned his own flying service, which included a flight school charter operation, and that he had had a lease with Curtis-Wright Corporation to operate the Caldwell-Wright Airport in northeastern New Jersey. I knew the airport. I hadn't been there in years, not since the days when I worked for Bethlehem Steel. I remembered it as a small airport on the side of a hill.

Anyway, Clarey insisted on telling me that Vesco, whom he apparently regarded as a captain of industry, had bought him out and installed him as president of Fairfield Aviation. The deal brought Clarey little cash, but a lot of paper. It remained to be seen whether the title was worth the job or vice versa. Vesco's intention, Clarey said, was to continue the airport leasing arrangement with Curtis-Wright and use the airport, which was just a few minutes' drive from Vesco's ICC headquarters.

The way Clarey described things, I felt a little more optimistic. I was interested enough to agree to travel from Nebraska to Caldwell, New Jersey, for an interview. I have to admit that the real deciding factor was that the trip would be at their expense.

"When do you want me to come?" I asked.

"Tomorrow, if that's not too soon," Clarey said.

"No problem," I said.

Clarey would arrange for a motel. He would see me there to discuss my qualifications. It was his responsibility, he told me, to "weed out" the applicants because "Mr. Vesco is a very busy man." Vesco would make the final selection himself from those few recommended by Clarey.

In the aviation industry, whatever is not military or commerical—that is, airline—is lumped under the term "general aviation." This includes everything from a guy flying something he made out of a mail-order kit up to the multi-engine, luxury, executive jets operated by the likes of IBM or Standard Oil.

The "general-aviation" category includes more than ninety percent of all aircraft, civilian and military, operating now in the United States. The elite of the "general-aviation" category is that which serves corporate America. Corporate-owned aircraft log more air miles and fly more hours than all of the country's domestic airlines, scheduled and non-scheduled combined. Entire service industries have grown up devoted exclusively to catering to the needs and whims of corporate aviation. There are literally thousands of pilots, mechanics, and service personnel who have never worked even a day for commerical carriers. There are aircraft design and manufacturing companies, totally unknown to the general public, that are dependent solely on corporate customers. Competing with them are the better-known manufacturers such as Boeing and Douglas, even major airlines with service and modification facilities and, in some cases, aircraft-sales franchises such as Pan Am's Falcon Jet program.

Corporate-aviation operations are expensive. A modest executive aircraft will cost in the neighborhood of a million and a half dollars, and it will cost another half a million dollars a year to operate. This includes crew salaries, fuel, maintenance, insurance, airport fees, support costs, and the like. And no self-respecting corporation would operate only one lousy airplane.

The Big Three of the automotive industry, General Motors, Ford, and Chrysler, have a combined air fleet that is larger than some regional carriers. A Grumman Gulfstream Two, for example, carries only twelve passengers and costs more than five million dollars. Yet, that's almost ten times the cost of the standard turboprop used by regional carriers, and they carry over forty passengers. It's not hard to figure the cost per passenger-mile for each.

Corporate aircraft are, in the strict sense, non—revenue producing, contrary to two myths perpetuated by the aircraft-operating corporations. One, that the use of these aircraft by executives and "corporate friends" generates sales and thereby justifies itself. And two, because of the "fiscal benefits" derived from the first myth and "executive time/dollar savings," these operations are self-supporting. The truth is that corporate aviation provides an exotic "fringe benefit" to favored executives. The sucker who pays for this ego massage, this air-age "stroking" of VIPs' conceit, is your good friend and mine, John Q. Taxpayer. Corporate aviation is carried on the books as a tax-deductible operating expense.

Next morning I drove to Lincoln and caught a United Airlines flight to Newark. I didn't have the vaguest idea of where the hell I was going. All Clarey had told me was the location and name of the motel I would be staying at. He had mentioned Caldwell Airport. The motel was in Wayne, New Jersey, on Route 46. He said, "You can't miss it, take a cab." He didn't tell me that I could have bought a car for the cost of the cab ride. The motel was thirty miles from Newark Airport.

In case my cab driver was unfamiliar with the northeastern United States I had bought a road map at the airport and together we found the motel. It occurred to me that since it was still light I might just as well look at the airport.

I asked the driver if he knew where it was. He said he didn't. We checked the map and located it. The airport was even further away from Newark Airport. I hadn't paid him yet, so we agreed on a price for the whole trip, including his empty run back to Newark, then started for Caldwell Airport.

All I had was the address Clarey had given me over the phone for Fairfield Aviation. 171 Passaic Avenue. It was just turning dark when I spotted the turnoff from Route 46. We went along Passaic for about a quarter of a mile when I saw a rotating beacon, something that every pilot recognizes, and we used it as a homing device to find the airport. About half a mile farther on, we pulled into the parking lot and I began to search for Fairfield Aviation. Looking around I thought that either we had found the wrong airport or the wrong side of the right one.

What I saw looked like something that was under demolition for an urban-renewal project. In front of me were two forlorn buildings. One was a sad-looking World War II-style wooden hangar on top of which was a pole holding a shredded wind sock, lighted by what looked to me to be a fifty-watt bulb. Near it was obviously an abandoned operations building and control tower. I saw a sign that said "Restaurant" but there were no lights on. The rotating beacon we had seen was on top of the tower. I couldn't believe my eyes. I got out of the cab to take a look around, certain I was in the wrong place. The driver got out too, and it was him who spotted the sign in the driveway that announced that this dreary dump was indeed the home of Fairfield Aviation.

"Let's get the hell out of here," I told the driver. During the ten-minute ride to the motel I considered catching the first plane back to Lincoln. My second thought, and the one I acted on, was to hang in there.

Tomorrow will be different, I assured myself. That old hangar is where they store old parts and wrecked airplanes. When I come back in the morning I will see a modern facility made with yards of glass, a large clean hangar, and mechanics in white coveralls climbing all over spotless aircraft. I will see bright offices and efficient secretaries. There will be veteran pilots huddling with their students over lesson plans and briefings for flight-training sessions. I will be greeted by a smartly dressed Jack Clarey in his carpeted office, and he will show me around his operation with pride and enthusiasm. Tomorrow will be a clear sunny day, and I will meet the kind of people I have become used to in the corporate-aviation industry. Sure I would. I felt better after the psych job and maybe I really believed it.

My self-induced euphoria lasted all of one night.

At about nine o'clock the next morning Clarey called me from the lobby.

"Ike," he said, "I'm downstairs. I'll be right outside in the car waiting for you."

In corporate aviation, when someobody says "the car," the least I had come to expect was a black station wagon with a dome light. Sometimes it was a Cadillac and sometimes it would be a no-more-than-two-year-old sedan, all slick and shiny. Despite my misgivings of the night before there was still the very real possibility that I was dealing with people who knew what they were about. With that in mind, I dressed conservatively in a most acceptable, "sincere," gray suit, shirt, and tie. I looked as I intended to, like an IBM salesman. I went down the stairs to the front of the motel. I didn't see "the car."

At one time, I was in the used-car business and there was a grade of vehicle that was referred to as "iron." A few yards from where I was standing, in the driveway of the motel, sat such a vehicle. It was a Chevy that I guessed to be about seven years old. I would have estimated its trade-in value at about $1.19. It was classic iron. If I was still in the used-car business I wouldn't take it. I waited. There was a guy in the Chevy and the engine was running, making one hell of a racket. I honestly thought that the old heap belonged to some boiler mechanic and was simply blocking the way of "the car." I expected a guy in blue jeans and a checkered shirt to come out of the motel with a bag of tools and get into the Chevy, which would then pull away, allowing Jack Clarey to drive up under the canopy in "the car." But the guy with the tools didn't come out. Instead the guy in the iron started waving at me. I went over to see what he wanted.

"Ike?"

Jesus! it was Clarey and that was "the car."

My sporting blood turned to horse piss. Everything I had feared the night before came back. Jack must have sensed my mood.

"Heh! Heh! (sniff)," he said, "this is our airport (sniff) courtesy car." I went along with the joke. "My (sniff) wife's got mine." He meant to reassure me but I thought that, whether his wife had his car or not, the wreck we were in was a poor bit of public relations. I said nothing.

"We'll go to the airport (sniff) office where we can talk," he said. "I have a lot of questions (sniff) to ask you."

Two things made that ride to the airport miserable. The first one was Jack Clarey's constant sniffling. I couldn't tell whether it was a temporary situation due to a cold or simply a nervous tic. But it drove me crazy. The second was the view.

I remember as a kid the few times I drove from my home in Coopersburg, Pa., to the Big City. The roads were not the superhighways of today. They were not as remote. The memory of how the neatness and the cleanness and the beauty of the Lehigh Valley would slowly disappear the closer I got to New York came back to me on that drive to Caldwell.

New Jersey is called the Garden State and parts of it are truly beautiful. Like Denville in Morris County, where I live today. What we were passing through now was anything but beautiful. It was ugly and depressing. It was November, which is not my favorite month and the roads were lined with cinders and debris. The buildings, drab single-story blobs, looked sad and very lonesome. I remember thinking what an awful place to have to make a living in. It didn't matter that this was industrialized, northeastern New Jersey, where the money was made. It was downright sickening. I was in a hell of a mood when we got to Caldwell, the same goddamn place I was the night before.

All the way to the airport Clarey kept talking. But I didn't hear anything he said. I was too absorbed in what I saw. I was used to steel towns where there was grime but not filth. I thought to myself, *What the hell am I doing here?* There was no way I could work, live, survive in this kind of atmosphere. I can't remember a time when I was so down. Clarey's babbling was just another noise like the tappets in the engine.

Jack's office was about as cruddy as the hangar and the parking lot. There was a beat-up desk in the middle of a ratty-looking rug with a big oil stain on it. There was a spavined couch against the dingy wall. There were the usual aircraft photographs scattered around and the windows were dirty. It reminded me of a bad, 1940's Regis Toomey movie.

I don't know why Jack brought me there. It certainly wasn't impressive. He blathered about "the future." I let him talk. It was very obvious to me that, as far as the corporate aviation business was concerned, his credentials were nil—or close to it. Of course there was no way of assessing how he stood with Vesco, who, after all was the guy I would have to deal with.

The impression I got from this so-called interview was that Jack Clarey considered himself to be Vesco's aviation consultant. He tried to get me to believe that as far as Vesco was concerned, his word was Holy Writ and that I was just another applicant for a flying job. He talked grandiosely about the kind of aircraft he would advise Mr. Vesco to buy. Of course, I would have a crack at the left seat until he checked out and qualified as Captain.

I read the Gospel to him.

"Jack," I said, "I am here because I was told that Mr. Vesco is looking for somebody to run an aviation division. If I get the job, if I take the job, that is exactly what I am going to do. If I am mistaken in my concept of why I'm here, tell me right fucking now and I will go home."

"Let's go see Mr. Vesco," he said. On the way out of the office he kind of grinned at me. "You can't blame me for trying."

"Right!"

Vesco's offices at that time were in a converted garage. By now I was pretty well immune to shock. Vesco headquarters in Fairfield, as modest as they were, were palatial when compared with the setup at Caldwell. All I wanted to do was to go through the motions and get back to Nebraska.

Jack took me to a little anteroom and disappeared. There were a couple of other guys there waiting to be seen. We didn't talk to each other, which was just as well. About a half hour later things started happening. Clarey came out and brought me into an office—a tiny one—where I met a man called Ralph Dodd. I was to get to know Ralph pretty well in the ensuing years. We looked at each other. I'm sure he knew why I was there but I had no idea why he was involved at that time. We didn't talk flying, or airplanes, or anything. All I saw was a handsome guy in shirt-sleeves, about my age, with sky-blue eyes, an Elvis Presley hairdo, television teeth, and a hell of a personality—at least at first encounter.

"Shirrrrrrl!" The shout came from down the hall. Dodd grinned.

"We don't have an intercom," he said. "That's how we communicate around here."

"Ralph!"

"That's me." He left the room. He was gone about a minute and a half. When he came back he sat down at his desk. "About a minute, Mr. Eisenhauer." Almost immediately Shirley came into the room. Shirley was the first person I saw since I got to the Garden State of New Jersey who looked like she knew what she was doing.

Shirley Bailey was a striking woman. I began to think at that moment that there was more here than met the eye. She was a small woman but compact. She gave me a searching visual check. I felt like an overaged Constellation under the scrutiny of a 50,000-hour Captain. But she smiled as she evaluated. She stuck out her hand.

"Captain Eisenhauer," she said very pleasantly, "I'm happy to meet you. Mr. Vesco will be with you in a minute."

She had just the right touch and it wasn't a put-on. I sensed her efficiency and her competence, two qualities she demonstrated time and again while she was with Vesco.

"Shirrrrrrrrl!" She went back to Vesco's office. There was not a wisp of a change in her composure. Apparently Vesco was ready to see me. I sure as hell was ready to see him. I did not exactly have my right hand cocked like a drunk in a gin mill but I was running pretty short of patience. I was by now convinced that I was dealing with a bunch of people whose ambitions far outweighed both their wallets and their experience. Shirrrrrl beckoned to me. And I met Robert Lee Vesco, President and Chairman of the Board of something called International Controls Corporation.

What I saw was a 35-year-old guy with a skinny mustache in an office that was no more impressive than anything else I had seen at this place. He sat behind what looked like a dining-room table with enough leaves in it for an Italian wedding, piled high with papers. He got up to shake hands, and I was surprised at his height—over six feet.

I don't know if he sensed my mood. But he made me feel that, at that moment, I was the most important person in his life.

"Hi, I'm Bob Vesco!"

It would be nice to be able to say that that interview was one of the high points of my life; that, suddenly, upon meeting Robert Vesco, I "saw the mountaintop," that all my doubts were dispelled, and all my misgivings were laid to rest.

But that's not the way it was. The air didn't crackle with dynamism. Vesco did not come on like Burt Lancaster, all charisma and bursting with energy. There was no ninety-piece orchestra blaring music at moments of high drama. There was no posturing for effect.

Considering the subject of the meeting, how to go about spending a couple of million dollars to build a company airline—that's what he was really talking about—I expected the conversation to be serious, but we talked like two guys killing time in the local saloon.

It was "Enjoy your trip?" and "How are the wife and kids?" for openers. He told me matter-of-factly that his company was going places.

He showed some familiarity with aircraft but from the standpoint of the passenger. In the broad sense he knew what he wanted, and understood the costs involved. As we talked I revised my negative opinion that, for all the highblown talk up to now, these people thought that $50,000 would be about right for a company plane. He didn't try to "sell me." As a matter of fact if he had come on like Dynamite Dan I would have walked out. He gave the clear impression that he felt he didn't have to prove anything to anybody. He outlined his plans as if the decision had already been made to go ahead. There was no talk of clearing anything with any committee. He told me flatly that he was the boss. I was in that office because he was looking for the right man to give *him* what *he* wanted.

We talked about airplanes for a while. I gave him my background, including the bad parts, which didn't seem to faze him. Then he asked me, "Are you interested?"

"Yes," I told him, "but on my terms." He nodded.

"What are they?" he asked.

He surprised me again with his calm acceptance of what he could have regarded as smart-ass arrogance. I even surprised myself by my hard-nosed attitude. But I knew then what I had to do. I hadn't gone through the corporate experience without learning something. No corporate hotshot would ever again come between me and the job I was qualified for. This is about how I laid it out to Vesco.

"If I'm going to run this thing," I said, "I'm going to run it. You tell me what you want and I'll see that you get it. But you tell me. I don't want anyone between us especially some executive type who doesn't know anything about aviation." He smiled and I realized that he knew precisely what I was talking about.

"Okay, Ike," he said, "what do you think?" I knew right then that the job was mine. But, for whatever reason, possibly because I did not want to appear over-anxious, I waffled.

"I'd like a little time to think, Mr. Vesco," I said. Again he smiled.

"Why don't you go to lunch?" he said. "There are still a couple of people I ought to talk to. Come back about one o'clock?"

Vesco sent me to a local restaurant in his own car. At ten minutes to one his driver came to get me. I walked back into Vesco's office at precisely one o'clock. Apparently he had the same regard for punctuality that I did.

"Well?" was all he said.

"Yes," I said.

"Right," he said. "The papers are already in the mill. When can you start?"

"I need a couple of days," I told him. He agreed and then we talked about money and such. I was out of there in five minutes, picking up expense money from Ralph Dodd.

Shirley, Ralph, and Clarey gathered around me and welcomed me aboard. They hadn't been in the office when Vesco and I shook hands. I knew that before I got back from lunch he had told them, "We have our Captain."

On the flight back to Lincoln I had a chance to reflect on the 180-degree turn in my fortunes. The Vesco operation was like nothing I had ever seen before in my life. The only real thing about it was the 2,000 dollars of Vesco's money in my pants pocket. As drained as I was, I couldn't help feeling some excitement at this new venture.

3

1952—1968

My career in corporate aviation began back when the field was still a haven for ex-military pilots from World War II and Korea. Aircraft were usually converted bombers and military transports, fairly primitive by today's standards. The hot shot throttle jockey booting around a slicked-up B-25, B-26, even a B-24 "Liberator" was the image of the corporate pilot. There was little or no transitional training and newly developed flight systems were ignored in favor of the old, "needle ball and airspeed."

After the Korean War, during which I served as a Navy jet pilot, I was faced with the choice of a Navy or civilian career. Whatever choice I made I was determined to continue my flying career. For personal reasons I chose to return to civilian life and before my separation from active duty I did some job hunting. More quickly than I expected, I got two offers. One was from American Airlines as a First Officer trainee. The other came from Bethlehem Steel, not as a trainee but as a Captain in command of a Lockheed Lodestar, a plane I had flown in the Navy.

The choice was really an easy one. I had done a

little research into airline advancement policies. Like the military, the airlines were seniority oriented. Skill, experience, and ambition ran a poor second to time with the company, not only for promotion but to choice of routes as well. It was no contest. I took the Bethlehem Steel job at Allentown, Pa., only fifteen minutes from my home in Coopersburg, Pa.

The most important man in my aviation career was my friend and former boss at Bethlehem Steel, Al Junker. He was really my mentor and teacher and how we met is a story in itself.

While I was still in the Navy I had heard a rumor that Bethlehem Steel, was getting a second Lockheed. At the time, the Navy allowed me (and other senior squadron officers due for separation) to combine proficiency training flights with personal business such as arranging housing for their families in their hometown areas. I had made a couple of flights to Allentown-Bethlehem-Easton Airport where Bethlehem Steel's aviation operation was located. When I heard about the Lockheed, instead of writing a letter of application, I simply flew up to A-B-E Airport and taxied my Corsair right up to Bethlehem Steel's hangar. I got out of the airplane and asked to see the Chief Pilot. I must have caught everybody by surprise because I was ushered right into Al Junker's office. Nobody even asked me what my business was with the Chief Pilot.

If Al Junker was impressed by my stunt, he didn't show it. I apologized for looking so "grungy." He said that he hadn't looked much better when he was pushing Navy fighters around. Besides breaking the ice, I don't believe our common Navy bond played any part in his judgment of me as a candidate for a pilot's job. Al was a tough and probing inquisitor. He put me through the wringer but I felt like a goddamn king when I left him. I still didn't have the job. I had one more step to go. If I passed, the job was mine.

The final decision rested with one of the last of the old-line rugged individualists, Eugene Grace, chairman of the board of Bethlehem Steel. Grace regarded Bethlehem's aircraft as his personal property. I needed the old man's blessing. Less than a week later, I got it.

Two weeks later I left the Navy. That was on a Friday. I went to work for Al on Monday. I stayed with him for more than fourteen years.

The day I went to work for Bethlehem Steel I felt that I had landed in the best of all possible worlds. I had married my schoolgirl sweetheart while I was in the Navy and had a two-year-old son, David. I had bought a small farm outside Coopersburg with my savings plus some help from my father-in-law. I was a working pilot when there was a glut of pilots on the market.

I didn't realize then the battering my marriage would take from the demands of my work, demands that would grow more numerous and insistent as the size and complexity of corporate aviation grew over the years. My marriage ended just about the time I left Bethlehem Steel, but my career and changing jobs would not change the life-style that had become an integral part of my work.

Al Junker was a man of vision, and he took it upon himself to open my eyes to the developing industry we were a part of. He made me his protégé. I had always considered myself something of an innovator even in an activity in which, to most people, the book is *all* and creative initiative is dangerous boat-rocking. Al lit a fire under my ambition. As the Bethlehem fleet of aircraft and its range of operations expanded I took on added responsibilities and my work load increased enormously—but I ate it up. During those years I qualified for and received my rating as an Airline Transport Pilot at a time when it was not considered necessary or even desirable. I also devoted five years to on-the-job training as a working mechanic trainee to qualify for, and receive, my FAA mechanic's license. Even today there are probably not more than a handful of Airline Transport Pilots holding both ratings.

In five years things started to happen as Al had predicted. By 1960 we were operating brand-new airline-type aircraft. When I had started with Bethlehem, there had been three pilots. By 1960 we had about fifteen flight personnel at any one time. Plans were made to operate out of a brand-new multimillion-dollar hangar with the most modern maintenance and service facilities in the country and with a vastly expanded general service activity. We had progressed from flying old man Grace and his friends around to the kind of executive transport service I mentioned briefly earlier. Then, somewhere along the line, the corporate sharks discovered the prestige value of "the company plane." Al had been left pretty much alone to run his operation as he saw fit. But it wasn't long before he became just another "middle-management" executive on the corporate pegboard.

Being part of Bethlehem Steel's booming aviation department provided me with a great deal of insight, insight that would years later lead me to understand Robert L. Vesco's ambition to build an aviation division.

I ultimately came to appreciate Vesco—apart from anything else, as the only business executive I have ever known who clearly understood the value of the airplane as a twentieth-century business device. It gave him mobility. He used it to move troops where they were needed, when they were needed, in the best military-logistics sense of the word. Along with his personal brilliance, his ruthlessness, and his money, he used his aircraft to surprise and intimidate his adversaries.

As I stated before, Bethlehem's aviation operation, for all intents and purposes, was under the direct control of Eugene Grace. Al Junker ran the department independently of the corporation, reporting directly and only to the top. I don't recall exactly when things began to change. It was certainly in the early Sixties during the period that Arthur Homer was chairman of the board and Edward Martin was president.

At that time the General Services Department concerned itself with overall supervision of offices and plants, housekeeping, real-estate acquisitions and sales, building construction, restaurant operation, and ground transport plus a lot of other small activities of a service nature to the company. The general manager of the General Services Department was a man I'll call Fred Baldur. Baldur was a "company man." Oh! Was he ever a company man! I had been told that he had been a company man from the day he entered Lehigh University as a freshman. Lehigh is a beneficiary of Bethlehem Steel to the degree that, around Bethelem, Lehigh is considered a division of Bethlehem Steel. At any rate, Baldur worked part time for the company during his college years and, upon graduation, joined the company full-time.

The pilots in the Bethlehem aviation division were, I admit, a privileged bunch. We dealt only with Al, were given membership in the country club for a nominal fee, and stayed pretty much to ourselves. In fact we seldom set foot on Bethlehem property, except for the airport. That included Al. Whenever we wanted to talk with him we could always find him at his desk or somewhere around the hangar if he wasn't flying. So it was highly unusual when, in 1960, Al began paying more and more visits "downtown" to the front office.

Al's trips downtown bothered us. We didn't know what they meant. Soon we began to see people from General Services around the hangar who, as far as we were concerned, didn't belong. They were nosy. They asked a lot of questions, not only about how we operated, but about what was needed to improve our operation and what we might recommend for the construction of a new hangar. These were questions that should have been directed to Al. He was the boss of the aviation division.

Then Baldur himself began to come around. We had no way of guessing what was happening. All we knew was that it wasn't good. Certainly whatever was happening, it was hurting Al. We could all see the change.

Of all the pilots, I was probably closest to Al. He was a guy who thought he could hide his feelings. But I could see him suffering and I wondered what was going on downtown that could shake Al that way. He told me that Baldur was making a pitch to take over the aviation division. Yet he was loyal enough not to say how he felt about it. He didn't need to. I could read it right on his face.

Six months later the roof caved in. Aviation was placed under the direct supervision of General Services.

That meant Baldur. From now on he would be Al's boss and ours.

Baldur had had the reputation of doing favors for the right people. In his General Services Department he had the goodies, the people, and the authority to dispense them. What he expected in return is something I can't testify to. But I said earlier that the use of corporate aircraft is an executive fringe benefit. It also confers status upon the user. The guy who controls and authorizes the use of these aircraft is dealing primarily with ego—and he knows it.

Ultimately Baldur humiliated and undercut Al in a number of ways. He bypassed him constantly in dealing with flight and ground crews. He dictated how, when, and by whom the airplanes would be used and, finally, he banished Al to a cubbyhole of an office downtown. It was an unnecessary and spiteful move designed to intimidate the one man Baldur felt was in his way.

Al's enforced move downtown pissed me off and I resolved to do something about it. Despite his power Baldur couldn't do much about me at that time. He disliked me and distrusted me because I was Junker's man, and he understood that company loyalty or personal ambition would not change that. I was Senior Captain then and I had some clout of my own but I knew I had to tread carefully because Baldur considered me a personal threat and I was next on his list.

Al's move downtown created a confidence vacuum at the airport. Baldur replaced Al with two of his own men. Neither one knew a thing about corporate aviation. The top man was an ex-Air Force colonel who, in my opinion, was nothing more than window dressing. The new Chief Pilot was a former United Airlines Junior Captain. Baldur would never have offered me the Chief Pilot's job because I would have told him to shove it out of loyalty to Al. He found it easier and probably more to his liking to install his own men.

Within weeks aircrew morale and proficiency began to suffer. I admit I was hostile to my new bosses but I honestly felt, as a professional, that they were either incompetent or unconcerned about what was happening.

On top of that the Junior Captain from the airlines behaved like a martinet. We needed Al. I began to collect data on all operational deficiencies, both human and technical, then passed this information on to Al downtown.

When Al felt he had enough ammunition, he went directly to top management and laid it out for them. They were sensible men. None of them wanted to die in an airplane crash because of sloppy maintainence or deteriorated pilot performance. Baldur got the word—"bring Al Junker back." When Al resumed his old seat the two Baldur men who had replaced him became superfluous. Even Baldur could not do anything about that. One of them remained with the company in another capacity and the other was asked to resign. Things improved almost immediately. The aviation department was still under Baldur's thumb, and it would stay that way. But we felt we had won a victory of sorts.

Despite our experience with Baldur, we in the aviation department had really learned nothing about how the mind of a dedicated corporation bureaucrat works. We did not understand the techniques of personal empire-building. Any corporate executive needs to add to his domain, to build it, to acquire as many departments to supervise as possible. This gives him a certain amount of insulation. It also gives him power. There is a dehumanization factor built into the corporate psyche. Everything is done by the numbers. The good and welfare of the corporation is paramount and when you get right down to it the corporation is nothing more than real estate and a bank account.

If Baldur disliked me before Al came back, he now hated my guts. He knew that I had fed Al the information that got him his job back. As far as Baldur was concerned, I was not a "team player," had no loyalty to the company, and was insubordinate to him, the captain of "the team." The only way he could exercise complete domination over the aviation division was to remove Al permanently, and he did not care how he accomplished that. Al, to protect his pension, had no choice but to take whatever Baldur threw at him.

As I said, things changed somewhat for the better after Al came back to the airport. But the mood was different and Baldur made his authority known in many ways. Looking back, I realize that, like Al, I was taking a lot of shit that I should not have tolerated. I had become locked into a way of life that I did not want to give up. I had a stake in the community. I was the all-American citizen. Not only did I coach Little League baseball but I was a member of the district school board, taught an adult-education course on aviation at the local community college, and was very much involved with my naval reserve unit. Because of all this I was vulnerable to a man like Baldur. Maybe it was because he was really in the same boat that he understood power and how to use it to control people. In my opinion he totally lacked human compassion. That's how men like him survive and prosper. He's like a riverboat gambler who knows the size of your bankroll and how close you are to being tapped out. And, for him, that's when the game gets interesting.

I had resolved that what had happened to Al Junkor would never happen to Ike Eisenhauer. I really believed that my role in short-circuiting Baldur had demonstrated my guts and independence. Sure, it did take a certain amount of courage to buck a guy like Baldur. It set me apart. But I was kidding myself. I had a lot to protect and, for the next two years, I did my share of knuckling under and tolerating the kind of humiliation that a Baldur can dish out. Frankly, I wasn't very pleased with myself. I didn't know it then but those two years were an annealing process for me and prepared me for my later encounter with Robert Vesco.

They say the best way to stop a dog from chasing cars is to let him catch one. He is so shocked that he doesn't know what the hell to do with it. In a way that's how I felt the first time I consciously bucked the corporate presence.

Forget for a minute the wishful "sea-captain" image that a lot of airplane drivers would like the public to see them in. The function of a corporation aircraft pilot, whether he sits in the left seat—command seat—or in the right seat, is to not only see to the operation of the aircraft, but to the comfort and convenience of his passengers. Like a good chauffeur, he is there. He loses nothing of his self-esteem unless someone he is required to serve abuses his privilege.

Enter one vice-president.

In the summer of 1966, Bethlehem decided to acquire its first pure jet aircraft, a North American Sabreliner. Very often the sales organization sends a pilot, a "demonstrator," to familiarize the buyer's crew with the operating characteristics of the airplane. That pilot ordinarily remains with the aircraft for the duration of the loan period. He functions as if he were employed as a crew member for the buyer's corporation under the buyer's chief pilot or senior Captain. Ordinarily this is no problem. There are seldom any confrontations between passengers and crew.

I took off from A-B-E Airport one August morning in 1966 with four passengers. They were Mr. and Mrs. Steward S. Cort (the president of Bethlehem Steel and his wife), a vice-president of a subsidiary whom we will call Dan, and a vice-president of the parent corporation whom we will call Mr. Jones. My co-Captain on this trip was with the company that had loaned the airplane to Bethlehem. It was to be a normal, routine, round-robin business trip between Allentown and the West Coast with a number of stops along the way. The flight was fairly uneventful until we started home.

The other pilot, whom I will call Joe, alternated in the left seat from point to point. I was at the controls when we left Monterey, California. We had agreed that since this was the windup of the trip I would take the Sabreliner all the way back to Allentown. The only stop before we unloaded our first passenger would be Grand Island, Nebraska, for refueling. From Grand Island, about all we really had to do was put the airplane on automatic-pilot until we started descent for Allentown where we would drop off Mr. Jones.

There is a progression of passenger activity on these executive flights. Shortly after takeoff they usually talk business—for about a minute and a half. Then someone says, "Let's have a drink." From that point on the suffocating boredom of the flight is smothered in food and drowned in booze. On short flights it's not so bad. On long flights you usually wind up with a cargo of comatose or legless passengers. This flight was no exception. By the time we had reached Grand Island, my four passengers were feeling a little buzz. From experience, and considering that we had another two and a half hours to go to Allentown, I knew they would be barely ambulatory by the time we got there.

About a hundred miles out of Allentown Mr. Cort came forward and changed our flight plan. Initially we were to stop at Allentown, drop off Mr. Jones, then continue on to LaGuardia where Mr. Cort and his wife would leave the aircraft. Then I would take Dan to Westchester County Airport. From there Joe and I would deadhead back to St. Louis, the home base of the borrowed Sabreliner, still stopping at Allentown on the way.

Now, Mr. Cort wanted to go to LaGuardia first. Accordingly, I contacted traffic control and revised my flight plan.

Mr. Cort apparently had not cleared his plans with Mr. Jones, which is not unusual because Mr. Cort was—lets' face it—the boss.

A few minutes after Mr. Cort left, I felt the heavy breath of Mr. Jones on my right ear.

"How soon do we land?" I did not realize he was referring to Allentown.

"We're due in LaGuardia in about thirty minutes."

"LaGuardia?"

"Yes, LaGuardia." He didn't give me a chance to explain. I knew he had a load on but I wasn't prepared for the Niagara of abuse he hit me with. I kept my mouth shut. Actually, the guy had a gripe. He had plans, and Mr. Cort's decision screwed them up. There was nothing I could say that would change anything. I figured he would eventually calm down and accept the situation. After a few more obscenities, he went back to his seat. As far as I was concerned, the matter was closed. Oh boy! Was I ever wrong!

We duly landed at LaGuardia. Conscious of Jones' anxiety to get to Allentown as fast as possible, I diplomatically hurried Mr. Cort and his wife through the Marine Terminal at LaGuardia and saw them into their limousine. I hustled my fanny back to the airplane, under the assumption that by now Jones knew all the details of the change in schedule. I did not realize that he didn't know Mr. Cort had suggested that I drop Dan off first at Westchester County, which was only eight minutes north of LaGuardia, and then continue on to Allentown with him. Thus is the pecking order in the corporate world. I tried to break it to Jones gently.

"Mr. Cort wants me to drop off Dan first," I told him.

It didn't help. He was still mad but for the moment he controlled his temper.

I did the best I could. My plan was to get to Westchester County the quickest possible way, dump Dan, and take off immediately. But I had a fuel problem brought about by the change in flight plans. It seemed logical to refuel at Westchester County. Hell—it was necessary. I was down to the fumes. It didn't occur to me that this would be a problem. I had been cleared tower to tower—LaGuardia to Westchester County. There was no traffic in the area. It was well after midnight. Naturally, when we got to Westchester County, the place was closed up tight except for one dispatcher and one janitor. I was lucky to find a cab for Dan.

I told Joe I'd take care of the fuel situation. The dispatcher told me we had at least a half hour's wait. Shit! It was one o'-goddamn-clock in the sonofabitching morning, and I had an irate vice-president on my hands whose indignation increased in geometric proportions to his booze intake.

Jones went totally bananas. Joe told me he knocked off a tumbler full of gin, left the airplane, and just disappeared. Joe had no idea where the hell he had gone. The coffee shop was closed. The bar was closed. There were no taxis. And the nearest wateringhole had to be ten miles away.

I was busy in operations filing my flight plan and checking Allentown weather. I had gotten reports en route to LaGuardia of possible fog conditions at A-B-

E. That's all I needed. By the time I finished at operations, fueling was completed and I went out to the airplane, ready to take off. In fact I was closing the door when Joe told me that Jones had vanished.

"Jee-zus!" At that moment I saw the dispatcher running toward the airplane.

"Hey, Ike," he yelled, "you'd better get your passenger before he gets his ass slung in the can!"

"What's going on?"

"That clown—whoever he is—is in the parking lot screaming his head off and swearing. If the cops see him they'll lock him up. They won't give a shit who he is."

I took off like a shot for the parking lot and there—sure enough—was the old ball buster himself doing exactly what the dispatcher said he was doing and waving his arms like a guy fighting a swarm of bees.

This is not the most unusual behavior in the world for somebody who has partaken of more than his share of strong waters. And we have all dealt with it. The procedure is to make a reasoned approach to the individual and, gaining his confidence, persuade him into more decorous behavior. The words usually used would go something like this. "C'mon! Quit fuckin' around." But I couldn't say that. I was dealing with an alcoholically spastic vice-president. What I said was, "We're ready to take off, sir. I'll have you home in twenty minutes."

Following standard operating procedure, I grasped his elbow in what I intended to be a friendly and encouraging grip. He pulled away and gave me a shove.

"I wouldn't get on that airplane with you if I had to walk!" he said. "Get me a fucking cab!"

Oh, shit! Now I had a problem. I really wanted to help the guy but he was in no mood or shape to be dealt with reasonably. "I'm not going anyplace with you!" he babbled.

"Why?" I asked him.

"You did that to me on purpose!" he shouted. "Goddamn you, Al, you're a prick!" I knew he was thinking of Junker.

"I'm not Al," I said. "I'm Ike!"

"Same thing!"

This was getting ridiculous! I didn't need this kind of shit. This was above and beyond the call of duty.

"You're going with me if I have to carry you," I told him. Drunk as he was, he got the message. He staggered back to the Sabreliner and got on board. I followed, fully aware that the whole scene was witnessed by the dispatcher and the janitor. I was so shaken I asked Joe to fly the airplane to Allentown.

I kind of collapsed into the right-hand seat beside him. I assumed that Jones would do the manly thing and pass out. Wrong!

We had just about cleared the Hudson River when he sounded off.

"Al!" he bellowed, "C'mere!"

I looked at Joe and shrugged. I got up out of my seat and went back to Jones. He was slumped in his seat, as loose as a Chinaman's slipper. He fixed his bleary eyes on me.

As I said, executive jets are not roomy. The easiest way to carry on a conversation at eyeball level with a passenger—a frequent occurrence—is to get down on one knee. Which I did.

"You're fuckin fired!" I got up to go back to my seat. This shithead was getting tiresome.

"Come back here!" I went back and got back down on one knee.

"I'm sick and tired of you and Fred (Baldur)! I've had it! What you did to me tonight made up my mind!" I suggested he think his decision over.

"Maybe you have the wrong guy," I said. He looked at me out of his bloodshot eyes. "Get off your knees, Captain. I don't want any man to beg for his job." I went back to my seat. The rest of the flight was uneventful. Joe suggested that I coldcock the guy but you don't do that kind of thing in an airplane just to establish your manhood.

The crunch came at Allentown. Jones literally fell out of the airplane. I was at the foot of the steps and grabbed him to keep him from landing on his skull. I don't know what he was thinking of but he tossed one from center field and caught me in the belly. My reaction was instinctive. I wanted to cream him. But the silly shit was so drunk I might have killed him.

Somebody dumped him in the waiting limousine and took him home. I stood on the ramp feeling like a jerk for not having asserted myself with him. But when I thought more about it, I didn't really need to hit him. It would have been a human—but stupid—thing to do. I was grateful for the fact that the Sabreliner had to go back to St. Louis that night.

I climbed into the airplane to wait for Joe, who had gone in to file a flight plan.

Surprisingly, there was no explosion at Bethlehem Steel. I think that everybody wanted to forget the whole incident. Any probe into this affair could only hurt Jones. Nobody wanted to embarrass the company by exposing the kind of behavior that Jones, a high-ranking executive, was guilty of. Of course Baldur got his licks in. He called me into his office and indicated to me that "because of Mr. Jones' generosity" he would not fire me. But I was on the toboggan.

It took a year before I finally reached the end of my tolerance. Baldur and his minions had put the blocks to me at every opportunity and I took it. I was treated like a leper. And I took it. And then I just had enough. The specific incident took place in Baldur's office in the late summer of '67. Al had been pushing for my promotion and had been turned down flat. I was called in because Al wanted me there for the final confrontation. That was Al's way. There would be no misrepresentations. We would all hear the truth. After the usual bullshit, Baldur told Al to wait outside. Now it was between Baldur and me.

There was some preliminary dancing around, each of us trying to justify our position. Then it got down to the bottom line. In effect, Baldur told me that for the good of the company, I was frozen in my job. If I behaved myself, he might even decide to keep me on. I knew what he was doing. Whatever I said, whatever I agreed to, would not prevent the inevitable. He just didn't have the guts to say flat out, "Fuck off, Ike. You're fired!" I knew what I had to do, and I suppose

I had spent two years getting ready for this moment. The last words I remember were Baldur saying, "If you leave without a fuss I won't do anything to stop you from getting a job. . . . Otherwise . . ."

I got up out of my chair, leaned across his desk, and suggested, eyeball to eyeball, that he perpetrate upon himself a physical impossibility—and a flying one at that.

The following week I went to work for Sperry Rand's Flight System Division based at Westchester County Airport as an instructor pilot and service representative. I stayed with Sperry about a year and, after a lot of romancing, succumbed to an "offer I couldn't refuse" from Gates Learjet. That was in August of 1968.

The Gates job seemed very promising. I was to be made director of flight operations, headquartered in Denver, Colorado. Promotion to a vice-presidency was to follow in a reasonable period of time. I moved into a motel and had just about settled on a house to buy when the bomb went off.

I was called into the office of the president of Gates Learjet—Hig Gould. He told me that the signals were changed. I was being shifted back to New York, back to Westchester County Airport. One of the main reasons I took the Gates job was to get out of Westchester, but what he said next really shocked me. I was to fire the guy who ran the Westchester operation, a guy who had become my friend while I was with Sperry. Hig's demand violated my sense of professional ethics. I'd had my fill of that at Bethlehem. I was not about to stick the shaft into a good friend and fellow pilot, "Torch" Lewis, even though my reward would be the job they had promised me in the first place. After I had reorganized everything at Westchester, *if* they liked the way things turned out, there was a very good chance that I would wind up back in Denver as part of the Gates Learjet executive team. Horseshit!

I told him so, and I reminded Hig of our original deal. I didn't have to go back to Westchester to "prove myself." For three months I had been carrying a double work load. The particular vice-president who had romanced me away from Sperry had been mugged and hospitalized. I had taken on his duties. I knew that I had done a good job, and I knew they knew it too. Maybe that was the trouble. The vice-president in question knew it too. I told Hig to his face that the guy was probably scared shitless that he would be out of a job so he conned Hig into making me a hatchet man. Hig denied it. He said it was his decision because he felt that I had been a little too aggressive in my approach to my work. Again—horseshit! Hig kept his cool, and I backed off a little. He asked me to talk to the vice-president to see if we couldn't work things out. Oh, boy! Here was the corporate stuff at its purest. Hig was not about to pull the trigger. That was the vice-president's job just the way the vice-president tried to put me in command of the firing squad at Westchester County. I went along with him for the moment. Maybe I was wrong.

I went to see the vice-president at his home where he was recuperating. I was right. They guy *was* scared shitless. He apparently had been pretty badly hurt. Still, I felt at a serious disadvantage. And the message came through loud and clear—do it his way or get out. I told him what I thought and I left. Back at the office Hig said, in effect, "Sorry, Ike."

I picked up my briefcase and went back to the motel.

Almost as if the devil had decided to give me an extra cheap shot, somebody bombed my car with rocks during the night. I was not in a very happy frame of mind when I left Denver for York, Nebraska.

I began to think that I was snake bitten. First there was the shattering experience at Bethlehem. Then, perhaps because of greed and ambition, I blew the Sperry job, which could have been a "home." It would have taken some compromises on my part as far as the corporate pace was concerned. The pay was good, the work was satisfying if not too challenging, and the people were decent. Now this. Maybe even at Sperry I would have found myself to be the square peg.

My future looked absolutely hopeless. My life was a

bunch of jigsaw puzzle pieces and they were all one color—black. And that's why I was sitting at the kitchen table early that morning trying to compose a job résumé when the call came from Ken Spinney.

One of the last things I did before I left Gates Learjet was to make a bunch of phone calls around the country. Ken was one of the guys I contacted. I knew he wasn't calling out of sympathy. He had a job in mind for me. I felt the gods were smiling for a change.

Clarey's call, so soon after Ken's, had to be an omen no matter how unimpressive Clarey came across. I owed it to myself to at least take a closeup look.

4

November, 1968

My first assignment for Vesco was to buy him an airplane. For the kind of traveling that he planned to do and the numbers of people he wanted to carry, we agreed that a Grumman Gulfstream One was the right airplane for the job. Between the day Vesco hired me and the day I came back from York, Nebraska with my worldly goods to start this new job, Clarey had been doing some bird-dogging. The aircraft he had located were unsuitable for a variety of reasons: too old, and high flight time and mileage, or, by my standards, badly maintained. I owed Ken Spinney a favor but that was just coincidental. I knew that Ken would give me grade-A service.

Ken's company, Atlantic Aviation, had just sold a brand new Grumman Gulfstream Two to CBS to replace their Gulfstream One . . . which Atlantic had also sold them, and which they had serviced. I knew that that airplane would be in tip-top condition. But, it would not be available until the Gulfstream Two came out of the shop where it was undergoing "dealer prep." This could take months.

I checked with the CBS Chief Pilot and found out

how much they wanted for the airplane. The price was no problem. All that had to be done was to break it loose ahead of schedule. I dropped that problem in Vesco's lap.

The following day Ralph Dodd told me we had the airplane. The only condition to the sale was that I would fly William Paley, CBS board chairman and his family to Nassau for their annual Christmas vacation. Until that time the Gulfstream would undergo an inspection and interior modification at Atlantic's facility in Wilmington, Delaware. I also had to find a copilot.

Harry J. Werner, Jr., was working as an instructor at Wings Field outside Philadelphia. He had impressed me when I had first met him a year or so earlier. He had no heavy aircraft experience but what I had liked about him was his professional approach to his work. A guy like Harry, who learned thoroughly and fast, would give me what I needed when I needed it. Of course Harry had to pass through the interview mill. I had the final say but I felt I ought not make any unilateral decisions at this point. I asked Jack Clarey to interview the applicants along with me and independently rate them. Fortunately for Harry, and for me, Clarey also rated Harry number one. I was fully aware of how important a job like this was for Harry. Harry served in the U.S. Air Force as a mechanic. But in the Air Force Harry had been bitten by the flying bug. While working on the Philadelphia police force Harry used his G.I.-bill benefits to become a licensed pilot and get his instructor's rating.

I sent Harry to Flight Safety for a cram course in the operation of the Gulfstream. He took to it like a duck to water. Both Harry and the Gulfstream were ready on schedule and on the appointed day we were at LaGuardia to pick up the Paleys for the flight to Nassau.

The Paleys showed up on time with a ton of luggage. Their Chief Pilot was there to help. He introduced Harry and me to the Paleys and helped generally in getting them on their way. The three-hour trip to Nassau was a bus ride. Harry would have liked to stay over in Nassau but we had a schedule to meet. We were home for Christmas.

Vesco had seen his Gulfstream the day before I took the Paleys to Nassau. It was a gala day. He came out to the airport with Shirley and Ralph. Clarey was already there. I gave them the grand tour. Vesco was delighted.

According to instructions Vesco had given me the day he bought the Gulfstream, on the day after Christmas I had the airplane at Caldwell ready to go. Vesco had planned a trip to California. It was a business trip but the whole Vesco family would make the inaugural flight. That included Vesco's wife Pat, their four children, Danny, Tony, Dawn, and Bobby, Vesco's mother and father, and his sister and her husband whom we picked up en route, as well as Shirley Bailey. We had no stewardess. At Wilmington I had had the existing galley expanded so that meals could be prepared on board. No precooked, flash-frozen airline fare for Vesco. I had been told about Vesco's eating habits. He has the appetite of a goat. His personal preferences run to pizza with pepperoni, chili, chili dogs, roquefort-burgers, and steaks so rare that you can hear them breathe. He could tolerate *haute cuisine* but his preference was at the bottom of the ladder. It was understood that I would do the cooking.

I had long since lost the capacity to be emotionally stirred by an airplane. But the reaction of the Vesco family to the prospect of flying in this magnificent machine was a joy to behold. Vesco had been a wealthy man for a few years and provided his family with every luxury. Time enough had passed for them to become used to money. But there's a big difference between old money and new money. The old-money people don't have the capacity any longer to be awed. New-money people don't have the capacity to hide their awe in situations like this. They really couldn't believe it. They tried, the adults that is. But their emotions could not be held in. It was the grandest Christmas present of them all.

Our flight plan called for stops at Detroit to pick up Vesco's sister and her husband; Pueblo, Colorado, for fuel; and then on to Palm Springs, California.

We took off from Caldwell before noon. The

weather was crisp and clear. Flight between Caldwell and Detroit is relatively along well-traveled air routes, therefore, I had to stay in the cockpit. I could hear a lot of "oohing" and "aahing" in the back of the airplane, and I could tell from the movement of the elevator trim wheel that there was a lot of walking about.

Our flight to Detroit took a little less than two hours. We were on the ground about thirty minutes. We picked up our two additional passengers and I had the fuel topped off. The next leg of our flight to Pueblo, Colorado, about four hours, gave me the chance to go back and mingle with my passengers. I took off my Captain's hat and put on my chef's hat and served a mixed menu. By this time everybody had become fairly used to being in the airplane and the atmosphere was relaxed and happy like a family party. Vesco himself acted like the proud *paterfamilias*. I've rarely seen him that way since. We touched down at Pueblo on schedule. It was already dark and cold. I left a small jet auxiliary engine in the tail of the plane on to keep the interior of the airplane warm. During refueling the passengers went into the terminal. In about an hour I was ready to go. The passengers boarded tired and ready for a snooze on the last leg to Palm Springs.

Takeoff was normal and I climbed to my assigned altitude. The weather at my cruising altitude was not clear of clouds. We could see from the reflection of the navigation lights that we were flying through light snow and there was a moderate amount of turbulence. But conditions like these are more uncomfortable than worrisome. We were over the San Juan Mountains about 150 miles southwest of Pueblo. The passenger cabin was dark except for one lone reading light—Vesco's. Harry went back to Vesco's seat. He returned to the galley to fix a drink for Vesco. I was talking to air-traffic control about the weather ahead. As usual my eyes swept the instrument panel. Suddenly—trouble!

The master caution warning lights came on. These are lights, one on each side of the cockpit at eye level, that serve to warn the pilot that there is a malfunction in one or more of the aircraft or engine systems. From this point on every action of the crew should be instinctive and automatic. I looked to my left at a console that is a trouble indicator. It's called an annunciator panel and it's made up of many small lights called annunciator capsules. Each is connected to an electrical circuit that monitors one specific vital function of the airplane. The annunicator capsule for the left engine oil pressure was on. I checked the left engine oil pressure gauge on the panel in front of me. Pressure was low—very low. I turned toward the cabin.

"Harry!" I yelled. "Come up here! I need you!" I made it sound as casual as I could. We were not in a panic mode yet. And until I knew exactly what was wrong I wanted to avoid alarming my passengers. Harry came forward. He saw the lights.

"Buckle in and get the checklist," I told him. "This is no drill!"

For the next thirty seconds we followed the standard procedure that would tell us if we really had a problem or a false indication. Apart from the oil pressure gauge everything was normal. Then the torque indicator for the left engine started to drop. We were indeed in trouble—bad trouble!

"Harry, we have to shut her down," I said. We went through the standard shutdown procedures item by item. As Harry read the checklist I accomplished the job. This is not to indicate that I did not know the procedure from memory. But, working as a team using a written checklist, the chance of missing something, especially under pressure, is virtually eliminated. Shutting down an engine in flight means, basically, turning off its fuel supply and accessories and stopping it from turning by "feathering" its propeller. This turns the blades so they knife into the wind and don't create a lot of drag that makes the airplane difficult to control. The propeller wouldn't feather! We went through the entire procedure again—nothing! Christ!

The propeller on a turboprop engine has several built-in safety devices called pitch locks. They restrict the angle to which the propeller can decrease in flight to prevent an overspeed. They operate by oil pressure. My gauge showed I had no oil pressure. This meant I was left with a potential time bomb. If I can't stop it from turning, can't control it without oil pressure, and can't lubricate it while it's spinning wildly, it can only do one of two things. It can spin faster and faster, heat up and break off, throwing itself through the side of the airplane, or it can seize and stop turning. We tried a third time. No soap.

"Oh, shit!" I said aloud. Harry agreed. All I could do now was to slow the airplane down to a minimum speed and still stay airborne. The idea was to slow the propeller down to reduce the chances of overspeeding and breaking off. But reducing airspeed had no effect. I couldn't believe it. Here was a fail-safe procedure that failed. I had practiced this feathering procedure in simulators and in the air, taught it to hundreds of students as an instructor. It always worked before. I never heard or read of a failure of this system. Any malfunction that occurs in aircraft operation in the United States must, by FAA regulation, be reported and the details circulated throughout the industry. That is mandatory. No report and no manual has ever, to my knowledge, dealt with the particular situation I was in. I would have said that a failure of this kind, especially on a Rolls-Royce power system which is probably the most dependable in the world, was impossible. This was one hell of a time to find out I was wrong. The only thing left was to get the airplane on the ground safely!

I contacted air traffic control and told them I was unable to maintain altitude.

"One November Charlie, what is your status?"

"Got one out, can't feather it," I replied.

"Roger, squawk ident." This meant that, by pushing a little button in the cockpit, our airplane would show up boldly on their radarscope.

"Gotcha!"

"Find me the nearest suitable airport," I requested.

"Are you declaring an emergency?" they asked.

"Not at this time," I told them. There was no point to it. And there was no need. I had by no means exhausted all of the possibilities for dealing with the situation. I still had control of the airplane and perhaps at a lower altitude that control would increase, although I didn't know for sure. Declaring an emergency would do nothing for me in the cockpit. A ship or a boat at sea can holler for help and help can be provided. A helicopter or a Coast Guard cutter can be dispatched to the scene. The vessel can be taken in tow, passengers and crew removed to saftey. You cannot park an airplane and wait. You can't heave to. The airplane will come down. It's up to the Captain, using all his skills, to make sure that the airplane comes down in one piece. The only thing that declaring an emergency would achieve would be to get a lot of people on the ground excited. If there was conflicting traffic in the area, I would be routinely informed and given instructions for avoiding it without declaring an emergency. In addition, any other aircraft in the area would be notified of my situation. I knew that if a suitable airport was close enough I'd have no trouble with a single-engine landing.

"You are fifty miles west of Alamosa," I was advised. Harry checked the numbers for Alamosa—runway length, field elevation, type of approach, etc.—in the airport information manual, which is required equipment in any aircraft. I was satisfied so I informed air-traffic control that we wanted to be cleared to Alamosa.

"Reverse course, this will be radar vectors," they told me. This meant I didn't have to navigate. Air-traffic control radar would guide me to Alamosa. I was cleared at my discretion to descend to 18,000 feet. This would keep me well above the tops of the mountains in the vicinity, provided I could maintain 18,000 feet. I started a gentle turn. Suddenly Vesco was in the cockpit.

Whether or not Vesco had, up to this point, any inkling of trouble, I couldn't tell. If the feathering procedure had worked, the stopped propeller would be clearly visible from the passenger cabin. But our prop was still turning. There was an appreciable change in the noise level when I reduced power and maybe this caught his attention. But it was probably the turn that got him out of his seat. He knew that there were no major turns scheduled between Pueblo and Palm

Springs. All the red lights showing in the cockpit confirmed his suspicion that something was wrong.

"What's happening?" he said. I needed him in the cockpit like I needed a boil on my ass. I told him simply that I was having trouble with the left engine and had to shut it down. I didn't have time for any lengthy explanations. But he persisted.

"Why is it still turning?" he asked.

"Yeah—well—that's part of the problem," I told him. "I'm going to land. Everything is under control." I don't think he believed me. At that moment I didn't care. I wanted him out of there. I suggested he go back to the cabin and tell the passengers to buckle up. He must have sensed my annoyance. He left, but not for long.

In the middle of the turn things started to happen. The airplane began to skid and yaw and I began to sweat in secret places. I tried to control the erratic movement, with only partial success. I had to reduce power on the good engine. Then I checked the panel again. The left-engine tachometer was oscillating wildly, indicating that the left propeller was going completely bananas. The effect was that of an 11½ foot disc stuck on the front of the left engine. We began to lose altitude fast. And I wished that Alamosa were right under me instead of fifty miles away on the other side of the San Juan Mountains. At that moment the possibility of a crash landing became very real. Even if the Utah salt flats were under us the prospects for a safe belly landing in a high-performance airplane are little more than minimal. I did not have much hope of survival in the terrain I would have to set down in. I needed a break.

I fought the airplane and my mind raced along like an IBM computer seeking and discarding solutions. It seemed like an hour, but actually it was only a very few minutes before the break came. I heard it before I saw it. The left engine had been whining like a mountain lion with his balls caught in the crotch of a tree, and was getting louder and louder. Now the noise began to subside. The drag eased off. The airplane was Dutch-rolling—sloshing around the sky like a trawler in a rough sea. I checked the tachometer. It was spinning down. Then I wasn't working quite so hard to keep the airplane in reasonably level flight. Suddenly, with a shudder that damn near tore the engine off the wing, that big propeller came to a dead stop. Whew! Now all I had to worry about was fire.

With the airplane back under control I could think again about landing at Alamosa. Even though the propeller was still not feathered and exerted considerable drag, I was able to hold my own.

During the previous few minutes we had descended through clouds. We broke out at about 16,000 feet under the overcast—2,000 feet lower than air-traffic control had cleared us to. However, even though we were flying through fairly heavy snow we could see the mountaintops beneath us. And what can be seen can be avoided. That's when Vesco came back to the cockpit again. He was white-faced. He grabbed me by the shoulder.

"Don't you see those fucking mountains out there?" he screamed. The well-modulated corporate tone had become a soprano screech.

"Of course I see those fucking mountains out there," I said. "Don't worry about them." His grip tightened on my shoulder. I forced my attention away from him and back to the things I had to do.

"I'm going to slow the airplane down," I told Harry. "I want to see how she behaves." I had to find out how slow I could fly and still control the airplane for a landing. It would be inviting disaster to try to land the Gulfstream at 200 miles an hour. Landing speed for this type of airplane with the load I was carrying and under optimum conditions would be around 110 knots. The closest I could come was 130 knots—a speed I could live with. I eased back the power on the good engine.

"What are you doing? What are you doing?" Vesco yelled. I thought he was going to pull my shoulder off.

"Mr. Vesco," I said, "please go sit down and let me fly the airplane," I told him. He didn't argue.

I put power back on the good engine and concentrated on finding Alamosa, which was not easy. I was beginning to get below radio-reception level for air traffic control. I told them I was passing through 16,000 feet and that this had to be a one-shot approach. Apparently they were worried that I was too low.

"One November Charlie," they said, "Alamosa is twelve o'clock twenty miles. Switch over to Alamosa, they have been alerted."

"Alamosa, this is One November Charlie, twenty west, descending." They acknowledged and told me some things I didn't really want to hear. There was a strong crosswind and the runway was slippery with patches of frozen snow and ice—braking action poor! But I had no choice.

We located the rotating beacon, and for the first time I was conscious of taking a breath. Now that I had found the airport I knew I could land on it. I set up my approach pattern. It had to be right.

Because of the mountains and my unfamiliarity with the area I had to make a fairly steep turn onto the final approach.

"Are we gonna make it?" Vesco's voice almost shattered my concentration. I didn't even look back.

"Yeah!" I yelled. "That fuckin' idiot," I muttered to Harry. I was ready to tell him to shove his airplane up his ass. Did he expect me to tell him *no?*

For the next thirty seconds I was busier than a one-legged man in an ass-kicking contest. The approach end of the runway whizzed under the aircraft. I knew I was hot. I had to be. As soon as the wheels touched the ground I got on the brakes and felt the anti-skids doing their job. Thank God something was working! I used every sonofabitching foot of runway. When the airplane finally stopped, I looked at Harry. He was rigid! I had to laugh.

"What's the matter, Harry?" I asked. He couldn't even squeak.

The standard procedure here would have been to evacuate the airplane because of the possibility of fire resulting from the overheated brakes. However, we were three-quarters of a mile from the terminal building and the outside temperature was below freezing. No emergency vehicle had come out and from what I could see none were on the way. Since there was no indication of immediate danger from fire I taxied back to the airport building as quickly as I could.

Vesco, gray faced and shaken, herded his confused and frightened family off the airplane. He was the last to leave except for Harry and myself. He left the airplane without a word. Harry followed the passengers into the terminal and I stayed behind to look at the engine. Walking around in that cold I became acutely aware of my bladder. I had to take a leak very badly. I was also getting very angry at serial number 97—this particular Gulfstream. I was standing near the nosewheel well away from the overheated main gears. I peed on the airplane. I felt relieved.

I walked back to the terminal fully expecting a confrontation with Robert Vesco. I felt personally and solely responsible for what had happened and I wouldn't have blamed him if he fired me on the spot.

The terminal building was a one-story cement-block affair that looked like a jail. Besides the Vesco entourage and a few airport and airline personnel there were a couple of cowboy types and an Indian or two, braids and all. I found Vesco at a public telephone hanging on the wall. Shirley was with him. As soon as he saw me he handed the phone to Shirley and came over to me.

"How do we get to Palm Springs?" he asked. It was the last thing I expected to hear.

"I'll take care of that right now," I said. I left him with mixed emotions. Despite my willingness to accept full responsibility for the near-disaster, I knew I had done a hell of a job getting the airplane down and saving a lot of lives, including my own. I think Vesco knew it too. Even if he was ready to fire me, a small compliment or a simple "thanks" would not have been out of order. But, what the hell!

I had considered the matter of getting Vesco and his family to Palm Springs while we were still in the air. As unusual as this might seem, considering the circumstances, that's the way a corporate-aviation pilot must operate. It's an essential part of his job—to consider all his passenger's needs, especially in situations like this.

An airline Captain, on the other hand, sees his responsibilities to his passengers and crew end as soon as they leave the airplane.

The moment that the left engine had failed the prospects of going on to Palm Springs diminished steadily and rapidly to zero. During the less frantic minutes I had given some thought about how I would get my passengers to California. A lot would depend on where I set the airplane down.

There were a number of charter services that could provide aircraft and crews to take care of my passengers. The closest outfit was in Denver only 150 miles away. That was Gates Learjet. I wasn't too thrilled with the idea of contacting them after my unpleasant association had ended less than two months before. I would have to holler to them for help. No matter what they thought of me, business is still business. And, I was pretty sure that Robert Vesco would demand that I get him out of Alamosa one way or another, post-goddamn-haste, even if I had to make a deal with the Devil.

I still had one friend at Gates, my only friend, Ned Heppenstall, the senior vice-president. I called him at his home, just a little nervous about how he might greet me. After all, corporate politics can blot out the closest friendships. But Ned was glad to hear from me. I told him what happened and that I needed transportation for a dozen people to Palm Springs—right away. He reminded me it was still holiday season and it would take some doing to dig up a couple of crews but he promised that he would get on it right away and stay on it until my problem was solved, even though it was then nine o'clock at night.

I told Vesco what I had done.

"How long do you think it will take?" Vesco said. I told him I couldn't even guess but that it would be a couple of hours anyway. He thought for a moment, then called Shirley over and told her to arrange for some wheels and rooms at a local motel where his family could keep warm and rest. He seemed especially concerned about the children. He would follow later on. Then he asked me about the Gulfstream. I told him that we obviously needed another engine. He looked surprised.

"Wasn't that sonofabitch inspected?" he asked. "Wasn't it supposed to be in tip-top shape? What the hell happened?" I had to tell him the truth.

"Mr. Vesco, I just don't know," I said. I felt like a real klutz. After all, it was my job to know. He looked at me for a minute.

"Go buy a new engine," was all he said.

Ned called me back about an hour after Vesco went to the motel and told me he had arranged everything and that two Lear jets would arrive at Alamosa sometime during the night. He would call me as soon as they left Denver.

While waiting for the aircraft from Gates I went out to assess the damage to the Gulfstream. It was pitch black. The airport had no facilities for a proper inspection. We gave up the idea of anything more than a flashlight look-see. But we did check the propellor of the left engine. As mentioned earlier the prop on this type of engine should move freely like the blade on an electric fan. Harry and I strained our balls off. We couldn't budge it. It was as if the goddamn thing had been welded to the nose case. This meant only one thing to me. We had had a massive internal failure somewhere. I had no way of knowing what it was but indications were that it had to be in the nose case. When the engine was disassembled for repairs later on, the inside of the nose case was a junkyard.

Harry and I stood looking at the engine. We were absolutely helpless. Harry had this silly grin on his face. He was shivering like I was. His teeth were chattering like mine were. His shoulders were hunched like mine. And I'm sure he felt that if he bent his foot his toes would break off. But the two of us stood there with a lousy little flashlight looking at that super-perfect Rolls-Royce engine like a couple of farmers at a burlesque show.

"I just don't believe it," I told Harry. Harry was new to the airplane and he didn't know what I didn't believe.

"There must be thousands of these fucking engines

flying all over the goddamn world and 200 of these same fucking airplanes with the same engines flying all over the goddamn world and, on my first fucking flight, with my new fucking boss and his whole fucking family, I have to draw the only fucking one of these goddamn airplanes with this idiot-fucking-proof engine that goes bananas. And I don't fucking A-well know why!"

"It's a goddamn-fucking shame!" Harry said. I could have killed him.

Whatever happened should never have happened. I've never heard of it happening before or since—not like this. A couple of hours later when the Lear jets came in from Denver the pilots were equally baffled.

Harry and I went back to the terminal. Following Vesco's instructions I set about finding an engine for the Gulfstream. I called Ken Spinney—dependable Ken Spinney—at his home. I told him what the problem was.

"I don't fucking believe it!" Ken said.

"It's fucking true!" I told him. "Where can I get another one of those goddamn engines?"

If, from the foregoing, it is deduced that the adjective "fucking" is an integral and necessary part of the aviation vocabulary, you are absolutely right—especially in situations like this.

Ken had nothing available. He put me on to Dallas Airmotive and told me who to call.

Contrary to Vesco's instructions I would not "buy" a new engine. Unless an engine is totally destroyed it is usually repaired and rebuilt. To keep the airplane in service a replacement engine is installed while the damaged engine is being overhauled. What I had to locate was someone with the kind of engine I was looking for. If Dallas Airmotive could not help me they could probably hand me off to somebody else.

Dallas Airmotive had what I needed and I arranged to have it flown from Dallas to Alamosa with two mechanics. It would arrive sometime the next day. Now all I had to do was sit and wait for the Learjets that would get the Vesco party out of the way.

Harry called his wife and told her what happened. She had planned to meet us at Palm Springs. We agreed that since it would take a couple of days to get the airplane fixed that she could come to Alamosa and accompany us to California when everything was finished.

By now the airport, which resembled a Pony Express way station, was deserted except for Harry and me. I was in a lousy frame of mind. The fact that it was the engine that had failed did not, in my view, relieve me of full responsibility. My professional pride was fractured. And all the consoling noises that Harry made during those miserable hours didn't help one goddamn bit. On top of that the airport coffee tasted like something drained out of a radiator.

About three A.M., Denver called and told me that two Lear jets were on their way. I alerted Vesco at the motel to gather up the clan. The jets arrived before Vesco got to the airport. As soon as they arrived Harry and I transferred the baggage from the Gulfstream to the jets, glad for something to do. Waiting for Vesco, the crews of the Learjets, marveled over the Rolls-Royce failure. It was like discussing a terminal cancer case. I was relieved when the Vesco party arrived—but only briefly.

I've described Shirley Bailey as a pert little woman. Over the years with Vesco I came to see how Vesco minions tended to assume Vesco attitudes. I also came to recognize a quality in Shirley that can best be described as cataclysmic. She was like the guy in the comic strip with the black cloud over his head. She was Madame Doom herself.

The Vesco party swept into the airport. Vesco himself assumed the duties of assigning his entourage to the different aircraft. Shirley hung back in the terminal. I don't know why, but I had the feeling that she wanted to talk to me in private. At one point I had to go back to the terminal. Shirley beckoned to me, and I went over to her.

"Captain Eisenhauer," she said. "I don't know quite how to tell you this."

Oh, Jesus! What now? Shirley was a little bitty woman, but she could convey with one look a message of eternal damnation.

"I'm afraid the aviation department is finished," she said. "I'm sorry for you," she said, "but I think you and Mr. Werner ought to see about flights back to New Jersey." Then she walked out to the waiting airplanes.

I followed her. My brain was absolutely dead. The trouble was that I agreed with her. Nothing that happened since the Gulfstream had left Caldwell that morning could possibly have supported the creation of an aviation operation for ICC.

Vesco was the last person to board a Lear jet. I stood there by the wing tank like Algernon Asshole, flopping my hand at him. "Bye! Bye!" I remember thinking that freezing to death was a pleasant way to go. Vesco turned toward me.

"See you in Palm Springs," he shouted, above the noise of the one engine that had been started. "We'll have your rooms ready. Call Ralph."

Sonofabitch!

Call Ralph. I didn't know what it meant. The handoff. Vesco didn't have the balls to fire me himself. Ralph Dodd would do it. I waited until the airplanes reached the end of the runway and I went back to the terminal. Harry was there.

"What's happening?" he asked.

"Beats the shit out of me," I said. "I have to call Ralph Dodd." I didn't want to tell him that I thought we would both be looking for work in the morning. I called Dodd.

Surprise! Surprise! I was a fucking hero.

"Ike, you have it made!" Ralph shouted over the telephone. "Bob thinks you're the greatest thing since Lindbergh! What the hell happened?" I gave him a quick rundown. I told him about getting another engine, and he told me that Vesco had mentioned it. "You're in charge, Ike," he said. "Yessir! You sure are!" I felt like the guy who learned the difference between circumcision and castration in the nick of time.

The mechanics of an engine change are fairly simple. Especially a change like the one needed on the Grumman. A couple of mounting bolts and a few connections. But that's in a heated hangar with lots of light, all the mechanics and tools you need, and time.

It's a different bag of snakes in a desolate valley between two mountain ranges at an airport with minimal facilities. I'd been through engine changes before—scheduled engine changes—and even away from home base they only took a day with a little time to kill. But this was rather nonstandard. As events proved later it was strictly a Vesco-type situation.

Harry went into town to get some decent hot coffee, long Johns, a couple of pairs of coveralls and cold-weather gear for the two of us. We needed something to sling the broken engine off the Grumman and hang its replacement in so we could nail it on. The only equipment available at the airport were two strong Indians and a muscle-bound cowboy—not enough for a one-ton engine. A bunch of people were standing along the fence beside the terminal. They had heard about the "emergency" landing and had come out to see the fun. I had already asked everybody at the airport—official, that is—if there were a hoist, a derrick, a crane, anything I could use to handle the engine change. All I got was, "Sheeeeee-it!"

I saw a guy in coveralls with dirt on them that looked like grease. He wore a cowboy hat, pacs and a sheepskin coat. I figured anybody with grease on them would have some idea of what I was talking about. I made it simple.

"I need something that can handle a ton," I told him. I pointed to the Gulfstream. "I want to take an engine from an airplane that will land here soon and move it to that airplane over there, take the busted engine off of that airplane so I can put the new engine on to that there airplane." He looked at me like I was a simpleton.

"Why don't you call the telephone company?" he said. Somehow I had the feeling that I was the dumbest asshole in creation. But I had to ask.

"Why?" I said.

"They got a piece of work that looks like a bull's pecker," he said. "It can reach out way yonder or suck way in. I seen it pick up a whole bunch of telephone poles. That what you're looking for?"

It took me a couple of minutes to find out how to

get in touch with the owner of the bull's pecker—the local phone company. I did a little dickering, agreeing to pay bonus money to the crew and had the mobile crane ready when the DC-3 arrived from Dallas. After that it was all downhill—if you can call working in twenty degrees below zero downhill. It took two full working days—fourteen-hour working days. When all the bits and pieces that had gotten scattered around were finally accounted for, I climbed into the cockpit to see if everything worked. Beautiful! I was satisfied. The engine would get me to Palm Springs. There were still problems.

I knew my brakes would only be partially effective due to the abuse they had taken when I had landed. There was no way they could be fixed at Alamosa. But this was not a major problem. I took off from Alamosa late in the afternoon of the third day, still not knowing what the future held. But, shit! California here I come.

5

June 13, 1971—N728PA to N11RV

"Might as well go out and fly the sucker," I said to Captain Ned Brown, manager of flight training for Pan American in Miami, Florida. I had known since the day before that the airplane that would put Robert Vesco in the most exclusive club in the world had arrived from Tel Aviv. Within a very short time the official transfer of ownership would take place and Robert Lee Vesco would become one of two men in creation who had a Boeing 707 jet aircraft for his own personal and exclusive use. The other person was the president of the United States.

For two and a half years I had been hauling Vesco and his family, friends, business associates, and victims all over the world in the Grumman Gulfstream One. In the early days when most of Vesco's activities were confined to the Western hemisphere the Gulfstream was adequate. When his overseas ambitions began to flourish in 1970, Vesco's already furious pace increased to a point where he was pushing both the Gulfstream and its crew almost beyond their capabilities. We were living very dangerously.

The Gulfstream's range was less than 2,000 miles. It

was simply not designed for frequent transatlantic crossings on a regular schedule. Two fuel stops, Newfoundland and Iceland, were required most of the time on ocean crossings. But Vesco never made a trans-Atlantic crossing in the Gulfstream. He would fly commercially to Europe. When he got there he would expect the Gulfstream and its crew to be ready and waiting when he arrived. It made no difference to him, if he even thought about it, that the crew were red-eyed from lack of sleep and exhausted to the point of collapse. It was not unusual for Vesco to cover as many as six European cities in the same day and to do this three or four days in a row.

At one point my crew actually mutinied. My co-pilot Harry Werner actually left his seat during an ocean crossing, went back to the passenger cabin, and refused to have anything more to do with the operation of the airplane. He didn't give a damn if I fired him. I couldn't blame him. There were other pressures on Harry, besides the work load, that brought him to this point. They arose out of Vesco's character which was one of unrelenting vindictiveness toward any individual who displeased him for any reason whatsoever. Somewhere along the line he had done something to offend Vesco. Harry didn't have the vaguest idea of what he had done. I didn't blame him for getting up out of his seat and staging a sit-down strike. I didn't fire him.

A few months later I saw that Harry was going over the edge. We had just finished another one of our marathon trips. Vesco had been riding Harry unmercifully. I gave him a couple of weeks off. Not only did I hope that Harry could get his act together again but that Vesco, with Harry out of the way, would forget whatever it was that was bugging him.

I never found out how things might have worked out. Harry simply never came back to the crew. Vesco never said anything and neither did I. But I know that Vesco realized how valuable a crew member Harry was. Vesco would never admit a mistake. Worse, he would often make the same one over and over. From the time I went to work for him he held a grudge against every

stuck my finger under his oversized, spongy-looking horn.

"Vesco," I said, "don't you ever talk like that to me again—ever!" I walked away and went to my room. He never mentioned the incident again. Neither did I. But, he never repeated the routine.

It was the only head-butting we ever engaged in. Now it was time for another. A certain etiquette had evolved in my relationship with Vesco. My operational activities and problems were directed almost exclusively to Dodd. This included the frequent memoranda I wrote about the need for a new airplane. I don't want to give the impression that I was constantly whining into Vesco's ear. The system generally worked smoothly. But Ralph's function was little more than procedural. He was little more than an office manager. In the matter of the continuous and growing problem with the Gulfstream and my crew, dealing with Dodd was as futile as trying to whistle with a mouthful of mashed potatoes. I knew I wasn't getting through to him.

Any time my pipeline to Vesco got clogged I went directly to the man himself. This was infrequent enough so that he usually paid attention to what I had to say. But with regard to the plane even that didn't seem to work. In April of '71 I lowered the boom. It was in London. And again we were just winding up another mad excursion all over Europe immediately following another one of those ball-busting over-ocean hops. I did not like the idea of bracing Vesco on the aircraft. I would have preferred the more businesslike atmosphere of an office or even a hotel suite. But this time I had no choice. Vesco would be flying back to the United States aboard a commerical airliner in very few hours. I would take off in the Gulfstream and fight my way to Iceland, Newfoundland, and Caldwell only to find Vesco rested and full of piss and vinegar, ready to go again. Bullshit!

I asked Vesco if I could speak to him alone in the airplane. I sent the other crew members into operations. Our passengers left the airplane. When we were alone Vesco gave me one of his slaunchways looks. It was the look of a street guy who knows that someone is going to throw him a curve.

"What's on your mind, Ike?" he said. Like a grade-B actor in a grade-B movie he pulled out a Kool, tapped it on his thumbnail and casually stuck it in his mouth and set fire to it.

"This is my last fucking flight over water in this fucking airplane," I said. I got through to him. He kind of rutched around in his seat. I honestly thought I caught him completely by surprise. But, I didn't. He grinned at me.

"I'm way ahead of you, Ike," he said. "I've read all those goddamn memos you wrote. When you get back start looking around for what you want. Work it out with Ralph." I wasn't going to let him win this one. I played it cool too.

"Four-engine jet—right?" I said. "No more grasshoppers."

"That's right," he answered, "as soon as you can. I'm going to need a big airplane very soon." He got up and left the airplane.

Two hours after Vesco told me, in the Gulfstream, that we would get a four-engine jet, I took off from Heathrow Airport, London, on the last transatlantic flight I would make in that airplane. Even reports of rotten weather and strong head winds all the way across didn't dampen my spirits. I knew it would be a long grind but I didn't even consider the possibility of not making it.

Now, I'm not a believer in curses, omens, hexes and the like, even though I'm a Pennsylvania Dutchman. But it wouldn't take much to convince me that that son-of-a-bitching Gulfstream had a soul—and a mean one at that. It was waiting for the right moment to stick it to me for pissing on it back at Alamosa. That last over-ocean flight was the hairiest of all.

The distance between London and Caldwell, New Jersey, is roughly 3,200 nautical air miles broken up into three legs; London to Keflavic, Iceland, 1,000 miles; Keflavik to Gander, Newfoundland, 1,200 miles; and Gander to Caldwell, New Jersey, 1,000 miles. Scattered across the Atlantic both on land areas and at sea are navigation installations that transmit radio signals by which pilots can find their way accurately from point to point. Some of these installations have radar, make periodic weather reports and can, and do, talk directly with the pilot on special communication frequencies. The sea installations are ships, anchored, that maintain station all the time within a very limited area. Crews are changed periodically. Some of the land installations are manned—others are not. All are helpful and comforting as long as the airplane stays in the air.

The first leg from London to Keflavik was just about what I had expected, long and grinding. At Keflavik operations, the weather briefing I was given indicated diminished head winds to Gander. Wrong!

The first indication I had about how wrong Keflavik weather had been was over my first positive checkpoint, Ocean Station Alpha, about 300 miles west of Keflavik. I was way behind schedule.

But Alpha gave me the same information about the winds I would encounter as Keflavik. They told me that the head winds would slack off very shortly. My instinct told me that somebody had the wrong numbers but I hoped fervently that those people down below were right. They were the only source of information I had. I couldn't see anything. There was no way I could make even a rudimentary eyeball check of my progress. At this point I considered my situation and toyed with the idea of returning to Keflavik. I re-computed and decided that I could make Gander safely. It would simply take longer to get there. But, the winds did not diminish—instead, they increased.

My next checkpoint was off the southwestern tip of Greenland; Alpha Sierra, a radio beacon that was 100 miles off my right wing. I was even farther behind schedule. At that moment that perverse Gulfstream made its move against me. I thought fleetingly of the engine failure over Alamosa and wondered if this goddamn airplane had a death wish.

First a red light came on, the right AC generator was hot. No big deal. I switched it off to let it cool. The red light went out. After a short time I switched it back on. Then another red light came on—the AC generator had automatically switched itself off. Still no big deal. I had no anti-icing on the right engine but as long as the situation stayed the way it was I would not have to shut the engine down. Screw you, Gulfstream.

If the Gulfstream could have talked it would have said, "Oh, yeah? Try this on for size." Then my main navigation device died. This meant that I had no way of knowing exactly where I was over the water. And the sea and land stations couldn't help me unless they had radar and I was in range, which at that precise moment was not the case. I was reduced to a single navigation instrument, a Collins ADF (automatic direction finder). All it could do is show me in what direction a radio station was but not how far. It has an effective range of a couple of hundred miles if conditions are right. Their usefulness is limited close-in to a destination in today's highly sophisticated navigation network. In my present situation over the North Atlantic it was only a little better than nothing at all. But it was the only whccl in town.

The winds had taken their toll. My two checkpoints showed me that the winds reached upward of 100 knots. And it was all against me. My speed over the water was reduced to less than 150 knots, slower than that of an old piston whacker like a Constellation. My engines didn't know the troubles we had. They kept gulping fuel at their normal rate. As far as they knew we were tooling along at 250 knots. I knew there was simply not enough fuel to reach Gander. But, where the hell to go? Those friendly stations below were now useless to me. Even if I could find one of those ships, I couldn't land on it or even ditch in the ocean near it. The closest land was Greenland, 100 miles to the north.

It was easy to find Greenland. All I had to do was turn right. But I had to find an airport. And I had to be able to land when I found it.

As long as you have radio on board your aircraft, you're not completely lost. And I still had a couple of hours of fuel left. I switched over to high frequency and was actually able to reach Gander. I gave them my status and they suggested I attempt to reach

Narssarssuaq in Greenland. Their weather was hours old. The best they could do was to give me what they had. Now I was completely on my own. My first target was Alpha Sierra. If I could find that I would have, at least, a starting point. I made a turn to the right.

Months before I had told Dodd that our navigation systems were totally inadequate. I told Vesco. Dodd's excuse for not authorizing the installation of modern and redundant systems was cost. That's something pretty hard to argue with. The decision had to be made on the grounds of safety. This requires some understanding of aviation operations, and Vesco's response was always in the, "you-can-do-it-Ike" vein. That was something I always found hard to cope with. It was an absolute contradiction of what I knew to be his attitude toward flight. It terrified him. I think that if there was any other way to get around with the speed he demanded without leaving the ground he would never have set foot in an airplane. Still he constantly avoided dealing with matters of safety. For example, the runway lighting system at Caldwell was not only primitive, it was in a shocking state of disrepair. I had been on Clarey's back to improve it. His standard response was that he didn't need runway lights since the only night operation of high-performance aircraft was with Vesco's Gulfstream. If Vesco needed lights, he could pay for them. I finally got my lights by putting Vesco in the cockpit of the Gulfstream on a clear night and asking him to pick out the runway, which was right in front of us. With a great show of certainty he pointed to the Willow Brook shopping center. I pointed out his error and shortly thereafter I got my lights. Now, as I headed toward Greenland, I wished that I had Vesco and Dodd along with me. It would have taken seven hours to clean the shit out of the airplane.

Inside the limit of 100 miles, the ADF is a reliable piece of equipment for the most part. This was one of those times and I located Alpha Sierra. Since I now knew my exact position I was able to zero in on Narssarssuaq, which was some 70 miles to the north, about fifteen minutes' flying time. But, I did not know the terrain or anything about the airport. I couldn't see the ground because of the solid undercast. I would not begin my descent until I could contact somebody who could tell me what I needed to know. I made several attempts but did not get an answer from the tower until I was directly overhead at 26,000 feet. The bad news was that the overcast was practically on the deck. And that the airport was tucked in against a mountain at the end of a fjord. The only thing to do was to get back over the ocean, descend, and copy the approach information for the airport as it was read to me over the radio.

Suddenly, my fuel situation was critical. I could stooge around for a little bit if I had to, but it was Narssarssuaq or forget it. If I didn't make the airport I was hoping they had me on radar so they could get a fix on where to find the wreckage.

I broke out of the overcast at about 200 feet, not far from the airport and the runway I would use to land on. I was still over water. From the tower, I received the weirdest warning of my career.

"One November Charlie, watch out for icebergs off the end of the runway."

It was a week before Vesco settled in at Fairfield long enough for me to go looking at airplanes. My recommendation had been to buy a Boeing 720B from Northwest Orient and install long-range tanks. I had gone out to Minneapolis to look at such an airplane and had made tentative arrangements for inspection and modification. But somewhere along the line Vesco had raised his sights. When I got back to Fairfield I went to tell Vesco about the airplane I had found. I never got the chance. By this time Vesco had moved his entire operation into a new building at 200 Fairfield Road, designed in an architectural style I would describe as modern Chicken Delight.

Shirley announced me and told me to go in. Vesco came bounding out of the office followed by Ralph Dodd who was grinning like an idiot. Vesco put his hand on my shoulder and kind of turned me back in the direction of Shirley's office.

"You're going to Miami, Ike," he said. "I just

bought a 707 from Pan Am, and you're going to go to school down there to learn how to fly it. Everything is set for you and the crew. I'll see you in a couple of weeks. But keep me posted." That was that.

Vesco's new Boeing, a standard Pan American airliner, was promised for the middle of June. It had to undergo a pre-sale inspection. At the time negotiations were completed it was still in service. As soon as it could be released from scheduled operations it would be flown to Tel Aviv, Israel, where Pan Am had contract maintenance facilities. After inspection it would be delivered to Miami and its new owner. Then I would take command. That was a mere five and a half weeks away.

Vesco wanted me and my crew fully trained and certified to fly the airplane the day it arrived in Miami. Ned Brown, Pan Am's manager of flight training in Miami said it couldn't be done. At the very least it would take twice that time. But he was willing to try. He agreed to personally take charge of my training as aircraft commander. He made one thing clear; there would be no bending the rules. I and my crew would have to meet every standard. Period. It was a vicious grind but I made my deadline. Without Captain L.N. "Ned" Brown, I wouldn't have made it in the time allotted.

When Captain Ned and I went out to the Boeing that hot June morning, I didn't run up to it with a brush and a little can of paint to inscribe the name, Silver Phyllis, on its nose. The name came later and never actually appeared anywhere on the airplane. Before I could fly it up to Newark, there were still a number of things that had to be done.

The airplane would not belong to Vesco until an official transfer was accomplished. For tax purposes this would take place in Nassau, the Bahamas. It was a tricky bit of business that was, nonetheless, legal. Following that, registration had to be transferred, and the aircraft number changed. Then, finally, I would have to successfully complete my final check ride with an FAA Inspector.

That first flight was routine. If I felt anything at all,

it was relief that the intense period of training was coming to an end. Big as it was, and as important as it was to Vesco, that Boeing was just another airplane to me. It was more important to me to prove to that FAA Inspector the following day that I was a fully qualified Airline Transport Pilot—Pan Am style. In the training of flight crews, Pan Am is the Tiffany of the business. My second flight in the Boeing was my check ride the next day, and it lasted two grueling hours.

The highest practical rating for an Airline Transport Pilot is Category Two (CAT Two) in type of aircraft. This means that an aircraft commander may, when the occasion demands and at his own discretion, exceed minimum flight operation requirements to a different degree than that which is otherwise standard. All during training—in the simulator and in flight—Captain Ned had been guiding me at the CAT Two level of performance, his way of insuring that I would qualify at the normal level, CAT One.

I completed all of the required maneuvers. The FAA Inspector turned to Captain Ned, who sat in the right seat.

"I'm satisfied with your student, Captain Brown," he said. "Let's go home."

"I'm not," Ned said. I was as surprised as the FAA Inspector. In fact, I goddamn near went into shock. Ned winked at me. "We're going for CAT Two," he told the Inspector.

"On the first check ride?" the Inspector asked. He was flabbergasted.

"We can do it," Ned said very simply. The Inspector scratched his head.

"Okay," he said. "But, I'm telling you now, your student has his ticket. If he busts the CAT Two check, he busts the works."

"Understood," Ned said. Me? I didn't say a word.

We went through the routine. Just the way Ned figured it, I made the grade. If this sounds like I'm boasting, I sure as hell am. It's one of the proudest achievements of my career.

That afternoon I flew the Boeing to Nassau where a gang of lawyers, some of whom I had brought with me, legalized the rip-off of Uncle Sam's piece of the action. The procedure took a couple of hours, and I was back in Miami before dark. I called Vesco and told him I'd be up to Newark the next morning with his Boeing. During the night, all Pan American identification was obliterated and Nan Seven Two Eight Papa Alpha became Nan Eleven Romeo Victor.

It was still a long way in time and money from becoming that spectacular flying command post/ bordello that would help Vesco accumulate nearly half a billion dollars.

6

June 17, 1971 JFK—LBG

Vesco was in Paris.

His instructions to me when I had called to tell him that his Boeing had arrived in Miami were to pick him up in Paris around noontime on Friday (June 18, 1971). That's how certain he was that I would deliver.

I had arranged prior to the end of my training to hire an experienced Pan American 707 Captain and a flight engineer who would crew the Boeing for the first several weeks of operation. It was a matter of common sense. The Boeing would be operating within the worldwide Pan American structure and an experienced Pan Am Captain could fill me in on all those details that can't possibly be covered in training. He could tell me, for example, just how to deal with the chief of maintenance in Frankfurt or station manager in Pago Pago. The engineer would work with Herbie to improve his efficiency under actual working conditions. At Ned Brown's recommendation I signed up Captain Frank M. Briggs, a retired Pan American captain with 37 years of service. The engineer I hired was Peter H. Dolliver, currently on furlough from Pan Am, an ex-

Air Force pilot with three years experience with Pan Am.

With Ralph Dodd as our only passenger we made the flight to Newark. I had to leave Bob Brunelle, one of the crew, back in Miami for further training.

The next day, June 17, 1971, I made my first ocean crossing nonstop in Robert Vesco's service. I put the Boeing down at LeBourget Airport outside Paris shortly after sunup the next morning. The flight was a lot more comfortable and less hazardous than those made in the Gulfstream, but we all felt just as tired. I was grateful that Vesco was late getting to the airport. He didn't show up until almost six o'clock that evening. He had not yet seen the airplane he had bought.

We were on the aircraft waiting for him, much refreshed. We were all togged out in brand-new uniforms, Pan American style. It was the first time I had worn one since going to work for Vesco. Passenger service notified me on the radio that he was on his way. I gathered the crew to greet him at the top of the steps.

Vesco was accompanied by Dr. Milton Meissner, his recently acquired financial chief of staff. He got out of the airport van and, carrying his red clothes bag and a suitcase, literally bounded up the steps, two at a time. He was all smiles. Even before he said hello he looked back along that immense fuselage and up at the towering tail.

"Ooh! She's a *big* sonofabitch!" he said. Then he stuck out his hand. "Hiya, Ike, how do you like it?" What could I say?

"I like it, Bob," I said. He noted the uniforms and nodded his head approvingly. I introduced him to the crew, and he introduced Meissner all around. Herbie took his luggage, and Vesco looked the airplane over briefly, especially the flight deck. I knew he was tickled. He came back to me literally rubbing his hands together, pleased as punch.

"Okay, Ike," he said, "let's go show the goddamn Swiss what it's all about."

Luxury aircraft are commonplace at any major airport in the world. And airport personnel are very blasé about them and their passengers. But we really shook the shit out of everybody when we set down that Boeing at Geneva Airport. It is not the usual procedure to advise them of the number of passengers aboard, but only that ground service is indeed required, for example, baggage handling, passenger steps, passenger transportation, etc. I was directed to a parking area, located about a quarter of a mile from the main terminal building. I was concentrating on the "follow-me" jeep that was leading me to my parking stand and then the directions of the taximan's hand signals. It wasn't until he gave me the engine cut signal that I looked beyond him toward the terminal. Holy shit! It looked like a motorized lynch mob was approaching us.

Heading straight for the Boeing were the following: two motorized passenger ramps, two trains of baggage dollies, two huge passenger buses, three fuel trucks, a tug towing a power unit, an air-conditioning truck, two station wagons with passenger-service personnel in them, a van loaded with a cleaning crew, a catering truck, and a Swiss customs agent riding a bike. I pointed them out to Captain Briggs and he said, "Oh shoot!" I swear to God, that's what he said. We both burst out laughing. Pete Dolliver, my flight engineer, turned to see what was going on.

"Jesus H. Christ!" he said, "I've got to stop those people!" He left the flight deck in a flash.

His job as engineer required him to be the first one out of the airplane to check the nosewheel locking pin and signal the Captain that the airplane is properly chocked. Ordinarily he goes out the forward entrance door and down the steps. But Pete wasn't about to wait. He yanked up the deck hatch to lower 41, went down the ladder and went out through the belly door. Pete was a big man—six-foot, three-inches, and 200 pounds. That mode of exit was a tight squeeze for a guy as big as Pete. But he squirted through that opening like a judge caught in a cathouse raid. The next I saw of Pete he was running toward the advancing horde waving his arms like a maniac, signalling them to go back. Stop, we don't want any, arretons, go home, there's nobody here. It didn't do any good. They all swept past him except for the Customs agent who was still riding his bike and hadn't even reached him yet. Pete turned and made a gesture of futility in my direction. Briggs and I couldn't stop laughing. But, somebody had to open the goddamn door and face those people. That was my job. I left my seat.

Vesco was already standing near the door ready to go. I lifted the lever and swung the door open and there stood about forty people with their vehicles, arrayed around the airplane. All awaited what they thought would be a planeload of well-heeled American tourists. Vesco and Meissner stepped out of the airplane and went down the steps. They totally ignored the entire assemblage. He and Meissner walked over to one of the station wagons and got in. Herbie, just as confused and as nonplussed as we were, carried what little baggage there was over to the station wagon that held Vesco and Meissner, and threw it in back.

The departure of Vesco and Meissner apparently meant to all those service personnel that the VIPs on the airplane had been taken care of and that now all the passengers, all 200 of them, would leave the airplane and they could go to work. Respectfully, they waited. The passenger agents at the bottom of the steps, front and rear, clicked on their smiles. Nobody came out. Necks craned. There was a wait. Still, nobody came. Now I had to tell them that that was all there was; there weren't any more. I picked on the agent with the biggest smile and the most stripes. It was also very probably that he understood English.

"No more," I said. He didn't understand. I repeated my words. "No more, that's it." He was beginning to get the message. I tried French. "*Rien.*" I held up two fingers. "*Deux personnes, seulement.*" The light went on.

"I dun't bilif you, Captain!" he said. I indicated the steps.

"Take a look," I said. He regarded me for a moment as if trying to decide whether I was crazy or a *provocateur*. Suddenly he turned to another agent and exploded into French. I didn't understand what he was saying but from his gestures I got the meaning loud and clear. The gist of it was that Americans are so rich and so arrogant that they would transport *deux personnes seulement* in an airplane that big. *Merde!* That was one of the first French words I ever learned. It means—*shit!* We got out of there as fast as we could. But it wasn't over yet.

When we'd had the Gulfstream, I and my crew would usually put up at the Swissair Crew House at the Geneva Airport. It was a comfortable, friendly place, and I got to know a lot of the Swissair crews. The flight crews based in Geneva, for the most part, flew continental routes only. The international crews were based mostly in Zurich. We were somewhat unique in that we were not an airline, that we were American, and that we had made over-ocean flights in a Gulfstream One. We had a further distinction in that they believed us, the Gulfstream crew, to be very courageous in flying the Atlantic in such a small airplane.

I hadn't been in Geneva in over three months and I was greeted heartily by a dozen or so pilots, engineers, and stewardesses who were scattered around the lobby. The uniform impressed them. When the greetings subsided one of the pilots in heavily accented English asked me if I had seen the Boeing 707 with the two crazy Americans. "Imagine, only two passengers!"

"That was me," I said.

"You were one of the passengers?" he said.

"No, the Captain." I said. I was enjoying myself. The word spread quickly, and within seconds even the aircrew people I didn't know were gathered around me, Briggs, Dolliver, and Staretz.

I had received no other specific instructions from Vesco than to keep the airplane ready to go at a moment's notice. That was nothing new. It had been standard operating procedure in the Gulfstream. But, with an airplane as big as a Boeing, you simply didn't fly into an airport and say, "Fill her up and wipe the windshield." It became apparent very quickly, as a matter of fact on that first flight into Geneva, that new procedures for handling would have to be developed specifically to meet my needs if I were to keep Vesco's schedules.

For the past month or two I had heard the IOS situation crop up in conversations I couldn't help but overhear. A number of times Vesco had made not-so-veiled comments directly to me about his intention to grab hold of the entire IOS ball of wax. He had hinted pretty strongly that the Boeing would be a key factor for the coming IOS stockholders' meeting in Toronto, Canada, at the end of June.

I knew that he had already screwed Bernie Cornfeld out of his stockholdings and offices in IOS in a shell game I still don't understand, even though I later read explanations of it. Vesco had bragged about how he had, "fucked that sheeny bastard." Vesco was that kind of guy.

I only saw Bernie Cornfeld once in my life although, at the time, I didn't know it. It was in Geneva at the Hotel President where Vesco was staying. All I knew was that Vesco had a very important business meeting and wanted me handy in case things got muscular. I saw this chubby, bearded, bald, middle-aged hippie go into Vesco's suite. What the hell does Vesco have to fear from him? I remember wondering. At Vesco's orders I was in a room adjacent to his suite with the door open. Vesco was alone in his rooms. The discussion apparently started off at a high pitch. Generally the words were indistinct but the tone wasn't. They were two very angry men. The impression I got was that somebody was going to get fucked, but I couldn't tell who would wind up being the fucker, and who would be the fuckee. Even after Bernie stormed out of the suite breathing fire, what little hair he had all mussed up, I still didn't know who was which. Of course, I found out later on.

At the time of that confrontation Bernie had already been tossed out of IOS by his own people. Vesco wanted, and needed, Bernie's shares to lock up his control of IOS. But Vesco's complete victory over IOS was still nearly a year away. I would pin point the beginning of the assault around June of 1970 because of a seemingly unrelated event that took place in October of 1969.

Vesco had to have somebody inside IOS, if not on

his payroll, at least on his team. In the light of later developments I would have to finger that man as Christian Henry Buhl, III. Buhl was a director of IOS. Whatever Buhl might have testified to about his relationship with Robert Vesco, from my own experience I know that Vesco treated him with a great deal of deference.

On October 18, 1969, at one o'clock in the afternoon, I picked up Henry Buhl and his wife at LaGuardia Airport in New York and flew them to Detroit, Michigan. Uncharacteristically, Vesco had placed the Gulfstream completely at Buhl's disposal for as long as he might need it and ordered me to carry out any of Buhl's instructions. He had also told me to keep my mouth shut about this man and suggested that I disguise his identity on my passenger manifest.

In the early months of 1970, on our frequent visits to Geneva, I saw Buhl in Vesco's company—usually socially. On September 8, 1970, again on Vesco's specific instructions, the Gulfstream and its crew were placed at Buhl's disposal. I ferried Buhl and a man named Warren Avis from East Hampton, Long Island, to Montreal, and back to White Plains, New York. This was precisely at the time that the IOS board approved Vesco's loan proposal in principle.

Shortly before this flight Vesco told me how important Buhl was in his plans.

"Butter this shithead up, Ike," he said. "He hasn't got the brains to pour piss out of a boot but he does what I tell him. And, he's my man on the inside."

Ralph Dodd has a big mouth. Like a lot of small men, and I'm not talking physical stature, he would inflate the importance of his seemingly big job by dropping little bits of inside information on my head like sparrow shit. In June of 1970, back in New Jersey, he had been making noises about the fate of the Gulfstream. I didn't pay too much attention because I had been pushing for a new airplane and to me whatever he said was only so much stroking. I remembered these noises when in July he stated categorically that, "he" was putting the Gulfstream up for sale. This pissed me off immeasurably.

Considering Vesco's travel requirements you don't sell the only airplane you have that's worth a damn until you have another in hand better than the first one. Plus this action was in absolute violation of the terms Vesco and I had agreed upon when discussing the matter of who was running the aviation operation. If what Dodd said was true—about selling the Gulfstream as well as about his role in the sale—then I was seeing again the beginnings of a disease that infects the entire corporate-aviation industry. That is, the incursion by totally unqualified administrative hacks who are smitten with the mystique that surrounds aviation.

I had no beef with Ralph Dodd provided he stayed where he belonged, which was anyplace outside of my bailiwick. I recognized and accepted his right to review and sometimes reject my requests, which after all involved corporate money. But, once he stepped across the line, he was my enemy.

I laid my problem on Dick Clay. Richard Evans Clay was Vesco's general factotum. He traveled either with Vesco or in advance of him to thump the tub or smooth the road. He was an old and trusted friend of Vesco's, one of the few people Vesco believed he could rely on . . . and also one of the few people in his employ that Vesco did not regard with contempt. If there was any one man in the world who could put all the pieces of the Vesco puzzle together, it was Dick Clay. More than any man, at least in my time with Vesco, he had the king's ear. I liked Dick very much. And, I trusted him.

I cornered him in a bar in Cap D'Antibes on the French Riviera, where Vesco had gone for a couple of days of sun and sin. I had landed at Nice Airport a bare two hours earlier, after the usual skittering around the Continent. What Dodd had told me had been gnawing at me. He had also told me when I asked him what the hell we were going to use as a replacement for the Gulfstream that "we're getting Bernie Cornfeld's BAC 1-11," which didn't make any goddamn sense to me. It was even less adequate than the Grumman for our purposes. We would be going backward. Besides, as far as I knew, the IOS business was still very much up in the air and I knew goddamn well that Dodd did not rate high enough on Vesco's list to know more than, for example, Dick Clay.

"Dick," I asked, after I'd told him what was bugging me, "what does all this bullshit mean?" He kind of smiled at me.

"Don't worry about Ralph," he told me. "You're in charge. Bobby's got Ralph under control. And you know that won't change. Ralphy's just blowing dust."

He told me then that this casual meeting was not so casual.

"I'm not going to try to shit you, Ike," he said. "Bobby knows you've got a bug up your ass. He asked me to cool you down. Just remember one thing, you can get Ralph Dodds by the boxful. But, you—your kind of talent—ain't so plentiful. Bobby knows what he's got." I felt a hell of a lot better.

Vesco never did get Bernie's BAC 1-11. Bernie's creditors beat him to it. But he got everything else in the IOS inventory. In fact, a month after he got the 707, there was a general housecleaning of IOS headquarters in Geneva that my crew and I were involved in. But, that's another story.

Vesco used the Boeing as he did the Gulfstream for the next two weeks, zipping among the money centers of Europe, and toward the end of June, 1971 I flew him back to the United States where he put the final touches on his scheme to stampede the IOS stockholders into naming him chairman of the board. He was about to have his license to steal validated. And Silver Phyllis would help him do it.

7

June 27, 1971 GVA—EWR

Vesco left Geneva on the 27th of June, 1971, for the final assault on IOS.

An hour or so before he arrived at the airport, a mid-sized delivery truck drove up to the Boeing. I didn't pay a hell of a lot of attention to it at first. After all, trucks at an airport are just about as common as airplanes. What made me notice it, finally, was that it veered out of the mainstream of traffic and made a beeline for the Boeing, which was parked a fair distance out. A few moments after it had stopped an IOS security officer whom I had met a couple of times came onto the flight deck.

"*Bon jour*, *Capitaine*," he said. He was a cheerful guy who spoke about half a dozen languages, sometimes all at once.

"I have some boxes for you." I didn't know what the hell he meant. The way he mixed his languages, *boxes* could have been a Bulgarian word for something I really didn't want.

"What do you mean, boxes?" I asked him. He tried to describe them with his hands.

"Boxes!" he said. He looked at me like I was some

kind of nut. "Paper boxes! You know what paper *boxes* are."

"Right!"

"Meester Vesco sent them out," he explained. "They are very important. They are to be put in the cabin."

"How many?" I asked.

"About five hundred kilos," he said.

I didn't want five hundred kilos worth of cardboard boxes flopping around in the cabin.

"In the belly," I told him.

"But—"

"In the belly!" He shrugged his shoulders and left. I turned to Pete Dolliver, my engineer, and told him to open up the rear belly. After a minute or two it occurred to me that as Captain of this airplane I ought to have some idea of what I was carrying. I left the flight deck and went down onto the ramp and watched while two men, under the overseeing eyes of the security officer, loaded about twenty-five "transfiles," specially designed cartons for transporting records and office paper, onto the airplane. Pete estimated them to weigh about forty pounds each. They would not create a weight problem.

There were no markings on them to indicate where they came from or where they were going or to whom they belonged. There was nothing to indicate that they had been passed by the Swiss douane. I called the security officer over.

"What's in the boxes?" I asked. He made a typical Gallic gesture and smiled.

"What do I know?" he said.

"How'd you get in through the gate?" I asked him. He hesitated, looked away, looked back at me, and rubbed his thumb and forefinger together. I knew what he meant. He must have noticed my concern.

"Not to worry, Captain," he said. "They have been passed." He handed me an official-looking document. It had a stamp on it, which was all I was looking for.

"One must pay, always, for quick service," the security officer said. What the hell, I thought. It's Vesco's money, and his ass if somebody wanted to make something out of it.

I had no way of knowing at the time how those boxes would affect Vesco's life. He was later accused of actually stealing a large number of IOS shares from a bank vault to use in the all-important Toronto meeting of IOS stockholders. Those shares constituted a large chunk of his victory margin. I have no doubt that it was the IOS shares that were in those boxes. At least some of them. Later when Vesco showed up at the airplane he made certain that the boxes were on board even to the point of looking into the rear cargo area.

"Those boxes stay on the airplane," he said, "all the way to Toronto."

"Toronto?" I asked.

"Yeah," Vesco said. He held back while the others boarded the airplane and indicated to me that I should wait with him.

After nearly three years I got so I could read Vesco's moods pretty well just by looking at him. When the pressure was on he became withdrawn. His acquired social graces went out the window. He spoke in short, clipped sentences. He treated everybody with a disdain that bordered on nastiness. He always had a habit of twisting his head as if to relieve a tightness in his neck that I called his Ollie-the-dragon syndrome. Whenever I saw this I knew that Vesco was in his night-before-the-battle mood. Now his head was going like a speed bag in a gym.

"Ike," he said, with an unaccustomed seriousness, "You're going to be pretty busy for the next few days. This is 'big casino.' You and your crew are on full alert until further notice. You can bitch all you want when it's over."

"That's what you're paying me for, Bob," I said. It was the kind of thing he liked to hear.

Nobody mentioned IOS. But, Vesco's reference to Toronto had to mean the big stockholders' meeting scheduled for June 30th, something we all knew about.

Vesco, as it is now known, had a secret. And it was that without complete control of IOS, he was dead in the water. Hell—he was dead *period.* International Controls, which he had neglected in his IOS campaign, was now in a state of chaos. ICC was deeply in debt and damn near broke. Whatever else can be said about Vesco he never lost his nerve or his balls.

The flight back to Newark, as far as Vesco's behavior is concerned, was the grimmest I had ever experienced. He sat by himself covered with papers, ledgers, and note pads, all of which he studied with the intensity of someone cramming for a final exam that will make or break him. I don't think he ate a bite of food or had a single drink all the way across. It had become routine for Vesco to visit with me in the cockpit during these long flights. Not this time. I can't say even now whether his self-imposed isolation stemmed from that quality of concentration on detail that is said to be the mark of genius, or whether he simply wanted to be alone with the terrible fear that he might fail. I don't doubt that he was afraid. A street guy like Vesco, however, had to learn to cope with fear. He reminded me of some feisty guy who refuses to stay licked. By the time we landed in Newark Vesco had a snarl on his face that made him look as mean as a cornered Doberman. He was ready for a fight—and God help the other guy.

We landed in Newark about five in the afternoon. Vesco was the last one off the airplane. Before he left he asked me to come back and talk to him. We were well out of earshot of the rest of the crew. He was so tense his shoulders were hunched. He didn't waste any words.

"Get the airplane serviced before you leave," he said. "I want that plane ready to go—now. Then, you go home and stay by the phone and wait for my call." He brushed past me and left the airplane. I didn't see him again until three days later—in Toronto.

I didn't get a call until late the following morning. It was from Shirley Bailey. She read me a passenger list and told me that Vesco wanted me to leave for Toronto at five P.M. He would not be on the flight. I remembered his remarks of months earlier about how he intended to use the Boeing to further his plans. I had the feeling after Shirley's call that his going on to Toronto by himself was a calculated maneuver to that end.

Besides Vesco's wife, Pat, there were seven passengers on the Toronto flight. Four of them were ICC executives. The other three were IOS officers including C. Henry Buhl, all of whom Vesco had boasted were in his hip pocket.

My instructions from Vesco via Shirley were to drop my passengers and get back to Newark and wait. However, when I arrived in Newark I got further instructions to go, instead, to Kennedy and wait. This convinced me that Vesco was playing his game. We sat there biting our nails for thirty hours. At one-thirty in the morning, on June 30, the day of the IOS stockholders' meeting, we got our marching orders. Fly the Boeing to Toronto and report on arrival.

I called Ralph Dodd at the Royal York Hotel from Toronto Airport about four in the morning. He told me that Vesco wanted the airplane fully serviced, which means 160,000 pounds of fuel—enough for a flight of 5,000 miles or more. The crew was to stay at a motel near the airport. I was to wait for a call. Another thirty hours! This business was driving me and the crew crazy. Apart from not knowing what our next move would be, we didn't have a clue as to what was happening in Toronto. From the reports we read in the paper Vesco was about to get his head handed to him. This didn't help morale. We could all be out of a job at any moment. It would not have surprised me to see the Royal Canadian Mounted Police clippity-clop up to the Boeing, chain it to the ground, and throw us all into the pokey.

Dodd finally called me about noontime on July 1.

"Ike, Bobby wants you to get your ass in a cab and get to the hotel right away," he said. "Wear your uniform. Bobby wants you to look impressive." I got mad as hell. More mystery. I wanted to spit in his ear but I'd only mess up the telephone. I think Ralph was having the time of his life. He said he'd meet me in the lobby of the Royal York Hotel.

The Royal York Hotel is a stately place that caters to a well-heeled clientele. When I reached the foyer outside the Ontario Room, the huge ballroom where the main sessions were being held, the place was a madhouse. People swarmed out of the Ontario Room. Many of them angry and swearing, even the ladies, of which there were a large number. I overheard one silver-haired *grande dame* in expensive-looking clothes say to no one in particular, "They ought to hang that sonofabitch." I don't know why, but I assumed she was talking about Vesco.

Ralph Dodd appeared out of that mass of humanity, and I knew why Vesco had insisted I wear my uniform. The white cap, the four gold stripes, gave me high visibility. Ralph had his mechanical smile locked onto his face but I could see that he was worried and hassled. I asked him how things were going.

"Not good," he said. "It's a fucking war. Those Jew bastards are trying to bust our balls." He was talking about the dissidents, a group of former IOS big shots who were fighting like tigers to keep Vesco from taking control. They were all part of the old guard and probably had as much to do as Bernie Cornfeld did with the sorry state of IOS that gave Vesco his opportunity to move in. It was a toss-up as to which group was worse for the future of IOS, the dissidents or the Vesco gang. Dodd had mentioned a number of times, as did Vesco, that all the dissidents were Jews. That was not true, of course. But, enough of them were to give Vesco—and Dodd, who parroted all of Vesco's opinions—a handy tag to hang on them.

Almost as soon as Dodd made his anti-Jewish remark, Vesco and a bunch of his cohorts stormed out of the Ontario Room, bulled through the crowd, and disappeared into another, smaller conference room. Dodd broke off and scurried after Vesco yelling at me to stay where I was. There were two uniformed guards stationed outside the room Vesco had entered. They were checking credentials. A knot of angry people gathered around them. They allowed some to enter and barred others, sometimes physically removing them from the entrance. After a few minutes and obviously at a signal from inside the doors were closed.

I wandered among that crowd for almost an hour taking it all in. The tension grew as the minutes ticked away. I drifted over toward the smaller conference room and became aware that people were watching me. When I drew near a small group, all conversation would cease. After I passed one group I heard a male voice say, "Who the hell *is* he?" One thing Dodd had told me when I came into the hotel was that Vesco wanted me to be noticed. That's exactly what was happening. In fact, my presence there seemed to worry some of the people. Nobody spoke to me nor did I talk to anybody.

I took a position between the small conference room and the entrance to the Ontario Room. The doors to the small conference suddenly swung open. It was like a scene from a Mack Sennett movie. Vesco was first out of the room. He strode across to the Ontario Room and everybody else tumbled out of the room behind him. There was a lot of shouting and swearing, and I thought a couple of times that fist fights would break out. Vesco spotted me. His face lit up. He winked and gave me the thumbs-up sign. That meant that the war was all but over and he had won. I watched as he entered the Ontario Room and marched up to the dais.

Dodd, looking like he had been squeezed through a key hole, came by. He handed me a stockholder's pass.

"Bobby wants you to come in and watch the fun," he said and split.

According to reports there were about 350 stockholders at the two-day session. But it looked to me like half the population of Toronto was in that lobby and they were all trying to get into the Ontario Room at the same time. I was not about to join the pack. I waited. I'm glad I did. One of Vesco's ICC people, who had been in the small conference room, came over to me. He was grinning like a shit-eating cat.

"Ike, you should have been there!" the man said. "Bobby really stuck it to them. He clubbed those bastards right into the ground, and he used you and that big fucking airplane to do it." He went on to explain in a rush of words.

Vesco knew that he was involved in a cliff-hanger. He had forced an adjournment of the main session to regroup and work out a deal with the dissidents.

It was common knowledge—a sort of open secret—

that Vesco's victory at that point hinged on his being able to vote a great number of shares in the IOS stock-option plan. But the dissidents had gotten a court injunction that blocked Vesco from doing this. He had three options. One was to fight it out on the floor and probably lose. Two was to stall for time so that he could work out a way to get around the injunction (which he ultimately did although the maneuver still did not give him enough votes to ensure a victory). The third was to garner shares and proxies not represented at the meeting. And that's where the Silver Phyllis and I came in.

In the small conference room Vesco told the dissidents that he could force a twenty-four-hour adjournment of the main meeting if he had to break heads to do it. He told them that his Captain and his airplane were standing by to fly anywhere in the world to pick up shares and/or options, which were then being acquired by his agents, and be back in Toronto the following day. If the dissidents did not agree right then to come to terms, Vesco would, the next day, have the votes to assure him total victory and they, the dissidents, would get a serving of shit. On top of that Vesco said he would see to it that the dissidents would get the blame for preventing an orderly reorganization of IOS. The dissidents would be lucky to get out of the hotel alive.

My informant told me that Vesco was ready to call me into the room and hand me my itinerary. If it was a bluff, it worked.

Vesco did not convince all of the dissidents but he scared the shit out of enough of them to carry the day.

I went inside the Ontario Room to watch the show. There was still a lot of shouting and carrying on. Vesco even had one of the dissident leaders tossed out. Sometime during the meeting Vesco had one of his people bring me a note that instructed me to go to the airplane and stand by. To me, despite all the pandemonium, Vesco looked confident. No vote had yet been taken and my own observations were that there was no way that anybody could read anything out of what was going on. It looked like absolute chaos.

Because of the situation I simply could not understand what the note meant. Was Vesco getting ready for a fast getaway? Or, was he planning a swoop on Geneva's IOS headquarters as soon as he had won?

About four-thirty that afternoon I got a call from Dodd stating Vesco now owned IOS and would be leaving for Geneva within the hour. Vesco showed up at the airport a totally different man from the one who got off the plane in Newark three days earlier. He looked exhausted but his spirits were high. He was accompanied by his wife and three IOS people, who had helped him in the fight. Without giving any reason he told me we were going to Rome instead of Geneva, which was a surprise. I had really expected that Vesco would waste no time in occupying the IOS complex in Geneva and claiming title to the entire contents thereof. It had happened before.

Electronic Speciality Company (ELS) was a Pasadena, California, manufacturer of high-strength metal products mostly for the aerospace industry. Sometime in 1968 Vesco decided to go after it. He also had his eye on a couple of other California operations including Golden West, a small regional airline operating in and around the greater Los Angeles area.

The purpose of that first nearly disastrous flight on the Gulfstream the day after Christmas, 1968, was to look into the Golden West possibility and lock up the ELS takeover. I had followed Vesco out to Palm Springs from Alamosa and had the Gulfstream repaired. Vesco had arranged for accomodations for the crew at his Palm Springs hotel. It was all sun and fun for the first few days.

The only unusual occurence that first week in California was an invitation by Vesco to attend the Rose Bowl game on New Year's Day. What made it memorable, however, was that Vesco sat with the newly elected President of the United States, Richard Milhous Nixon. Vesco had boasted a number of times how tight he was with Nixon and was proud of the fact that a few months before he had sat on the dais of the prestigious Al Smith Memorial Dinner in New York. He even showed me a photograph of the event which pictured him sitting immediately behind Lyndon B. Johnson, James J. Farley, and Richard M. Nixon.

I wasn't very impressed with Golden West Airlines. I told Vesco so. I suggested that he might give it to Jack Clarey to play with but he went ahead with the acquisition anyway. It's one of the few times Vesco took a bath on a venture. He unloaded Golden West about six months later at a loss of almost a million and a half dollars.

Sometime around the end of January, 1969 Vesco, armed with boxes and boxes of proxies descended on the ELS stockhholders' meeting in Pasadena. In a show of strength Vesco had the proxies brought into the meeting room and stationed me and my copilot as guards over them. We were very conspicuous. Vesco literally bludgeoned William H. Burgess, founder and chairman of ELS, into submission. The boxes contained Vesco's authority. There wasn't even a vote. Vesco simply took over the meeting, declared himself chairman and chief executive officer, and announced his slate of directors and closed the meeting. Burgess was told to immediately vacate his offices and take his personal possessions with him. Vesco then left for the ELS executive offices nearby. His ICC people, including Harry and ,me, and a few of the ELS executives who had been at the meeting, went with him. I had become somewhat used to corporate coldheartedness. But I was not prepared for what happened when we got to ELS.

The ELS headquarters were located on an upper floor of a large and modern office building in Pasadena. Vesco led his "troops" through the lobby and up to the ELS suite. He barged through the reception area into the office area. Burgess and C. Ray Harmon, ELS president, were waiting in the hallway. Vesco ignored them. He turned to Dodd.

"Where's a fucking screwdriver, Ralph?" he yelled. It was an obvious attempt to shock and intimidate. And it succeeded. Dodd scurried around and found what Vesco wanted. Vesco then toured the offices instructing Dodd while he ripped the nameplates from the doors of ELS officers and executives. His language was foul. His manner, brutal. Secretaries, clerks, and so forth, who had turned out to welcome the new management, were thoroughly cowed. They could not believe what was happening. The only executive whose office was not violated was that of Elmer A. Sticco, ELS executive vice-president, who had sold out to Vesco and was largely instrumental in sandbagging Burgess. The spectacle was something I did not want to witness. I was angry, but there was nothing I could do. I left and went back to Van Nuys to wait for Vesco.

The ELS thing had left a sour taste in my mouth and maybe Vesco noticed it. He prodded me a couple of times asking if I had a bug up my ass. But I just kept my mouth shut. We were doing a lot of traveling up and down the West Coast and into Texas, where Vesco was butting heads with S. Mort Zimmerman, chairman of Intercontinental Industries, Inc. of Dallas. Intercontinental made bomb and rocket casings, a profitable business with the Vietnamese war in high gear. The bone of contention, as I understood it, was that Zimmerman charged that Vesco had bought the bomb company with bad paper. The deal was eventually straightened out.

At the same time Vesco was bouncing around to various locations owned by ELS doing pretty much the same thing he had done at the executive offices. Toward the end of our West Coast stay, an incident occurred that I like to think of as some sort of retribution for Vesco's barbarism. It's telling also serves to illustrate fairly clearly the two Robert Vescos whom I saw constantly over the next five years. He was a bully boy on the ground; in the air, however, he was a total coward.

Vesco had scheduled a flight from Pasadena to San Francisco for ELS business on the 5th of February, 1969. Early weather reports indicated a hundred-mile-wide, north-south line of thunderstorms all the way up the coast. I told Vesco that it would be wiser to postpone the trip to late afternoon or at least until such time as the frontal system had moved eastward.

"Goddamn it, Ike!" Vesco said, "go around the fucking things."

"No problem going around," I said. "But we're going to have to punch right through them to get into San Francisco."

"That's what we'll do," he said. I told him he wouldn't like it. But he insisted. All right, old buddy, I thought, you are going for a ride you will never forget.

The weather pattern required me to fly the Gulfstream along the eastern side of the San Joaquin Valley. We could see the frontal system to our left for the entire flight. About fifteen minutes out of San Francisco my radar showed that there would be no way of avoiding very heavy turbulence. I personally have no fear of thunderstorms. I respect them and I wouldn't fly through one for kicks. But, in general, modern aircraft are built to withstand even the most violent, provided the crew fully understand the limitations of the machine. My main objective then was to get on the ground as quickly as possible.

In corporate aviation the boss always sits in the same seat regardless of the type of airplane. You can make book on it. Vesco's roost was in the second seat on the right side of the airplane. In the Gulfstream I could look over my right shoulder and see him.

The first few bumps on the fringe of the thunderstorms didn't seem to disturb Vesco too much. As we got deeper into the cells I kept glancing back to see how he was taking it. Conversation in the back gradually stopped. Then I noticed that Vesco had both hands clamped on the armrests and was staring out the window at the flapping wings. He was trying desperately to play it cool.

Suddenly the Gulfstream slammed into a wall of water. The airplane seemed to stop dead momentarily. It hadn't, of course. Then it was carried up at a terrific rate that pegged the vertical speed indicator which, by the way, shows a maximum rate of six thousand feet per minute. We were in the shit and no mistake—driving rain, hail, and violent wind shear. But, I had braced myself for this. I had my radar operating in "contour" mode and it forewarned me of what to expect. I couldn't keep up a running commentary for the benefit of my passengers. They had no way of preparing themselves for the shock. I had made certain that they paid attention to the seat-belt sign and I was pretty sure then that nobody in the back would be stupid enough not to be firmly strapped in.

I had my hands full controlling the Gulfstream and forgot, for the moment, about Vesco. In the midst of all the turmoil I heard a plaintive bellow.

"Hey, Eisenhauer!" Vesco yelled above the noise, "let's get out of this shit, huh?" He tried to sound casual—but came across sounding about as casual as a guy who's just backed into a buzz saw. I didn't answer him but explored alternate routes to maneuver around San Francisco in an attempt to skirt as many of the thunderstorms as possible. No go. Approach control told me to follow their vectoring. Plenty of other planes were in the same boat, and we had no special priority in spite of Vesco's panic. I didn't dare tell Vesco that what lay ahead would be worse than what we were in. And was it ever! We were slammed up, down, and sideways.

Vesco never left his seat. He had that much sense. But he sure as hell made himself heard.

"Ike, get the fuck out of this shit right now!" he yelled.

"The people on the ground are calling the shots!" I hollered back. "We have to wait our turn."

"I don't give a fuck!" he screamed, "buy the sons of bitches." I looked back to see if he was serious, to see if he really meant for me to offer a bribe to the controllers on the ground, federal employees, to allow him to land ahead of everybody else.

"Goddamit, buy them!" he repeated. *"Buy them! Buy them! Buy them!"* He was absolutely terror stricken. But, I honestly believe he meant exactly what he said. I decided not to follow his orders.

Needless to say we landed safely a few minutes later. There was enough time during the final approach for Vesco to regain enough of his composure to behave as if nothing had ever happened. At one point, about a mile from the runway, Mother Nature gave Vesco her final shot. We had broken out of the heavy turbulence and the final approach was relatively smooth. Vesco had lighted a cigarette and was sitting in a relaxed manner. Then—whap! whap! The airplane felt like a car slamming into a pair of potholes. I threw a quick glance back at Vesco. The cigarette was gone. Maybe he swallowed the damn thing. He was sitting bolt upright and had resumed his death grip on the armrests. I looked away quickly before he saw my grin.

July 1, 1971

Vesco's Toronto Victory was less than total. When Dodd had called me from the Royal York Hotel to advise me of the Geneva departure within the hour, I asked him how things went.

"We won with the stockholders," he said, "but the Heebs are still in it. I don't know how he did it but that sonofabitch Schiowitz (Morton Schiowitz, former Cornfeld associate at IOS) talked some hick judge in New Brunswick into issuing some kind of injunction against Vesco. I don't know what it means but somebody ought to take care of that Jew bastard. He's a troublemaker."

That may have been why Vesco switched our destination from Geneva to Rome. For all I knew the injunction might have forbidden him to go near IOS headquarters.

I was just as happy. When we got to Rome, Vesco disappeared. Since there was nothing on Vesco's flight schedule for a couple of days the crew and I rented a bunch of motorcycles and did some sight-seeing.

We had acquired a new full-time crew member, Dorothy Elizabeth McCarty. She was not new to me or Vesco. She had made several flights in the Grumman. I first worked with Dottie McCarty back in 1968. She was, at that time, Chief Stewardess for Arthur Godfrey's aviation operation known as Luxaire. We, that is ICC, had occasion to lease Godfrey's Gulfstream One from time to time. Vesco was very impressed with Dottie's work and her personal appearance. When Godfrey sold his Gulfstream and shut down his aviation operation, Dottie worked part time for me on the ICC Gulfstream. She became the obvious choice of both Vesco and me for full time employment as chief stewardess on Vesco's Boeing.

Her first flight with us was the Newark to Toronto run just before the IOS meeting. What a way to start a job! In less than a week she had been on more than sixty hours of standby. Those three days of blitzing around Rome and the surrounding countryside sort of made up for her first week. The three days served another purpose. The entire crew had been pretty much under the gun from the day I first saw the Boeing. There had been little, or no, relaxation and no chance to learn how we would function off the job away from home. On the airplane the unifying factor is the authority of the Captain. On the ground the unifying factor has got to be mutual respect and liking. By the time we were ready to take off again, we were a unit of friends.

I was wrong in thinking that the Canadian injunction was intended to keep Vesco away from IOS in Geneva. We arrived in Geneva from Rome on July 3rd, 1971. Vesco presented himself as the conquering hero, acting as if he had won control not only of IOS, but of Switzerland as well.

As in the case of ELS, Vesco spent the next week or so taking inventory of IOS real estate and "portable assets" found in Geneva, Fernay-Voltaire on the Swiss-French border, and the major cities of Europe. The Boeing was carrying only two passengers, Vesco and Meissner, and four crew members. Everywhere we landed we received the same reception as on that first landing in Geneva. Nobody could cope with the idea of that much goddamn airplane for two lousy passengers. But Vesco ate it up. He was king of the hill.

July 15, 1971

I flew Vesco and a bunch of his people from Geneva to Bangor, Maine. Something was up. Norman LeBlanc filled me in. Vesco intended to take care of Schiowitz once and for all. But there was a problem. Each member of Vesco's gang was afraid to enter Canada and it was boiling down to drawing straws.

"What's he going to do, kill him?" I asked. I had known LeBlanc casually for about a year. Vesco got involved with him when he started to investigate the IOS financial picture in the summer of 1970. LeBlanc, although being paid by his accounting firm, Coopers & Lybrand, was in reality a Vesco operative. He provided the ammunition that Vesco needed to give credibility to his "bailout" offer. When Vesco won the proxy fight in Toronto, he made LeBlanc financial vice-president of IOS. In spite of his ability as an accountant, LeBlanc impressed me as being something approaching a giggling nitwit. I think he would talk in his giggling fashion to a fence post. The kind of information he delighted in imparting would be the quality of his morning stool. Or he would rhapsodize about a new pair of jockey shorts. Only occasionally, would he drop something useful or important.

LeBlanc looked astonished when I asked about Vesco doing away with Schiowitz. He couldn't comprehend that I was putting him on.

"Nothing like that, y'know," he said. "Like—about that injunction. Bobby's going to quash it. He got Beatty (Frank G. Beatty, ICC vice-president) to write this—y'know—letter calling in this—y'know—loan. It's a blackjack job. The old—heh! heh!—daisy-chain effect. Schiowitz and his gang either pay up or drop the injunction. And they can't pay. You know."

I didn't know. I had no idea what the hell he was talking about although it came out later that Vesco was using the terms of his original loan agreement to put the screws on the dissidents.

During the flight Vesco came forward and told me that his ultimate destination was St. Johns, New Brunswick, but that he and his group would drive up, or go some other way, not in the Boeing because he did not want attention called to his being in Canada. I don't know how he ultimately got to St. Johns. I don't believe he actually ever went.

We landed at Bangor, Maine, at eleven o'clock at night on July 15, 1971. Vesco and his eight-man entourage left the Boeing and disappeared into the darkness. I didn't see them again until five o'clock the following afternoon. We returned to Geneva. This time there was a lot of drinking and carrying on, and I assumed that whatever Vesco had in mind had worked. Strangely enough, LeBlanc avoided me and got quietly drunk.

After the Bangor excursion, Vesco continued to use the Boeing like a shuttlecock in a silk mill. The only interesting flight I can recall in this period was when I brought a bunch of ICC directors from Newark to Geneva for the annual ICC meeting. Vesco had decided to switch the site from New York to Geneva and to hold the meeting in Bernie Cornfeld's palatial headquarters right on the shores of Lac Leman, the Bella Vista. I had flown all the way from Geneva to Newark empty to collect the group. I knew all of the passengers on that flight except one. He was a young man conservatively dressed and serious looking. His name was Robert Odle. At the time he was just another passenger. He shot into brief national prominence when, as a member of the finance committee of Nixon's CREEP (committee to re-elect the president) he testified before the Senate Committee investigating the Watergate scandals.

IOS was an enormous operation. It had offices, warehouses, depots, hotels, clubs, apartments, and resorts all around the world. In the Geneva area alone it had dozens of locations. I only got to see one really close up at that time. It was the Bella Vista.

One morning in August—August 5, 1971—Vesco

called me at the Hotel du Lac in Coppet, a suburb of Geneva, where the crew stayed regularly. He wanted me to run someone up to Zurich right away, which was not an unusual assignment. But then he told me that he wanted me, Chuck and Pete to bring some old clothes along and get into them as soon as we got back to the Geneva airport where we would be picked up by somebody from IOS.

"I have a job for you," was the only explanation I got.

I returned from Zurich around noon. The only old clothes that the crew owned were dungarees and flannel shirts. Whatever Vesco had in mind it probably involved some muscle work and what we had would do.

The vehicle Vesco had sent out to pick us up turned out to be a stake-body Mercedes truck with only a driver. Chuck, Pete, and I looked at each other. This was strictly nonstandard transportation for a flight crew. I went over to speak to the driver.

"Are you from IOS?" I asked.

"Yes," he said. "I am here to fetch you to Bella Vista."

Fetch my ass. I had a Mercedes 250 sitting in the auto parking lot right outside the terminal. I wasn't about to climb into the cab of that truck when I had my own wheels. I told the driver to take us as far as my car and I would follow him back to IOS headquarters. He agreed.

I parked the Mercedes on the street outside Bella Vista and walked through the gate behind the truck. I checked with security and they called Vesco's office to tell him we had arrived. The three of us were instructed to go to Vesco's new office in a small but elegant chalet next to Bella Vista and within the same compound.

The main building in this compound that was called Bella Vista was a gray stone "palace." It had been adapted for business use. The chalet, also of stone, had been Bernie Cornfeld's personal headquarters where he had operated in almost regal privacy. Now it was Vesco's.

I suppose the three of us looked kind of klutzy in

those surroundings. We were greeted by Vesco's new and beautiful Swiss secretary. The sight of three guys in jeans and work shirts didn't phase her. She led us into a huge reception area richly furnished and decorated. We sat in huge leather chairs to wait for Vesco.

He showed up almost immediately.

"Ike, I've got some personal stuff I want humped over from the main building to here," he said. "I don't trust the local moving guys."

We hauled a bunch of heavy file cabinets from Bella Vista. Some went in the back of the truck, some went into Vesco's new office. All told, the job took about half an hour. I figured that was it, but Vesco had other plans. There were other "things" to be taken out of Bella Vista. Vesco insisted that only the crew load these items. They consisted mostly of wooden crates, some of which were very heavy and some of which looked as if they could hold paintings. Vesco told me that it was my personal responsibility to see that these particular items were stowed safely on the airplane. In addition, the truck would make several stops on the way back to the airport to pick up more special cargo. These were also my responsibility. Before we left, another truck appeared. It was bigger than the first one. This too, would make a number of pickups around the Geneva area and would then proceed to the airport. Its contents would also be loaded aboard. "Come back here when you're finished and I'll give you guys the grand tour," he said. Almost as an afterthought, he added, "if you run into any trouble call me on my private line right away."

I don't know how many stops we made but we went all over the place. We picked up crates, boxes, barrels, cartons, paper-wrapped packages—you name it. Nothing was marked but everybody seemed to know what went where. Our asses were dragging by the time our truck headed for the airport, and we still had to off load the sonofabitch.

As we approached the Boeing I saw a Mercedes sedan parked near it. A man whom I recognized as a senior IOS security man leaned against the side of the car. I got out of the truck and he introduced himself.

The airplane was locked up tight and he obviously was waiting for me to open it up. We opened the cargo hatches and the security officer and I supervised the transfer. When the job was done and the hatches secured, he reached in his pocket and pulled out a sheaf of documents all officially stamped. He suggested that I take note that all of the cargo was destined for Nassau in the Bahamas. Then he got in his car and left. I reported back to Vesco that the airplane was loaded. We got our grand tour and we also got our cold beer. Half jokingly, when the tour was over, I asked Vesco if we were carrying bullion. He smirked at me.

"Company documents as far as I know," he said.

It was perhaps a year later that I read that Bernie had accused Vesco and his gang of doing a Hermann Goering job on IOS. Bernie claimed that the ICC'ers had looted every IOS location of paintings, sculpture, silverware, crystal, expensive bolts of fabric, gold cigarette lighters, electric appliances, carpets, luggage, game sets, attaché cases, tape recorders, video sets, radios, golf clubs, cameras—anything of any value whatever, even a quantity of children's watches. But, the prize bag of booty, which I verified later, included a quarter of a million dollars' worth of specially made Patek Phillipe watches. Bernie used to reward his super-salesmen with them and presented them as gifts to favored international dignitaries. I saw several of these watches later in Nassau. The wristwatches, as well as the pocket watches were both about the size of a fifty-cent piece and had been unobtrusively engraved with the IOS logotype.

My observations at the gate had been that Swiss officials know goddamn well who's getting away with what. But then, Switzerland is a country where money is a religion and bribery is a sacrament.

That was the last time I handled cargo. Shortly after this incident the Vesco gang acquired a new member, one of whose duties would be to handle special cargo for Vesco and other ICC/IOS big shots. He was a young, overbearing twit with a genius for irritating people. One day in Nassau I saw him wearing one of those precious IOS watches and I almost had a heart attack out of sheer rage. He would, for the next two years, be a problem.

The new member of the "team" who so quickly acquired a piece of the IOS booty was Donald Nixon, Jr., a nephew of the president of the United States. I remember wondering if Uncle Dick had an IOS watch too.

8

September 8, 1971 0055Z IAD—GVA

It was a typical "red-eye" flight. We left Dulles International Airport at about nine o'clock at night. My four passengers ate a lot, drank a lot, talked a lot, and went to bed early. By the time we touched down in Geneva I was feeling a little cranky, as was the rest of the crew. All I wanted was a light snack before I grabbed a few hours' sleep. Later that day I would have to make arrangements to take the Boeing to England on the next day, to Aviation Traders Engineering Ltd., Southend-on-Sea. Before my flight engineer even had a chance to put the pin in the nosewheel a Swiss airport official delivered a snack I hadn't ordered. It was a particularly unpalatable Swiss combination sandwich—noise abatement-pepperoni-chicken shit—between two thick slices of bureaucratic bread.

The first I knew of his presence on the flight deck was when he shouted at me.

"Captain!" I turned around in my seat and saw a Swiss official in a blue blazer, wearing a scowl. "You will come with me immediately to the *airport director*." He said airport director with great emphasis.

"Right away," I told him, "as soon as I'm ready." I

didn't like the way he busted onto the flight deck but he seemed agitated about something. I spoke in what I believe was a reasonable tone. However, he apparently didn't think so.

"You will come now—this instant!" he said.

"In a pig's ass," I told him. I got out of my seat ready to drop-kick the little clown clear back to operations. He read my thoughts and backed off a few feet right into Vesco who was on his way out of the airplane.

"What's up, Ike?" he asked.

"Don't know, Bob," I said. "This guy's busting my balls."

"Tell him to go fuck himself," Vesco said.

"For Chrissakes, Bob, he understands English!" I said. Vesco labored under the illusion that only Americans and Englishmen spoke English and the English didn't do too good a job of it, either. He waved off my warning and left the airplane.

The little man in the blazer was rigid with anger. He glared at Vesco's back. I ignored him and took care of the few routine chores that had to be done before I could leave the aircraft. They took only a few minutes. I told the crew not to service the aircraft. That would be taken care of later in the day.

"I've got to go to the airport director's office with this cat," I told the crew. "I'll see you inside."

Contrary to my expectations the airport director greeted me affably. I had met him once, the first time I brought the Boeing into Geneva a few months before. He was one of a group of Swiss and French airport-management people who came aboard to marvel at the only privately owned Boeing 707 in the world.

"Captain Eisenhauer," he said, "it appears from this report I have that on several takeoffs recently you have exceeded the maximum allowable noise levels for our airport."

"I don't see how that could happen," I told him. "I follow your noise-abatement procedures to the letter." He showed me the report, which was written in French. I couldn't read the language, but I could read the numbers. He indicated with a pencil three dates on which I was supposed to have "rung the bell."

I wasn't going to argue with him. He merely passed on what his staff told him. My beef was with the guys who wrote the report. I told the director that I felt there was some mistake and that I would like to discuss the matter with the staff. I asked for his authorization to look at the recording strips and departure log. He agreed and instructed my escort that I was to be given every cooperation. I thanked him and left his office.

His manner took some of the edge off my annoyance at having my ass jumped the way it was. I had cooled down enough to accept responsibility for actual violations of noise regulations. But before I did that I wanted to see for myself.

Noise abatement is the pilot's bane.

On one hand he is charged with the safety and comfort of his passengers. On the other he is beset by the demands of conflicting, and sometimes dangerous, regulations and procedures developed as chaotically as our tax structure. Probably the most potentially disastrous procedure is for noise abatement.

Let's face it—we can't turn the clock back. The airplane is here to stay. They will get bigger, faster, safer and noisier. The main problem is that aircraft technology has always developed at a faster pace and with better planning than that of airport locations and airway traffic control. The fault lies with government. In every country in the world it is the government which claims authority over its airspace. Its bureaucracy determines, by regulation, how aircraft will operate within its borders. No problem. It's the only way to keep airplanes from running into each other and falling on the citizenry. On a world-wide basis international air traffic is regulated and controlled by agreement, through ICAO, International Civil Aviation Organization. Almost every government in the world is a member. Again, no problem—in principle. Unfortunately the gap between principle and practice is enormous.

Private companies developed the airplane to its present state. Competition in a fast growing industry is the spur. Sure, in wartime, for example, the government gets involved in technological development but usually only by laying a set of requirements for specific needs before the civilian operated company. When the bureaucrats take a hand in the actual design function, disaster usually results.

The difference between the private sector and the bureaucracy is talent. In the private sector you produce or get out. In the government sector if you *do* produce beyond an established level of performance, you're in trouble.

Most air disasters occur in, and around, airports. Takeoffs and landings are the most critical parts of flight. And airports and the sky over them are the most congested areas. The need for intelligent regulations, not only of traffic but of airport location and design, is critical. That is government's function. But bureaucratic ineptitude, departmental jealousies, and local community demands prevent any kind of sane, practical, and fail-safe solutions. The Geneva Airport operation illustrates this as well as any. It's the same all over the world.

Noise-abatement procedures are usually set locally and depend almost exclusively on the population concentration around an airport. This is because the takeoff of a large modern jet extends for several miles beyond the airport boundary. The takeoff is also the noisiest part of flight. The irony is that those living in the path of the takeoff seem to be more concerned about the momentary aural discomfort than they are about the possibility of an airplane flying at a dangerously reduced speed to cut noise falling on them. It is a fact that the only way, at present, to reduce aircraft noise on takeoff, is to cut speed. Cutting speed reduces the margin of safety during takeoff and increases the danger, not only to the aircraft, but to the people on the ground.

The safest procedure for any takeoff is for the pilot to utilize all the designed thrust, or power, to accomplish lift-off, acceleration, and climb away from the ground and surrounding obstructions as quickly as possible. The procedures required by most airports around the world have the ridiculous effect of prolonging the time that the heavily laden jet remains close to the ground over populated communities. The battle over safety and comfort in highly impacted areas will not be solved by government regulations but by the technological development of built-in noise-control devices. However, there are airports that incorporate noise-abatement procedures arbitrarily. At such locations there is no heavy concentration of people and homes around the airport or in the flight paths.

The International Airport in Geneva sits astride the Swiss-French border in a fairly remote section. Large jets are limited to a single runway which runs in a northeast-southwest direction. Almost immediately after takeoff, from either direction, the airplane passes out of Swiss air space and is over France. Therefore, the noisiest part of any takeoff from Geneva occurs over French territory.

Straddling the border as it does, Geneva Airport is technically under two flags. It has dual Customs and joint administration. However, actual airport management seems to be in the hands of the Swiss. This means that the Swiss control the noise abatement monitoring system.

Measurements of aircraft-noise levels are standard and the unit used is the decibel. One or more microphones are located at specific points along the departure path of a runway. They are hooked into a monitor/recording device that is usually located in either operations or the control tower. As an aircraft passes over a microphone, its noise level is recorded on a graphed paper strip similar to that used by a seismograph or an EKG unit. The stylus that makes the tracings is connected to an alarm system. When an aircraft generates a noise above the local acceptable level, the stylus arm is driven to a point where a bell rings. Obviously it is not necessary for an operator to continuously monitor this device visually for violators. When the bell rings it alerts traffic-control personnel that a violation has occurred. All that is required is for someone to check the strip of paper and enter into a log the time, date, reading and the identity of the aircraft owner or operator. Following this, the usual procedure is for the tower to notify the pilot immediately during the takeoff that he has exceeded the prescribed limits. When the pilot is told that he has rung the bell his usual response is, "Sorry about that. I'll watch it next time." The incident is usually dropped. Or, at best, in the case of scheduled airline operations, the company is routinely notified and takes whatever action is required—if any.

When I left the Geneva Airport director's office my first officer was in the hall waiting for me. I explained the situation and told him to come along with me. We followed Fatty up to a control room where the records and logs were kept. There I was introduced rather sniffily to the man in charge whom I'll call Schissel. Schissel was another bureaucratic cipher. With a great show of importance he trotted out the logs and, referring to the report, located the relevant pages. Sure enough on the occasions they indicated I indeed had rung the bell. But on the same pages I noted that I wasn't alone by any means. TWA, for example, showed at least half a dozen violations. So did other airlines including Swissair, which operated some aircraft smaller than the Boeing.

I was particularly interested in TWA, since they were operating Boeing 707s identical to Silver Phyllis on exactly the same type of over-water flights, and they would naturally weigh close to the same and have identical takeoff characteristics. I pointed this out to the official and asked him what action they had taken in these instances.

"That is not the point," he said. "*You* are in violation and we will speak only about you." That's when I got mad.

"Bullshit!" I said. In the two and a half months since we had acquired the Boeing I had made approximately eighty takeoffs from airports in the United States and Europe, including cities with equally as stringent procedures as those at Geneva. Included in these eighty were thirteen takeoffs from Geneva. Until this particular time I had not been cited for any noise-abatement violation in any manner. These guys were talking about three specific takeoffs within the previous month, all of which were transatlantic flights where I was heavy with a full load (160,000 pounds) of fuel. Now, noise abatement has never been my primary concern on any takeoff. But, I was very much aware of it and went by the book—Pan Am's book. Having no evidence to the contrary I would naturally assume that my techniques were within the limits. Now I'm told I'm a scofflaw.

As angry as I was at the manner in which I was notified of my violations, I decided not to make an issue of the obvious special treatment I was getting. One of the reasons I cooled it was that I wanted to survey some of the other pilots, airline people especially, to see if they were getting flak. I agreed to take extra precautions on subsequent departures. Schissel was very patronizing.

"I strongly urge you to do that, Captain," he said, "for Mr. Vesco's good." That was the zinger—Vesco. It wasn't noise abatement at all. It was the pepperoni business all over again.

Every time we got ready for an overseas flight, Vesco made damn sure he had a plentiful supply of his favorite foods—chili fixin's, hamburger, pizza fixings, roquefort cheese, Tab, and pepperoni. Lots of pepperoni. At the end of a flight we usually had a fairly good supply left over. Instead of throwing it away or giving it to ground-service people for themselves Vesco insisted on taking it with him—especially the pepperoni. But Vesco himself left the job of moving his personal baggage and traveling delicatessen through Customs to the crew.

From our first flight we had problems with foodstuffs, especially that goddamned pepperoni. There was always an argument. But that was not unusual. At any port of entry the Customs people take special pains with foodstuffs, plants, and the like. There were good reasons for this I suppose. But the Swiss *douane* at Geneva seemed to take a special delight in hassling me over—at the most—ten lousy pounds of American pepperoni. It usually cost twenty to a hundred dollars' worth of persuasion to endanger the Swiss economy.

Thus Vesco's palate would be soothed but this had to be the most expensive pepperoni on record.

Bribery, like any other business transaction, has its limits. Usually the briber and the bribee reach an understanding on the numbers and everybody stays happy for as long as the arrangement is required. There are the occasional disruptions. For example, you get a new guy on the gate and the price is negotiated either up or down depending on how dumb, smart, greedy, or patriotic the new man is.

About a month after we started to come into Geneva on a fairly regular schedule the "arrangement" broke down. There were interminable delays that even extra incentive could not break. Suddenly the aircraft commander was required to discuss the importation of proscribed foodstuffs with a senior Customs official. If this was a high-level rip-off I was not about to get involved. I tried to argue the pepperoni case on its merits. What difference to the Swiss economy or danger to the Swiss national health could a few pounds of pepperoni make? It was to be taken directly to Mr. Vesco's dwelling where it would be quickly consumed. I was damn careful to avoid even a hint that I was prepared to "settle the matter" for the sake of Vesco's belly.

On one arrival the crew and I were delayed for more than two hours. The usual emolument was refused. This was a new wrinkle. The pepperoni, along with the other stuff, would not move. Again I was called up front. The senior Customs officer insisted Mr. Vesco could no longer import edibles into Switzerland without complying with existing regulations. Finally, totally exasperated, I dumped the Tab, the roquefort, the hamburger, the chili, and a greasy bag of pepperoni off the baggage cart and told the Customs officer what he could do with it. I am sure that the Customs officer did not ingest any of those goodies through the orifice I had recommended.

But that was not the end of our importing activities. I found another clandestine means of getting the pepperoni. It didn't cost half as much.

I found a butcher shop in a village on the other side of the border near the airport. It was close to Ferney-

Voltaire where IOS had one of its office complexes. I arranged with the butcher for regular deliveries at a "premium price" of ten pounds of pepperoni a week to an address in Geneva. It was his problem to get it across the border—payment on delivery.

As I left with my first officer, I was positive that the Swiss intended to make trouble for Robert Vesco one way or the other and this was just the beginning. When Vesco took over Bernie Cornfeld's empire he inherited an official hostility that had been building for years. It was no secret that the Swiss wanted IOS out of the country. And I don't think that Vesco created a good first impression the day the Boeing arrived at Geneva with *deux personnes seulement.*

September 9, 1971 0806Z GVA—SND

Dennis Dearlove's call woke me at six o'clock in the morning. His Cockney voice sounded cheery and excited.

"Everything is laid on, Ike," he said. "Weather is fine and will hold all day."

Dennis was technical assistant to the directors of Aviation Traders Engineering Limited (ATEL), an aircraft-service and -modification center situated thirty miles east of London. ATEL was at the municipal airport at Southend-on-Sea, Essex, England, on the Thames Estuary.

I first made contact with Dennis through Pan Am's New York office about a month before. I was very unhappy, at the time, with Pan Am's contract-maintenance program. It was too expensive, so much so that I considered it as a rip-off. And I said so. Vesco was in complete agreement. It might seem strange for a guy who would use a four engine jet to fly two people half way around the world at an enormous cost to worry about the price of keeping the airplane in shape. There's no doubt about it, Vesco was a spender. He was willing to pay a fair price, no matter how high it was. But, he didn't like getting screwed. And he felt as I did that Pan American was screwing him. Vesco is no dummy. He knew what costs were all about. Reluctantly, Pan Am's New York rep put me on to Aviation Traders.

On my next flight to Europe I phoned Aviation Traders, explained what I was after, and was routed to Dennis Dearlove. Dennis agreed to meet me in Geneva to discuss terms.

Dennis was a tall, reedy Londoner with a fine sense of humor and impressive credentials. We got along very well. It was the only time I had fun talking business. It almost seemed as if that, to Dennis, the business aspects were secondary to the enjoyment of good conversation and good wine.

Our talks were broken off a number of times in order that Dennis could conduct telephone consultation with his home office. After one of these calls Dennis returned with a peculiar glint in his eye.

"Ike, old boy, we have this idea," he said. "We would like you to bring the Boeing into Southend. What do you say?"

Oh boy!

ATEL's primary, heavy-jet maintenance center was located at Stansted Airport. But its shops and major facility was located at Southend-on-Sea, about sixty miles away. The problem with Southend was that the British Aircraft Registry Board insisted that the Southend runway length was insufficient to accommodate the landing requirements of a Boeing 707 jet aircraft. In fact, none had ever landed there.

The idea appealed to me. Hell, it was exciting. Too many people in this business of mine seemed to believe that the era of new discovery in aviation is over. It all went the way of the airmail pilot and barnstormer. I don't believe it. And apparently the people at ATEL didn't believe it either. Before I had a chance to answer Dennis drove on.

"We realize that this is strictly nonstandard," he said. "But, it's a grand opportunity for the both of us."

He had brought with him a package of material about ATEL and its facilities. Included was an approach chart for Southend. He whipped it out and put it in front of me. He kept on talking as I checked the numbers. "Apart from the fun of the thing," he said, "this could be of great value to us to prove, beyond doubt, that a Boeing can be safely and legally landed at Southend. It would save us a great deal of money and time."

"And you know, Ike, it could be advantageous to you," he said. "If you're successful—with good margins of course—we are prepared to provide all the service you need at a price that will reflect our appreciation." Again, he hesitated.

"And—we'll—you'll be making history, Ike," he said. He seemed embarrassed at saying something so corny. If nothing else, his concern for something that can't be put into the computer or read off a slide rule, plus the sheer adventure of the thing, would have sold me. To get as corn ball as he was, he dropped the gauntlet and I picked it up.

"Dennis," I said to him, "you have a deal." He immediately left to call the home office.

The plan called for me to be over the Southend Airport at about ten o'clock on the morning of September 9, 1971. At this time all the necessary monitoring equipment, cameras and the photo chase plane were to position themselves for the purpose of following and photographing my entire approach through to landing and stopping. In addition all the executive staff of ATEL would be on hand as well as government officials who would attest to the legality and safety of the landing.

Most commercial airline operations around the world are conducted from airports with more than ample runway for almost any conditions. The aircraft manufacturer goes one of two routes in designing and building any particular aircraft. Either he studies the route over which his aircraft will be operated, including the length of runways at airports along that route, and ensures that his aircraft is capable of using those facilities—or he determines the requirements of the customer and appeals to the governmental agencies involved to improve and lengthen the existing runways or build new airports.

The Southend runway, at a little over 4,000 feet and built originally to accommodate World War II aircraft, was shorter by more than half of the shortest runways in use around the world for heavy commercial jet operation. If there is a standard by which both manufacturer and pilots of aircraft are guided, it is that the minimum safe operating length for a runway for heavy jets should be two miles.

I circled Southend a couple of times at 3,000 feet waiting for the "go" signal. Even to me, a carrier pilot, that runway looked awfully short. To the crew it looked like a suburban driveway. Pete Dolliver, my flight engineer, a product of "The World's Most Experienced Airline" squeezed over my left shoulder and peered out my side window.

"Holy Jesus, Ike!" he said. "You're kidding."

Chuck, my first officer, turned in his seat and looked at Pete.

"You just relax, Pete," he said, "and leave this here carrier landing to a couple of old Navy pilots."

"I'm sure as shit glad I'm not shooting it with Pan Am," Pete said. He took another look and shook his head. "We're gonna die," he muttered. I had to laugh. I heard that a lot from gunners during my carrier days. Pete tightened his shoulder harness and picked up a paperback book he had been reading.

"Ike!" he hollered, "just give me time to see how this fucking thing comes out." Southend Tower called me.

"Sky One Zero Nine," the controller said, "you may begin your approach at your convenience."

The approach was no different from any other—with two exceptions. The first was that the main landing gear of the aircraft had to touch the runway "on the numbers," the runway-direction indicators painted at the very end of the runway. The second exception was that I had to have reverse thrust available just before touchdown. In carrier parlance, as I told the crew, I was shooting for the number-one wire, not the standard touchdown point at the thousand-foot mark. The only other difference between this approach and a standard approach was that my first officer called out my reference speeds at shorter intervals.

The flight engineer's seat in a Boeing tracks side to side, fore and aft and swivels. This gives him the mobility he needs to attend to his panel which is on the right side of the airplane behind the first officer and perform his duties on takeoffs and landings at the pedestal between the pilot and co-pilot and still remain strapped into his seat.

As we neared touchdown Pete was in position between myself and my first officer. I looked at his face. He was bug-eyed. For a fleeting second I saw Harry Werner all over again at Alamosa.

The main gear touched exactly where I'd intended. Pete hollered, "Four lights!" which indicated I had reverse on all four engines and damn near blew my right ear drum out in the process. I popped the ground spoilers full out and planted the nose gear on the runway. I applied full brakes, felt the anti-skids cycle, and immediately went to maximum reverse thrust. Phyllis behaved like a perfect lady. She stayed dead center on the runway and came to a dead stop with a kind of curtsy on the mark. I felt very smug when the tower, at my request, gave me a readout on my landing distance.

"You are slightly over 2,000 feet, Captain," the controller said. "Congratulations!"

On instructions from ground control I taxied toward the main ramp. As I approached my parking place I saw a huge crowd of people standing on the ATEL ramp. More people were standing outside the fence. Behind them were cars parked every which way with people standing on the cars. Frankly, I wondered what the hell they were all there for. I soon found out. As I came down the steps from the airplane there was a reception committee headed by G. H. C. Fisher, managing director of ATEL, and Tony Cusworth, airport commandant. Grinning broadly with them was Dennis Dearlove. I found out that my landing had been billed in the local press as a major aviation event. Southend is the home of a Royal Air Force Museum and was a military base during the war. From it, fighters had gone up to glory in the Battle of Britain. Southend was a very aviation-conscious town. We were greeted like heroes. I have to admit that I was completely bowled over. For the first time since I'd gotten into the corporate-aviation business I experienced a real sense of achievement. And I was aware that these professionals who greeted me had fully appreciated what I had done. I donated to the museum one of my wheels and a tire from that landing.

There was a small lunch party in the airport dining room at which some flattering speeches were made. I was given a letter of appreciation and was toasted by Tony Cusworth.

I was very much moved by Tony's gesture and his words which I won't repeat. Tony is an old RAF hand and a veteran of the air war in Europe. He is an urbane and extremely civilized English gentleman in the very best sense.

The hope had been that this "experiment" would give rise to a regular flow of heavy jet aircraft into and out of Southend in order that they could receive maintenance and service. The landing *did* achieve certification for Southend.

Before I left Geneva for Southend I had invited Bob Vesco to come along. He refused.

"Shit, no!" he said. "Tell me all about it when you come back." I did just that and the white-knuckle champ of corporate aviation, who listened to every word I said, told me he was sorry he had missed it. I believed him.

It was a true adventure in a time when there are few in the predictable world of civilian aviation. Tony Cusworth had said at our little dinner party that it took a Yank to do the job. But it took the British to initiate it. Amen!

September 10, 1971 12222Z GVA—EWR

I rang the bell again at Geneva. Before takeoff I had told the tower that I would take extra precautions—what I call Noise Abatement Ridiculous—to stay well within their noise limits. I also requested that they give me the courtesy of a call on the radio with my actual decibel reading as I passed over the locations of the pickup microphones.

The takeoff scared the shit out of Vesco. According to procedure I reduced power at 400 feet altitude. But this time I cut way back on the power levers to such a degree that Vesco thought all four engines had quit. He was up on the flight deck like a shot.

"What the fuck is going on?" he asked.

"Noise abatement," I told him.

"Fuck noise abatement!" he shouted. "The sons of bitches are trying to kill me!" Maybe it didn't occur to him that there were other people on that airplane too.

September 30, 1971 1239Z GVA—EWR

We didn't get back to Geneva again until September 27. We had been back in the states for almost two weeks.

On the morning of September 30 the crew and I left the Hotel du Lac to get the plane ready for a flight back to the United States. This, of course, meant a full load of fuel. We arrived at the airport about ten o'clock in the morning and boarded Silver Phyllis.

Pete, Chuck, and I worked out the flight plan for the ocean crossing. When we finished, I sent Chuck to operations to file our flight plan and get the weather folder. He came back about a half hour later angry and swearing just like a Louisiana croco-gator.

"They won't accept my goddamned clearance," he said. "They want to see you, Ike. I have a car waiting."

"See me?" I asked. "For what?"

"I don't goddamned know, Ike," he replied. "They won't goddamned tell me." I grabbed my Captain's hat and took off with Chuck. I had a sneaking suspicion that it was the noise-abatement bullshit again. If it was, someone was going to get his ass tore out. I was fed up.

The operations duty officer was apologetic.

"I am only following orders, Captain," he said. "I was ordered not to give clearance to Captain Eisenhauer."

"Who ordered you?" I asked him.

"The order came from the airport director's office," he replied. I turned to Chuck.

"You come with me, Chuck," I said. "I know where he is." But the director was not in. I asked his secretary who I could see to straighten things out. When I told her my name she became a little apprehensive. She made an interoffice phone call. A few moments later a snotty-looking character, whom I will identify as Mr. Belp, marched into the office like he was on two weeks' active duty

"Come with me, Captain Eisenhauer," he said. And I followed him into the director's office. Chuck stayed in the outer office.

Belp enthroned himself in the director's chair. He held a sheet of paper in his hand, then carefully took out a pair of glasses and put them on. He let me stew a bit and when he looked up at me he had a kind of smirk on his face.

"Captain Eisenhauer," he said in an accent more German than French, "I must inform you that you may not command an aircraft departing Switzerland until further notice."

"What the hell do you mean?" I shouted at him. "I have a load of passengers coming out here in less than an hour and they fully expect me to fly them in that Boeing to the United States—today."

"Mr. Vesco will simply have to make other arrangements," Belp said. "You have a record of five noise-abatement violations within the past six weeks." This cannot go unpunished. Your landing rights are also revoked. You can appeal my decision at a hearing but you must remain in Switzerland until such a hearing is held and a decision is made as to your status." He put the paper down and stood up as if that were the end of it.

"You sit down, Mr. Belp!" I told him. I stuck my finger under his nose. "We're going to settle this once and for all." He sat down.

I cited the violations I had seen not only for TWA, but for Swissair as well, and pointed out that, as far as I was able to learn, no similar action had been taken in any case. I also told him and challenged him to come and see that there was no way an airplane such as a Boeing 707-300, fully loaded for an over-ocean flight to the United States, could leave Geneva without ringing that fucking bell and still operate safely. He backed off a little. But the smirk stayed.

"What are you suggesting, Captain?" he said. I had the feeling he was baiting me.

"I'm suggesting one of two things, Mr. Belp," I said. "Either you are trying to hold me up for a bribe or you are following a course of deliberate intimidation of Mr. Vesco. That goddamned bell is set too low and I think you know it. You seem to be pretty goddamned selective in enforcing your noise-abatement regulations. You either clear me now to leave this country or I will call the United States consulate in Bern on this fucking phone and charge you with the following." I ticked off my fingers in front of his face. "One—you are interfering with the duties and charges of an aircraft commander. Two—you are deliberately and maliciously disrupting the operation of an American flag aircraft owned by an American citizen engaged in legitimate international commerce. Three—you have arbitrarily and without warning taken punitive action against me without a fair hearing." I said a lot more and so did he but I had him on the run. I think what convinced him was my threat to bring an American FAA inspector to

Geneva to examine the logs of their noise-abatement monitoring system to prove my charges that I was being selectively disciplined.

"If I have to do that," I told him, "I will sue your ass—yours Mr. Belp—for any loss I incur and any discomfort I suffer."

By the time I finished Belp was in shock. I'm sure he wasn't used to that kind of attack and I had the feeling that he wished he had seized the opportunity to make a little profit when I suggested that he was looking for a bribe.

I waited while he phoned operations and lifted the hold on my clearance. After I left operations with my clearance I thought about what had happened and got madder and madder. By the time I boarded the Boeing I had worked out a plan that would shake the livers out of those Switzers. But I made sure to warn Vesco first that I would be following a new noise abatement procedure on this takeoff and told him not to be concerned whatever happened. What I intended to do was to demonstrate just how ridiculous and dangerous noise abatement can be when the parameters are unrealistic.

I knew where the microphones were located. During my takeoff, just prior to coming abreast of the first one, I reduced power to 1.7 EPR, which is very little power for a 300,000-pound jet on takeoff. I whispered past the first microphone and dropped the nose slightly. The Boeing could go only one way—down. And it did just that.

I slid past the second microphone—still coming down—but quietly. Ahead and about 100 feet below I saw a road-construction crew at work. They obviously didn't hear me coming up on them. That's how quiet it was.

"Takeoff power all four," I yelled to Pete. The engines roared to life and spewed more than 70,000 pounds of thrust across the countryside. The construction crew stopped work and ran off in every direction—shovels, pick axes, crowbars flying.

"Jeeeee-zus!" Chuck yelled, "look at them scatter."

I eased the nose to a normal-climb deck angle and went on my merry way. That was the end of complaints about noise abatement at Geneva. I was told later that my procedure, taken because of the unreasonable Swiss attitude, caused one hell of a flap at the airport. In fact, one excited controller pushed the crash alarm. Somebody, and I hope the hell it was Mr. Belp, would have a hell of a time explaining the Keystone comedy that must have followed.

After this flight, I was to make only one more "heavy" takeoff from Geneva Airport. And that was to take Vesco on a 'round-the-world flight, then Silver Phyllis was returned to the United States for extensive modification. Before the modification was finished, however, Vesco would have lost his taste for Switzerland. Vesco got his ass slung into a Swiss jail. When he got out he left Switzerland as fast as he could and vowed never to return.

9

November 8, 1971 0042Z JFK—GVA

The governor was late and Vesco was furious.

Governor William T. Cahill's tardiness was the insult added to an earlier injury to Vesco's pride. Vesco had been denied permission by JFK operations to land his Jet Ranger helicopter next to the Silver Phyllis. He was required to land at the Port Authority Terminal and then take a station wagon to his airplane, a distance of about three miles on the airport perimeter road. The governor, on the other hand, arrived in a New Jersey state police helicopter—identical to Vesco's. The state police helicopter deposited Governor Cahill within a few yards of the Boeing. To Vesco this was patently unfair.

Not only had Vesco contributed to Cahill's election campaign and to the New Jersey Republican party, but he was also a personal friend of the president of the United States, Richard M. Nixon. That in itself should have granted him status superior to a lousy governor. But he was also, now, the employer of the governor's daughter, Regina. And he was flying two of the governor's other children to Europe for a vacation. So who the hell was Cahill to get the special privilege denied to the only private citizen of the U.S. to own his own Boeing 707?

True to his character Vesco hid his irritation and his fundamental contempt for politicians from Cahill. Conversely, he greeted the governor like an old friend, personally conducted him and Mrs. Cahill on the grand tour of the airplane, then sat with him and chatted over drinks in the main lounge of the Boeing for almost an hour.

As I said earlier Vesco believed that a lot of his success resulted from the greed for money or power of other men. The attitude was never more apparent than when he dealt with politicians. He might boast of his friendship for Nixon or a clutch of congressmen, a prime minister or two, assorted dictators, and even a couple of governors. But his basic concern was always what his political contribution or special favor (such as free transportation in the Boeing, or the hiring of a relative) bought him. Vesco never did favors. Whatever he provided in cash or courtesies was a down payment or the full price for services rendered or to be rendered in return.

For example, Vesco made the Grumman Gulfstream available, at a modest cost, to Milton T. Shapp, present governor of Pennsylvania, for his 1970 campaign. The only condition that Vesco placed on this "arrangement" was that Shapp use his influence to get Vesco's eldest son, Danny, into Lehigh University. At least this is the only one I know of. I personally conveyed *that* request to Shapp's campaign manager. I was also responsible for the billing. To my knowledge only a small portion of the bills run up by the Shapp-Kline Campaign Committee were ever paid. All attempts to collect were met by the same kind of runaround one gets from a bankrupt corporation. There is nothing deader or broker than a political campaign committee after the election. Then a politician's pockets are as empty as his promises. Vesco never shared my concern over the unpaid bills. He regarded them as an investment in the future.

To me, Cahill's visit to the Boeing with his wife was simply that of a loving father seeing his children off on a vacation. He and his wife were pleasant and chatty. When they left, their wishes for a safe trip were genuine. As the governor's helicopter lifted off the ramp beside the Boeing, Vesco, still with a smile on his face, said only one word: "Jerk!"

I looked around to see if the girls were anywhere near. But they were well out of earshot. Vesco turned and headed back to the Boeing.

"Let's get the hell out of here," he said.

It was vintage Vesco. Vesco hated men like Cahill, men of power or position. In Vesco's world, however, men like Cahill had a price, and it was a challenge to Vesco to find out what it was, then pay it. Once that happened the man would become his property and he would treat that man as he did the Ralph Dodds and the Norman LeBlancs, with a vile disregard for their humanity.

I don't think this is a harsh judgment. I had already spent three years with Robert Lee Vesco and that is more than enough time to take the measure of a man.

I had long since ceased to think of him as my employer. Sure, he paid my salary and then some, and because of that I was able to take care of my responsibilities. But that often-useful barrier between employer and employee had disappeared very soon after we shook hands that day in his office in Fairfield in 1968.

In sixteen years of corporate aviation, I had met and served corporate executives at every level. I've seen them drunk, scared, officious, timid, and colorless. I have put up with their eccentricities. I have toted their baggage, walked their dogs, and been nice to their wives—and girl friends. I have met some monumental bastards and some blithering idiots. But one thing they all had in common was an understanding of the need for elementary courtesy, the "rules" of the game. But I had never encountered a personality like Vesco.

I was lucky. Maybe instinct had forced me to lay down ground rules at the very outset that were designed to protect my position as a member of Vesco's executive staff. But I was thinking then in traditional corporate terms. The net effect, however, of these ground rules was to insulate myself as a person against being Vescoized. By that I mean being sucked into the swamp of greed, fear, and degradation that Vesco created around himself. Like most people Vesco accorded some respect to, and held somewhat in awe, what he did not understand. Flying is still a mystery to a great number of people. Maybe Vesco saw in me some power he could never master. Perhaps it would have been the same with any pilot. But I like to think it would not be. Whatever it was it kept me out of that swamp and allowed me to be a buffer between Vesco and my crew.

As far as I know I was the only person in the Vesco inner circle who ever said *no* to him. LeBlanc, Straub, Strickler, and even Dodd, might argue and disagree with him in matters of business but when Vesco shut off debate and made a decision, they did what they were told. It would make no difference whether the decision was right or wrong—in the business sense.

I could not function that way. Vesco knew that and it bothered him. In fact the only times that Vesco was unsure of himself were in dealing with me. He never let me forget that the Boeing was *his* airplane and that I would take it when and where he told me. And yet I always knew that I had the option of refusing. The reasons I could give were simply beyond his comprehension. Business he could understand. Lawyers and accountants and salesmen and deal-makers were his daily fare. But with me there was still that veil of mystique.

Dozens of times Vesco complimented my performance. And those times were usually involved with actions and results that were within his comprehension like a landing or takeoff under difficult conditions. Sometimes it involved a chore that was not connected to my flying activities. It was always a case of, "I knew you could do it, Ike." Sometimes, however, we clashed on what could or should be done or not be done. This didn't happen too often, but when it did I invariably won my point. And I did it with "loaded" dice.

For example, Vesco might insist on a takeoff under adverse weather conditions. He had complete confidence in my ability to overcome any flying hazard. There would be no point in explaining the real dangers that might lie ahead. He would simply dismiss my reasoning with a wave of the hand. So, I usually double-talked him.

"Bob," I would say to him, "weather along the route is very bad. I suggest we lay over awhile or do it tomorrow."

"For Chrissakes, Ike," he would say, "I want to go now! You can do it." This is when I would go into my act.

"But, Bob," I would say, "it's not only the weather. The Flidner solenoids in number one and number four are stuck in the open position. And you know, Bob, that without these solenoids I'll never get pressure in the mernals." He would think this over a minute.

"Well, get some new ones," he would say.

"I'll have to phone Pan Am and see if they have any in Europe."

"Okay," he would say, "but for Jesus' sake, hurry it up."

He would walk away muttering to himself.

But there were other times when a flat *no* with no explanation was all he got. He would scream and yell and threaten to fire me on the spot but he knew that my decisions were never capricious, and he would accept my refusals.

Vesco offered to fly Juan Perón from Madrid to Buenos Aires for the dictator's triumphal return to power in Argentina. He didn't tell me about it until he had made the offer and it had been accepted. This is one of the times when I refused his direct order and made it stick.

The Silver Phyllis is a 707-300 series Boeing that puts it in the long-range class. However, there is a limit to the safe range of any airplane. And I knew that the distance from Madrid to Buenos Aires was out of the question for a nonstop flight. And because of the politics involved the flight had to be nonstop. I told this to Vesco.

He cited other long-distance over-water flights that we had made particularly between Madrid and Nassau and one from Tokyo to San Francisco. But the distance between Madrid and Buenos Aires was nearly 1800 miles longer and better than three hours' additional flying time compared to the distance between Tokyo and San Francisco. We could handle part of that extra distance—but not all of it.

"Do you want to tell that gaucho that he's going to have to swim the last 500 miles?" I said. Vesco blinked.

"You wouldn't shit me, Ike?" he asked.

"I wouldn't shit you, Bob," I told him. We were sitting at the bar in the Sheraton Hotel overlooking the Plaza San Martin in Buenos Aires. As I got it Vesco had met secretly with Perón's representatives in another part of the city—either earlier that morning or the day before. He had already committed himself and now he had to go back and get uncommitted. He was really upset.

"They aren't going to like that one goddamned bit," he said.

"Bob, I'll go tell them and give them the reason," I said.

"No way!" he said. "This is heavy business. I have to handle it myself. You keep that airplane ready—just in case."

"In case of what?" I asked him. "Are we in some kind of a jam?" He shot me a look that indicated I was poking my nose where it didn't belong.

Sitting with us was the son-in-law of the president of Paraguay, who had accompanied us on the South American jaunt that originated in Nassau. The whole trip, I thought at the time, had something to do with Vesco's wheeling and dealing in Spain. But after I had put the kibosh on the Perón flight, the Paraguayan president's son-in-law was even more agitated than Vesco. He seemed downright scared shitless. He started to say something. Vesco raised his hand to shut the man up. Then he got up from the table and took the guy's arm.

"Stick around the hotel, Ike," he said. "I'll call you." He and the Paraguayan left the bar in a hurry.

Now he had me worried. My imagination went into high gear. A day or two before we got to Buenos Aires a terrorist bomb had been set off in one of the guest rooms of our hotel, killing a young American tourist, a woman. Buenos Aires itself was an armed camp. Everywhere there were soldiers and police armed to the teeth and squads of tough-looking *federales* patrolled the streets looking for trouble. There were sporadic riots everywhere. U.S. installations such as the embassy offices and the U.S.I.A. Library on Calle Florida, across the street from the hotel, had double guards in front of them. There was a lot of anti-American propaganda. I put this all together with a couple of other incidents that had happened since we got to Buenos Aires. Sitting in the hotel bar one afternoon, a waiter who knew I was *norteamericano* pointed directly toward a corner table where there were four men talking quietly.

"C.I.A.," the waiter said—grinning. I dismissed this as being just another one of those ploys used by the waiters, taxi drivers and the like to spice up a tourist's visit. For all I knew those four might have been beef buyers. Then I remembered that the Paraguayan had expressed his worry that, "*SIDE* (pronounced see-day) might have people watching us." *SIDE,* I learned, are the initials for Argentine state security. I was also told that they are a tough bunch of sons of bitches. I did not know much about Argentine politics. And I didn't want to. I found myself wondering whether Vesco was involving himself in "foreign relations" that had nothing to do with any specific business venture. That kind of thing is illegal for an American citizen and can also get you killed. But Vesco, on more than one occasion, had dropped some pretty ponderous hints that he had some sort of secret mandate from his "good old buddy," Dick Nixon.

I did not see Vesco again that day. I got a call the following morning from him telling me we would be leaving Buenos Aires later that afternoon for Asuncion, Paraguay. He didn't mention the Perón business, nor did I, but he sounded pretty calm.

The flight from JFK to Geneva with the Cahill kids presented no problems. As usual, after his ration of Crown Royals, Vesco wandered up to the flight deck and took his position behind me. This was his signal that he wanted to talk. Vesco had the right as the owner to go wherever he wanted on the airplane. Of course, as Captain, I could have kept him off the flight deck if I wanted to. But I maintained an "open-door" policy not only for Vesco but for any passenger who wanted to come up and look around. Usually, with the average passenger, the visits were of short duration. Not much happens on a flight deck especially at night when there isn't a hell of a lot to see. But Vesco seemed to find some sort of purging quality in the reality of the lights, gauges, and controls.

He used his seat behind me almost as a confessional. He would rest one arm on the back of my seat and lean forward so that his head was between my left shoulder and the side of the airplane. Often he would sit there without saying a word, staring out at the empty sky. Then he would begin to talk in a low confidential tone in my left ear about whatever was on his mind. Sometimes he would bet me that we would or would not touch the top of a cloud up ahead.

"Don't touch anything, Ike," he would say. "I have a grand that says we'll hit that cloud."

I'd study and sight the cloud before I took the bet. Clouds are not just fluffy things floating in the sky. They're dynamic. They're alive. They're in constant internal turmoil. They change shape and, of course, they move with the air. After so many years of flying I could pretty well predict the behavior of any cloud. So I had an edge on Vesco. But that didn't seem to bother him. Very often, when I knew I could trap him into a sucker bet, I'd up the ante to 5,000 dollars. The number didn't shock Vesco. He would drop twice that much on a single roll of the dice. My raise made the bet more exciting to him. He would then go into a series of gyrations rechecking his computations by whatever standards of measurement he used. He would wait until the last possible second before he took the bet.

If we missed the cloud he would watch it go by with a look of disgust on his face.

"Sonofabitch!" he would say. I'd stick out my hand

for my winnings. "Put it on my tab," he would say, and look for another cloud to get even on.

When Vesco and I parted company permanently in 1973 his "tab" amounted to 33,000 dollars—U.S. American.

In the dark of the flight deck Vesco would very often bleed all over me. He would tell me things I didn't really want to know or voice complaints I didn't want to hear. I had my own problems. Most often I would listen with only half an ear. But there were times when he would drop something that would perk up my attention.

One night over the Atlantic he was staring out at a full moon and cloudless sky. He had been silent for almost five minutes. I thought he had fallen asleep. Suddenly he erupted.

"That dirty Jew sonofabitch," he said. I thought he was talking about Bernie Cornfeld because that is the way he usually referred to Cornfeld. "You just can't trust a Heeb," he went on.

"C'mon, Bob," I said, "Bernie can't bother you anymore."

"Sporkin," Vesco said. "I'm talking about that rat bastard Sporkin from the SEC." I knew that Vesco was having troubles with the Securities and Exchange Commission. Not only was it in all the papers but I had actually flown Vesco's lawyer, Edward Bennett Williams, from Washington to Nassau right after the SEC announced its suit against Vesco. I didn't know who Sporkin was.

"Who's Sporkin?" I asked.

"He's that sheeny prick at the SEC who's trying to stick it to me," he said. "I laid out 200 fucking thousand dollars to take care of that business but that bastard Sporkin won't play ball. I ought to have his lights put out. I could do that—you know." This was the kind of thing I didn't want to hear.

"I don't think that's the smartest idea in the world, Bob," I said. I don't know if he heard me.

"I just don't understand it," he went on. "I paid, Ike, goddamnit, and I expect delivery." He was quiet for a couple of seconds. "Fucking politicians!" I kept my mouth shut hoping it would discourage him. It did. He went back to the cabin.

Our arrival at Geneva was notable only because the crew met, for the first time, the newest member of the Vesco team: Donald Nixon, Jr., or Kid or Idiot or Junior, as he came to be known. The choice of nickname was dependent upon the mood at any given time of the person who was talking to him or about him. He was the first person aboard the airplane after we landed. He even beat the handling agent in the door—which takes some doing. The first I knew he was aboard was when he bounded onto the flight deck and announced himself.

"Hi, gang!" he said, "I'm Don Nixon." I don't know what he expected but his breathless announcement was received with a massive display of mild interest. I had met Donald Nixon, Jr. briefly in Vesco's office in Fairfield a month or so before. He seemed like a pleasant kid. Tall, slender, and moderately good looking. His features, unfortunately, bore more than a slight resemblance to those of Alfred E. Neumann, the cover boy of *Mad* magazine. After my introduction to him back in New Jersey, Shirley Bailey and Ralph Dodd had some uncomplimentary things to say about the nephew of the president. But they, like everybody else around Vesco, would have found it hard to say anything positive about Santa Claus. I paid no attention to their judgments. As a matter of fact, I forgot completely about Donald Nixon, Jr., and was as surprised as anybody when he showed up in Geneva. I knew he had been working with Gil Straub (Gilbert R. J. Straub) somewhere in Europe. Straub was one of Vesco's top-echelon front men from the early days of the IOS adventure. All I knew about Don Nixon, Jr. was that he had been hired as an "executive trainee" under the tutelage of Straub in Europe. I was soon to learn that Junior not only had an entirely different view of his function in the Vesco operation, but he had a shattering genius for provoking crisis.

We were polite enough to the president's nephew although we were a little amused at his bouncy enthusiasm. He went off with the Vesco party practically arm in arm with Vesco himself. Vesco didn't look too happy at having an "executive trainee" behaving as if he were an equal. If Gil Straub had been anywhere in the vicinity I think that Vesco would have flayed him and told him to "teach this mutt to heel!"

I won't say that Junior did not have some impact on the crew. We were aware that he was the nephew of the president. That information came right after, "Hi, gang! I'm Don Nixon." This was at the time Richard Nixon still enjoyed the power and prestige of the office of the president of the United States. He had his political enemies and there were those who distrusted him. But the "Tricky Dick" identity was beginning to fade. So the antics of young Donald Nixon, Jr. were judged by those who came in contact with him totally apart from his relationship with his famous uncle. He proved to be an asshole in his own right. He didn't need his uncle for that.

As Junior Nixon left with Vesco and his party, it did not even occur to me or any of the crew that we would have any further contact with him except in the most sporadic way. Wrong!

That very night at the hotel where the crew stayed when in Geneva, we had a visitation from this once-removed celebrity. We were in the dining room talking about everything except airplanes—Vesco, Nixon, politics, and especially Donald Nixon, Jr. Suddenly, he appeared wearing sunglasses pushed over his forehead. He strode across the floor like a used-car salesman greeting the first customer of the day. He had his hand stuck out ready to shake anything.

"Hi, gang!" he said, "I'm Don Nixon. Remember? The nephew of the president." Oh, shit!

10

November 9, 1971 0830Z GVA—BEY

I never thought I'd regard a flight around the world as a dismal prospect.

Before we left JFK on what I'll call the Cahill Flight, Vesco had told me that he intended to take his wife Pat around the world in the Boeing—just the two of them. This was quite a jolt. Since I had known the Vescos I had the feeling that after twenty odd years of marriage, Bob and Pat no longer even liked each other. The crew and I were embarrassed witnesses to many family fights carried out at high pitch in public. These fights ended, usually in grim and protracted silence, and each seemed to carry a grudge afterward. So it was with a certain amount of optimism that I announced the plans to the crew.

"A second honeymoon," someone suggested. Maybe. And maybe Robert Lee Vesco had taken a long look at himself and realized that he had more than enough money for a guy in his late thirties and now could turn to the business of enriching his marriage. Just maybe.

Any hint of a "second honeymoon" vanished as soon as we left Geneva for our first destination: Beirut, Lebanon. The two Vescos arrived showing about as much enthusiasm as they would have if they were on their way from their home in Boonton Township to the center of Denville for a day's shopping. On top of that they brought a hitchhiker with them, one Dr. Hanspeter Brunner, about whom I remember nothing. He would be with us as far as Bangkok, Thailand. Gil Straub and his fiancée, Barbara Rossner, would accompany us as far as Beirut.

We stayed in Beirut for two days. Although it was well within the range of the Boeing's capability to fly nonstop from Beirut to Bangkok, the rip-off syndrome infecting many governments required me to make two totally unneccessary stops.

Incredible as it sounds, no private aircraft may overfly Syria or India. An airplane entering Syrian or Indian airspace must land, pay whatever fees are levied, and buy fuel that is unneeded and criminally overpriced before it can proceed to its next destination. The only way to avoid this rip-off is to fly around the country, a detour which could be costly in time and which could use up more fuel than would be taken aboard during the required landing. And don't think these countries haven't figured this all out. But that's not the end of it. Then to ensure speedy servicing of the airplane and prompt handling of clearances, it is not only advisable but downright necessary to bribe an endless parade of airport officials. The Damascus, Syria, stop cost a flat 2,000 dollars above the standard airport fees and the cost of fuel. That was the price. There was no haggling and no receipt. I laid the two grand on a man who, from the way he was treated by other airport personnel, was obviously the boss.

And then there is India.

I landed at Bombay about four-twenty in the morning, local time. It was a black night. My passengers were sound asleep. Dottie McCarty, our chief stewardess, routinely opened the forward passenger door expecting to see a ground-service representative waiting at the top of the stairs. The door had not swung open more than a few inches when a skinny, brown arm thrust into the cabin. The hand, bony and filthy, clutched an unlabeled aerosol can. The sudden appearance of this hand and arm frightened Dottie, and she recoiled a step or two.

Spritz! Spritz! A finger depressed a valve on the can and two piddling squirts of something dribbled onto the floor. Dottie had uttered a little cry at the first appearance of that hand and arm. Pete, the flight engineer, heard her. The crew was always on the alert, especially in the more primitive areas of the world, for any sign of danger, or a possible hijacking.

Pete, busy at his panel shutting things down, stopped what he was doing, launched himself out of his seat, and was at Dottie's side with one long step. He grabbed the door edge and swung it open ready to do battle with whatever the hell was on the other side. An incredibly wizened Indian wearing what looked like a stained and tattered British-World War I army uniform, a soiled turban, and no shoes stood in the doorway. Immediately behind him were two other Indians in less ancient but equally dirty uniforms. They were shod and wore service caps that indicated they were government employees.

The little man with the aerosol can stood there with a toothless grin on his face. He held out his hand, palm up. By this time I had joined the party.

"*Dis afet! Dis afet!*" The little man said, making a gathering motion with his hand.

"What the hell is he saying?" I asked.

"How the hell do I know, Ike?" Pete said. "I don't understand the language either."

One of the other uniformed men stepped forward. He spoke with a clipped singsong imitation-English accent.

"Disinfect, Captain," he said. "He has only just disinfected your aircraft and he is waiting for his fee. It is 500 rupees. You must pay him immediately."

With the memory of Damascus still very fresh in my mind, I was sore as hell.

"And just who the hell are you?" I asked.

"I am Customs," he said. I ignored the little man with the aerosol can. I took Dottie's clipboard, which held the declaration form and other pertinent documents for an around-the-world flight, and pointed out to the

Customs officer that the aircraft had already been disinfected in flight according to international regulations. The Customs man was insistent.

"You must pay 500 rupees," he said. "It is required." It was too hot and muggy and late to argue with these people for what I figured was a few dollars. All I wanted to do was fuel up, get clearance, and leave. I turned to Dottie and asked her to look in her World Guide and give me the figure in U.S. currency.

"Ike," she said, "that's more than fifty dollars." I blew up. Twenty-five dollars a spritz is highway robbery.

"I'm not going to give him a goddamn cent!" I told the Customs man. "We complied with the regulations. Now tell him to get the hell off this airplane!"

"But you must . . ." the Customs man began. I spun the little man around and shoved him out onto the stairway, then pointed down to the ramp. He was frightened enough, despite the presence of the two Customs officers, to scurry down the steps. Before he disappeared into the darkness he turned and shook his fist up at me, screaming what I took to be obscenities.

The Customs men were startled but they didn't interfere. I interpreted their silence as tacit agreement that the little guy tried to pull a swindle. I expected them to leave. I went to get my briefcase since I had to go to operations to file my flight plan and get clearance papers to continue on to Bangkok. As I stepped away the two Customs men moved to enter the airplane. I turned back.

"Where're you going?" I asked them.

"We must inspect the airplane," one of them said. "It is required." For Christ's sake! I pointed out to them that a Customs inspection was *not*—repeat, *not*—required. We were a transient aircraft. Nobody would be leaving the plane except the Captain. Nobody would be arriving aboard the aircraft, and nothing would be taken from it or put aboard. It didn't make any difference.

While I watched, the Customs men strolled through the airplane brazenly picking up whatever took their fancy as if daring me to do something about it. They woke my passengers, getting a barrage of obscenities from Vesco. I wanted to kick both of them right square in the ass as they left the airplane. I was really helpless, not knowing what kind of trouble these two men could cause. We were foreigners, and foreigners—especially Americans—are always wrong.

I gave fueling instructions to Pete, grabbed my briefcase again, and set out for operations.

Silver Phyllis was parked a couple of hundred yards from the hangar line. I asked one of the fuelers for directions. He pointed to a group of hangars and buildings. On the ramp side of one of the buildings I saw a sign lighted by a single bulb that said OPERATIONS and had an arrow. I would have to pass through an unlighted alley. At the end of the alley I saw the operations building on my left, a hundred feet away. The only illumination came from a single light over the entrance to the operations building. About halfway along the passageway I became aware of two men backed up against the building to my left. I'm not spooky by nature, especially around airports. But a sixth sense told me that these guys had no business being there at that time of the morning. I tightened my grip on my briefcase. I was carrying more than 20,000 dollars of Vesco's money. It was standard to carry large amounts of cash on a trip like this because most often cash was the only way you could pay for services—including bribes. I didn't really believe that these guys were going to take a run at me. But suddenly, without a sound, one of them broke from the shadows and made a beeline for me. In his right hand he held a knife with a six-inch blade. The other guy cut across my path to swing around and take me from the other side.

This was too goddamn much! First Damascus, then the little guy with the can, then the Customs thieves—and now this! The adrenalin began to flow. These two raggedy-ass runts were not about to take me. Right then I felt as if I could walk through a concrete wall. When the guy with the knife got in range I swung the briefcase, a 4½-inch-deep vinyl-covered metal Samsonite that, with everything I had in it, weighed close to 25 pounds. It felt like a feather. A corner of the briefcase caught the guy with the knife on the side of the head. The knife flew one way and he was propelled, all arms and legs, in another. He collapsed to the ground out cold. The other guy had stopped dead in his tracks. I was so fucking angry that I charged him. I must have been a frightening sight. He was about five-feet two and couldn't have weighed more than 100 pounds. I am close to six feet and weigh close to one-ninety. That little squirt took off like he was fired from a slingshot. There was no hope of catching him. I gave up the chase at the foot of the steps into operations.

Once inside operations, I raised 60 kinds of unshirted hell about what had happened, about everything. All I got were shrugs. The only satisfaction I got was a police escort back to the airplane. The oaf who showed up for escort duty had apparently been rousted from a sound sleep. He wasn't too happy with the assignment but then I doubt whether his presence would have intimidated even an aggressive cat. I kept the incident of the would be muggers to myself. There was no point in alarming passengers or crew. I did not want to implant, in their minds, that this was the kind of thing we could expect from here on out.

It might seem that wherever I go I attract trouble. These kinds of hassles occur regularly. Aircraft commanders are responsible for the observance of all regulations, laws, and procedures as well as for paying the bills en route. They are the most visible, the perfect targets. Captains have been beaten up, shot, jailed, and thrown out of countries because they protested officially condoned harassment and corruption. Good-bye India!

November 11, 1971 2318Z BOM—BKK

Our arrival in Bangkok was, for me anyway, a shocker. The airspace over Bangkok Airport was aswarm with United States military aircraft—jet fighters, heavy transports and, very high and heading east, a pair of B-52 bombers that left their black, smoky trail across that gorgeous blue sky. The airport itself was crammed with more of the same and there were military vehicles everywhere. Until that moment I had forgotten about the war in Vietnam. I remembered, then, that not far from Bangkok was an American bomber base from which B-52's sortied into North Vietnam, a mere 500 miles to the northeast.

When Vesco and I had planned the trip back in the States, neither one of us considered the likelihood that for part of our trip, not only would we pass through a war zone but we would fly within eyeball range of Red China.

"Play this one cool, Chuck," I told my first officer who had seen and commented on U.S. military presence. "I don't want to spook Vesco." Taxiing in, I called Dottie on the flight deck and warned both her and Pete Dolliver to make no mention of the Vietnamese war or all the military hardware at the airport to the Vescos. If Vesco brought the subject up, I would handle him.

We all stayed at the same hotel in Bangkok, the Siam Inter-Continental. This was not always the case. Both Vesco and I preferred that the crew lodge separately from the boss and his associates. But when he was traveling with Pat, he wanted the crew in the same hotel.

The routine when Pat Vesco was not along was that any playing around took place out of sight of the crew. On a couple of occasions, however, our paths crossed. Sometimes these accidental encounters in restaurants and nightclubs were an embarrassment to all of us. Other times we were invited to join the boss and his party.

Once, in Munich, when we had no flight scheduled for the following day, the crew opted for an evening of fun. We were staying at the new Holiday Inn that featured an exotic discothèque called the "Yellow Submarine," which boasted a stainless-steel dance floor.

I was dancing with Dottie McCarty. Suddenly someone grabbed my shoulder, spun me half around, and shoved a woman at me. A look of utter surprise came over Dottie's face. Then I spotted Vesco, a big grin on his face, jiggling like an eel. He danced off with Dottie without missing a beat.

The woman he shoved at me was no stranger. She was a young, very attractive and well-built Londoner. She was a passenger-service representative for Pan Am working at Heathrow Airport. I had seen her only a few days before and there wasn't the slightest indication then that she and Vesco were joined together in unholy hanky-panky. When the music stopped, Vesco invited the whole crew to join him. The other two guys in my crew became uncomfortable and mumbled something about other plans and departed. Dottie and I joined Vesco's group which was, apart from the Pan Am gal, an all-male party. When Vesco got up again to dance and Dottie went to the powder room, one of the men complained.

"We have to scout up our own ass," he said. "Bobby flies his in first class."

"The trouble is," another said, "we can't go sniffing until the boss toddles off." An hour later Vesco did just that, taking his girl friend with him. The other guys split as soon as he disappeared through the door. I never learned how they made out.

There would, of course, be no hanky-panky in Bangkok. But there would be no "togetherness" either. The crew arrived at the hotel a couple of hours after the Vescos. Vesco, looking refreshed and wearing a complete change of clothes, was in the lobby, carrying a briefcase and chatting with a couple of people I guessed to be IOS executives in Thailand. He just waved his hand and said, "Pat's in the sack," and left the hotel. I didn't see him again until we were ready to leave.

The crew got some rest and did some sightseeing and shopping in the afternoon. Pat Vesco, on the other hand, seemed totally disinterested in the culture or the products of foreign locales. The routine she followed in Bangkok, when she finally did leave the hotel suite, was the one she followed for the rest of the trip.

A Mercedes-Benz picked her up at the hotel that afternoon. She sat in the back all by herself and the car moved away. As with her husband, that was the last we saw of her until departure time at the airport. She would arrive at the plane with a few cheap souvenirs that she'd purchased either at the hotel shops or at the airport. I once saw her considering buying a picture of a Chinese-looking Jesus whose eyes followed you around the room.

Vesco was not interested in souvenirs, sightseeing or shopping for exotic bargains. When he showed up at the aircraft, he had with him a second briefcase that he carefully stowed by his seat. His working briefcase, the one he usually carried, he placed in the passenger luggage compartment in the cabin. Before the trip was over there was no doubt that this was no second honeymoon for the Vescos. Vesco was checking the IOS trap line and collecting "pelts."

Singapore, two hours' flying time to the south, turned into nothing more than another briefcase stop. My problem was the trip ahead—from Singapore to Hong Kong.

November 16, 1971 0126Z SIN—HKE

The briefing at Singapore operations was more extensive and intensive than usual. We would be flying right through the Vietnam war zone and at one point we would pass very close to Red Chinese territory, specifically Hainan Island where there were a number of Red Chinese jet-interceptor bases. Chinese Communist pilots have been known to extend their range of operations and harrass passing aircraft.

Modern jet aircraft like the Boeing do not need or carry navigators. That job is performed by computers programmed by the Captain or first officer, who constantly monitor and update as the flight progresses. At the time, our primary long-range navigation system was the self-contained Doppler System. It is a system that operates on the principle of transmitting radar-frequency impulses to the surface of the earth and measuring the time they take to return to the aircraft.

Fighter aircraft, especially those used by the Red Chinese, do not utilize anything that approaches the accuracy of the equipment carried by commercial aircraft. Whether or not an airplane is "violating" Red China's sovereignty depends on the on-the-spot judgment of a fighter pilot whose only reference points are what he can see. There is, of course, continuous monitoring of passing aircraft by radar ground stations. But I didn't have a hell of a lot of confidence in the judgment of some unseen Chinese private.

At the Phon Thiet beacon I crossed the south coast of Vietnam, east of Saigon, and continued on to Qui Nhon. As we approached the Mekong Delta the air traffic was as bad as the Long Island Expressway on a weekday morning. We turned northeast at Qui Nhon, where the air was clear. I had an unobstructed view of the ground. Flying at 40,000 feet I could see for over 100 miles in any direction. It was easy to pick out Saigon, and I could trace the Mekong River into Cambodia. Here and there on the ground I could make out the smoke of perhaps half a dozen battles. Occasionally we observed aircraft attacking ground targets. Chuck and Pete got out of their seats to look out the window.

"I feel so goddamn guilty," I said to Chuck. "Guys are getting killed down there."

We watched in silence, fascinated by what we were looking at. Contrary to movies, you can't hear explosions on the ground. You can't hear aircraft that fly near you. All you hear are your own engines and the whip of air over the surface of the airplane. It's like watching a silent movie.

Each of us had had experience with war, and our sympathies were with the guys who were doing the fighting. We had talked about Vietnam many times. We were against it. But we had the kind of background that allowed us to make informed judgments. We didn't buy the lies of our own government about Vietnam and we *knew* they were lying. We didn't need to wait for the release of the "Pentagon Papers." I felt all along that our involvement in Southeast Asia, our military involvement, was a stupid and unsupportable adventure. Ideology had nothing to do with it. My opposition was practical and, I admit, emotional. I have three sons, two of them at that time draftable. I would expect them to honor their obligation to their country when their country is in danger. But I did not want to see them down there in that smoke for no goddamn good reason.

Chuck, Pete, and I were not radicals. We all hated the violent radicals, the hate-America Peaceniks and "crazies" who caused so much trouble back home. But I think that we represented a growing number of Americans who needed to let their opposition to the Vietnamese war be known.

Vesco suddenly appeared on the flight deck behind me. He jerked his thumb toward the window.

"There's a lot of goddamn airplanes out there, Ike," he said. "What's going on? Where are we?"

"That, Bob," I informed him, "is Vietnam."

"Jee-zus Christ!" he yelled. "What the hell are we doing here? Get out of here! Get out of here!"

"No can do, Bob," I said. "Unless you want to go to Manila this is the road to Hong Kong." He went back to his seat. Later Dottie told me that he and Pat sat with their faces pressed against the left side windows until we had passed out of sight of land. I realized after he had left the flight deck that Vesco claimed a close friendship with the man who was running that goddamn war—Richard Nixon. I wanted to go after him and tell him to tell his shifty-eyed friend to put a stop to it. But I don't believe that, other than during that one brief span, between Saigon and Da Nang, where we turned out to sea, that the Vietnam tragedy had ever disturbed Robert Lee Vesco.

I felt pretty helpless and very angry. The thought had crossed my mind, briefly, that I could make one gesture to show our opposition despite the fact that I had two women aboard. I had the impulse to dump that big, sleek, comfortable but unarmed 707 down to grass level and buzz the whole damned political playground. No doubt somebody would have noticed and my explanation for the act would have gotten worldwide attention. If I didn't get shot down, they probably would have put me in a room with rubber walls.

The last point of personal interest I located before I headed out across the South China Sea was the city of Hue, which would figure so prominently in the final disintegration of South Vietnam.

Even before we lost sight of Vietnam I saw the Red Chinese island of Hainan off in the distance. I hoped that Vesco would not reappear to ask me about it. In fact I wished he would go to sleep.

I spotted the two jet fighters, which had to be Red Chinese, slightly above me at about eleven o'clock. They were heading right at me. I pointed them out to the crew. If they were making a run at us there was nothing I could do. If I turned to the right, I couldn't outrun them, and such a maneuver might indicate to the two pilots that I was admitting that I had entered Chinese airspace. I held my course and double-checked my Doppler position. At a distance of about three miles they suddenly broke off to their right and we could clearly see the Red Chinese markings on the underwings and tail surfaces. This was to happen a couple of times before I finally got well inside the Hong Kong control area. I knew that I must have been identified by ground radar as a nonhostile. So I figured that the Chinese pilots were having their fun at my expense. I'm glad Vesco didn't see them.

Vesco picked up another briefcase in Hong Kong.

I had filed originally for Tokyo, Japan, but was diverted to Osaka. Vesco and his wife took the high-speed express on up to Tokyo.

We spent three days in Japan. The Vescos came back to Osaka earlier than they had planned, and Dottie and I had dinner with them at the new Plaza hotel. Dottie asked Pat Vesco about her trip to Tokyo. I felt a little sad that the only impression she brought back with her was that there were too many cars in Tokyo. I invited the Vescos to join Dottie and me at the Shin-Kabukiza Theater to see a traditional Japanese Kabuki play. They both refused. Vesco had business and Pat wanted to take a nap.

November 21, 1971 0745Z OSA—SFO

The question that Pat Vesco asked almost constantly ever since we'd left Geneva was, "When do you think we'll get to Las Vegas?" A question I would not be able to answer until we landed in the United States. Vesco had never even mentioned Las Vegas and I didn't know why Pat Vesco thought we were going there. Our destination was Monterey, California, for reasons that were unknown to me. We would first have to land at an airport of entry for Customs clearance and Monterey was not an airport of entry.

After Monterey we were scheduled to return to Newark after which I would fly the airplane to Ft. Worth, Texas, to begin major modifications to the interior.

Ever since we acquired the Boeing, Vesco and I had discussed the changes he wanted in the aircraft interior and the changes I wanted in the basic structure and components. On long flights I would sit with Vesco in the back of the Boeing and we'd take measurements, rough out sketches, argue, and make notes. When we agreed on any particular change, it would be put in writing with an appropriate sketch. I would, upon landing, contact Qualitron Aero Design, send along the notes and sketches, and ask them to send back an engineering drawing. When that came back, if it met with Vesco's approval, he would initial it as authorization to proceed.

The interior modification would be made in phases. To do the job all at once as was the industry practice would have kept the Boeing out of service for more than six months. Vesco couldn't tolerate something like this. He could have kept the Gulfstream until the Boeing was completed but he had schedules to meet that demanded the use of the 707. In addition, the modifications we wanted could be determined in detail only after we had become familiar with the airplane. I worked out a schedule that would allow the work to be done in phases. By knowing in advance when the plane would be out of service and for how long—5½ weeks at the outside—Vesco could make other arrangements.

Qualitron resisted this program. They had never done work that way before. What convinced them to go along was the ability of Jack Prewitt, the marketing vice-president, to sell his own people on it. He understood the benefits to Qualitron to be the first to take on a job of such magnitude. Nobody had ever tackled such extensive alterations to a Boeing 707 before.

Since the work would be done at both Ft. Worth and Burbank, California, it was necessary to keep the crew intact. Even if I could have let them go home I would have to stay with the airplane because dozens of decisions had to be made daily. I needed to personally supervise some of the installations because only Vesco and I understood what we wanted. Dottie McCarty had a sure talent for color and design. She knew fabrics and textiles and developed the basic color and design theme for the interior and also took on the responsibility for functional location and design of all passenger-service related components.

On the flight from Osaka, Vesco and I again went over the plans for the first phase of modification. Pat Vesco was never consulted. Nor did she seem to have any interest in what was to be done to the airplane. That certainly was a switch. I had been involved with the modification of corporate aircraft many times. In the interior-design area, especially in the selection of fabrics and colors, executive wives invariably insinuated themselves. They are responsible for some of the most hideous and tasteless interiors I've ever seen.

Shortly before we landed at San Francisco, Vesco asked me to come back to the cabin. I had reminded him that we had to clear Customs before we could continue to Monterey. As we walked to the rear of the Boeing I was suddenly worried that what he had on his mind was a gimmick that he had used once before to my knowledge to slip something past Customs without the danger of a possible arrest if his plan should fail.

The year before Vesco and some of his associates returned from Europe via commercial carrier to JFK Airport. This was before we had the Boeing. I was to have the Gulfstream at the airport when he arrived. I waited outside the Customs area of the International Arrivals Building. The first one through the doors was one of Vesco's associates. He spotted me and came over. He dropped his bag and for a minute I thought he expected me to pick it up. Instead he reached into his overcoat pocket and pulled out a flat, gold-tooled leather box.

"Ike, hang onto this for Bob," he said. "He'll be out in a minute." I took the box, looked at it and stuck it in my pocket. Since Vesco was on the ground and would be ready to move shortly, I went to telephone Port Authority for transportation from the IAB to where the Gulfstream was parked at the General Aviation Terminal. The station wagon that would be sent to pick us up would be on the ramp side of the International Arrivals Building. To get onto the ramp it was necessary to pass a guard. This meant that I had to identify myself and vouch for the passengers. By the time I finished calling, Vesco appeared and all of us went out to the ramp. We had to wait for our transportation. There was some small talk about the trip. Then the man who had given me the leather box poked me lightly on the arm.

"Give Bob the box," he said. I took the box out of my pocket and handed it to Vesco. He opened it. It was empty. The guy who had given me the box in the first place giggled. Then he reached inside his suit jacket, fiddled a bit, and pulled out a lady's watch. It was a beautiful piece of jewelry, solid gold, and studded with diamonds. I would not even attempt to estimate its value. But it was not the kind of thing you could get with Green Stamps. Vesco began to laugh. He put the watch in the box and tucked into his pocket.

"Hey, Ike, look at this!" the other guy said. He opened his coat and there, hanging from a pin fastened to the lining of his jacket, was another watch, also a beauty, but less elegant. I wanted to run away from these two clowns. The Customs Service regularly assigns plainclothes agents to mingle with the public. More than once they have nailed some smart-ass who didn't have the brains to wait until he was well clear of the airport before showing somebody what he'd just smuggled through.

"Did you *smuggle* those things in?" I asked. They were enjoying themselves immensely.

"Who, me?" Vesco asked with a mock-innocent look on his face. He pointed at the other guy who thought it was the greatest joke in the world. I wonder how funny that asshole would have thought it was if a Customs agent had put the arm on him right then. Vesco could have said—and I would be his unwitting witness—that *he* didn't smuggle anything. The other guy did.

The next time I saw that watch it was on Pat Vesco's wrist nearly three years later. At the time Vesco was in deep trouble. He was under indictment for fraud and faced a raft of civil suits. He had been out of the country for months. He would not allow the Boeing to be flown to the United States for fear that it would be impounded on behalf of creditors, which included the U.S. government. He had leased a Grumman Gulfstream Two from the Union Bank and Trust of Chicago whose president, Allen Dorfman, was serving time for misuse of Teamsters' union pension funds.

I had flown Pat Vesco and some of the children up from Nassau and landed at Teterboro Airport in New Jersey at six thirty in the evening. I was using Dorfman's Gulfstream Two. Since Teterboro handles international corporate traffic it had Customs available. The usual procedure for private aircraft is for a Customs agent to come on board the aircraft and perform the necessary duties. When he's finished he clears the passengers and baggage to leave. Normally it is a perfunctory and speedy procedure. Customs Agents who deal with corporate and privately owned aircraft know that they are dealing with people in the upper economic level. They are used to seeing the accoutrements of wealth—expensive jewelry, coutourier clothing and the like. The Customs people, for the most part, are courteous and business-like. There is no doubt that people of wealth are treated more deferentially and with more leniency than the average commercial passenger. Under normal circumstances I have never seen more than a single uniformed Customs agent come aboard an aircraft like the Gulfstream Two I was flying.

On this occasion, May 28, 1973, there were only four passengers on the Gulfstream, Pat Vesco and three children, all minors. One agent was certainly sufficient.

I parked the Gulfstream in front of the corporate-aviation hangar and passenger lounge. As expected, Pat's limousine drove onto the ramp and stopped at the foot of the steps. I left my seat and waited at the top of the steps for the Customs agent to arrive from the hangar. I saw him walking toward the airplane but I was surprised to see that he had three other men, in civilian clothes, with him. About the time they reached the steps of the Gulfstream another car, a Ford, pulled up behind the limousine. There were two men in the front seat. They didn't get out.

The first man up the steps and into the Gulfstream was a black man in civilian clothes. He was followed by the Customs Inspector in uniform. Then came the other two in civilian clothes. They all entered the airplane. I was puzzled. I thought maybe it was a training session for new agents. The man in uniform, however, left us and went back into the cabin where he began his routine. I asked the others what was happening.

One of the men standing behind the black man stepped forward.

"Is Vesco on this airplane?" he asked. I didn't like his tone. He looked like a hard nose.

"No!" I told him. "But his family is."

"Where'd you come from?" he asked. I stuck the General Declaration in front of him.

"Nassau," I said.

"Did you land anyplace else?" he asked. His manner was brusque and aggressive.

"Who are you?" I asked. He repeated his question. From everything about him I figured him for some kind of federal cop.

"I didn't land anywhere else," I said.

"You're sure of that," he said.

"Hey pal," I said, "do you have some trouble with your hearing? I asked you who you are." He reached into his pocket and took out a paper and waved it at me.

"I've got a warrant for his arrest," he said, "a federal warrant. When was the last time you saw him?"

"A day or two ago," I said.

"Where? What were you doing?" he asked.

"In Nassau," I told him.

"I asked you what you were doing?" he said. I didn't like what was happening. This guy was coming on like Kojak.

"How the hell do I know what we were doing?" I said. "Playing ice hockey for Christ's sake!" All through this the black guy and the other guy said nothing. Then I heard Pat Vesco's voice. It was high pitched and angry.

"This is ridiculous!" she said.

The three men—let's call them federal agents—had positioned themselves between me and the cabin. When I heard Pat's voice I shoved them aside and went to see what was the matter. One of the agents grabbed my arm. I stopped, faced the three of them, and pointed my finger at each one of them individually.

"You! You! You!" I said, "get the fuck off this airplane—now!" I was perfectly within my rights as aircraft commander. Without specific authorization they had no business on that airplane. In addition, none of the three had shown any identification. I had exactly the same authority on that airplane as the Captain of a seagoing vessel. My two crew members were ready to physically eject the three men from the airplane on my signal. We had done it before. The explosive situation was defused by the black man who showed me his shield and ID card. I knew that at least he was a bona fide federal employee. For all I knew, the other two guys could have been local warrant squad flunkies.

"You can stay," I told the black man, "they go. They either walk off or they get thrown off." There was a moment of absolute stillness. Nobody spoke. Nobody moved. Then the black guy nodded his head and the other two left. The black man followed me back to where Pat Vesco, with her three children watching in wonder and fright, argued with the Customs agent. Arguing is not the word. She was talking *at* him and he was ignoring her. He had *all* the luggage open. He had pulled everything apart and was meticulously examining a toy that belonged to Vesco's youngest son, little Bobby. When he finished, he picked up another toy and examined it like a monkey picking over a coconut.

Pat had her hands up in supplication.

"What is this man doing?" she said. "He won't even talk to me." The uniformed Customs agent stopped what he was doing and looked around. He was about to say something but instead took hold of Pat Vesco's left arm. At that moment the watch she was wearing caught my eye. It was the one I had seen on the ramp at Kennedy.

"Where'd you get this watch, lady?" the Customs agent asked Pat. Pat wrenched her arm from the agent's grasp. She looked absolutely panic stricken.

"From my husband!" she yelled. "My husband gave it to me."

"Take it off. I want to look at it," the agent said.

You might get the idea that I don't like the Customs people of the world. In most countries this would be true. Along with the British, the United States Customs agents are generally outstanding. They have a difficult, almost impossible job. They deal with an awful lot of people and their patience and courtesy is remarkable. But occasionally you come across some clown who either has a wild hair up his ass or is trying to impress a superior officer. This particular agent was certainly well within his "manual" rights in examining anything he wanted in as thorough a way as he chose. But he is required by department rules to exercise courtesy, discretion, and good judgment. This guy was a loser on all three counts.

Pat took the watch off and handed it to him. He examined it carefully and handed it to the black man.

"This is foreign merchandise," he said. "What do you think?" The black man looked at the watch, said nothing and handed it back. One thing that I've learned is that your average experienced Customs agent is as good an appraiser of almost any type of product as you can get. This agent, despite his attrocious manner, knew his business.

"You got a receipt for this watch, lady?" he asked. By now Pat was crying with anger and embarrassment. She was not by any standards a sophisticated woman but she was a mother who was being humiliated in front of her children. She began to turn defiant.

"My husband declared this watch," she yelled at the agent. "You can check your records." She snatched the watch from his hand.

"I'm going to do just that, lady," the agent said. He demanded that she tell him when she got the watch. It took her a minute or two but she came up with a date. He went back to his minute and infuriating examination of the Vesco family's luggage. It took him another hour but he finally allowed Pat Vesco and her children to leave. Then, when she had gone, he turned to me.

"You guys are next," he said, "where's your stuff?"

"We don't have anything," I told him. He didn't believe me.

"Don't give me that," he said. "Where's your stuff?"

"You don't hear well either?" I asked him. "I told you we don't have anything. When you get finished fucking around I'm going to fly this airplane right back to Nassau and finish my fucking ice hockey game." He had no idea what I was talking about but the black guy did. He chuckled. He was on my side. The Customs agent looked like a kid who had just dropped his ice-cream cone into a pile of dog shit. He left the airplane. The black federal agent apologized for what had happened, although his behavior was exemplary. He explained that he could not really interfere because of departmental jealousies.

"How come six people showed up at this airplane tonight?" I asked him. "Why the big hassle?"

"We got a tip," he said.

"About what?" I asked.

"That Vesco was coming into the country," he said. That explained him and the two guys with him and maybe even the two guys sitting in the Ford. But it didn't explain the attitude and behavior of the Customs agent. I asked the black guy about it. He shrugged.

"What can I tell you?" he said. "Maybe he got a tip too. Or maybe his wife shut him off." We both laughed at that. And I was in a better mood.

We remained at San Francisco Airport only long enough to clear Customs and refuel and then hopped over to Monterey, 40 minutes south on the California coast.

It remains a mystery to me why Vesco had insisted from the beginning of the trip that we stop at Monterey. There was no business interest he had there as far as I know. There was no gambling and, with his wife along, there was no hope of horsing around.

It had been reported that Junior Nixon had been siphoned out of a hippie commune by Anthony Ulasewicz, the former New York detective who worked for John Ehrlichman and for CREEP on cloak-and-dagger assignments. Ehrlichman had dispatched Ulasewicz to bundle Junior off to other surroundings less embarrassing to the president of the United States. But I don't see any connection between that event and Vesco's brief stay at Monterey. After all, Junior had been bathed and shaved before Vesco was asked to employ him.

The collection of briefcases that somehow passed Customs without disturbance, as far as I knew, remained on the airplane. The following afternoon Vesco called me at my hotel near the airport and told me we were going to, "jump over to Vegas" for a couple of hours. And that he would be at the airport in an hour. I thought of Pat Vesco's plaintive queries about Vegas. But I couldn't believe that Vesco would make the stop just for her. He just didn't do that kind of thing. Vesco is a gambler. He's a barracks crapshooter who likes to play with thousand-dollar markers. It's a real show to watch him shoot. He gets loud, raw, and excited. He can bring any casino to life. Maybe he was feeling the itch. Maybe it was all those "pelts."

We arrived in Las Vegas about six o'clock in the evening on November 22, 1971. Vesco did not tell me how long we would stay. The crew and I were totally exhausted, and I told Vesco that we had to get some sleep, so we would stay aboard the airplane. Vesco and his wife took off.

I had arranged with a line boy working the night shift at Hughes air operations at McCarren Airport to keep an eye out for Vesco's return and to hotfoot it out to the airplane to wake me the moment he saw Vesco. As it was I woke up without his help. I roused the rest of the crew and we were ready to go when Vesco and his wife arrived at two o'clock in the morning on November 23, 1971.

All in all I racked up maybe four hours' sleep. It was barely enough but I felt pretty good. Vesco came aboard bright eyed and bushy tailed. Pat Vesco looked plumb tuckered out. All she wanted to do was go to sleep.

"How'd they roll, Bob?" I asked. "Hot or cold?" Vesco was the kind of gambler who, if he won big, you'd hear about it. If he lost big you'd hear about that too. A so-so night at the table produced a so-so reaction. From Vesco's mood I guessed that he had done pretty well. But if he did he didn't mention it. He winked at me.

"We're still solvent," he said. I didn't know what the hell he meant. It was an out-of-character statement. It was only later when the airplane was in Ft. Worth that I thought about the briefcases. I didn't remember seeing them at Newark.

The Vescos slept all the way back to Newark. We arrived at 6:25 A.M. Since the Boeing was going directly to Ft. Worth we tried to make certain that the Vescos took with them all of their belongings, especially any valuables. As it turned out Pat Vesco had completely forgotten a package of souvenirs she had picked up in Tokyo. We found them later in the carry-on luggage bin. Vesco was not to set foot on the airplane again for a month. When he and his wife drove away in the limousine it was the last time I saw him until the day I watched him being led along the prisoners' walk in St. Antoine Prison in Geneva.

11

November 23, 1971 1313Z EWR—GSW

Lou Notte had a bunch of messages for me, as usual. Lou was my traffic coordinator at Newark Airport. Every time and anytime we came into Newark, Lou was there. His job was to make all the arrangements necessary to move the Boeing and its crew from country to country, and when we were in Newark to take care of all the services, including those required by the passengers. He was the first person aboard the airplane and usually carried with him any messages for Vesco or myself.

Vesco's aviation operations included more than the Boeing and the crew who operated it. And my duties for Vesco were not confined to flying the Boeing. As director of aviation for International Controls Corporation I maintained an office and small staff at Caldwell Airport and an office of convenience at Newark Airport that Lou used.

Vesco's aviation activities fell into two separate and distinct categories. One was the ICC corporate-aviation division. The other was Fairfield Aviation, a fixed-base operation that operated both a flying school and a charter service. Fairfield Aviation was a wholly owned subsidiary of ICC. It was run, autonomously, by Jack Clarey. I ran the ICC corporate-aviation division. Under the terms of my agreement with Vesco I had nominal supervision over Clarey's operation. However, because I had no interest, nor the time to involve myself, I never exercised my authority. Clarey dealt directly with Ralph Dodd. In the Grumman days I used the facilities at Caldwell but was billed for them like any other tenant.

Under the ICC umbrella, there were about fifteen aircraft at any one time, most of them assigned to Fairfield Aviation. Under my supervision were the larger aircraft servicing ICC corporate needs. In the beginning ICC owned perhaps three aircraft outright in its own name. When other aircraft were needed they were usually leased. The three aircraft owned by ICC were the Grumman Gulfstream One, a Bell Jet Ranger helicopter, and a Grand Commander. However before we acquired the Boeing Vesco had worked out a scheme to get it for nothing. This required setting up another dummy company called Skyways Leasing Corporation of which I was made general manager.

Skyways Leasing became a subsidiary of Fairfield General Corporation. Robert Vesco was the major stockholder of Fairfield General. At the time Vesco was beginning to have trouble with his board of directors at ICC. The company had grown rapidly, and he was out of the country a lot. His control had been weakened. He could not operate as freely as he had in the early days. He had set up Fairfield General as a safe haven across the street from ICC, against the day he lost all of his clout at the company he started.

Vesco's original agreement with Pan American for the lease-purchase of the Boeing called for an initial down payment of 343,750 dollars against a total purchase price of 1,375,000 dollars. The balance was to be paid over a five-year period in twenty quarterly payments of 66,152 dollars for a total purchase price of 1,666,790 dollars for Silver Phyllis.

When Vesco told me in the spring of 1971 that we were acquiring a four-engine long-range jet, he had just formed Skyways a few months earlier. Ralph Dodd was president. There were no employees and no payroll of record although I was installed as general manager. My salary and the salaries of all my staff were paid by ICC. This last fact is significant.

ICC entered into a lease-back agreement with Skyways. This agreement required ICC to pay Skyways an initial 100,000 dollars upon execution of the contract. ICC would then lease the Boeing on the following terms:

a. 100,000 dollars per month for the first three months
b. 83,000 dollars per month for the next twelve months
c. 47,000 dollars per month for the next three years

This amounted to an aggregate of 3.08 million dollars over 4¼-year period. All ICC bought for this money was the right to use the Boeing. The agreement between Skyways and ICC also required ICC to pay all of the operating costs including salaries of all flight and support personnel.

Over the life of the agreement (4¼ years), ICC would pay an additional 3½ million dollars in operating costs. And they still would not own the Silver Phyllis.

Enter IOS.

Vesco conned his ICC board of directors into approving the Skyways agreement by telling them that he had a surefire plan to lay these costs off on somebody else. In effect he told them that the Boeing would not cost ICC a penny. This was before he stampeded the IOS stockholders in Toronto and got himself "elected" board chairman and chief executive officer.

On the day after Vesco's victory in Toronto, the first payment on his promise to his ICC board of directors was due, or so it seemed. Vesco told Ralph Dodd that now that he was the chief executive officer of IOS and he was traveling on IOS business Dodd was to bill IOS for the expenses of this and future flights. But Dodd didn't bill on ICC invoices even though ICC was entitled to any revenues generated through the use of the Boeing it leased from Skyways. Dodd billed IOS on Skyways invoices causing any payments due ICC for the use of *its* aircraft to, in effect, be redirected into the Skyways coffers. This was done on Vesco's direct order to Dodd even though no agreement covering Vesco's traveling expenses via the Boeing existed, or could legally exist, between Skyways Leasing and IOS. This was no problem to Vesco. He didn't need an agreement. One of the first moves that Vesco made in regard to new management at IOS was to install Norman LeBlanc as chief financial officer. This put LeBlanc in charge of the checkbook. Vesco told LeBlanc to honor any invoices coming from Skyways. And that took care of that.

Shortly after the Toronto-to-Rome flight Ralph Dodd called me to ICC headquarters in Fairfield. When I got into his office he closed the door, which was unusual.

"Ike," he said, "what does it cost to run the Boeing?"

"I can't tell you, Ralph," I said. "we haven't had the airplane long enough. I can't use Pan Am's figures because there are no similarities in the way we operate." I told Dodd I needed a few months of operating analysis behind me before I could come up with a figure I could live with.

"I need something now, Ike," he said. "Give me a ball-park figure."

"You're asking me to guess, Ralph," I said. "If I knew what you wanted them for I could probably come up with something."

"We're billing IOS for the use of the Boeing," he said. My impression at the time was that Ralph, on Vesco's instructions, was working up some sort of agreement between ICC and IOS covering Vesco's travel for IOS. This is not unusual in corporations. It is a simple matter of in-house billing between departments and subsidiaries to keep the record straight. The common practice is to keep an accurate record of actual hours which are reasonably billable to a department or subsidiary.

"Don't hold me to this figure, Ralph," I said. "But, since you're pushing for an answer, I'll go for two grand an hour." He smiled.

"Great!" he said. "That's all I need."

About a month later, when I was catching up on some paper work at my office at Caldwell Airport, included in the stack on my desk was a sheaf of Skyways Leasing invoices clipped together and marked "file copy—Ike." Something was wrong. In the first place Skyways had no business billing IOS for anything. In the second place all of the invoices were addressed to Norman LeBlanc. But the thing that shocked me were the items on the invoices. Skyways Leasing was charging IOS for the use of the Boeing including an hourly charge, a crew-layover charge, and airport fees. The hourly charge to IOS was listed at 3,500 dollars per hour. This was highway robbery. Since the time Dodd had asked me to come up with an hourly cost of operation I had been able to develop a more accurate figure—1,805 dollars per hour. I called Ralph Dodd.

"Ralph!" I yelled into the phone, "what the hell is going on?" I told him what I had in front of me.

"Forget it, Ike," he said. "It's none of your goddamn business." That was the first time Dodd ever spoke to me like that.

"It is my business, Ralph," I said. "My name is down as general manager. I don't want anything to do with a rip-off like this." His attitude changed slightly. There was a nervous laugh on the other end of the wire.

"Cool it, Ike," Ralph said. "This is Bobby's baby. I'd advise you to stay the hell out of it. Don't even bring it up."

After I hung up I did a little addition. That flight from Toronto to Rome, the very first one after Vesco's Toronto victory, cost IOS exactly $25,583.31. Incredibly for that month of July, 1971, invoice number 54, the actual invoice to be presented to IOS, totalled $143,372.32. Below this total on the invoice was a note that stated that "any additional landing fees will be billed at a later date." How's that for balls?

Until Vesco finally lost the use of the Boeing, Skyways Leasing Corporation, whatever the hell it really was, launched its moneymaking efforts out of sight. I learned later in a prospectus of Fairfield General Corporation dated January 17, 1972, on page 10, that 439,000 dollars was recorded as income from the lease agreement in effect with ICC. This was supposed to cover the period through September 30, 1971. But I couldn't find a single mention of the $559,941.06 reflected in invoices 46 through 55 for this same period sent to Norman LeBlanc at IOS for their use of the Boeing. What added to the total confusion of the information contained in the prospectus was the fact that, "the company has no employees licensed or authorized to operate 707 aircraft." Skyways Leasing was a wholly owned subsidiary of Fairfield General. I was general manager of Skyways Leasing paid by ICC. I was not only authorized to operate the 707—I did it.

The board of directors of ICC who gave Vesco their approval were not only stupid, but they couldn't do their arithmetic. They were swallowing the operating costs of the Boeing inflated to an astronomical figure without so much as a cough. And Skyways was hauling in money faster than it could be counted and it was going out the other end—so it appeared. Skyways was pulling in over a million each from ICC and IOS with no more overhead than the insurance on the 707 and the quarterly payments due Pan Am of 66,152 dollars. That's profit! Fairfield General's board—Vesco, Beatty, Clay and Dodd—had every reason in the world to be proud of that kind of an operation.

There may exist some kind of document which gives the foregoing scheme legitimacy. I don't know of it. I don't even know for sure that Skyways or Fairfield General ever saw a dime from IOS. Again, it might be a case of in-house billing. But if any money actually did flow, the question is, "What ever happened to it?"

But, a little speculation is in order.

The 200,000 dollars that Vesco illegally provided for the 1972 re-election of Richard Nixon was his own money. There is no record of any corporate transaction involving ICC. In 1968, for example, Vesco used ICC corporate funds to make a donation to the Nixon-Agnew finance committee. A check for 25,000 dollars against ICC account number 021 000 6375, check number 7561, dated November 1, 1968, was drawn against Trust Company National Bank of Morristown, New Jersey, (now American National Bank and Trust). The bank then issued, on the very same day, five of its own treasurer's checks—numbers 0000176,-77,-79, 0000180, and 0000181—for 5,000 dollars each to the Nixon-Agnew finance committee through five separate entities. It was a violation of the Hatch Act even then.

Apart from showing the change in Vesco's approach to political campaign contributions, this gift to Nixon came at the time that Vesco was making his plans to start an aviation department. After the contribution was made, the corporate balance for ICC was listed at $440,863.17. Yet a mere six weeks later ICC paid 950,000 dollars cash for the Gulfstream One. It was common knowledge that ICC was in a very short cash position. Vesco had started his move to take over ELS and every spare dime went to buy up ELS shares. After the SEC bomb fell on Vesco I was told that the money for the Gulfstream came from a source, a Wall Street source, that was described to me as being "connected." The story I got was that an individual at this "connected" Wall Street brokerage house objected strenuously. He hated Vesco's guts. But the "connection" laid down the law. "Bobby wants his airplane and he's going to get it." So Bobby got his airplane.

It hardly seems possible that there would be anybody who would not understand what "connected" means. In law enforcement circles it means "associated with Organized Crime," the Mob. Such a charge would be made against Vesco frequently.

Vesco's political shenanigans were not confined to the continental United States.

In July of 1973 the Bahamas gained independence from Great Britain. Among those who aspired to political leadership in the independent Bahamas was the then prime minister under the Crown, Lynden O. Pindling. Pindling, who headed the PLP, had long fought against the power of the Bay Street boys and for Bahamian independence. He looked like the front runner and Vesco, who had big plans of his own for the Bahamas, decided to pocket Pindling and his party.

Vesco did this in two ways. He arranged through his Bahamas Commonwealth Bank for unsecured loans to be made to the top PLP people including Pindling. These were personal loans to be used as the borrower saw fit. They bought homes and cars and businesses and mistresses. Vesco also openly threw around a lot of cash for Pindling's campaign. He provided Pindling with mobility, allowing him and his party members to cover all of the out islands that make up the Bahamas, something rival politicians could not do. Vesco, through the newly formed flag carrier of the Bahamas—Bahamas World Airways—in which he reportedly had substantial financial interest, gave Pindling a Learjet. He also made less exotic aircraft available to PLP fat cats to help with their campaigning through leasing arrangements with Executive Air Courier Incorporated, Somerville, New Jersey.

The Bahamas have no law similar to the Hatch Act so it was perfectly legal for corporations to openly support political candidates and parties. ICC paid for Vesco's political actions in 1968. In the Bahamas, however, these contributions were made by Skyways Leasing Incorporated. They paid the bills for the use of the aircraft by the PLP and perhaps even handled cash disbursements and indirectly bestowed favors.

Perhaps the apparently enormous sums of money coming into Skyways from ICC and IOS provided Vesco with the means to initiate a mini-Watergate situation in the Bahamas.

But all of that was still in the future when we landed at Newark after the around-the-world flight. Among the messages that Lou Notte brought aboard the airplane was a flash from Jack Prewitt at Qualitron Aero that he expected the Boeing to arrive at Greater Southwest Airport in Ft. Worth at noon that same day. Oh, shit!

I had planned to go home, throw my dirty laundry into the hamper, pet my dog, and pick up my mail. And I had hoped to stop by my office to clear up a backlog of work. Now I had to take Silver Phyllis off again as soon as she could be serviced. Lou took care of servicing while I went into Butler operations at Newark to file my flight plan.

When I got back to the Boeing everything was go even though the crew was far from gruntled. I don't know how much more they would have taken before they mutinied. But as pissed off as they were collectively I could see that they would go "one more time."

Lou was in the galley brewing up some fresh coffee. He had told Dottie to sit down and relax. It was the kind of thing Lou did well. He handed me the fuel slip.

"She's full across the wings, Ike," he said.

I had planned all along to take Lou with me to Ft. Worth. He was a "can-do" guy who always seemed a jump ahead of me and he would be exactly the person I needed in Ft. Worth.

"Lou, how long will it take you to pack a bag and get back?" I asked him. "You're coming with us."

"About a minute and a half, Ike," he replied, with a grin. "I've got it in the car." Like I said, he seemed always a jump ahead of me. I might have mentioned at some time that I would need him in Ft. Worth but at that time I didn't remember if I had. Lou eventually joined the crew as assistant to Dottie.

Like any lady, Silver Phyllis decided to show her displeasure at being misused at the wrong time—in flight. We were coming up on Washington, D.C., when the fuel flow gauge for number-one engine went crazy. Then Pete noticed that the number-one fuel quantity was lower than normal. It could have been just a bad gauge or a faulty fuel-flow transmitter, but the quantity had me guessing. I sent Pete back to take a look out the window at the number-one engine. Just a precaution. He came back in a matter of seconds white faced and stuttering.

"The . . . the . . . the . . . the . . ." He pointed toward the number-one engine on the left outboard wing. I craned my neck for a look.

"Jee-zus!" I yelled. I shut the engine down immediately. The entire number-one nacelle was enveloped in a fine white mist of escaping raw kerosene that mixed with the hot exhaust gases coming out the tail pipe of the engine. If that mist ignited we would have blown the wing off the Boeing. There was no time for checklist procedures. It was a case of do it or die.

There is a constant build-up of carbon deposits inside any internal combustion engine. A jet engine purges itself of these deposits constantly in flight. In the daytime an observant passenger might see occasional puffs of black smoke emitted from the engines. At night he would see intermittent sparks. This simply means that these carbon deposits are being spewed out. But they are red hot.

If Phyllis had decided at that moment to fart a little out of number one she would have destroyed herself and us too. We went on to Ft. Worth on three engines.

I've often wondered what Vesco would have thought if his new toy had scattered herself over several dozen acres of Nixonland on the Potomac.

The first order of business after we turned the airplane over to Qualitron was for the crew to get some sleep. Lou stayed with the Boeing to take inventory while the rest of us went to a motel. I was actually too tired to sleep. After a shower, a shave, and a clean shirt, I went back out to Qualitron and met with various department heads until nearly midnight. I guess it was then that somebody mentioned Thanksgiving Day. I had completely forgotten about it. I faced a dilemma. Vesco wanted his airplane ready before Christmas. The actual date set by Vesco was December 23, 1971. He had plans. Even with the extra help that Qualitron had hired and assigned to the modification project it would be a cliff-hanger. But they would be shut down on Thanksgiving—so they thought. I decided the crew would spend Thanksgiving Day with their families. Lou and I would stay with the airplane and, at my insistence, some Qualitron people would come into work on Turkey Day. I didn't release the crew until I got a solid morning's work out of them that day.

There was no point in me going home for Thanksgiving. I had critical scheduling problems to solve with the Qualitron engineers. But I did have to get back to New Jersey for a couple of days. By Saturday morning it looked pretty safe for me to leave Ft. Worth until the following Tuesday—November 30, 1971. I left everything in the hands of "can-do" Lou.

I'm not rootless. The house I had in Denville is the one I still own and live in. What needs doing I do. I don't like hiring somebody to do the work, the satisfying work, around the house and grounds. It's too much like letting a nursemaid care for and educate your children. As for the paper backlog at Caldwell, I could handle it all in one afternoon. My secretary, Karen Federowicz, organized things to the point where all that was needed was my signature except where my personal attention was required for invoices involving unusual expenditures. My house and my dog Sancha were the real reasons I wanted to get back to New Jersey.

I got to Newark Airport about four o'clock in the afternoon.

Every man has his own favorite hangout. Mine was the Flintlock which stands at the side of Route 46 at the entrance to the little community in which I live. As I turned onto my lake road, I saw a number of cars I recognized parked in the Flintlock parking lot. I suddenly felt the need to be with friends. I had been too much with hot shot horseshitters who not only did not speak the language I spoke literally and figuratively, but whose values were no deeper than a saucer.

The first face I saw in that comfortable, dimly lighted bar was that of Don Mueller, the bartender. Don is a big man frontways and sideways. He would be upset if I said he was bald so I won't mention that. He wears a fifty-eight inch belt—at least, and a smile to match. He is a true friend of mine.

So is Gene Feyl, who owned the joint. If I expected a warm greeting, I got it. As soon as Don saw me he turned around, picked up a piece of paper next to the cash register and dropped it on the bar.

"When are you going to take care of this, Ike?" he said with a straight face. "It's a month overdue." I looked. It was a bar tab for 26 dollars and change that belonged to somebody else. It was his way of saying, "Where the hell you been for the last month?" I decided to play it straight. I took out a hundred-rupee bill, a souvenir of Bombay, and tossed it on the bar.

"Take it out of this," I said, "and give the house a drink."

He took one look at the bill and said, "We don't take Canadian money." Without my ordering he set me up with what he calls a "mustache," in honor of my own mustache. It's nothing more than Ballantine Scotch and soda—my usual drink. This was a good start for my weekend at home.

As I expected, my work backlog at the office took only a few hours to complete. It took an entire day to get the storm windows up but I enjoyed every minute of it.

I had planned to go back to Ft. Worth late Tuesday, November 30, 1971. I had a few things to clear up at the office in Fairfield and decided to use the opportunity to stop in to see Jack Russell, who owned a restaurant called the Chez Leon. Jack was particularly close to Vesco and, although it was through Vesco that I had met him, I considered him my friend as well.

Even today Jack Russell is one guy you can't knock Vesco in front of. They say a real citizen is a guy who pays his bookie, his bartender, and has spent at least one night in jail. At that point, Vesco was good for two out of three. At least with Jack. When Vesco was struggling to turn Captive Seal into ICC, Jack not only extended him charge privileges at Chez Leon, but treated Vesco's clients with a deference that had to add luster to Vesco himself. He "carried" Vesco far beyond practical limits purely on Vesco's promise to pay "sometime." To Vesco's credit he not only paid his bills when things got better, but he did everything he possibly could to steer business to Chez Leon. As Vesco's fortunes waxed strong the Chez Leon became, more or less, the ICC executive dining club.

But I never got to see Jack Russell that day. I didn't get to the Fairfield offices to finish my chores. Nor did I get back to Ft. Worth until I had made a side trip to Geneva—as a passenger.

I packed my belongings and poured a Scotch and soda for myself before I left for Fairfield. I saw a couple of things I could have done around the house but for which there just wasn't enough time. The telephone rang. It was Helen Force, Ralph Dodd's secretary. She sounded a little breathless. Ralph wanted to talk to me. Ralph was agitated.

"Ike," he said, "pack a bag and meet me at Caldwell right away."

"Ralph," I said, "I am packed and I'm going to Newark and then Ft. Worth."

"No! Geneva!" Ralph said. He sounded weird, panicky. He seemed looney enough to have forgotten that Silver Phyllis was in Ft. Worth at the beauty farm. I reminded him.

"I know that, goddamnit!" he said. "This is something else. It's an emergency." His voice dropped to little more than a whisper. And he sounded as if he were talking through his teeth, "I—can't—talk—on—this—telephone! Just get out to Caldwell as fast as you can. I'll explain later." He hesitated. "Bobby wants you in Geneva." He hung up. What the hell. If Bobby wanted me in Geneva then that's where I would go but I was goddamned if I could figure out why.

The urgency in Ralph's voice was enough to warrant my doing some hustling. I didn't bother calling Lou in Ft. Worth. I'd have Karen take care of it when I got to Caldwell.

Ralph was waiting at the helicopter when I arrived. I told one of the line service boys to tell Karen to call Lou. The rotors were already turning and Ralph was frantically beckoning for me to climb aboard. I slung my bag in the baggage compartment and jumped into the rear of the helicopter. Before I even had my seat belt fastened we were twenty feet in the air.

"For Christ's sake, Ralph, what's the problem?" I asked. He put one finger to his lips and pointed to the pilot, Ron Barone. There is nothing in this whole wide world that would shock or startle Ron. I had known him for a long time and I not only liked the guy but I knew he could be trusted—absolutely. He was Chief Pilot for the Alexander Department Store chain and he and I had a working agreement to cover each other when possible. He did more covering for me than I ever did for him.

"I'll tell you later," Ralph said.

Later proved to be inside the International building at JFK. We were met there by a trio of Vesco lawyers including Howard Cerny. All of them looked grim and nervous. Ralph conferred with them off to one side, then came back and told me we were confirmed on Swissair to Geneva leaving at eight o'clock and arriving in Geneva at nine in the morning, Geneva time. That pissed me off. I had busted my ass to get to Caldwell. We had taken off in a helicopter like we were on a rescue mission out of a forward fire base in Vietnam. And here we were at JFK with a 2½-hour wait.

"Stop the cloak-and-dagger shit, Ralph," I said. "What the hell is this all about?" Ralph looked at the lawyers. They looked back at him. They all looked over their shoulders and then at each other again. With the forthrightness typical of the legal profession the lawyers let Ralph break the news.

"Vesco's in jail," Ralph said. "They arrested him and put him in the pokey in Geneva." He said it with a mixture of awe and outrage, as if he were announcing that the Swiss had arrested God.

"No shit!" was the only thing I could think of to say. Then I started laughing. It was not the smartest thing to do, but I couldn't help myself. I looked at those four solemn faces. They were trying to impress upon me that they really felt badly that their meal ticket, Robert Lee Vesco, multimillionaire, the brightest comet in the global money sky, had got his ass slung into a Swiss dungeon. Actually they reminded me of guys who stopped off at a funeral on their way to a whorehouse. They were putting on an act just in case the deceased riz up. I thought it was a real howl. I could actually visualize that smart-ass Vesco, the Prince of Pepperoni, the Sultan of Swindle, with his 300-dollar suit and his hand made 150-dollar shoes sitting on a steel bunk in a cruddy Geneva jail without a belt, tie, shoelaces, or his nail file, just like an ordinary chicken thief. I tried but I just couldn't stop laughing.

No man is a hero to his valet or his personal pilot.

These guys were afraid of Vesco. I wasn't. I had seen him with his guard up and his pants down.

Ralph was indignant.

"C'mon, Ike," he said, "I don't think it's very funny."

"Wrong!" I said, trying to keep from choking. "I think it's a fucking ball buster! Hoo! Hoo! Hoo! He! He! He! Oh—Jesus" I actually walked away from them. I couldn't cope with my vision of Vesco in the slammer, nor could I handle those four poor bastards who were dead serious—for the moment anyway—about the indignity visited upon their leader.

I walked around for a couple of minutes. I felt sorry for Vesco. I really did. Sure, I thought it was funny that, despite his wealth and position, he would get himself canned. But he wouldn't be the first millionaire to lose an argument with a cop. I didn't know yet why Vesco was in the slammer. He might have gotten caught by a jealous husband. He could have gotten picked up in a raid on a cathouse but that didn't happen in Europe very often. It defied reason. What made the whole thing so goddamn ludicrous was the solemnity of Dodd, Cerny, and the other lawyers.

People began to look at me and I realized that I was making a spectacle of myself. I had all but staggered away from Dodd and the others. Every time I turned to go back to them I would see those hound-dog expressions and start laughing again. I finally had to stop and turn my back and crank up my command attitude. It took a minute but I was able to turn back and face them. I matched their solemnity although I could feel my cheeks twitching.

"Sorry about that, men," I said. I looked each of them square in the eye, determined to play their game. I could just see Vesco's reaction when Dodd told him that I laughed like an idiot. (Maybe I could convince Dodd between JFK and Geneva that I had become hysterical with grief.) Hee! Hee! Hee!

"What does Bob want with me?" I asked Ralph. I just assumed that Ralph would not have called me if Vesco hadn't ordered it. I had visions of myself rounding up a gang of goons to storm the jail and deliver Vesco from durance vile.

"Dick Clay is organizing things in Geneva," Ralph said. "He'll brief us when we get there. He's the line commander." I couldn't believe my ears. Ralph was an ex-Marine and it was beginning to show.

The Swissair DC-8 was less than half full so Ralph and I had plenty of room and an abundance of privacy. Ralph filled me in on the details as he knew them. What it all boiled down to was that Vesco was jailed because of his big mouth.

The whole thing went back to the IOS take-over in Toronto. Those paper boxes that Vesco had made certain were on board the Boeing at Geneva on June 27, 1971, apparently did contain IOS shares that he used in the proxy fight. Specifically, Vesco was charged with actually stealing from a vault of the Overseas Development Bank—the IOS bank in Geneva—135,000 IOS shares on Saturday June 26, 1971, when the bank was closed for business. Vesco's cohorts in this caper were Milton Meissner and Ulrich Strickler. Included in these 135,000 shares of IOS limited preferred were 56,000 shares that belonged to a former IOS sales manager, David Tucker. Tucker's shares were being held by the bank as collateral for a loan. Somehow, although Tucker was making regular payments on his loan, his shares had been physically placed with the others . . . or so Vesco claimed, which entitled the bank to sell them. This was untrue because Tucker was not in default. The reason that Vesco, Meissner, and Strickler could even enter the bank on a Saturday, much less haul away boxes and boxes of negotiable securities, was that Vesco controlled the bank through IOS.

Vesco knew what he was doing. He had been in Geneva since June 21, a Monday. The "removal" of the shares, including Tucker's, took place on a Saturday. It was obvious that Vesco, despite his claims that he was entitled to remove and sell IOS shares held by the bank, waited until Saturday because there was no legal or other way that he could take Tuckers' shares. If he had gone in during the week, during business hours, he might have been able to get away with 79,-

000 shares. His claim that Tucker's shares were "inadvertently" stored in the wrong place has got to be so much bullshit.

Vesco sold Tucker's shares but, when Tucker threatened to holler cop, Vesco returned the shares in the hopes that Tucker would forgive and forget. But Tucker did neither. He filed suit in Geneva two weeks later accusing Vesco, Meissner, and Strickler of fraud and attempted embezzlement.

What probably pissed Tucker off as much as anything was the brazenness of Vesco's caper. He probably didn't even learn of the removal and sale of his shares until the Toronto stockholders' meeting had begun. As explained earlier, Vesco's edge was very thin. The purloined shares from the Overseas Development Bank were sold to a Vesco-controlled company, to be later added to those of another Vesco company called Linkink Progressive Corporation, S.A., a shell corporation registered in Panama that existed only in a file box on some lawyer's shelf. Linkink, in turn, would vote these shares in favor of Vesco. It was in Toronto that Tucker learned he had been jobbed and subsequently threatened Vesco with a criminal complaint. Vesco backed off in a hurry and called off the sale of Tucker's stock. Tucker then was able to vote his shares in favor of the dissidents, if that is what he did.

It took 4½ months for Swiss justice to catch up with Vesco. He had been in and out of Switzerland, Geneva specifically, twenty times in his Boeing for durations of up to nine days' since Tucker's complaint was filed. I had seen him last on November 23, 1971, when we returned from our around-the-world flight. I knew then that his plan was to go to Geneva but I didn't know the date. I don't know that Vesco had even an inkling that Tucker had sworn out a complaint. But whether or not he did know, it was Vesco's style to treat something like this with complete indifference. And that's what landed him in the clink.

According to Dodd, who got his information from Dick Clay, who in turn got his information from Vesco's Swiss attorney, Alain Farina (I met him later), Vesco had voluntarily appeared before Judge Robert

Pagan, the dean of Geneva's examining magistrates, to be questioned by him about the Tucker charge. Pagan fouled off all of Vesco's reasons for his actions. Then Vesco's mouth ran away with him. He tried to impress the judge with his importance and his wealth. I guess the old bird got sick of that kind of crap. A complication was that Pagan spoke little or no English and Vesco spoke no French. His attorney was with him but I would guess that he had one hell of a time translating whatever Vesco had to say. Unfortunately he would have had to cover Vesco with a blanket to hide from the judge the manner that Vesco very probably displayed. From what happened later I have to believe that Meissner and Strickler kept a very low profile. The trouble was that they were tagging along with Vesco and when the judge lowered the boom, it hit them too.

After two hours Judge Pagan, fed up to the eyeballs with Vesco's litany of his international connections, his wealth, and his general importance, pulled the string on Vesco. He called over a court attendant. He fixed Vesco with a baleful eye.

"Il est dans votre intérêt propre donc que je vous decerne une mandat d'arrêt." Vesco looked at the attendant and then at Farina, his lawyer.

"Wha'd he say?" Vesco asked. Farina, astounded at the judge's decision, gave Vesco only the meat.

"You're under arrest," the lawyer said. "You must go to jail." Poor Bobby Vesco didn't even get to pass "go."

Farina protested the judge's decision but Pagan, who intended to make an example of Vesco for bringing disrepute to the sacred institution of Swiss banking, stood firm. Meissner and Strickler were included in the judge's *mandat d'arrêt*. The three men, shocked beyond belief, were led directly from Pagan's chambers into the centuries'-old St. Antoine Prison, smack in the middle of the very Swiss town Vesco had believed came with the lease when he took over IOS.

Somebody, perhaps Farina, pleaded with the judge to show some deference to Vesco's importance. It would not be proper for a man of his stature to be lodged with common criminals. So they stuck poor

Bobby Vesco in solitary confinement. Meissner and Strickler were lucky. They did not receive such favored treatment. They were thrown into the bullpen.

As I've indicated I'm a lousy airline passenger. Ralph Dodd zonked off to sleep for most of the flight. Me, I read everything on the airplane to keep my mind off all of the things I was certain the flight crew were doing wrong. Maybe that's unfair but I am very jealous of my profession and it grinds my guts when I am confronted by the mechanical and sometimes too casual approach to flying taken by most airline pilots—even, and maybe especially, senior Captains.

The Swissair DC-8 literally slammed onto the runway at Geneva. I half expected to see the outboard engines bounce off the concrete. It may not have been the Captain's fault entirely. But that goddamned noise abatement again. We had talked about noise abatement on takeoff. But the procedures for noise abatement on approach can be equally as dangerous. Modern jet aircraft are designed for nominal values set forth by the applicable regulations found in government publications—FAR's (Federal Aviation Regulations). An approach, for example, is predicated on a reasonable approach angle to a runway from which the transition to actual touchdown is a simple matter. However, noise abatement keeps an aircraft high and close in on approach, forcing the pilot to descend at a rapid rate with little or no power on the engines, in order to keep the decibel level very low. The average universal 2½- to 3-degree glide slope with a corresponding rate of descent of seven to eight hundred feet per minute suddenly becomes a dive virtually, with the rate of descent as high as 3,000 feet per minute. Herein lies the basic problem again. The safe design parameters are compromised for political reasons and the loser ends up being the crew and passengers.

I was in a bad mood when I got off the airplane. For the first time upon entering Switzerland I would have to pass through Customs as an ordinary passenger. I guess I had gotten too accustomed to the speedier routine accorded flight crews. Queueing up and shuffling forward a few inches at a time was not my idea of how to end a long boring flight. Ralph, of course, was used to this and displayed what I deemed an amazing degree of patience and forbearance. It was a side of him I had never seen before.

Waiting beyond the Customs area was Vince Bordoni, one of Vesco's security men inherited from IOS. I had met Vince on my very first flight into Geneva back in June when Hal Simpson, chief of security at IOS, had dispatched him to meet me at Geneva Airport. He was to familiarize himself with procedures that would minimize the hassle and maximize the efficiency of the Boeing's passengers and crew landing and taking off from Switzerland. That first time he impressed me as a Swiss Lou Notte. He was good-natured, capable, and accommodating. I never saw him get excited or rattled.

He had all of the finesse of a proper majordomo and initially that's how I rated him. But as I followed him to the car he had waiting for us on that first visit, I noticed that he was packing a pistol. This caused me to make a new and swift evaluation of those hard-looking eyes and that hooked nose, which looked as if it had been forcibly leaned on a number of times. I came to appreciate Vince as a very tough professional who knew exactly how good he was.

On the way into the city Vince told us how Vesco got the word out from his cell in St. Antoine Prison that he wanted me and Ralph in Geneva. Prison authorities apparently allowed Vesco to keep his cigarettes and matches. He also had with him a pencil and a rubber band, which I thought was a peculiar item for Vesco to be carrying.

Vesco's minions in Geneva, chiefly Dick Clay, had ordered Hal Simpson to station people outside the prison. Vesco spotted them from his cell. He printed the words: GET IKE AND RALPH on the inside of the matchbook cover. He folded the matchbook up and shot it into the street with the rubber band.

The matchbook cover was one of his own from the Silver Phyllis. Like a lot of suddenly rich people, and even not so rich people, Vesco went ape with his initials. His personal identification mark was an arrangement with a large V flanked by a small R and L. It was on everything he owned except maybe the butter pats in the galley. In a way Vesco didn't know how lucky he was in having that matchbook cover. Paper matches are not in general use in Europe. And Vesco, whom I have caught reading self-improvement books on the airplane, might have been carrying one of those matchbooks, that advertise, "EARN MORE $s WITHOUT COLLEGE!" and with the inside completely printed over with a coupon offering a "FREE BROCHURE!" he might still be in jail.

Vince drove Ralph and me directly to the IOS duplex apartment at 147 Rue de Lausanne. IOS security people were all over the place. Vince passed us through the cordon of guards quickly. I had noticed that there were an unusual number of cars parked in the immediate vicinity of the apartment building. Some of them were even up on the sidewalk and there were a lot of people standing around. Several of them had cameras hanging around their necks. And I realized that an awful lot of people considered Vesco's jailing of major importance. I still thought it was funny.

Dick Clay looked like he was on the tag end of a four-day bender. He was unshaven, red-eyed, and testy. Dick is usually an impeccable dresser. But he looked as if he had slept in his clothes. The rooms on the lower level of the apartment were jammed with lawyers and IOS executives. Everybody was mad as hell at the judge. Dick hadn't seen Ralph and me when we'd first come into the apartment. Now Vince went over to Dick, who was talking with some men, and told him we were here. Apparently our arrival was a signal for some plan of action. Dick came over.

"Christ!" he said, "am I glad to see you two! Especially you, Ike." He turned and hollered at the crowd.

"Quiet!" he yelled, "everybody in here. Ike and Ralph just got in."

When the room quieted down Clay announced that Judge Pagan had set a bail hearing for Vesco, Meissner, and Strickler for two o'clock that same afternoon.

"We've been working all night to get our ducks lined

up," he said. "Now that Ike is here I can start working up a couple of contingency plans." He then outlined what had been going on and what the over-all program for the day would be.

Harry Sears had already established contact, direct contact, with John N. Mitchell, the attorney general of the United States. Sears had been told to squeeze Mitchell hard to personally intervene. Mitchell was to call the American ambassador in Bern, Switzerland, and have him use diplomatic pressure to bring Judge Pagan to heel. What shocked me was the crassness of Clay's statements. It was not a matter of "requesting" or even "strongly urging" the attorney general or U.S. ambassador to help. Orders were being, and had been, issued almost as if the Department of Justice and the Diplomatic Service were subsidiaries of IOS and ICC.

If Alain Farina, Vesco's Swiss lawyer, found this display of cynicism distasteful, he said nothing. But there's no doubt he was impressed.

"The intervention of your Attorney General Mitchell will be most helpful," he said cautiously. "I am sure that Judge Pagan will tender the utmost respect to such a request. The American ambassador will certainly know how to convey Mr. Mitchell's interest in Mr. Vesco's problem to Judge Pagan. What we cannot, at this moment, know is the amount of the bond the Judge will require in order to free Mr. Vesco."

"Do you think the Judge will spring him today?" Clay asked Farina.

"I would hope so," Farina said. "But I cannot speak for Judge Pagan." Clay swore.

Dick went on to the rest of the program. His main concern was what might happen when Vesco walked out of St. Antoine Prison. His arrest and detention might have opened a Pandora's box. Tucker was only one of a large number of people who had a beef either with IOS or Vesco himself. Clay raised the specter of a queue of process servers waiting to slap more paper on Vesco the second he stepped through the prison gates onto the street. He turned to me.

"This is where you come in, Ike," he said. "I've got

a Learjet waiting at the airport. You can fly one of them can't you?"

"Certainly," I said.

"Okay," Dick said. "That takes care of that."

"Takes care of what, Dick?" I said.

"We might have to make a quick exit from the country," Clay explained. "I want to be ready if we do." I held up my hand.

"Wait a minute, Dick," I said. "One—you don't just jump into a Learjet and drive away like in a rented car. I need at least one more crew member." Dick looked impatient.

"You can fly the goddamned thing all by yourself if you have to," he snapped at me. "Let's take this up later on."

Clay had more to say but it didn't involve me. Dick thought it would be a good idea if I got a couple of hours' sleep. He did tell me that he would be occupied with rounding up enough cash—over a million dollars in Swiss francs—to meet any number that Pagan might come up with. Clay told me and Ralph to report back to the apartment at one o'clock for a final briefing. I thought about Ralph's description of Dick as the commander on the line.

Of course I got no sleep. Vince had taken Ralph and me to La Reserve, the deluxe hotel near the Villa. I laid down on the bed with my shoes off but the adrenalin was flowing. I got up, showered, shaved, and dressed. Some instinct told me that I would not forget the next 24 hours. I guess Ralph couldn't sleep either. He called my room and asked me to meet him in the dining room.

Ralph's concern for Vesco didn't affect his appetite. He ate like a journalist at a press luncheon. All I had was coffee while Ralph shoveled in the calories and carbohydrates. By the time we finished in the dining room we were approaching H-hour at the apartment. Vince was already in the lobby. If any of this bothered him, it didn't show.

On the way back to the apartment I had decided that I would brace Dick Clay on one aspect of his scheme. It concerned the getaway Learjet. If I read

Dick Clay right, I would fly Vesco out of Switzerland in a hurry only in case of immediate danger. The danger could come from the aforementioned process servers. That wouldn't bother me. The sticking point could be any restrictions imposed by Judge Pagan on Vesco's movements. A condition of release might very well be that Vesco remain in Geneva, or at least Switzerland. I was not about to become an accomplice to a patently criminal act by flying Vesco out of Switzerland against a court order. I intended to tell Clay that if that was what he wanted—if that's what Vesco wanted—I would take the next plane back to the States. They could get themselves another boy.

When we got to the apartment there was no talking to Dick Clay. He had undergone a transformation. He looked fresh and sharp, and he was running the show. The same people were there and maybe a few new faces. Clay reported that the "green machines" were still on the road. This meant that all of the money had not yet been amassed. He also told us that he "had gotten to somebody" and that Pagan intended to slap Vesco for a bond of 175,000 dollars. He allowed for the possibility that the same number would apply to both Meissner and Strickler. Clay again addressed Farina.

"Can we count on Bob's release today?" he asked. Farina considered his answer.

"I am confident that Judge Pagan will release them," he said in his precise English. "However, Judge Pagan might deem the case to be more seriously criminal. He is a very independent man and might possibly resent representations from your attorney general and the embassy." He fell silent a moment. The room was tense. I think that Farina was making absolutely certain that if things went sour, he would not be the fall guy. As impressed as I was with Farina, I could see that he was just another lawyer. And the first rule of law is to cover your ass. "It is entirely in the judge's hands," he said.

Clay looked exasperated.

"I don't know whether to laugh, cry, shit, or go blind," someone said. Clay glared his disapproval of the comment. He was really uptight and I felt sorry for him. Of all the people around Vesco he was the only guy who had the balls and the smarts to handle a situation like this. If there was one thing he did not need then, it was a smart-ass making witty remarks.

An important part of Clay's strategy was to jam the hearing room with Vesco people. His thinking was that even an iron-ass like Pagan would be intimidated by a show of strength. In addition, he intended to capitalize on the amount of attention the press was paying to the arrest of Robert Vesco. Clay knew what he was doing. The fact that a businessman could be harassed by an overly moralistic judge could have an adverse effect on the Swiss banking community. The last thing those people wanted, the Swiss bankers, was some "man of principle" rising up in public in their behalf. It could be bad for business. Christ, anybody with an illegal buck to protect would think twice before dumping it in a country where even one judge was worried about a thing called honor. Clay wanted all the attention he could get without undue harrassment of Vesco.

The hearing room was small, comfortably accommodating about forty to fifty people. There were that many alone in the motorcade from the apartment to St. Antoine in which the hearing room was located. The press was there in force so that there were nearly, by my estimate, 200 people sardined into the spectator area. It was a madhouse.

Farina had gone on ahead. He entered the hearing room through a side door in his traditional lawyer's gown. He was a handsome man and the gown added a touch of drama to his appearance. By contrast to the spectator area the section in front of the railing where the actual hearing would take place was an oasis of dignity and decorum. Farina spoke quietly to the government attorney and to the attorney for Tucker, who had brought the charges in the first place. Both were opposed to bail. They wanted Vesco's ass. And I assume Farina was trying to persuade them to back off.

I was wedged into a corner and, to get a good look at what was going on, I had to stand on tiptoe. Jammed up against me was a ratty-looking woman.

From the comments she made to a bearded man with her I took her to be an American. I would have ignored her except for the fact that she stank like the men's room in the BMT subway in New York. She was wearing a perfume. I knew that because there was a second scent that was not natural. I would call it *Spanish Onion No. 44*. The girl needed a bath, a sandblasting. She made my eyes burn. I was looking for a way out.

Her companion moved in front of me and, if possible, he was even more malodorous than she. I've never smelled stale camel piss but I imagine that it would smell like this guy's hair, of which he had a lot. He looked at me directly. I could see what looked like some of his lunch in his beard, which was full and greasy looking. There was enough of it to harbor a family of wombats except that I understand they are relatively clean animals. He had a gang of cameras hanging from his neck. I realized then, that he and the broad were from the press.

"I know you," the guy said.

"No, you don't," I told him.

"Oh, yeah," the girl whom I now regarded as Smelly said, "you're with them."

"I'm with nobody, lady," I said. And tried to move away.

"I'm with the *Times,*" she said. "I want to talk with you."

The *Times*. There must be a hundred cities in the United States with a newspaper called the *Times*. She looked more like the perversion editor of *Screw*.

"No way, baby," I said. I had to get away from them. As I moved away she took my arm.

"I'm gonna stay close to you, Buster," she said. I pulled my arm away.

"Then you'd better stick a rocket up your ass," I told her. I am pretty straight laced when it comes to talking to a woman. But this broad was as sexless as a sack of sawdust. I pushed through the crowd and actually found one buttock's worth of a seat on a front bench near a window, through which I could see the prison itself.

"There they are!" somebody yelled. The courtroom came alive. Press people jammed against the windows to look out at the walkway from the cells. Photographers raised their cameras and shot wildly. I caught a quick glimpse of Vesco, Meissner, and Strickler. What a sight. They were three very defeated and bedraggled-looking men, except that Vesco had his tie on and that must have cost him a few francs. They passed out of sight. A moment later the side door to the courtroom opened and the three prisoners entered. Strickler looked penitent. But he was Swiss. Meissner was angry and looked around the room defiantly. Vesco was looking at his shoes. He didn't look particularly humble and on a hunch I kind of raised up a little to see what he was looking at. He was the only one of the three with laces. Another fifty francs.

The three miscreants were directed to stand near the judge's bench in front of the defense table. Farina greeted all three of them solemnly. The Swiss equivalent of a bailiff hollered out a stream of French. The room fell silent and everybody seated stood up. Pagan came out of his chambers. He was everything I had been led to expect. He was in his sixties and had a face that would look good on Mount Rushmore. I had a feeling that nobody could push this guy up against the wall.

The entire proceeding was in French and I didn't understand all of what was going on. Altogether the session lasted about an hour. If it was not for Farina the hearing would have been dull and boring. Everytime Tucker's attorney would get up to make a point Farina would quietly shoot him down. The judge kept silent, listening impassively. Unlike U.S. courtrooms the attorneys behaved with civility. After the basic arguments were disposed of, the time came for each attorney to make a plea directly to Judge Pagan. Tucker's attorney was first. He was both earnest and brief as if he realized that, against Farina, he was way out of his league. When Farina's turn came he put on a virtuoso performance that impressed everybody in the courtroom. He was grand opera without music. When he finished I half expected the spectators to applaud.

Instead the silence continued. There was a brief conference between the attorneys and the judge after which Pagan retired to mull his decision.

The Vescoites, including me, retired to a restaurant across the street to wait. I had very little in common with these IOS people. They broke off in bunches and sat in booths or at tables. I went directly to the bar and sat by myself. I ordered a Campari and soda. Farina came in. He stopped inside the door, looked around, spotted me, and came directly over. He was smiling.

"Captain," he said, "what did you think of my performance?"

I laughed. Here was a guy I could relate to.

"Beautiful," I told him.

"A lawyer must also be a good actor," he said. "I think you understand. There are times when you must deliberately behave as a Captain." He was absolutely right. More than once I waved those four stripes around to get what I wanted.

"What happens now?" I asked. He shrugged.

"Judge Pagan will give his decision within the hour," he said. "I cannot make a prediction. You must understand, Captain, that Swiss justice is quite different from American justice. Here the judge is supreme. His decision is final and absolute. There is no appeal. If he decides against us, then Mr. Vesco will remain in prison until such time as the judge decides to release him. We have no habeas corpus procedure."

During this exchange the others of the Vesco crowd had noticed that Farina had come over to me. Clay, Dodd, and one or two others drifted over. Farina seemed annoyed at their appearance. He sipped his drink, quietly responding to their questions in the vaguest of terms. The only time he dealt with the situation in any concrete way was when he asked Dick Clay about the availability of funds. Dick told him that the money had been collected and was at the apartment. Farina seemed satisfied.

"Very good," he said.

A young Swiss attorney entered the restaurant and came toward Farina, stopping several yards away. Farina left us and went to where the young man was standing. After a moment or two of conversation, he turned, nodded his head at us, and left the restaurant with the young attorney. Apparently the judge had reached a decision.

Farina had told Clay what to expect. When the judge had made up his mind he would summon the attorneys. As soon as he learned the result he would pass the details on to Clay and tell him the necessary procedures for the payment of the bond. He could not tell Clay how long he would be closeted with Pagan. I didn't see any point in staying at the restaurant. The best place for me would be back at the apartment. Clay agreed. And I left.

Back at the apartment a number of IOS secretaries were tidying up and preparing a light snack for the gang. I relaxed in a chair with a Scotch. I wasn't worried about flying that Lear but I'd made up my mind I would fly it only by the rules.

About twenty minutes later Clay and Dodd and the entourage stormed into the apartment all excited. Judge Pagan had agreed to release Vesco, Meissner, and Strickler sometime that evening. Bond for Vesco was set at 125,000 dollars and, for the other two, 25,000 dollars a piece. Everybody was ready for a party but Clay scotched that. He called for attention.

"The war isn't over," he said. "We've got some mopping up to do. Gather 'round." He came on like John Wayne.

He was still concerned about process servers. Clay did not want to have Vesco bounce right back into Judge Pagan's courtroom on another criminal complaint. Pagan would have buried Vesco. That was the immediate problem. Happily for me the judge had placed no restrictions on Vesco's movements. Pagan was the long range problem.

"We've got to do something about that sonofabitch," Clay said. "Even after he's released Bobby, he could put him back in the can anytime he wants as long as those charges are hanging over him." Clay seemed to have a personal grudge against Pagan. Maybe it was the professional public-relations man's penchant for taking on his client's problems as his own. "They got their fucking money," Clay went on. "But that won't do the job. We've got to have some insurance."

When he mentioned the money I realized that the guys who had charge of the loot had not been in the apartment when I got back. I guessed that sometime after I left the restaurant Clay had learned the judge's decision and phoned the apartment to get them on station at the prison.

"Speaking of money," someone said, "there's still over three-quarters of a million left. Why not lay a bundle on his honor?" This made Clay angry.

"Don't be an asshole," Clay said. "Even if Pagan was on the take the chance of exposure is too great. It won't work." There were some more suggestions, none of them practical. Then one of the lawyers stood up.

"Discredit him," he said. "You can talk about muscle all you want but that takes time to organize. Sure—we can buy pressure but the best thing to do is to disgrace the guy." He had something on his mind but seemed reluctant to come out with it.

"Great!" Clay said sarcastically. "You got any suggestions?" The man hemmed and hawed. Clay banged the table with his hand. "C'mon," he said.

"Pagan's a fag," the lawyer said. There was utter silence in the room.

"No shit!" Clay said.

"I don't know," the lawyer said. "All I'm doing is playing devil's advocate. You're looking for something to nail this guy with. Being a fag in Europe isn't that big a deal unless you're a judge with Pagan's reputation. We've got the channels to the press. Just feed that into the pipeline and they'll do the rest. It doesn't have to be true." Nobody said anything. This was a little sticky even for that bunch of sharks.

"I think we'd better table that," somebody else said, "and let Bobby decide if we have to go that far." Another voice piped up.

"Wouldn't it be funny if old Pagan really turned out to be monkey hump?" Everybody laughed. But it was a nervous kind of laughter.

"All right, guys," Clay said, "let's get it in gear." Clay was a pretty no-nonsense guy, and I'm sure he

Robert L. Vesco, young financial wizard, in a photo taken before his investment manipulations began to catapult him into international notoriety...

Laurence Richardson, Jr., former president and director of Vesco's International Controls Corporation.

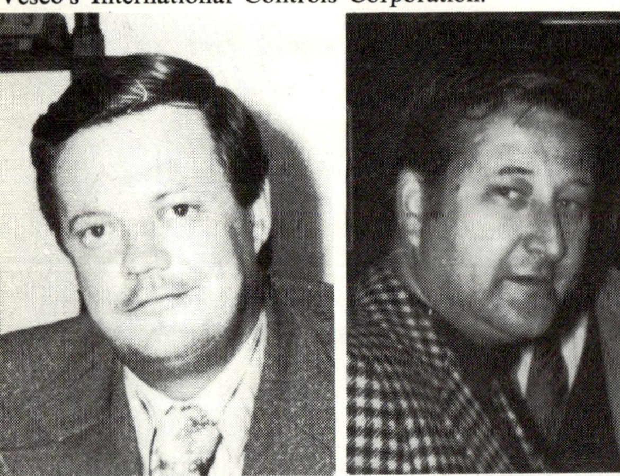

Norman Le Blanc, the top Vesco aide and "hatchetman," who helped engineer the IOS takeover. Le Blanc later barely escaped death when his car was tampered with and crashed in the Bahamas. Gil Straub in the main salon of the multimillion dollar Boeing. One of Vesco's inner circle, he now lives in exile in Costa Rica with his wife. Like Vesco, he is also under indictment in several countries.

Thomas P. "Tommy" Richardson, Los Angeles investment broker, and personal friend of Vesco. He owned Learjet N33TR, which he leased to Vesco; it also figured in a narcotics investigation and was seized by the U.S. Drug Enforcement Agency. The aircraft is now being used by the DEA as an investigative tool. Richardson was subpoenaed by the Senate subcommittee on investigations looking into Vesco's alleged gun-running and other illegal activities. He cited the Fifth Amendment in refusing to answer questions.

Harry L. Sears, former New Jersey State Senator, was a top Vesco attorney. He was later indicted with former U.S. Attorney General John Mitchell and former Commerce Secretary Maurice Stans on conspiracy charges involving an illegal contribution of $200,000 by Vesco to the 1972 Nixon Re-Election Campaign Fund.

The Honorable Lynden Oscar Pindling, Prime Minister of the Bahamas. Vesco provided money and aircraft to Pindling for his election campaign to become first Prime Minister of newly independent Bahamas in 1973. Vesco also arranged for unsecured personal loans for Pindling and some of his top associates. Jose "Don Pepe" Figueres, former President of Costa Rica. He is reported to be a close business associate of Robert Vesco and is preparing to run for a third term.

Robert L. Vesco in cabin of North American Sabreliner, N44SB, once owned by Allan Butler of Butler's Bank, Ltd., Nassau, Bahamas, later taken over by Vesco. Aircraft was en route to San Jose, Costa Rica, May, 1973. Robert Vesco during his 1973 extradition proceedings brought against him by United States in Bahamas. Vesco won his case. The attorney hired by the U.S. was once employed by Vesco.

Captain A. L. "Ike" Eisenhauer with Denis Dearlove of Aviation Traders Engineering, Ltd., after record-breaking landing (under 2000 feet!) of Vesco's Boeing at Southend-on-Sea, England. Captain Eisenhauer at his home on Lake Arrowhead, Denville, N.J.

The Silver Phyllis with the International Controls Corporation logotype on its tail, (they were later removed).

The flight deck of Vesco's Boeing 707, *The Silver Phyllis*. The Aircraft Commander occupies the left seat, the First Officer the right seat, and the Flight Engineer is stationed behind First Officer.

The huge vertical stabilizer of *The Silver Phyllis,* dwarfs the sedan below. Note absence of ICC logo. Eleven signifies lucky roll at dice. RV are Vesco's initials.

Main salon of *The Silver Phyllis*. The divan opened into a large bed. The salon was also equipped for in-flight motion pictures. The table in left foreground could be raised or lowered electronically for cocktails or card games.

The "discotheque" aboard *The Silver Phyllis* with stand-up bar and "flight stabilized" bar stools. Part of the special parquet dance-floor is visible. The discotheque featured "black" and strobe lighting and the latest quadraphonic sound systems.

The crew lounge and galley. All meals were prepared here, from fresh foods, and Vesco's favorite pepperoni pizza and chili dogs, to gourmet meals of seven or more courses with appropriate wines. The galley was connected by telephone to the flight deck and every passenger compartment. Vesco's "flying office" with full-sized teakwood desk which opened into a conference table. The office was equipped with an air-to-ground communications system, and the seats "tracked" fore and aft, side to side, swiveled and reclined.

Patricia III, Vesco's plush $1,400,000 yacht, named after his wife. Yacht was seized by U.S. Customs after Vesco was indicted on same charges for which John Mitchell, former U.S. Attorney General, and Maurice Stans, former Commerce Secretary, were tried.

Bella Vista, the former Lake Geneva, Switzerland, headquarters of IOS. The Board and Executive Committee met here.

The Vesco home in Boonton Township, New Jersey, where Vesco's two eldest sons now live.

The former Vesco compound in Nassau, the Bahamas. Security guards were called "groundskeepers." Visitors required an "escort" to main house. Frequently the escort was Donald A. Nixon, Jr., nephew of former President Richard M. Nixon.

Vesco's house outside San Jose, Costa Rica, reportedly one of eight different hideouts used by the fugitive financier.

This, one of the latest photographs of Robert Vesco, was taken on his secret "estancia" in Northern Costa Rica during filming of ABC-TV's "The Reasoner Report" in January, 1974.

didn't intend any dramatics. But the gathering of eagles attended his words like a bunch of platoon commanders in the field. I don't think the effect went unnoticed by Clay. I thought back to Farina's remark about acting like a Captain when the occasion arose. Dick pointed at me.

"Ike, you're the key in Phase One." He explained that contact had already been made with somebody inside St. Antoine. There were only two ways that Vesco could exit the prison. One was through the main-yard gate to St. Antoine. The other was via the entrance we had used earlier in the day, which is on a side street. St. Antoine Prison occupies a full square block on a hill in the old part of Geneva. It can be seen in all its ugliness from almost any part of the old city. Clay's plan required me to pick Vesco up at one of the exits, then go like hell in the direction away from St. Antoine. I was to be certain that I was not followed. It was immaterial how long it took to get Vesco back to the Rue de Lausanne apartment. The important thing was that nobody would have an opportunity to photograph Vesco leaving the jail. The second most important thing was that nobody could shove a piece of legal paper into his hands.

"Phase Two," Clay said, "diversion." Clay held his chin in his hand and thought a bit. If he was acting, he was doing a very good job of it. Everybody in the room hung on his words. "The press. That's our problem. We have to screw the bastards up. I've arranged for a dummy crew with lights and cameras to cover the main-yard entrance at precisely seven-thirty. This will draw the attention of the other press people, and they will converge on the main-yard gate. But, we have already arranged for Bobby and the others to exit via the entrance you saw today." It was typical of the Vesco mob that Meissner and Strickler were referred to as "the others." It was really a ridiculous scene. They treated the whole thing like a breakout from Folsom. If the machine guns opened up and Meissner and Strickler fell mortally wounded, I could visualize one of the Vescoites shouting "Never mind them! Take care of the boss!" Clay went on.

"I have arranged for one of the inside people to create a diversion at the gate where the newspeople will be gathered to create the impression that Vesco's exit is imminent. While they are focused on that action—" he turned and pointed directly at me—"Ike, who will be circling the prison constantly, will make the pickup on the run as soon as he gets the signal. This signal will come at precisely the same time as the false indication of Bobby's release at the main entrance." He turned to me once more. I found myself swept up in the excitement of the thing. It was all bullshit but it was fun. Here were a bunch of grown men, business types, plotting a caper of James Bond-ian proportions.

"Ike," Clay said very seriously, "this is the critical point. The signal for your move will be a guard sticking his head out the door of the side entrance. This will mean that our targets will be inside the door and ready to move upon your arrival. They will not appear, I repeat, will not appear, until the car is directly opposite the door. As soon as you come abreast of the door you will brake to a stop, make certain the doors are not locked, and survey the area to make certain that you are not being observed. You should be at that gate no later than eight-o-two." He explained that it would take at least two minutes for all those press suckers to race around the corner and reach the side entrance in time to catch Vesco. He'd had somebody time it. Wow!

Once more he singled me out.

"What kind of a car do you think will do the job, Ike?" he said with all seriousness. I couldn't believe it. I thought I'd jerk him around a little. Everybody was waiting to hear what I said. I let them wait. I made a big show of considering the problem.

"A 427 Chevy with a stick," I said, matching his solemnity. "I need the acceleration." Dick took me at my word.

"Jesus, Ike. Be reasonable," Dick said. "We'd never find one of them in the time we have available. Won't a Mercedes do?"

"Okay," I said.

"Way to go, Ike!" somebody said. What a bunch of

turkeys. If they'd have given me a '39 Hupmobile I could have done the job.

Dick Clay is a very sharp guy. I think that he was having as much fun as I was. We had a captive audience who were caught up in a caper. His next instruction convinced me that we were both on the same wavelength.

"Captain," he said, "you know what you have to do. You might as well go out on station now." That deserved a salute. If I had my hat on I would have. But as it was I simply said, "Right, Dick!" and got up to leave. When I got to the door I had a thought. I turned around. Forty or so pairs of eyes were watching me. I raised my left hand.

"Hey, Dick," I said, "I think we should synchronize our watches." From Clay's expression I knew that he knew we were in a jerk-off mode.

"Right!" he said. And made the most of the situation. Forty or so wrists were raised and Dick tolled the seconds.

"Mark!" he shouted. Jesus, that can be an exciting moment in any lawyer's life.

"Hack!" somebody in the back yelled. I figured him for a second lieutenant in the artillery. Gung ho! Hi-ho Silver! I got out of there before I wet myself.

I took the elevator down to the garage where Vince was waiting.

"Vince," I said, "you wouldn't believe what's going on upstairs." Vince smiled and nodded his head.

"I would believe it," he said. "What do I do?"

"You stay here and wait for the others," I said. "I'm going alone to pick up Mr. Vesco and the other two men." Now I was doing it too, treating Meissner and Strickler, whom I respected, as also-rans. "Vince, you know these cars. Which is the best one?"

"You gonna do some driving?" he asked.

"I got a feeling," I said.

"Take the Mercedes 280," Vince said. "It's the one I use." That was enough for me.

It was still 45 minutes to zero hour. I drove to the prison and made one full circuit to familiarize myself with the area. Dick had done a good job. The place looked like a movie set—lights, cameras, the works. As he predicted it sucked all the press people to the wrong side of the prison.

I had forgotten about Smelly. She might have been dirty, but she wasn't stupid. On my first pass by the pickup door I saw a Peugeot parked at the curb right opposite Vesco's escape hatch. Ordinarily I wouldn't have given it a tumble. It was pretty cruddy looking. But as I passed I got a glimpse of two familiar profiles. It was Smelly all right, and her gamey companion. They hadn't fallen for Clay's diversion. Or they were covered at the other entrance by somebody else and were playing the odds. I had to think this one through. I made a second circuit to be sure. There was no doubt about it. It was Smelly. A third pass might have alerted them so I stooged around until a couple of minutes before zero hour. I had arranged with Vince for him to relay the signal from the door rattler where the press was gathered. He would be on the corner, well removed from the crowd. At his nod I would begin my "run."

At precisely eight I pulled abreast of Vince and he gave me the nod. I rounded the corner and there was that damn Peugeot still parked across from the prison, its lights out. I knew what I had to do and that was to give Smelly and her bearded friend something to occupy themselves while I gathered up Vesco, Meissner, and Strickler.

I switched off my lights and crept up behind the Peugeot. Smelly and Camel-Piss were so intent on watching that side door that they were not even aware of my approach. When I was about a foot from their car I touched the accelerator just enough to make firm contact with the Peugeot. I increased the pressure on the accelerator. The Peugeot resisted for a fraction of a second. I kept the pressure on. The Peugeot mounted the curb. I could see Smelly and her buddy looking at each other in wonderment. I shoved that little heap between a light pole and the wall of the building. There wasn't a hell of a lot of room there and the Peugeot was *hors de combat* at least for the moment. I saw the side door open. I backed away from the Peugeot, flipped on my lights and whipped over to the opposite curb. Before I even had a chance to reach across to open the doors, Vesco, Meissner, and Strickler appeared. Vesco opened the front door and dove into the seat beside me. Strickler yanked open the rear door and tumbled in, Meissner right behind him.

"Go!" Vesco yelled needlessly—the car was already moving. Before I reached the corner, the Peugeot's lights came on and Smelly was on my tail. Clay's specific instructions were to lose any tail. That's precisely what I intended to do. But not until I had a little fun.

I had raced stock cars in my youth and the prospect of a movie-type chase through the streets of Geneva was a welcome one. I didn't know how good a driver the bearded one in the Peugeot was. I was pretty sure I wouldn't have to break any Swiss traffic laws to shake him. But this was fun time for me and I figured I'd give the guy a run for his money. What I didn't count on was a dinky Geneva police car squatting on a side street hoping for bad people like me. They soon joined the chase behind the Peugeot. That added a new dimension. I not only didn't dare get caught but I didn't dare let them get close enough to read the plate number on the car. That's when the real race began.

Up to this point Vesco was having a real good time. He was aware that we had a tail, and he hooted and hollered at me to shake it. When the cops joined the party he got worried. When he got a look at the speedometer he got spastic.

"For Chrissakes, Ike," he yelled, "you're gonna' kill us."

"Don't sweat it, Bob," I assured him, "I'm just earning my keep."

"You earned it! You earned it!" he yelled. "For God's sake, pull over and let me drive."

"You want to go back to jail?" I asked him. He shut up and scrunched down in the seat and after about fifteen minutes we arrived at the apartment—without our escort.

The apartment was still under siege by the press and both the garage and the lobby were patrolled by IOS security people. Old Faithful Vince was right there in the garage looking pleasantly mean. He opened Vesco's door but winked at me.

Vesco hurried off without even a word of thanks. He was back in charge. Meissner took his time getting out of the car as if he were trying to muster up his lost dignity. He was a big man, a huge man. He smiled tightly at me, shook my hand, and walked away in the direction taken by Vesco. It had been a tough experience for him but he carried off his return to freedom with class.

Ulrich Strickler was the most human of the trio. I did not know Stricker well. It was standard for me to keep a distance between myself and my passengers. But Ulrich Strickler was a decent man whose character insisted itself on whomever he came in contact with. He never intruded. Yet you always knew when he was around. He was a nice guy. He shook my hand as well.

"Thank you, Captain," he said. "Of course I did wrong but it is very good to be outside." He walked away slowly and, I thought, a little sadly. I felt really sorry for the guy. After all he was jugged in his own homeland having been suckered by a foreigner.

When I got up to the apartment the place was in an uproar. Vesco had changed his clothes. He had shaved and looked as fresh as a daisy. He was King of the Hill. Now it was really party time. And the booze flowed like booze. The IOS secretaries had laid out a buffet fit for a medieval baron on the huge dining-room table. All of the IOS big shots, including a couple of front runners I hadn't seen before, were gathered near Vesco who held a yard and a half of Crown Royal in one hand and a pepperoni hero sandwich in the other. The shit was flying like sleet in a high wind. And most of it came out of Vesco. From where I stood just outside the door I could hear his version of the saga of St. Antoine. He looks somewhat like a dime-store Errol Flynn, and right then he sounded like one with a twenty percent discount. To hear him tell it he was Lionel Strongjaw or the Count of Monte Cristo. What the hell. He was entitled. It could have been the most exciting thing that ever happened to him. And who the hell was I to judge?

It was close to ten at night and my batteries were just about run down. I thought I would just disappear and go back to La Reserve and die for about eight hours. But Vesco spotted me.

"Hey! Mario Andretti," he yelled across the room, "come over and have a drink. You've earned it." I put on my party smile and walked in. I didn't want to break any balloons. But the guy had a dig coming.

"I can't leave you alone for a minute, can I, Bob?" I said. Everybody waited to see how Vesco would take it. It wasn't a long wait. He gave me a whack on the shoulder and broke up. The room erupted in laughter. After a minute or two I backed away from the dining-room table and headed for the door. The party was getting heavy. There were more secretaries than before. From the amount of grab-ass that was going on they weren't secretaries. I ducked out into the hallway. A couple of security guards stood outside the entrance to the apartment. For no particular reason I took them for ex-cops, garden-variety foot patrolmen, flatfeet. It was the way they stood. Ramrod straight. Feet a little bit apart. Hands clasped behind their backs. They saw me without looking at me and rocked forward slightly on their toes.

Vince drove me back to La Reserve. In the short span of time that I knew Vince, he seldom if ever initiated a conversation. However on the trip back to La Reserve he asked me about the celebration of "Mr. Vesco's liberation." He was curious as to why I left so quickly.

"They're not my kind of crowd, Vince," I told him.

"I feel sorry for them," he said. "Me and you, we are different." He was silent for a few more miles. "There was no party when I came out of jail."

"When was that, Vince?" I asked him. He said nothing. When he dropped me at the hotel we shook hands. I didn't realize then that that was the last time I would lay eyes on Vince Bordoni.

Dodd called me early in the morning and told me that we were booked on a flight back to the United States that day.

There were reporters and photographers waiting to ambush Vesco at Geneva's Cointrin Airport. They had obviously been tipped off by airline personnel. This is common practice.

Vesco, Dodd, and I ran the gauntlet without comment of any kind. Strobes flashed everywhere. I saw Smelly and the beard. They were trying to redeem their failure of the night before. I caught her eye and winked at her. She must have taken this as a signal that I would speak with her, and she came over.

"You forgot your rocket, baby," I said. And hurried past her.

Vesco was not a hanger-arounder. He invariably arrived at an airport within minutes of flight time whether he was taking Silver Phyllis or commercial. We quickly passed through flight check-in into the departure hall. At Cointrin we had to pass through a long tunnel under the ramp to get to the airplane.

It was on that long walk through the tunnel that I noticed there was a subtle difference in Vesco's demeanor. I was walking behind him. The same long firm stride was there, but he did not hold his head as high as he usually did. One of the things that had always struck me about Vesco was the way his eyes darted about. The head would move left and right taking in everything, even while he carried on a rapid-fire conversation. Today his head was down slightly, and his concentration seemed to be focused straight ahead. He didn't mention St. Antoine or his courtroom experience once during the flight. We sat together part of the way while Ralph slept. Uncharacteristically Vesco avoided any lengthy conversations. He just wouldn't respond with any show of interest to my attempts to draw him out. After one protracted period of silence during which his neck twitch became pronounced, he put his hand on the back of his neck and stared at the overhead.

"Ike," he said, "I'm never going back there again!" I knew he was talking about Switzerland.

He said it quietly. The anger, the outrage was gone. He was a man who had been deeply humiliated. Every man judges himself according to his own standards. Spending a night in jail is not the worst thing that can happen to someone unless that kind of thing has a secret meaning. Vesco's inner armor had been pierced. Looking back I think the Geneva experience was a turning point in the life of Robert Vesco, the person. He was vulnerable. It could happen again—and again. To some men one night in jail creates a thousand nights of fear. More than anything else I believe that the dread of another jail sentence haunts Robert Vesco.

Robert Lee Vesco, self-made multimillionaire, friend of a president, brilliant businessman, international "fixer," had just lost his first country. None of us realized it at the time but Robert Vesco had become a man on the run.

12

December 23, 1971 1509Z GSW—JAX—EWR

Phase One of Silver Phyllis' beauty treatments was finished on schedule. I was ready to pick up Robert Vesco in Jacksonville, Florida, and get him home to New Jersey for Christmas. The day before I had taken Phyllis up for a test flight and I was very pleased with what Qualitron had done.

Jack Prewitt would come along as far as Newark in case any hitches developed with the new interior. Any trouble that might occur would make itself known in flight. Whatever could not be taken care of immediately or with minor maintenance would be corrected when Silver Phyllis returned to Qualitron for Phase Two in a little over two weeks.

After takeoff Jack and I inspected the area that had been modified. We listened for squeaks. We worked everything that could be worked, pushed all the buttons, flipped all the switches. Dottie did the same with the galley. I went forward to the vestibule and jumped up and down on the floor a couple of times. Jack knew what I was up to. I did the same thing in the forward lavatories and in Dottie's new kitchen. Jack watched while my nearly 200 pounds bounced off his new floor. When I finished stomping he smiled.

"Y'all satisfied?" he asked.

"Yup," I said.

The floor area I had jumped on had been a sore point with me since the day we got the airplane. My first step into N728PA had felt to me like I had just walked onto a trampoline. The floor inside the door had sagged at least two inches. When I inspected it by lifting the carpeting I could see that the interior structure of the floor panel was completely shot. These floor panels come in various sizes. They are of a sandwich-type construction which can be filled with anything from balsa wood to honeycomb of a variety of materials most of which, at that time, were subject to rot or corrosion when exposed to certain fluids and chemicals. I also found that the same sponginess existed in the floor panels in the forward lavatories and in the galley area. Water from passengers' wet shoes or blown in while the door is open during wet weather would account for the wetness in the vestibule. Splattered urine and spillage from lavatory sinks would be enough to damage the lavatory floor panels. And spilt coffee, liquor, ice and chicken soup would do the job nicely in the galley. On-board flight crews, especially the flight service personnel, do not clean up. It isn't in their contract. Ground cleaning personnel attack only what can be seen. That's in their contract. Maintenance personnel are guided by two major concerns. The first one is mandatory inspection procedures required by law. The second is profit and loss. The airplane must be kept in service. Floor panels are way down on the list of priorities. If a panel is discovered to be sub-standard it's usually a case of "we'll handle it next time."

Passenger safety on an aircraft is not merely a matter of mid-air collisions, crashes or engines falling off. Aircraft designers worry about sharp corners, exposed wires, the tension in the springs in the up-right return of passengers seats. They even worry about the floors. It just wouldn't do to have a passenger suddenly disappear into the cargo hold. A stewardess might run her panty-hose serving him his drink. Besides which, passengers are not allowed in the cargo hold during flight. Aircraft designers try to apply Murphy's First Law which states that "if anything can go wrong, it will." Or words to that effect.

It's the operator of the aircraft who fails the passenger. I had noticed the same condition on a number of Pan American 707's. Because almost every 707 is almost identical in its construction and in its various parts the probability is that the same condition exists with every airline using the same type equipment. I don't mean to suggest that passengers boarding modern jet aircraft need to leap the first three feet from the doorway but, if someone is traveling with a fat companion, it might be a good idea to let the fat companion precede him into the airplane.

Before the remodeling, the floor inside the doorway of Silver Phyllis was like a goddam tiger trap. More than once I wanted to warn Bob Vesco to step across that first panel. I had considered laying down a couple of two-by-sixes or shoring up with a lolly column from lower forty-one, doing a little repair work myself before Qualitron got Phyllis.

Changes have been made in the core materials used in floor-panels. They are highly resistant to rot and corrosion and even have greater strength. This is what Qualitron put into Silver Phyllis.

All the modifications in Phase One took place inside the Boeing except for the new paint job. Silver Phyllis now wore a dress of virginal white with a blue stripe down the side along the window line.

Most of the engineering modifications, of course, were not visible. The galley was enlarged and redesigned to cope with Vesco's demand for freshly prepared foods in flight. A main salon was installed, luxurious in appearance and functional in every respect. Facilities for in-flight movies were provided. The overstuffed chairs swiveled, reclined, and tracked inboard and outboard. Hideaway, pull-up, wood tables allowed for eating, gaming, and additional work areas. When Pan Am delivered the Boeing to Israel prior to sale, it had an interior configuration of 143 legal seats. Other models of this aircraft contained as many as 177 or 189 legal seats. When it arrived in Miami there were on board only 54 legal seats, including the divans Vesco ordered installed for the interim period of initial operation. Now, after Phase One, the number of legal seats aboard had been reduced to 40. Vesco did not like to travel in crowds.

At Jacksonville Vesco boarded the airplane like a man who had designed his own home and hadn't seen it until the day it was finished. I could see that he was thoroughly pleased. He didn't say much. He stood in the middle of the main salon looking around, a smile on his face, and nodding his head.

"Nice job," was all he said. In our design discussions he had indicated where his own personal seat would be located. He also insisted that his initials be displayed on the seat so that nobody would mistakenly sit in the king's place. Dottie had the initials made of leather and sewn onto the fabric covering the headrest. He spotted his chair, walked over, and sat down. He rutched in the seat and leaned back. He ran his hand over the console containing the buttons, knobs, and lights. The street kid from Detroit knew exactly where he was. He smiled the broadest smile I had ever seen. This was a long way from the jail cell at St. Antoine.

The aft bulkhead of the salon ended at station 782. In aircraft, measurements are made from a point in inches so that a station means nothing more than a specific measurement from some point of reference. In the Boeing, for example, the forward part of the salon began at station 540. This meant that Vesco's private salon was a compartment twenty feet long and as wide as a 707. It was at least as large as the living room in a good-sized apartment. Yet it occupied only one-sixth of the effective passenger cabin space of the airplane. And we had only completed the first of six phases.

Prewitt returned to Ft. Worth shortly after we landed at Newark. He was proud of his work and pleased with Vesco's reaction. Vesco still had some Christmas shopping to do. And so did I. And I had less than half a day to do it in. That's what I was thinking about as Vesco left the Boeing. Then the zinger came.

"I'm taking the family to Africa on safari," he said.

"When?" I asked.

"Sunday," he replied and left. That was the day after Christmas. Sonofabitch!

I had intended to spend a couple of days with my sons in Pennsylvania where they were living with their mother, my ex-wife Jeanne. It was the one time of the year when differences were forgotten and we could immerse ourselves in the goodwill of the season. I was very close to my sons and still am. It was difficult being away from them for such long periods of time. So I looked forward to my Christmas visit. And now Bobby Vesco had blown that one for me because he wanted to take potshots with a Polaroid Swinger at setups on the African plains.

For a few hours I was able to forget Vesco, airplanes, flight plans, and Africa. But only for a few hours. Most of the afternoon I spent on the telephone organizing the flight and sending telegrams. Needless to say my crew was not overjoyed at the prospect of spending the next ten days in the land of the tsetse fly.

December 26, 1971 1717Z EWR—QX—BEY

First stop was Gander, Newfoundland. I would have preferred to fly nonstop to Beirut but, because of the short runways at Newark, I couldn't take on a full load of fuel and Gander was "LAST GAS BEFORE TURNPIKE" the North Atlantic Turnpike, that is.

Aboard the Boeing were the entire Vesco family, a family friend, and two teen-aged friends of the Vesco kids. I've got to say this for Vesco. He loved his children, and he treated their friends with generosity and consideration. Many times, in the Grumman days too, I hauled teen-agers between Newark and Nassau and Newark and Europe. I always enjoyed these flights and I even brought my own sons along occasionally.

December 28, 1971 0700Z BEY—CAI—NBO

The memory of my last visit to the Middle East and the Damascus rip-off was still very fresh in my mind. It was a relief to know that my route to Nairobi, Kenya, would pass well clear of Syria. In fact I was looking forward to a trouble-free six-hour nonstop flight. The route I told Chuck to file for would carry me over our only ally in the Middle East, Israel. I would fly over the Gulf of Aqaba down along the Red Sea and then turn inland over the Sudan between Khartoum to the north and Addis Ababa, Ethiopia, to the south, straight into Nairobi. The only problem I could foresee was that the airport at Nairobi might have weather problems. There are few navigation aids in Africa and only fragmented weather information. Although the area I was flying over was generally hot and dry, Nairobi is close enough to the Indian Ocean and Mt. Kilimanjaro to be affected by rapid weather changes—especially in the afternoon, which was when I expected to arrive. If that happened, I had to be certain of being able to divert to another airport such as Salisbury, Rhodesia, or possibly as far south as Johannesburg, South Africa. I ordered a full fuel load for the trip.

To make sure that there would be no hang-ups on the route I wanted to fly to Nairobi, I sent Chuck to the United States FAA representative attached to the American embassy in Beirut the day before. To be absolutely certain that I could safely follow this route.

Normally, in the more stable parts of the world, the only concern I had was to ensure that I followed the international flight procedures that were outlined, in detail, in my international manuals. However, we were in a very hot part of the globe. The Jeppesen Manuals are regularly updated. But the Middle Eastern/African political complexion changes faster than a printer can reset type. It seemed logical that the U.S. State Department would be able to provide up-to-the-minute information regarding air traffic as well as lend assistance through its consular officials to prevent incidents.

After a full and frustrating day at the Embassy, Chuck returned mad as a hornet and totally confused. The guts of what he was told was that we would not be permitted to fly through any Israeli-controlled airspace.

"Permitted by whom?" I asked.

"I don't know," Chuck said. "The FAA guy talked in circles. I don't think he knows what the hell our problem is." I calmed Chuck down and got the story straight.

Lebanon is an Arab country, and hostile to Israel. To fly over Israeli territory would be an offense against Lebanon. It was not a matter of getting anyone's permission to fly over Israel except that of Israel itself. But the Lebanese would deny me any future landing rights in Lebanon if I flew over Israel. I didn't like that, but I understood it. Chuck's impression was that the FAA man was advising us to avoid an incident by bypassing Israel and flying to Nairobi via Cairo. In other words he and the United States government had no intention of using any pressure to get the Lebanese to soften their stand.

The least we expected was the FAA's assistance in seeing to it that the Egyptians not only knew that we would be flying over Egypt, but that they would treat us as a civil transient aircraft carrying the American flag. Before I left the United States I had considered that I might have to pass through Egyptian airspace. I therefore sent a number of cablegrams to the Egyptian civil aviation authorities asking for overflight permission. They never answered or acknowledged any of my communications.

What confused Chuck was the FAA man's laying out an alternate route to Nairobi. Considering that the man was a federal employee attached to the United States embassy, it would be logical to expect that the route he suggested had the blessing of the State Department.

I was unhappy with the way Chuck got jerked around on the assignment I had given him. I was looking for results based on what I wanted. What he brought back was something that not only forced me to rearrange my plans but was not clear cut.

I made two additional errors in judgment. The first is that I made an assumption, something I abhor. I assumed that the United States government would honor its obligation to protect its citizens in foreign lands and to defend those vessels and aircraft flying the American flag against insult and injury by foreign powers. I also erroneously assumed that in critical areas like the Middle East and North Africa, personnel assigned to diplomatic posts would have the intelligence and the information to know not only what the hell was going on but how best an American citizen could avoid trouble.

From recent experience I should have realized that Middle Eastern governments are about as dependable as a drunk locked in a liquor store and that the American flag in too many parts of the world is regarded with hatred and contempt.

I had to rely on Chuck's assessment of the FAA rep's words. The impression Chuck came away with, having been given the route by the FAA rep, was that somebody in Egypt would know that a privately owned, multiengine jet of American registry would be transitting Egyptian airspace on its way to another African country. I was in for a shock.

Beirut operations accepted the filed route recommended by the representative of the FAA. The route that I filed would go out over the teletype to every air-traffic control center in every country along my route. This is an "advisory" on an aircraft's movement solely for the purpose of the providing sufficient airspace for control while the aircraft is in any given sector. It is also a means whereby the aircraft can be "handed off" from control area to control area like a stick in a relay race. This procedure does not demand a response of permission on the part of a government to fly through its airspace. It is only when a government wants to prohibit such overflights that any response is given. Such prohibitions are usually made known before the aircraft in question starts its engines, unless a country wants to play a game of political football with an aircraft registered in another country—like Silver Phyllis. In cases like these original clearance is denied and a re-route is assigned.

Any pilot flying internationally who does not have the benefits of flying for a major international airline must himself see to all of the details of going from where he is to where he wants to be. In practice, it is a matter of referring to one of a number of available directories such as the Jeppesen Route Manual, which gives the essential information as to overflight requirements, entry requirements, hazards, restrictions, and warnings. The only other source of information available to the pilot is the daily newspaper, which he would check to be sure that there isn't a war or a revolution in progress along the route. In a doubtful area, even the dumbest pilot would probably seek the advice and guidance of his government through whatever representatives are at hand.

Anybody who wants to overfly Cuba, for example, knows that the required telegrams advising Cuban traffic control of an impending flight are futile in most cases. The moment that you know you are cleared to pass over Cuba is when you get there. If you are not cleared you are told to go away. If you are cleared they tell you it's alright. The lack of response from the Egyptians was not significant. Wrong!

Beirut ground control issued an air-traffic clearance to SKY Flight 128 at 0702 Zulu on December 28, 1971, exactly as it had been filed via Cairo with final destination Nairobi, Kenya. There was no apparent impediment to the flight and no grounds, legal or otherwise, for subsequent actions taken by the Egyptians.

The distance between Beirut and Cairo in flight time is a little under an hour The first indication of trouble came shortly after I was handed off by Cyprus control to Cairo control. I was approaching the Nile Delta. I had clear visual contact with the ground. There was no doubt that I was over Egyptian territory. I could pick out the Suez Canal off to my left and Alexandria to my right. The Nile Delta from that altitude appears exactly as it does on a map. I had Cairo dead ahead.

Cairo air traffic gave me a radio-frequency change. I

expected it. But not the one they gave me. Instead of a hand-off to a controller further down the line they put me onto Cairo approach control.

"SKY One Two Eight—descend to and maintain flight level two two zero."

"Cairo—SKY One Two Eight estimating the VOR on the hour—we are level three seven zero." Chuck was telling Cairo approach control, for what reason I did not know, that I was at an altitude of 37,000 feet and estimated to fly over the radio-navigation facility at Cairo exactly on the hour. It didn't make any sense. Cairo approach control and I had no business with each other. My flight plan did not call for a landing at Cairo. I was cleared nonstop to Nairobi. Then the situation began to get hairy.

"SKY One Two Eight—you are cleared to leave flight level three seven zero—report reaching level two two zero."

"Cairo—advise reason for lower level—I'm en route Nairobi."

"SKY One Two Eight—you will be landing at Cairo."

Up to this point Chuck had been handling the radio. I could hear what was going on. We were using the loudspeaker system on the flight deck instead of relying on individual earphones. Everybody up front could hear the dialogue. Chuck looked at me in utter disbelief.

"Land! What for?" he said. I think he was worried that what was happening was somehow his fault. Right then it made no difference whose fault it was. The screw-up in Beirut was over and done with. The clearance I got there had changed everything. As far as I could see there was not the slightest reason for Cairo's instructions to land the Boeing. I couldn't land safely even if I wanted to. I had too much fuel on board. A landing would very probably be fatal to everybody on board. I got on the mike.

"Cairo approach—this is the Captain—we do not wish to land at Cairo—we are en route flight level three seven zero to Nairobi, Kenya."

"SKY One Two Eight—Captain—please descend immediately to level two two zero."

"Negative! Do I have conflicting traffic?" At this point I did not believe they actually wanted me to land. But they were asking me to drop my altitude fifteen thousand feet immediately. This isn't done unless there is the danger of a midair collision or some other emergency.

"SKY One Two Eight—you are landing at Cairo."

"Negative—I am eighty thousand pounds over my landing weight."

"SKY One Two Eight—dump fuel and land."

"Negative—Cairo—do you understand I am forty tons over my landing weight?"

"SKY One Two Eight—follow instructions or we will take action!" I had a decision to make and I had to make it instantly.

"Pete!" I yelled to the flight engineer, "give me rated on all four—now." I reached up and flipped the seat belt sign on. But I couldn't wait to be sure that my passengers were buckled in. Pete had responded at my command. I laid that Boeing over and made a fast 180-degree turn and headed for the Mediterranean. Silver Phyllis buffeted and bucked her resentment at the treatment I gave her at that altitude but I needed time and space to think this thing through. The threat "action" could mean either that the Egyptians would send up fighter aircraft or use one of those United States-supplied SAM heat-seeker missiles. I told my crew to keep their eyes peeled for anything. As soon as the plane leveled off Vesco came storming onto the flight deck.

"What the hell are you doing, Ike?" he asked. I told him the situation.

"If I can get out of this hot-box," I told him, "I'm going to stooge around over the Med and try to work this thing out. I'll keep you posted." He went back and sat down.

"SKY One Two Eight—have you reversed course?" It was time to jerk them around a little.

"Cairo—I do not understand—say again." In the time it took for this brief exchange I had covered two miles back toward the Med. I wanted to dither around enough so that I would clear the Egyptian coast before they caught on to what I was up to. Back came Cairo.

"SKY One Two Eight—have you reversed course—repeat—have you reversed course?" I did not answer. I watched that coastline approaching.

"SKY One Two Eight—do you read Cairo?"

"Cairo—this is One Two Eight—you were blocked out—say your last transmission." They were getting angry. The coast was almost directly below me.

"SKY ONE TWO EIGHT—YOU—REVERSED—DIRECTION?" We were over the Med.

"Cairo—this is SKY One Two Eight—company requests I change my destination from Nairobi to Rome. Will you give me clearance out of the FIR and hand-off to Cyprus control?" This was not true, of course, but it sure as hell was confusing to them. In any subsequent development, such as a hearing, they would have no incriminating dialogue on tape from me. I did reverse without clearance. However, any aircraft commander can deviate from established procedures when he considers a situation warrants such action. Sooner or later he'll have to justify his action. I had no worries on that score. At least I'd *be* there.

After my request for a hand-off to Cyprus control and a change of destination, Cairo told me to stand by. There were no further threats. Maybe the Egyptians were having second thoughts. After a few minutes' delay I received a clearance from Cairo and was turned over to Cyprus control.

As soon as I was free of Cairo I contacted Cyprus control. The Rome business had screwed up Cairo. Cairo would have informed them in the hand-off that I had changed my destination. I didn't want to screw up Cyprus. I told them that I was not going to Rome and that I wanted an orbit over the Mediterranean.

Now that I was over neutral air I reviewed my situation. My intention was still to go to Nairobi by the most direct route or at least with the minimal detour, such as over another part of North Africa. If the Egyptians stuck to their guns the most direct route was out. But Libya and Algeria were sympathetic to Egypt and would no doubt refuse me passage. I could take the long way around skirting the west coast of Africa to approach Nairobi from the west across the fattest part of the African continent. This would be thousands of miles out of my way and would require a fuel stop. Of course I could fly over Israel and screw the Lebanese but Vesco would have to make that decision. The final alternative would be to call off the trip entirely and return to Beirut or land in Rome, Athens or some other European city. Of course I still had the option, when my fuel situation was safe, of knuckling under to the Egyptians.

Other aircraft commanders on the same frequency had heard what was going on. I got a call from a BOAC Captain.

"SKY One Two Eight—this is Speedbird," I heard. "Come up on one thirty point five." This meant that the Captain of the BOAC Speedbird wanted to talk to me on a different frequency from Cyprus control. "Hello chaps. Are you having trouble with the Arabs?"

"You'd better believe it, Speedbird." I answered.

"I've been listening," Speedbird said. "Why not contact Tel Aviv? The Israelis will be only too happy to help you. Of course, chaps, you could slip around Malta and run the UAR and refuel at Lagos." I explained to Speedbird that I had already ruled out that alternative for company reasons.

"Well, good luck, Captain," he said cheerfully, and signed off.

I went back to Cyprus control. Almost immediately I got a call from an El Al flight. El Al is the Israeli national airline. He gave me their company frequency and told me to contact Tel Aviv. El Al in Tel Aviv came back with an offer that, at first glance, seemed just the ticket.

"SKY One Two Eight—we understand your problem. Fighter escort is available to you to Elat—please advise." Wow! This was a new, and potentially dangerous, wrinkle. An American aircraft commander just doesn't accept another nation's fighter escort for his own convenience. I respect the Israelis and support their position in the Middle-east but occasionally they get chesty. Escorting the Silver Phyllis, even over their own territory, would be thumbing their noses at their Arab neighbors. It could be that some Israeli Air Force type saw an opportunity for a little combat practice. I was not about to make a decision that could involve the United States in an international incident. On the other hand the Israeli offer might have been a genuine guarantee of safe passage. I had to find out what acceptance of that offer would mean. I contacted Beirut control. It was like throwing a hand grenade into a chicken coop. The feathers began to fly.

First I insisted they verify my clearance to Nairobi via Cairo nonstop. They did. Then I told them that Cairo insisted I land. Their response indicated that that was my problem. Then I told them about the Israelis. They informed me that if I accepted their offer I would be banned from Lebanon. Forever. I insisted that they inform the United States embassy in Beirut of my situation. I was told to stand by. They came back to me a few minutes later.

"SKY One Two Eight—we have complied with your request—be advised you may *not* fly over Israeli territory. You may not accept Israeli escort." I was getting pretty angry at what was happening. Suddenly Silver Phyllis had become a shuttlecock in a dangerous game of Mideast badminton. It wasn't just that Vesco's airplanes had the whammy on them. It could have been any United States Flag carrier that happened to be in my spot at that time. This would not have happened to a commercial airliner. Silver Phyllis was the only privately owned 707 in the entire world, but the people on the ground in Beirut and Cairo did not seem to understand this. They regarded the plane as if it were a Sabreliner or a Learjet. It was bad enough that Cairo had some sort of piracy in mind. Their insistance that I land immediately was both unreasonable and unrealistic. It would be hours before I would be light enough to land safely. I could have dumped fuel—in a real emergency. It would not only be a waste but to dump fuel has its own element of risk. The fuel-dumping demand by Cairo fortified my belief that the whole issue was a swindle to garner landing fees and sell a bunch of kerosene—just like in Damascus.

I wanted to know the authority behind Beirut control's edict.

"Beirut—this is SKY One Two Eight—verify the authority for your last transmission." The Beirut controller simply repeated what he had said. I asked what the response from the American embassy had been. My transmission had not even been acknowledged. Therefore I had to believe that, if Beirut had indeed contacted the embassy, they were either taking a hands-off stance or had told Beirut that they were in agreement with Beirut's instructions but that I was not to be informed of this. Unfortunately there was no way that I could make direct contact with any American diplomatic representative.

There was one possiblity. But it was a wild one. The American Sixth Fleet maintains stations in the Mediterranean. I actually considered transmitting a PAN message. This would be done on a universally monitored distress frequency of one twenty one point five megahertz. It is one step below an all-out emergency. I would have asked assistance of carrier-based aircraft. I knew that the U.S. Navy would not respond with aircraft unless I were under attack. But merely making such a request would have shaken the shit out of those cookie pushers at embassies all over this part of the world. However, I soon scrapped the idea. I was in enough trouble.

It was time for Vesco. I told Dottie to go back and get him. He had been getting pretty upset at our seemingly endless circling and seemed glad to get into the act. I laid out all the alternatives and gave him the details of what I had done. Vesco was adamant. He wanted to go to Kenya to see the elephants and zebras. And he was goddamned if a bunch of fuckin' Arabs were going to spoil his safari. But he had to be realistic. Lebanon was important to his business plans. So were the UAR and other North African countries. He didn't give a shit about the Israelis.

"What happens if we land at Cairo, Ike?" he asked.

"It will cost us a buck or two," I told him. "On top of that, Bob, if they want to, they can hang me."

"For what?" he said.

"I refused to land," I said. "I couldn't land. I was too heavy. I'm still too heavy. We would have killed ourselves."

"When can we land?" he asked. He didn't seem to give a damn about my predicament.

"Not for at least three hours, Bob," I said. "By that time they'll be so goddamned annoyed that they'll have the firing squad waiting."

"It's not that bad, Ike," Vesco said.

"It *is* that bad, Bob," I said. "What the hell do we do about it?" My manner pulled him up short. He was silent a moment. He tapped me on the shoulder.

"Give me a little time, Ike," he said. He left the flight deck. Time for what? I thought. Now I was pissed off at Vesco.

There was nothing to do but keep circling and burn off fuel. After about an hour Vesco came back to the flight deck.

"We land in Cairo, Ike," he said. He was very assertive. "There won't be any hanging. I've got plenty of friends if it comes to that. You might have to take a lot of shit but that's what I'm paying you for. It will only hurt for a minute." He went back to his seat before I could say a word. I felt as if Vesco had stuck it in and turned it around. The crew realized my predicament. Pete grabbed my shoulder.

"Do we have to?" he asked.

"We have to," I told him. If I had refused Vesco the crew would have supported me, and we would have all been out of work.

I contacted Beirut control and advised them I was going to Cairo after all and that I was switching over to Cyprus control.

"Cyprus—this is SKY One Two Eight—can you get me a clearance from present position to Cairo with an E-T-A of eleven forty-five zulu?"

The Egyptian army was waiting for me when Silver Phyllis touched down at Cairo. At the end of my roll-out, the point in the landing run where the aircraft is slow enough to turn off the runway onto a taxiway, the tower controller called.

"SKY One Two Eight—watch for army vehicles clearing the runway—contact ground control." I looked ahead and saw about half a dozen armored vehicles waiting on both sides of the taxiway. At that time I did not know that this was my military escort. On the approach I could see antiaircraft emplacements surrounding the airport. One of the crew even remarked that we were being tracked. It didn't bother me. We were in the middle of a potential war zone, and I could understand the skittishness of the Egyptian troops. I began to think that maybe I misread Cairo's intentions at the very beginning when they demanded that I land. Just prior to takeoff from Beirut I had been handed a Pan Am telex communication to all stations in the Mideast. These advisories usually concern operational matters, but the contents of this one were a little nerve-wracking. It was in company code and warned of possible action by the Palestine Liberation Organization (PLO) or some such radical group.

The following is an exact copy of the message:

QL QAUOAPA QAMOAPA QANOAPA CPY BEYDSPA ROMDSPA HKGDSPA
NYCDSPA 282100 NYCXDPA
FOR INFO ONLY FAA ADV POPULAR FRONT FOR LIBERATION OF PALESTINE HAS ESTABLISHED SPECI SERVICE UNIT FOR PURPOSE OF BOMBING AND BLOWING UP AIRCRAFT STP WILL COOPERATE WITH AND USE NAME OF JORDANIAND LIBERATION MOVEMENT STP NO SPECIFIC INFOR AS TO TARGET OR MISSION STP DETAILS WILL BE REPORTED WHEN RECEIVED STP RECOMMEND GENERAL ALERT THIS MATTER 30 DECEMBER THROUGH 06 JANUARY END CARDMAN

(Above has been decoded)

The vehicles were parked off the taxiway itself. As I swung Silver Phyllis off the runway onto the taxiway I stopped. It appeared that my number four outboard engine might strike one of the vehicles. I noticed that the vehicles were of Russian design. A jeep pulled out ahead of me, and I was signalled to keep moving and follow him. At his direction, I applied sufficient power to get the Boeing moving again. Instant sandstorm. The vehicles were too close to me. The thrust of the engines blew up a cloud of grit and shit that buried all those poor bastards in the vehicles, except for the jeep in front of me. I followed it to the ramp where he handed me off to a regular airport-taxi director. At that moment, ground control called me.

"SKY One Two Eight—remain on your aircraft and shut down!"

The taxi director could not hear this transmission. He kept signalling me to follow his instructions. It was his job normally to spot the aircraft and give me the shut-down signal. The appearance of those armored vehicles that had been parked at the taxi turnoff told me to follow ground control's instructions. I stopped the Boeing. The taxi director continued to signal me ahead. He was on foot and held a pair of paddles. Clamped on his head were what are called "buns," which look like earphones but are actually noise mufflers. He did not understand why I had stopped. He continued to wave frantically and when Silver Phyllis did not move toward him he threw the paddles up in the air and walked away in disgust. At least he was standard. I've seen this kind of temper tantrum all over the world.

The jeep suddenly appeared whipping around from my left. Almost as if to make certain I saw it, it stopped, circled around and disappeared under the left wing. I had noticed there were four men in the jeep when I first saw it. Now I noticed that the two men in the back seat were carrying automatic weapons. Following the usual procedure Pete Dolliver went to open the door. Almost immediately he was back.

"They want you, Ike," he said. "They won't let me off the airplane." He had taken the nose pin with him. I took it from him and went back to the doorway. There I saw an Egyptian army officer. At the foot of the steps behind him stood the two guys with weapons—at the ready.

I started to go out. The officer held up his hands to stop me. Upon arrival at an airport it is not the usual practice to have a military officer greet you carrying a gun. I thought it best not to argue. A station wagon appeared and from it jumped an impressive-looking man in civilian clothes. The station wagon carried the TWA logotype on its door. The man bounded up the steps and pushed past the officer who didn't seem to mind. The new arrival turned out to be the TWA assistant station manager. He was an Egyptian.

"Captain," he said to me, "I received a call from your government. They recognize that this is a very serious situation. They would prefer that it be resolved without resort to diplomatic intervention. They have asked me to assist you and act as interpreter."

I knew the Egyptians were mad at me but what the hell had I done that would require "diplomatic intervention?"

"You will go with the officer and the rest of your crew and passengers must remain aboard the aircraft," he said. I looked at the nose pin in my hand.

"I'm not going anywhere until this airplane is secured," I said. He took the pin from my hand and tossed it down to a TWA mechanic in white coveralls who had come out with him in the station wagon. I told Dottie to go back and tell Vesco that nobody would be allowed off the airplane. It was a blistering hot day and already the temperature inside the airplane had begun to climb. I asked the TWA representative about a ground air-conditioning unit for my passengers. He said it was impossible and besides the matter would be finished quickly and we would be on our way. He didn't know what he was talking about.

When I got to the bottom of the steps I saw that Silver Phyllis was ringed by those armored vehicles. The soldiers had dismounted and formed a perimeter around the airplane. They all carried AK's. They were just kids and looked very uptight. They had no idea what the hell was going on. I knew that it would not take much to spook them into shooting indiscriminately. I made very certain that I appeared to be unconcerned and cooperative.

I followed the Egyptian army officer to the main terminal building. The TWA representative walked beside me. We were flanked by a couple of submachine-gun-toting soldiers who looked older and tougher than the ones in the armored vehicles. I followed the officer to the second floor of the terminal. I was brought into an ominous-looking room. There were benches along the walls. A large bare desk with a single chair behind it stood centered in front of a portrait of Abdul Gamal Nasser hanging on the wall. It was covered with a layer of brown dust. The army officer motioned for me to sit down on one of the benches. He had done his job of delivering the Captain from the Silver Phyllis to a room in which, I now had no doubt, my immediate fate would be decided. I sat on the bench, with my interpreter taking his place beside me. Neither of us made any attempt to remove the dust from the bench. My uniform trousers took on a sad appearance at every point of contact with the bench.

The army officer left the door open when he departed. For all I knew he could have been standing guard in the hallway. There was a lot of traffic back and forth past the open doorway. Occasionally somebody would stop and look into the hearing room and then go on. This sort of thing increased in frequency as the minutes ticked by. The word was getting around. Silver Phyllis would be a standout at any airport because it was obviously not a commerical airliner. At Cairo it took on the allure of a captured elephant and everybody wanted to get a look at the driver.

A half hour went by without anything happening. I had asked the TWA rep if he could find out what the routine would be. He refused. It was not his place, he explained, to inquire of anybody about what "the authorities" intended to do with me. He was a nice guy but obviously not very happy with his assignment. Maybe he felt that just by being with me he would be judged by "the authorities" as a turn-coat. I noticed that a number of men had gathered just outside the open door. They had a different look about them. They were neatly dressed and their faces were free of the glisten of sweat that marked almost everybody I had seen up to that point. I could feel it on my own face and my uniform was soggy. These men looked as if they had just come from an air-conditioned room. The TWA rep told me they were traffic controllers and that they were probably summoned to "testify."

Suddenly a short, fat, untidy little man strutted into the room. The men at the door had parted to allow him to pass. It was obvious that he was "the authorities." The TWA rep stood up the moment he appeared. The new arrival, whom I will call Mr. Moussa, was carrying a dog-eared file folder. Without a glance in my direction he sat behind the desk not bothering to wipe away the dust. He placed the file folder in front of him and beckoned the men at the door to come in. Nearly a dozen people filed into the room. The last one closed the door behind him. Everybody sat on the benches. Moussa opened the file folder and made a show of arranging the papers it contained. There were a lot of them. If they all referred to me they must have begun the file back in June when I made my first flight in the Silver Phyllis. I began to think that maybe he even had copies of the telexes I had sent requesting overflight permission.

Moussa suddenly looked up, made a gesture to one of the men, and spoke sharply in Arabic. The man went outside and came back a moment later with a straight-backed chair. Moussa indicated where he wanted the chair placed, smack in the middle of the room about four feet from the desk. It was only then that Moussa recognized my presence. He crooked his finger at me and pointed at the chair. I moved from the bench to the chair taking my briefcase with me. Moussa said something in Arabic. I looked at him. I didn't know what he was saying. I sat down and put my briefcase next to the chair. Moussa repeated, or so it seemed, whatever he had just said. I just sat there. Moussa had an angry look when he walked in and whatever was bugging him was getting him madder. The TWA rep came over to me.

"Captain, you are to put your bag on his desk," he said.

"No!" I said. "This is my personal property and nobody gets into it except me." The TWA rep did not have to translate since "no" sounds pretty much the same in any language except Turkish in which it sounds like the speaker is ready to puke, which is exactly what I would feel like doing before the session with Moussa was over. He glared at me and ripped off a stream of Arabic, which my interpreter didn't translate; I took what Moussa said to be uncomplimentary. He didn't repeat his demand that I put my briefcase on his desk. He turned his attention to the papers. He picked one up and read from it. When he had finished reading he said something to the TWA rep who interpreted.

"Captain," he said, "there are a number of charges against you. The document states that you entered Egyptian airspace without proper clearance, you disobeyed specific instructions to descend, you changed your course of flight, and also departed Egyptian airspace without clearance to do so."

This was just about what I expected. I knew what I did but the charge that I entered Egyptian airspace without clearance was so much horseshit. I began to feel my anger rising. How could I make this man understand that my actions were the direct result of an Egyptian mistake in the first place?

"Does Mr. Moussa speak any English at all?" I asked my interpreter.

"No, Captain," he said. I ticked off on my fingers all of the steps I had taken and all of the things that had happened, ending with a flat denial of all the charges.

"You tell him that!" I said. If I had felt that the TWA rep would be intimidated by his own people I was wrong. He must have not only conveyed my words to Moussa but also my anger. I watched Moussa's face while the TWA guy spoke. I thought Moussa would have an apoplectic fit. He shut the interpreter off with a wave of his hand. And launched into an angry tirade directed to the room in general while he waved the charge sheet at me. His voice rose in pitch. He stood up. He sat down again. He stood up again. He rattled the desk. And all the time he yelled. At one point he looked down at my briefcase on which there was an American flag decal. He pointed at it still carrying on then suddenly came around the desk and kicked at the bag, his foot knocking it over. I wanted to belt the sonofabitch. The TWA rep knew it and put his hand on my shoulder. Moussa stopped talking and looked at me as if daring me to do something. I looked around the room and saw that almost everybody was embarrassed. These guys, including the TWA rep, were not of Moussa's stripe. They were aviation people. Moussa was a political appointee and the worst kind of bureaucrat. I didn't need the interpreter to tell me that Moussa was using me to unload his hatred of my country and my people. At Moussa's instructions the TWA rep gave me the gist of his tirade. It was the same old bullshit that I had heard in almost every foreign country I'd been in. I heard it from bureaucrats, taxi drivers, even pilots. The United States was an arrogant, imperialistic bully. Americans were too rich and used their wealth to corrupt and dominate the poor countries. It went on like this. Nothing new. I felt sorry for the TWA rep who had to go on to tell me Moussa's opinion of me. I was the ugliest of all ugly Americans. All I could do was sit there and keep my mouth shut and match glares with Moussa. He could not understand what the TWA man was saying but he knew that he had gotten to me. From that point on it was all downhill.

There was not even a pretense of a hearing. Moussa held up various papers, said something to his compatriots, said something to me, and kept writing down strange notes on a sheet of brownish paper. After a while the TWA man didn't even bother to pass on to me what was being said. Moussa's performance went on for more than an hour. The other men in the room chafed and got out their "worry beads." If they had expected to be questioned they were disappointed. They served only as an audience for Moussa, and they didn't like it.

Suddenly the room was quiet. Moussa had shut up abruptly and went back to the desk. He made a busy show of going through the various papers and writing numbers in a column on a separate sheet. He added up the column of numbers and with a flourish of self-importance thrust the paper at the TWA rep who handed it to me. The paper was of poor quality and the lead in Moussa's pencil wasn't much. It was impossible for me to read the numbers. I asked the TWA rep to help me out. He must have thought I was asking him what it was.

"It is the total of your penalties, Captain," he said. "Five hundred Egyptian pounds." I told him I didn't have any Egyptian money. The slightest smile appeared on the TWA guy's face.

"He will take dollars, Captain," he said. He did some rapid calculations of his own. The total was a little over 1100 U.S. dollars. I stood up and picked up my briefcase.

"Where do I pay these penalties?" I asked the TWA rep. He indicated Moussa.

"Mr. Moussa will accept the money for the authorities," he said.

"Are you sure this guy doesn't understand English at all?" I asked. The TWA rep assured me that Moussa knew only one language, Arabic.

I walked to the desk where Moussa sat, fingers intertwined, looking very pleased with himself and also very righteous. I slapped that heavy briefcase on the desk and raised the lid so that the American flag was practically under his nose.

As usual I had quite a stack of Robert Vesco's hundred-dollar bills in the briefcase. The money was always kept in a green plastic, zippered bag provided by Peoples National Bank of Denville, New Jersey.

I zipped open the bag. Moussa tried to look over the edge of the lid to see what I was doing. That didn't work so he tried to turn the briefcase around. I held the briefcase still. He got the idea. As I counted out twelve 100-dollar bills I asked the TWA rep to tell Moussa the amount in dollars so there would be no mistakes. He did so. I zippered the money bag closed and shut my briefcase. I handed the money to Moussa one bill at a time. While Moussa was counting the money himself I turned to the TWA rep.

"I have something to say to this shithead," I told him. "And you can translate if you wish." When

Moussa looked up I stuck out my hand and put a smile on my face.

"Mr. Moussa," I said in as pleasant a sounding tone as I could muster, "you are without doubt the scabbiest asshole it has been my misfortune to ever have met." He nodded as we shook hands. He tried to pull his hand back but I held on firmly—very firmly. I wasn't finished. "Cat piss runs in your veins and your brain is made of camel dung. I hope you get boils on your balls, you offspring from a Mongolian gang bang." I turned him loose. He looked to the TWA guy for the translation. The poor guy was in shock. He said something to Moussa but it sure as hell wasn't what I had said. Moussa smiled once more, put the hundred-dollar bills in the folder and left.

The TWA rep and I followed Moussa out. All those traffic controllers who had sat in on the hearing spoke English. They would have either been trained in the U.S. or the U.K. I didn't know what kind of an effect my parting words to Moussa would have on them. When I turned to leave they were all smiling. My one hope is that some day, somehow, one of these guys would set the record straight with Moussa.

While I was gone Pete and the TWA mechanic fueled the Boeing. The troops and the vehicles still surrounded the airplane. Since I came back without a military escort I was free to conduct my business. I sent Chuck to operations, and I went with the TWA man to take care of all the charges. I thanked the TWA rep for all the help he had given me and told him I would be in touch with him from Nairobi in a day or two about overflight clearances on the return trip. I made it clear that under no circumstances would I land again in Egypt. If I had to I would take the long way around.

The interior of Silver Phyllis was like an oven. Dottie had done her best to ease the discomfort with iced drinks. She had opened all the doors of the Boeing in an attempt to capture any breeze that might pass by. Vesco met me at the main entrance the moment I stepped aboard the Boeing.

"When can we get out of here?" he snapped. I told him we'd leave as soon as Chuck got back. I offered to fill him in on what had happened.

"Later," he said. "Right now all I want to do is get the fuck out of this place."

When the start unit came out toward the Boeing it was a signal for the soldiers to get back into their vehicles and depart. I didn't waste any time in getting the hell out of Cairo.

January 4, 1972 0625Z NBO—BEY

Vesco and his party were in and out of Nairobi for the week. They had spent a couple of days "in the bush" at the famous Hotel in the Trees. Dottie and I got adventurous. We rented a VW beetle, intending to drive through one of Kenya's national parks to visit Mt. Kilimanjaro just over the border in Tanzania. Outside of the main cities and towns Kenya teemed with wildlife of every description. We drove around Lake Nakuru, which is in the middle of a huge bird sanctuary.

We had been warned at the entrance to this park to watch out for the Kenyan equivalent of highwaymen. These were small bands of Masai tribesmen who, on the approach of a lone vehicle like ours, would drive their cattle across the road. When the car was slowed down or forced to stop the renegade Masai would rob and sometimes kill the occupants. I really didn't foresee any trouble since we would be traveling between two tourist caravans, each numbering half a dozen Volkswagen minibuses. We would never be more than a mile or two from either group. Each caravan was in the care of an experienced guide who, I assumed, would be armed or at least have firearms at hand. Let's face it. There was always the possiblity of some camera toting tourist getting himself jammed up with something ferocious.

We traveled in a huge circle. Kilimanjaro was at the bottom. The first part of the trip was uneventful. We stopped for an hour or two for lunch and photographs.

We heard more talk about the renegade Masai. Again I felt there was nothing to worry about because I didn't expect to be getting off the main roads. Wrong!

About halfway back to Nairobi, after we had crossed back into Kenya, I saw the road blocked ahead by cattle just as we had been warned. There was no way of going around. I stopped the car. We rolled up the windows and locked the doors. Several Masai men carrying long spears and wearing coarse reddish-brown sheets ran toward the car and surrounded it.

They began to hammer and beat on the car with their spears, screaming at us in what I guess was Swahili. I never shut the engine off. I threw the VW into reverse making certain to spin the wheels enough to throw up a cloud of dust. I'm not a Hollywood stunt man, and I didn't want to break something on the VW and be stranded, but I didn't want my backward progress impeded by one of those Masai under my rear wheels. The short burst of acceleration to get the wheels spinning and the dust rising worked. The Masai in back of the VW scattered. Since I could back away faster than the Masai could run I outdistanced them quickly. I intended to get far enough away to turn and go back the way I came. Before I could do that the Masai screeched to a halt and began running away from me. In seconds, it seemed, they had cleared the cattle from the road and were taking off across the plain. I got out of the car and looked back and saw a Land Rover coming up on us. It contained a couple of park rangers, or whatever they call them, who asked us if we had had any trouble with the Masai. Since we hadn't been robbed there was nothing they could do. They followed us partway back to where we joined up with a caravan heading back to Nairobi.

New Year's Eve was spent at a private party given by some British flight crews we had met. They were all gracious and friendly and tried to show us a good time. We all would have preferred to have been someplace other than Kenya to celebrate the New Year.

Vesco made a couple of appearances in Nairobi during our one-week stay in Kenya. The evening of New

Year's Day I bumped into him in the casino in suburban Nairobi. As I've said, Vesco is a barracks gambler. He likes to make noise. But he was very subdued and disgusted with what he called the tight-ass European manner of gambling in absolute silence. He didn't stay long.

Before Dottie and I had left on our "safari" I had set the wheels in motion for clearance over Egyptian airspace. I had warned our embassy that I would either go over Egypt without incident, my safe passage guaranteed by my own government, or I would accept the Israeli offer of fighter escort over Israel. He didn't like my firmness but then he couldn't do anything about it either, except to work his telex overtime. Which is what he did. I didn't get the guarantee that I had demanded until just before takeoff. The embassy official apparently took me at my word. I had no trouble on the flight back to Beirut.

January 6, 1972 1305Z BEY—LHR

Donald A. Nixon, Jr. came out with the luggage shortly before takeoff for Heathrow Airport in London. The last time we had seen him he was Gil Straub's assistant. Today he exploded into the Boeing looking as if he were about to announce that he had been appointed ambassador to the Court of St. James. The entire crew was gathered in the forward crew lounge of Silver Phyllis. There was no escaping him.

"Hi, gang!" he said. "Great news! Bobby just appointed me his financial advisor, and I'll be traveling with you cats a lot." We demonstrated our joy at this announcement with a sincere display of apathy. But Junior, undaunted, forged ahead. He had some instructions for us for "our guidance."

"I don't want you to feel any different toward me because of my new position," he said. "For the sake of protocol, I expect you to address me as Mr. Nixon when we're with strangers. Among ourselves, of course," he went on, "you can call me Don." He singled out Dottie.

"Dottie," he said, "I want a pair, no make that a couple of pairs of those velour lounging suits like the ones Bobby wears. Color really doesn't matter but I prefer that they be somewhat different from Vesco's. First chance you get. Right? Dottie?" He said all this with a kind of breathless urgency and stifling good fellowship. I couldn't believe that the kid was serious. Calling himself Vesco's financial advisor was a little like calling a saloon swamper a restauranteur.

"I'm sorry, Don," Dottie said with all seriousness, "but those lounging suits came from Neiman-Marcus in Dallas—Texas, you know. As soon as we get back to the United States I'll teletype an order but I'll have to have a requisition from you." Junior whipped out a memo book and made a notation.

"Requisition—right!" he said. "Where do I get the forms?"

"Oh, you'll have to get them from Mr. Dodd," Dottie said, "but just tell him Mr. Vesco said it was all right and you won't have any trouble—I'm sure."

"Cool!" he said, and went about the business of supervising the loading of the Vesco family baggage. Just before he turned away I clicked my heels, bent slightly at the waist and snicked off what used to be called a "zoot salute." If Junior understood the mockery of it, it sure as hell didn't show. Naturally, there were a lot of snide comments by the crew. But it was leavened by the realization that we would have that pompous boob in our hair from now on.

After the Cairo flap, Junior Nixon's behavior was almost welcome, low-comedy relief. On the flight to London the more I thought about Junior the more ridiculous he seemed. It was my custom, when I had some work to do, to do it during one of my infrequent breaks from the flight deck. Shirley Bailey had her onboard secretarial offices temporarily located behind the newly renovated area. On official ICC stationery I used Shirley's IBM Executive to hammer out a truly impressive OPERATIONAL NOTICE TO THE CREW.

FROM: A. L. EISENHAUER, DIRECTOR OF AVIATION
TO: ALL FLIGHT PERSONNEL N11RV
RE: DONALD NIXON, JR., PROCEDURES RELATING TO

EFFECTIVE IMMEDIATELY, ALL CREW WILL ADDRESS JUNIOR NO LONGER AS JUNIOR BUT AS MR. NIXON, NEPHEW OF THE PRESIDENT. IN HIS NEW POST AS FINANCIAL ADVISOR TO MR. VESCO HE HAS REQUESTED TWO PAIRS OF DR. DENTON'S TO HELP HIM RELAX AND ADVISE WHEN ON BOARD THE BOEING. THESE WILL BE PROVIDED AT AN APPROPRIATE TIME AND HUNG IN A SPECIAL AREA FOR QUICK CHANGING IN ORDER TO AID HIM IN ADVISING MR. VESCO. INASMUCH AS HE HAS GIVEN FORMAL NOTICE THAT HE WILL BE HENCEFORTH A FREQUENT PASSENGER WHILE ADVISING MR. VESCO IN FINANCIAL MATTERS, IT IS OF PARAMOUNT IMPORTANCE THAT THE CREW COOPERATE IN EVERY WAY WITH JUNIOR—CORRECTION—MR. DONALD NIXON, JUNIOR, NEPHEW OF THE PRESIDENT—TO FOSTER AND MAINTAIN A PROPER BALANCE OF RESPECT AND FAMILIARITY AMONGST THE FLIGHT STAFF.

IN THIS LAST CONNECTION MR. DONALD NIXON, JUNIOR, NEPHEW OF THE PRESIDENT AND FINANCIAL ADVISOR TO MR. VESCO, HAS GRACIOUSLY WAIVED FORMALITY IN PRIVATE CIRCUMSTANCES. IN SUCH CASES HE HAS STATED THAT HE WILL NOT BE OFFENDED IF ADDRESSED BY MEMBERS OF THE FLIGHT STAFF AS "DON" OR SOME OTHER INTIMATE SOBRIQUET.

ALL FLIGHT PERSONNEL ARE ADMONISHED TO USE THE UTMOST DISCRETION IN CHOOSING THE APPELLATIONS THEY WILL APPLY TO MR. DONALD NIXON, JUNIOR, NEPHEW OF THE PRESIDENT AND FINANCIAL ADVISOR TO MR. VESCO.

6 JAN. '72 (SIGNED) CAPTAIN A. L. EISENHAUER
AIRCRAFT COMMANDER
DIRECTOR OF AVIATION

I posted the notice prominently on the door to the flight deck. Although the door was always secured open the notice was plainly visible not only to those entering the flight deck but to those using the forward lavatories. When Vesco saw it, he almost fell down laughing. I told him I intended to take it down after the flight crew had all seen it.

"Shit, no!" he said. "Leave the goddamn thing where it is. Put a piece of glass over it." The notice stayed up for more than a year. A lot of people all over the world got a chuckle out of reading it, including a member of the Spanish royal family.

Did it offend Donald Nixon, Jr., nephew of the president and financial advisor to Mr. Vesco? He saw it shortly after Vesco had seen it. The silly shit thanked me for my consideration and asked for a copy. To show his uncle?

February 16, 1972 2055Z EWR—IAD—NAS

According to schedule Silver Phyllis returned to Qualitron for modification Phase Two. From January 15 to the 30th she was out of service while Vesco's luxurious office was installed. It included a massive teakwood desk with a leaf that opened it into a large conference table. A secretarial unit, a model of space economy, was right across the aisle from his desk. His personal chair was larger than the one he used as a passenger. It was covered in dark-brown fabric and like his traveling seat had his initials prominently displayed on it. Vesco had exotic intercom facilities. The air-to-ground equipment was yet to be installed.

There were the usual flights for business and for the convenience and pleasure of friends to Europe and the Middle East. On one such flight Vesco visited Malaga, Spain, where he initiated steps to unload onto a Spanish consortium a huge IOS-owned condominium complex which was on the Playa del Sol. This may have been the beginning of dealings in Spain with people who included not only Franco but a brother of the present King Juan Carlos and a number of anti-Castro Cubans.

We left Spain on February 9, 1972, for Newark. There were a couple of flights between Newark and Nassau, the Bahamas, after our return. On February 11 I brought Vesco to Nassau and returned to Newark two days later with his family. Before I left, Vesco had told me that I would get instructions from Shirley Bailey about a couple of passengers I was to bring to Nassau, and a possible stop in Washington, D.C., on the way south.

About three-thirty on the afternoon of February 16 my passengers arrived. In addition to Dick Clay and his wife and son were Harry Sears and his son Ralph. Sears had been, and still was, a power in New Jersey state Republican party politics. He had been a state senator but declined to run for re-election in order to instead become New Jersey campaign manager for Richard Nixon's 1968 run for the presidency. Sears had also tried for the New Jersey governorship but failed. At this time he was New Jersey state finance chairman for Nixon's CREEP. When I first met him he was also one of Vesco's lawyers and served as a director of Vesco's International Controls Corporation.

Next stop was Dulles International Airport outside the nation's capital. We picked up a single passenger, a tall, striking, very well-dressed black man named Arthur McZair. McZair at that time was an assistant to the director of the Small Business Administration, and was in charge of a huge fund which was to provide assistance for minority-business ventures.

Sears had told me who we were picking up and what his position was. It confirmed, again, my judgment that corporate aircraft are a taxpayer hustle especially where government officials and employees are concerned. Vesco had balls to send into the nation's capital the biggest, most noticeable corporate aircraft in the world to pick up a government functionary who exercised a least some control over the disposition of more than two hundred and fifty million tax payer dollars to private businessmen, minority or not.

We landed in Nassau at 7:25 P.M. local time. As usual my passengers were met by cars that took them away.

My usual parking space in Nassau was either at the west side of the ramp near the firehouse or the east side near a hangar that was owned by a local air carrier, Out Island Airways, but leased to Howard Hughes. Hughes was a well enough known figure in his own right. I would have known he was in the Bahamas under any circumstances. All I had to do was read the papers or listen to the local gossip. However, almost from the day he hired me, Vesco had either expressed his admiration of Hughes or, as his international activities increased, bragged about how well he knew Hughes and how often he had met him either in Las Vegas or Nassau.

About midnight of the 16th I got a call from Junior Nixon at the Balmoral Hotel.

"Ike," he said, "Don Roberto is planning a very—uh—delicate trip for tomorrow. I got a list of VIPs. Tell me when you're ready to copy."

"Go ahead, kid," I said. He was silent for a moment. Calling him kid irritated the hell out of him.

"Numero uno," he came back, "is Hanna." Arthur Hanna was deputy prime minister of the Bahamas and the number-one aide to Pindling. He went on to give me some other names, none of which I recognized. He finished up with, "Hey—hey! Get this, Captain, a real live Limey peeress with lots and lots of rocks and a title—Lady Sassoon." I didn't know who Lady Sassoon was and I'm sure he didn't either.

"Is that all?" I asked him.

"Shit no, old buddy!" he said. His voice dropped to a conspiratorial whisper. *"Es mucho mysterioso!"* For Chrissakes! That short stop in Malaga, Spain, had him thinking he was Zorro.

"Hey, Don," I urged him, "don't play games. If you have a name give it to me."

"No can do," he said. "It's not firm. We'll know *mañana*—see ya'."

"Don!" I yelled into the phone. "Wait a goddamn minute! Where the hell are we going?"

"Uh—uh—oh, yeah," he stammered. "I forgot, Captain. It's San Jose, heh—heh."

"Which one, Donald?" I asked him. "There are about 140 San Joses in this part of the world."

"Gee, Ike," he said, "I'll have to find out." I didn't lose any sleep over Junior's secret-agent act. The kid probably got his jollies just saying the letters CIA.

A note from Junior was delivered to my room about nine-thirty the next morning. It read: "Mr. Hanna and party not coming. Mr. Strub (Straub?) not coming.

Lady Sassoon not coming. Change destination Newark. Nixon will be ten minutes late." I would not even have remembered this change in schedule if it were not for what happened later that morning.

I got to the airport about eleven with the crew and was driven directly to the airplane. Since I had a new First Officer I went to operations myself to handle the paper work. When I got back to the Boeing half an hour later I saw a U.S. Customs officer standing at the foot of the steps. It was not unusual to see a U.S. Customs officer at a foreign airport. Maybe the guy got curious about Silver Phyllis. Officially he had no business being where he was. I nodded to him and went up the steps into the aircraft. Inside were three Bahamian immigration officers. They were poking about everywhere lifting seat cushions, opening storage-cabinet doors, even the lavatories.

"What are you looking for?" I asked one of them.

"May I please see your passenger manifest?" one of them asked me. I showed it to him.

"If you'll tell me who or what you're looking for," I said, "maybe I can help."

"Are you certain these are all your passengers?" he asked.

"As far as I know," I said. "If any more show up I'll know as soon as they get here." Their presence on the Boeing was highly irregular for outbound flights. If it was a police matter, the cops would be there. I thought of the U.S. Customs man down on the ramp. There had to be a connection. It wouldn't be the first time that foreign government agents did the dirty work and the bidding of their American counterparts.

"You people don't belong here," I said. "Why don't you tell me what you want—why you're here?"

"Well, sir," he said, "we've had a tip that a very important resident of the islands is to leave today on your airplane."

"Robert Vesco is a very important resident of the islands," I said, "but as far as I know he's not leaving. And if he was it's none of your business—or my own government's."

"We were told that Mr. Howard Hughes is to be a passenger on this aircraft," he said.

"So what?" I said. The man said nothing. I indicated the door. "You can wait outside for him. We have work to do." The three Bahamians went down the steps and spoke to the U.S. Customs officer. Then they all walked back to the terminal.

I was in my seat when the passengers boarded. Dottie brought the manifest to me. There was Milton Meissner and his wife Lolly, Norman LeBlanc, Ken Beaugrand, a young IOS executive, Robbie Batton, an IOS secretary, Harry Sears, and his son Ralph. No Howard Hughes. Gee!

A couple of days later I read that Howard Hughes had, indeed, mysteriously left the Bahamas for Managua, Nicaragua. I know that he didn't leave on the Silver Phyllis even in lower 41. A very close Bahamian associate of mine who worked at the airport and who was in a good position to know what was going on on the island hinted that Vesco had arranged a "good rounder" for Hughes. He showed me a copy of a local newspaper called the *Tribune* dated Friday, February 18, 1972, in which a picture of the Silver Phyllis was shown along with the Hughes-leased hangar.

What spooked the Bahamian immigration people was the American Customs service. Customs service got their wind up because some newspaper reporter claimed he had gotten the tip about Hughes leaving on the Silver Phyllis. In the opinion of my Bahamian friend the whole thing was a deliberate attempt by "somebody" to divert attention from Hughes' real intent to leave the Bahamas by another route. He scoffed at the idea that Hughes would ever travel by boat and asked me if I had remembered a small jet which was parked practically under my wing. I just don't recall that particular airplane. My friend was pretty positive that Hughes had snuck out of the Bahamas while the U.S. Customs guys and the Bahamian Immigration people were sitting around the coffee table wondering what went wrong with the Vesco tip.

A remark made later by Junior brought the Hughes situation into a clearer focus. It also raised more questions than it answered. Junior had stated flatly that Vesco had met with Hughes before he left the island. This meeting may have taken place at the Britannia Beach Hotel before I got back to Nassau on the 16th. But Junior indicated that the meeting took place at the airport and involved "other" people. The only way this meeting could have been held in complete privacy at the airport was either in the Boeing, which was unattended except for a guard on the ramp, or inside Hughes' hangar. It is possible that Hughes was in the hangar before, during, and after the search of the Boeing by Bahamian immigration. Don Nixon, Jr.'s reference to "other people," because of the context in which he said it, could only refer to Sears. But I have never seen any reference to Harry Sears' involvement in the Howard Hughes contribution to the Nixon re-election fund. He was, however, involved with the illegal Vesco contribution. When the news of Vesco's 250,000-dollar gift broke later that year, I wondered whether Harry Sears had brokered not only the Vesco quarter of a million to Nixon's CREEP but Howard Hughes' hundred-thousand-dollar contribution as well.

Junior Nixon did not make the flight back to Newark. He showed up to send us off. He also supervised the loading of the baggage, then advised me that I would be bringing Pat Vesco, Shirley Bailey, and the Vesco children back to Nassau the following day and that he would have two limousines waiting. This sort of activity seemed to be the limit of his services to Robert Vesco. Maybe he was a financial advisor in on-the-job training. From what I saw of him he couldn't advise a three year old how to blow his nose.

I wanted to get word back to Vesco about the search of the Boeing by Bahamian immigration as quickly as possible. I had serious misgivings, but I entrusted the mission to Junior. He listened gravely and assured me that he would transmit my message exactly as I had given it. Vesco never mentioned the incident so I don't know whether or not Junior passed it on. Norman LeBlanc, who made the flight, had stopped to listen in on my conversation with Junior. Eavesdropping was a habit of his. He giggled as he listened and once inside the airplane pumped me for further details. I filled him in and he giggled some more. With Norman the giggle could mean anything—either that he knew some secret or that he knew nothing at all. I asked him what the hell was going on.

"It's very inside, Ike," he said, "very inside. Like—everybody is trying to fuck everybody else. Like—on the surface it's all palsy-walsy between Bobby and the other guy, y'know. Bobby runs a screen for him but he doesn't want to—y'know—reciprocate. But that's okay—y'know—because Bobby's got me—the secret weapon, like, y'know." This was vintage LeBlanc. It was all giggles and bullshit.

"I *don't* know, Norman," I said, "what do you mean?"

"Hughes," he said. "I'm the guy who can—like—fix his wagon. While he's watching Bobby—y'know—he's not watching me." He giggled and winked and went back to the cabin. I didn't know a damn thing more than I had before. But there was a report much later that Gil Straub and not LeBlanc was the one who pushed the Bahamian government into hassling Hughes into leaving the Bahamas permanently. If he did, it was on Vesco's specific instructions. In my opinion Nattering Norman didn't have brains enough to pour piss out of a boot—even after a training session.

February 22, 1972 2210Z NAS—EWR

Norman LeBlanc's hints about something going on between Hughes and Vesco tied in with some other rumors I had heard about Vesco's ambition to control gambling in the Bahamas. Junior had also been dropping this brand of sparrow shit. He let me know with wise looks that he knew that Vesco was "moving in." When I saw Hal Simpson, IOS security chief, boarding the airplane, I was surprised. I had met Hal a number of times in Geneva. We got along well. But Hal was the kind of guy who kept his mouth shut about his job.

It was Junior, again, who shot his mouth off. He told me that Hal had been flown over from Geneva to check on the security setup at the Paradise Island Casino.

Vesco, as was his habit, was the last to arrive at the Boeing. On this occasion he was accompanied by a man whom I was to see a lot of over the next several months. Vesco made a point of introducing the man to me and telling me precisely that.

Richard Chadwick Pistell has been described as an international promoter, and sometimes, as an international con man. He was with us all over Central America and Europe and was one of the happiest passengers I ever carried. He was a storyteller, a *bon vivant* and all-around good-time Charlie. He looked like a hammered-down fullback. He had a crushing handshake and a loud booming voice. He wore flashy but meticulously neat clothes. I never saw him drunk or angry. Whatever he was, he was one hell of a nice guy. Between Pistell and the crew it was a case of friendship at first sight.

It is a rule of mine never to pry into the background or affairs of my passengers. With Dick Pistell you didn't have to. He was his own biggest booster and talked freely of all the important people he knew around the world. It wasn't name dropping. You could make book on what he said. And this is what separated him from the bullshit artists.

February 28, 1972 1400Z EWR—PBI

Like every other get-rich-quicker, Robert Lee Vesco yearned for respectability. And he thought he could buy it. One of the most prestigious world organizations is the World Wildlife Fund, which is headed by Prince Bernhard of the Netherlands. It numbers among its exclusive membership some of the wealthiest and most influential persons of the international elite. One of the society's means of fund raising is an auction of items donated by the rich, the very rich, and the super rich. It is a supremely posh hoedown.

Vesco, who had been proposed and accepted as a member of the exclusive 1001 Club, had been looking forward to the auction to be held in Palm Beach that year. He intended to make the biggest splash of all the big fish in a very small pool. The invited guests arrive by yacht and private aircraft. In Vesco's book it was a case of big is best. He made one hell of an impression arriving in the Silver Phyllis. He paid the highest price for any object offered at the auction. He made a splash all right. The only problem was that in the news stories in the local paper the following day his name was misspelled. So much for store-bought class.

March 8, 1972 1340Z EWR—YZ

Donald A. Nixon, Jr., financial advisor to Robert L. Vesco, might have at times been an all-around pain in the ass and a self-made object of ridicule to those thrown into frequent association with him, but because of his built-in brashness and his status as the nephew of the president, he could pass through gates closed to ordinary mortals. He had a quick ear for gossip and rumor and a quicker mouth to spread what he heard.

Junior proved to have pretty accurate information about Vesco's plans for Paradise Island. There is no doubt that he picked up the information in the casino by accident. I could believe that the pitmen and the croupiers and even the current heavy management regarded him as the invisible man or considered him as not worth even lowering their voices for.

Young Nixon spent every free moment—and he had quite a lot of them between advisements—in the casino. He could wander around with the freedom of a puppy. One evening he accosted me while I was playing blackjack, waiting for Vesco. I was having a so-so run and was about ready to quit when Junior spotted me from across the casino. He smiled that Alfred E. Neumann smile of his, raised his arm, and yelled, "Hey—Capitan!" He bounded over to my table. He hooked his arm in mine.

"Ike," he said, "I've got a present for you." He pulled at me. Frankly I was embarrassed. Rather than tear his arm off at the shoulder I went along with him.

The blackjack tables in the Paradise Island Casino are laid out in a sort of horseshoe. The spaces between the tables are bridged by velvet ropes. There is a wide gap, also bridged by a velvet rope, facing the crap tables. Inside the horsehoe are, including the dealers, a number of pitmen who move around watching the play and the dealers. There is also the pit boss who watches the watchers and handles the chips. He usually is positioned near a console in which chips, cards, and other paraphernalia are stored.

Junior walked me around to the large gap in the horseshoe. He disengaged his arm from mine, unhooked the rope, and stepped into the pit area. With the balls of a burglar he strode up to the console, opened the door, took out a box of something and closed it again. Not one of the pitmen moved to intervene. The pit boss, who looked like a very hard case, actually stepped back and watched. Nixon showed the pit boss the box and apparently got his approval. Nixon brought the pit boss over and introduced him to me. Then he handed me a box of fifty fine Havana cigars. If it had been anybody else he would have been thrown through the wall.

Junior Nixon was typical of the kind of amateur that Vesco seemed to surround himself with. And this includes people like LeBlanc, Gil Straub, Dodd and Dick Clay. None of these people had the kind of background or experience that would qualify them for a top position, similar to the ones they occupied in the Vesco organization, with, say a conglomerate like ITT or Gulf and Western. They were purely Vesco creations and without Vesco to tell them what to do and often how to do it, they would flounder. I didn't need Junior to tell me that Vesco wanted to take over the Paradise Island Casino. Vesco told me himself—and so did Dodd, and so did Straub, and so did LeBlanc. Vesco's general staff was loaded with loose lips, besides which it was common talk on the island.

Taking over a casino is not like buying a piece of real estate or gobbling up a going corporation. Gambling means the Mob and the fact that a government is a major partner doesn't change anything. At that time the Bahamas were still under British rule and under the administration of a colonial governer-general. But business in the islands was controlled absolutely by a tightly knit group of lawyers, politicians, and businessmen known as the Bay Street Boys. The government granted permissions and issued licenses and permits but it was the Bay Street Boys who decided who would do business—of any kind—on the Islands. Huntington Hartford found this out the hard way.

The Bay Street Boys, of course, were not at all fond of the idea of independence for the Bahamas. They knew it was inevitable and that the next best thing would be to control the new government. The man they least wanted to head up the new government was the present prime minister, Pindling.

Vesco had told me that he intended to put Pindling in his hip pocket. If Pindling were elected, he would break the power of the Bay Street Boys which, in Vesco's opinion, would leave him a clear track. The only other stumbling block he ever mentioned was Howard Hughes. His intent, if he couldn't outmaneuver Hughes in buying not only the casino but the Britannia Beach Hotel and other choice properties, was to convince Hughes to form a partnership with him. Hughes had stated publicly that the best advice his father had ever given him was to "never take a partner if you can help it." There had been rumors that Hughes had been borrowing money for some of his hotel/gambling operations. That seemed kind of farfetched to me but Vesco apparently gave the rumors great credibilty. And maybe with good reason. Vesco could not have achieved what he had without reliable information. What he didn't mention was the Mob.

But Junior did. He used to delight in pointing out men in the casino who, he said, were "connected." Junior wasn't telling me anything I didn't suspect.

They were not the pitmen and dealers. They were the well-dressed quiet ones who stayed away from the tables. They were the ones who would disappear behind locked doors with Vesco.

Hughes had boasted that his entrance into the gambling scene in Las Vagas would drive out the mobsters. It never happened. Even Hughes, I am certain, had to make his deal with the "wise guys," even on Paradise Island.

There are people who get a vicarious thrill out of rubbing elbows with gangsters. LeBlanc was one of them and so was Dick Clay. But rubbing elbows with them and doing business with them are two entirely different propositions. I just couldn't see the likes of LeBlanc, Clay, and Straub being presented as principals in any negotiations. That had to be Vesco's personal domain. In Vesco's plan Straub and LeBlanc would be the out-front men, roles they could fill perfectly as long as they did what they were told and did not attempt any independent thinking. Tweedledum and Tweedledee. LeBlanc occasionally would break out of the corral, usually with negative and sometimes disastrous results.

Such an excursion almost cost him his life a year later. He was nearly killed when his car ran out of control and crashed into a stand of trees. The way I got the story was that the car was ready and waiting for him with the engine running in front of the casino. LeBlanc hopped in, put the car into drive, and stepped on the accelerator. The car shot forward at full throttle. LeBlanc tried to control the car without success. It was found later that the throttle, power steering, and brakes had been "fixed." The reason? LeBlanc had come on too strongly with those well-dressed quiet men.

If, as has been reported a number of times, Vesco was dealing with the Mob, he kept his lines well hidden. The reports had to stem from the obvious fact that organized crime controlled gambling on Paradise Island. The LeBlancs and the Straubs and the clutch of lawyers that Vesco always had handy could deal with the Bahamian government. That was strictly show. Vesco either had a *consiglieri* to represent him to the

Mob or filled that role himself. Either way, by simple reasoning, Vesco had to deal with the wise guys.

This certainly would not be beyond his capability. Vesco, as young as he was at the time—about 37—was no accidental millionaire. As far as I could see he was calling all the shots. In his business manipulations, the corporate take-overs, he made the decisions. For all their brilliance, Meissner and Strickler were merely advisors. They, along with the others in the Vesco high command, were totally useless when it came to dealing with the Mob.

There are ground rules for corporate piracy—all legal. Vesco could euchre Dodd out of his own company, Captive Seal, or destroy Burgess of ELS and not have to worry that either man would stick a knife in his guts or blow his brains out with four shots in the back of the head. Vesco knew precisely what he would be dealing with and who he would be dealing with and what standard industry procedures were.

Junior Nixon was in a class by himself. There is not one practical business reason why Vesco would allow himself to be saddled with such a total incompetent. Junior was a hostage. Vesco treated him with contempt even though he allowed him to assume whatever pose he wanted. As long as he didn't get in the way.

It was against this background of Vesco's Paradise Island ambitions that the March 8, 1972, flight from Newark to Toronto took on significance.

There were only two passengers, Vesco and James M. Crosby. Crosby was chairman of Resorts International, formerly Mary-Carter Paint Company, which bought Paradise Island in 1966 from George Huntington Hartford II. Hartford, the A & P heir, had dumped about thirty million dollars into what was once called Hog Island to create a lush vacation and gambling resort. He ran afoul of the Bay Street Boys and took a bath of twenty million dollars when he sold 75 percent of his holdings to Mary Carter for twelve million. Crosby immediately got into bed with the Bay Street Boys and got the certificate of exemption denied to Hartford. That certificate gave Mary Carter's Paradise Enterprises Limited exclusive gambling privileges.

In 1968 Paradise Enterprises Limited built the casino and a two-million-dollar toll bridge that connected Paradise Island and Nassau. Crosby also got into bed with the Mob. It was logical. There was nobody else around who knew how to run a casino. The first manager of the casino was a man named Eddie Cellini who, with his brother Dino, was reported to be tied in with Meyer Lansky. Lansky controls big-time gambling in the United States and very likely in Europe and around the Mediterranean. The man who got Vesco and Crosby together on the possible purchase of the casino was Dick Pistell.

Crosby had his Hughes connections too. In 1969 Mary Carter Paints made a strong effort to take over Pan American World Airways. The bid was frustrated when Congress passed a law barring airline ownership to anyone, or any entity, that did not have five years' commercial airline-operation experience. It had been reported that Crosby, operating through Mary Carter, was actually fronting for Howard Hughes, who had recently divested himself of TWA and wanted to get back into the airline business. The act of Congress was therefore aimed directly at Hughes.

Now here was Crosby, cheek by jowl with Vesco, who was in competition with Hughes for the casino. It seems improbable that Hughes, who had been living in the Bahamas for more than a year, would not have either bought the casino or made a very strong bid for it before the arrival of Vesco. Again, according to rumor, it was the Mob who dictated who would own the casino. And the Mob had no love for Howard Hughes. He couldn't be bought, and he couldn't be muscled.

One of the key moves in Vesco's plan was to buy the toll bridge. Once he owned it, he could shut it down and close off the heavy flow of tourist traffic to the tables and the hotel. The boats and light aircraft that operated between Nassau and Paradise simply could not bring in enough high rollers to keep the casino solvent.

Weeks before the Toronto flight Junior had stated that Vesco was going to buy the bridge. I remember kidding him about it.

"For Chrissakes, Don," I told him. "If Bobby wants a bridge, why doesn't he buy a decent one like the Brooklyn Bridge or the Oakland Bay Bridge?" He took me seriously.

"They wouldn't do him any good down here, Ike," he said.

"I hadn't thought of that, Don," I said, and let the matter drop before things got even more ridiculous.

During the seventy-minute flight between Newark and Toronto, Vesco and Crosby sat across from each other in Vesco's newly installed office. For the only time I can remember Vesco ordered that nobody come back to his office. No drinks and no food were served. The discussion was heavy and nonstop.

We shut the engines down in Toronto at exactly 9:50 A.M. Vesco and Crosby, still talking, disappeared into the terminal building. Vesco came back alone 2½ hours later. I had already filed a flight plan for my return trip to Newark. Vesco told me that we would be going to Washington, D.C., first for a few hours, and winked at me as if I understood what he was getting at. I notified ground control on my radio of the change from Newark to Washington and received a revised clearance.

About 25 minutes out of Toronto Vesco sent Dottie McCarty forward to summon me to his office. The desk was covered with papers, many of which were filled with numbers and notations in his handwriting. He had worked out a flight schedule for the next week. He wanted to know if I had any inspections coming up that would interfere with his travel plans. I told him the airplane was in good shape. He made it clear that it was very important that he be in London, Beirut, and Munich on the dates he had scribbled down on a piece of paper. I assured him that there would be no problems barring the unforeseen. He relaxed a little.

"You know, Ike, I don't have a single sonofabitch I can count on to do what has to be done," he said, "except you. And I can't use you for what I have in mind. Jesus! I wish I was two people. This thing with Crosby is big—and very hairy. But Crosby's all right. He's got balls and he knows who can pay the freight. It's those shitheads in Washington." He went into his Ollie-the-dragon act. "Larry (Richardson) just doesn't have the balls to stand up to a guy like Stans, and Mitchell (attorney general) would eat him alive." He twisted his neck again. "Goddamnit, I want a fucking guarantee for my money." He sat up straight and looked at me across the desk and smiled as if he realized he had said too much. He didn't need to tell me that the session was over.

We landed at Dulles International Airport at 1:35 P.M. local Washington time. Vesco returned to the Silver Phyllis at a little after seven that same evening with Larry Richardson in tow. Vesco was not in the best of moods and Richardson looked as if he had been thoroughly chewed out. I learned later that Vesco had met with both Stans and Mitchell and wrangled over whether his contribution to CREEP would be in cash or by check. Vesco also demanded a guarantee that Mitchell would stop an investigation of Vesco by the SEC. Vesco eventually paid out 200,000 dollars in cash and another 50,000 by check—a story in itself—but never got his guarantee.

On March 13, Vesco, Meissner, Straub, and another passenger named Parker flew to Beirut, Lebanon. Vesco and his party disappeared into the city. He had suggested that I take a look at the Casino Liban, the biggest gambling casino in the world, and to be sure to take in the floor show. I'd been in Beirut before but had never seen the famous casino nor its spectacular floor show—the biggest in the world.

I was literally overwhelmed. The casino is perched on a hill overlooking the Mediterranean. I saw it at night bathed in what looked like a thousand searchlights. But it is the floor show that gives the casino its reputation. It makes anything in Las Vegas look like community theater. There were hundreds of performers, dancers, swimmers, acrobats, and musicians. Beautiful girls and muscular men, painted gold and silver, were suspended from the ceiling. The stage surrounded the patrons. There were waterfalls, canals, boats, and live animals. It was an extravaganza the likes of which I had never seen in my life. And it was primarily designed for the diversion and entertainment of the wealthy oil sheikhs. I had wondered why Vesco had made it a point to have me go to the casino. The floor show erased any question from my mind.

But, two days later, while I was sitting in my room at the Phoenicia Hotel, I got a strange phone call. A French-accented voice speaking excellent English told me to stay in my room.

"Is there anyone with you?" the Frenchman asked. I assured him I was alone. He said that "we" will be up shortly to your room. "We have something to give you."

Ten minutes later there was a knock on the door. I opened it and saw two men. One I recognized as an old friend, a Lebanese, whom I will not identify for obvious reasons. The other was a tall, elegant-looking man in his forties, apparently the man who spoke to me on the telephone. They behaved as if they were anxious about being seen and pushed into the room. If my friend hadn't been there or it had been somebody else with the Frenchman I would have knocked somebody on his ass. I take a dim view of this Hollywood-style foreign-intrigue horseshit. The Frenchman took a chubby tickler-file folder from a briefcase and handed it to me.

"Captain Eisenhauer," he said very politely, "I was instructed to deliver this to you." He obviously expected me to examine the folder and its contents. Some of the papers were in Arabic. Some were in French. Some were in English. There were several large sheets folded twice that were filled with numbers. There were one or two small bits of paper with names written on them. None of it meant anything to me.

"What is it?" I asked. Both the Frenchman and my friend who had said not a word since I opened the door looked surprised.

"These are the records from the casino," the Frenchman said.

"Well, why'd you bring them to me?" I asked. I looked at my friend but he kept his mouth shut.

"I was told to deliver these papers to you," the

Frenchman insisted. "I was also to make certain that this was the information that was wanted."

"Who told you?" I asked. He made a gesture as if to say, "I can't tell you." I sat there not knowing what to do next. The Frenchman took the folder from my hands.

"Let me explain them to you," he said. He opened the folder and spread the papers all over the coffee table. It took hours and an entire bottle of Scotch, but by the time he'd finished explaining, I had gotten one hell of an education on how one gambling casino was used as a cover for illegal money manipulation involving individuals, governments, and corporations. I learned how the skim works and began to get some idea of why Robert Vesco would be interested in a piece of this kind of action. I didn't realize then that what he was really going after was the whole goddamn works.

The material that the Frenchman gave me was obviously intended for Vesco and had been taken—surreptitiously. As far as I could make out, and from the Frenchman's explanation only part of which I understood, the file contained not only actual records of the play in the casino on a daily basis for all games, but copies of contracts between the casino operators and those who provided services to the casino. One document listed in precise detail all the shareholders in the casino and how much each received from the reported gross income. Another document contained specifics on splits, cuts, and table-level skim involving pitmen, croupiers, headwaiters, and the like. I learned, for example, that all tips given by players to the tablemen belonged not to the man who gets the tip but to the organization through which he got his job—the Mob. As to the names found on the various bits and pieces of paper scattered throughout the file—the Frenchman told me that these were people who shared a skim that exceeded by far the reported gross income of the casino.

The Frenchman spoke as if I was supposed to understand everything he said. Most of it was unintelligible to me. But even the little that I did comprehend indicated that everybody involved in any way with the Casino Liban, the government, the workers, the officials, the investors, and quite a number of high rollers all made money. It seemed to me that here was one big conspiracy in which each participant knew what he was getting officially and also knew how much everybody was stealing. As long as the balance was maintained everybody was happy. The croupier, for example, who had to turn his tips over to his union, invariably found a way to siphon off something for himself, the Frenchman said.

I could see why the Frenchman and my friend were nervous. Men have been killed to protect information like this. I began to wonder if I was being set up—for what, I couldn't tell. There were some very important names thrown about. There was also a lot of innuendo about high-level, big-money skullduggery involving the oil millionaires, Air France, government officials, and other governments, including the good old U.S.A.

This seemed to be the core of what the Frenchman was telling me. All the numbers and the profit-and-loss information he threw at me, were supportive of something he seemed afraid to say directly—that the Casino Liban was a conduit through which flowed multimillions of dollars, pounds, and francs, ownership of which was known to only a very few.

The most exciting game in the world, especially for the rich and the crooked, is to avoid paying taxes. The search for hiding places, "laundries," and safe havens is constant and often frantic. The essential thing is that the money that is hidden or disguised must be kept available to the owner on demand. It doesn't do anybody any good buried in a pot in the backyard.

What the Frenchman detailed was a system by which any law in any country having to do with the control of money, especially out of the country, could be flouted with absolute immunity to being discovered. The key to the system was organization, which was Vesco's speciality.

To cite one single example, IOS was used by large-scale investors to hide enormous sums of black money, but since IOS had branches throughout the world and thereby generated a constant traffic of people, paper, and cash, money deposited in one country for example was available in another. Because of its operation IOS could also physically transport cash deposits for a client without that client's name appearing on a single document. This could be very convenient for, say, a politician who did not want it known that he was sending money out of his own country against the day he would retire from politics, even if he were getting rich honestly. By investing in IOS in his own country he was acting legally and, in principle at least, his money was staying home where it was being used for the good of the country. But the politician's investment gave him a line of credit anywhere that IOS had an office, or even a bank affiliation. This is what Vesco wanted IOS for. When IOS began to falter, Vesco immediately began to look for another device. It was obvious to me from the Frenchman's lecture that casino operation was Vesco's answer.

In connection with this I knew that Vesco was after Mideast Airlines, as his courier carrier. Because of certain international practices regarding confidentiality of company communications, which included not only interoffice correspondence but even large loads of freight, Vesco saw how great sums of cash could be freely moved wherever he wanted it. On more than one occasion Vesco had hinted that he would soon have an airline for me to run. I dismissed his boast, remembering the Golden West disaster.

My two visitors left. I was stuck with the folder. I had the feeling I should do something about security but I just stuck it in my briefcase. The next afternoon I got a handwritten memo from the Frenchman, which my Lebanese friend gave to me at the airplane. It was a sketchy outline of how the take-over of the Casino Liban could be accomplished.

He continued to believe that I was a principal in whatever was afoot. Vesco arrived with Straub and Meissner and a number of IOS executives who apparently had been in Beirut at Vesco's orders. Later developments proved that Vesco's visit to Beirut was for the purpose of negotiating for his acquisition of Intra Bank, which subsequently fell through. It was through Intra Bank that Vesco would not only gain ultimate control of the Casino Liban but also provide himself with the cover for his money manipulations and the financing of all his other casino ventures. I told him about the folder and the memo. He gave me a letter that he had written to Dr. Lucien Dahdah, chairman of Intra Investment Company, parent of Intra Bank. The letter, dated that same day, March 16, 1972, outlined in detail Vesco's investment offer. It helped to explain partially the Frenchman's visit. But I never found out why the documents were delivered to me or if it was at Vesco's orders. They were never mentioned again.

We returned to Newark from Munich on March 18, 1972. On March 21, Vesco made another trip to Washington, this time with Frank Beatty, financial vice-president of ICC. On March 30, I flew Vesco with his family and a load of passengers to Nassau. It was right after this that the matter of Vesco's contribution to Richard Nixon's 1972 political war chest came to a head.

13

April 6, 1972 1900Z NAS—EWR

Somebody is a liar—a perjurer.

I've read some of the testimony, a lot of newspaper accounts, and a description in a book about Robert Vesco—all about how 200,000 dollars of Vesco's cash got to Maurice Stans' office at 1701 Pennsylvania Avenue in Washington, D.C., on April 10, 1972.

At their trial Maurice Stans and John Mitchell claimed that the money was "constructively" on hand before April 7, 1972. Congress had passed a law that required all political contributions from whatever source to be publically identified. This law was to take effect on April 7, 1972. Prior to this contributors were guaranteed privacy and anonymity.

According to testimony in the Mitchell-Stans trial and later during the Senate Watergate hearings the amount and manner of Vesco's contribution had been discussed for well over a month, perhaps even longer. The impression one gets from the public record is that the amount involved—up to half a million dollars—was some kind of a big deal. Not so.

Consider. A few months earlier Vesco had been able to scrounge up two million dollars in cash in a matter of hours, which sat in a limousine outside St. Antoine prison while he waited to find out what his bail would be. It cost a half a million dollars just to pretty up the front *half* of his airplane. He could drop 40,000 dollars at the crap table in a single evening. The amount in question was, by Vesco's standards, walking-around money. At the first mention of a contribution to the Nixon campaign in 1972, Vesco could have had the cash in twenty minutes in whatever denominations were needed. There was no necessity, not even the slightest, for the matter of delivery to have gotten "down to the wire." Vesco wanted it that way. He engineered it. Vesco knew perfectly well that the kind of people who hustle contributions to political campaigns are impressed by numbers that he regards as piddling. And he's right. They made a big thing out of a lousy hundred grand from Howard Hughes, whose hotel bill for one year was ten times that.

The record shows that Vesco wanted to be an "up-front" contributor. This meant that he wanted his old buddy, the president of the United States, to know how much he was in for. And he had good reason—the SEC investigation. Vesco was a pretty good appraiser and the half million was his estimate of what it would cost to short-circuit the SEC. I'm convinced he would have doubled or tripled the amount if necessary. But everything is relative and half a mill was more than enough to dazzle the shit out of the grubby hustlers at CREEP.

The last time Vesco gave money to Nixon, he was buying political futures. I've already mentioned the 25,000 that I knew about in 1968. The total amount of Vesco's '68 contribution was double that and he was a hell of a lot less wealthy than he was in 1972. It bought him a seat on the dais at the Al Smith Memorial Dinner in New York along with President Johnson and President-elect Nixon. It also bought him an invitation to Nixon's inaugural ball and a seat in the presidential box at the Rose Bowl. The half million he was offering to the 1972 Nixon campaign would cost the Nixon administration a hell of a lot more than fun and games and a plate of roast beef, potatoes, and peas.

April 6, 1972, was the last day on which secret contributions could be made to candidates for public office. On that date Robert Vesco was in Nassau. So was Howard Cerney, one of his attorneys. In his book *Vesco*, Hutchison states that on April 5 Ralph Dodd phoned Harry Sears at his law office in Boonton, N.J., to tell him that the first half of Vesco's donation was en route. He doesn't explain what he means. Trial testimony revealed that Vesco would give 200,000 dollars in cash before April 7 and 50,000 dollars by check after. This ploy was intended to be a diversion. It would be expected that Vesco would contribute to Nixon and fifty grand was a big enough number to be impressive yet small enough not to arouse suspicion by curious parties such as Democrats or the SEC.

If it were true that 250,000 dollars were on their way, there was no reason why the money could not have been on Stans' desk in Washington early on the day of April 6. Hutchison does not state, nor does anybody else, where the cash originated and how it got from the point of origin to the point where it was taken possession of by Harry Sears and Larry Richardson, who delivered it to Stans on April 10, 1972.

Hutchison claims that Dodd "was instructed in a call from the Bahamas to pick up the money at Barclays Bank International and deliver it to Fairfield." Deliver it to whom? There was nobody there. To make matters more confusing Hutchison states that on April 6, the new law's cutoff date, Howard Cerney "hired a 270-pound private detective, Philip Beck, to accompany Dodd to Fairfield with the cash." Hutchison says that Beck was armed for the assignment and that he and Dodd entered Barclay's Wall Street branch just before the 3:00 P.M. closing and "saw the cash stashed in a corner behind the tellers' cages." According to Hutchison the money was in hundred-dollar bills wrapped in brown paper. Hutchison then goes on to state that the money was "loosely placed in an old brown leather briefcase" that Dodd carried. Dodd and Beck drove out to Jersey with the money to "Fairfield Airport, adjoining the International Controls headquarters." Hutchison states that a taxi was waiting to take

Beck back to the city and that as the taxi pulled away Beck saw Dodd "driving off with the money in the direction of the New Jersey hills." He follows that immediately with the news that Dodd took the money to Vesco's office and left it there. Bullshit—A to Z.

Let's take the last item first. If Dodd drove the money to Vesco's office, he would have traveled no more than a mile from *Caldwell* Airport, not Fairfield. The New Jersey hills are at least ten miles west of the airport and can't be seen from there.

Next is the matter of the 270-pound detective who served as an armed escort for Ralph Dodd. From the day I went to work for Vesco, cash money in large amounts was about as commonplace as paper clips. It was not unusual for Pat Vesco to carry as much as 60,000 dollars in an expensive tote bag when traveling. I've carried as much as 40,000. And so has Dodd. And never with an armed guard. The money was always carried in a standard executive briefcase or an attaché case.

But let's accept, in general, Hutchison's version of how the 200,000 that eventually wound up in Stans' safe got to New Jersey. Discounting the improbability of a heap of hundred-dollar bills amounting to 200 grand tossed in the corner of Barclays Bank in New York, it's too coincidental that the two men arrived to collect the boodle just before closing time. The whole operation has all the earmarks of a setup. Banks just don't leave money around like that. There is no way that Philip Beck or anybody else could have spotted hundred-dollar bills in brown-paper wrappers from a teller's cage.

The 200,000 dollars left Nassau at two in the afternoon on April 6, 1972, aboard the Silver Phyllis. It arrived at Newark Airport at 4:35 P.M. on the same day. Of this I am absolutely certain. It's the only thing that makes any sense whatsoever. I don't know who carried the money aboard but the briefcase containing it was stowed with other briefcases in the carry-on baggage rack in the forward crew-lounge area. It was carried on by somebody who knew that the Customs agents at Newark Airport never inspected businessmen's briefcases on milk runs from Nassau. The cash itself came from the casino, which would have no qualms about honoring a Vesco request for a 200,000-dollar line of credit. As for Howard Cerney, who has been identified elsewhere as having a hand in the transfer of the funds and whom Hutchison says hired Philip Beck, he was in Nassau on April 6 and made the flight back to Newark with Robert Vesco.

Considering all of this, I'd like to know what the hell "constructively" in hand *really* means. On the day that the money was supposed to be in Ralph Dodd's possession, it was still aboard the Boeing, an hour out of Nassau.

It's barely within the realm of possiblities that Barclays Bank would turn over that much money to Dodd on Vesco's behalf in such a casual manner in order that the CREEP deadline could be met "constructively." It might even be that the 200,000 on the Boeing was meant to go back to Barclays in New York. If the money had been picked up the day before by Dodd, that would have made some sense. But Dodd allegedly picked up the money only an hour and a half before the Boeing arrived at Newark. The hour-and-a-half difference didn't mean a thing. Even at 3:00 P.M. Dodd was too late for Stans. And at 4:35—actually it was 4:55 after Customs was cleared—it was too late to get any money back to Barclays. This would mean that 400,000 dollars would be sitting in limbo in New Jersey until Monday, April 10.

The original half million that Vesco offered was the bait. The 200,000 dollars' cash was the hook. Vesco knew what the law was. But he knew that the Nixon gang couldn't see past those dollars. They didn't realize that if that money were declared to have been illegally received, Nixon campaign managers would be accomplices in a criminal act.

If the money that was given to Stans, part of which incidentally helped to finance the Watergate break-in, actually came up on the Boeing, where does Philip Beck fit into the picture? Where does Ralph Dodd fit into the picture? At the time that Dodd was alleged to have been acting for Vesco as a courier he had no business association with Vesco or ICC. He had quit some weeks earlier and was associated with a New York brokerage firm. In fact he was at that very time engaged in a bitter dispute with Vesco over his severance pay. This was Vesco's alibi.

Whether Howard Cerney hired Beck before he arrived in Nassau or while he was there makes no difference. He would be a witness to the fact that Dodd appeared to receive 200,000 dollars before 3:00 P.M. on the 6th of April. Harry Sears testified that he telephoned Stans in Washington on April 6 to tell him that Vesco's money was on its way. Stans claimed that there was no way that he could accept the money that day. No matter how you slice it, Vesco's 200,000 dollars was not in the possession of any member of CREEP until eleven on the morning of April 10, 1972. How anybody could construe a telephone call as representing "constructive" delivery is beyond me. That has to rank up there with the other great American motto: "My check is in the mail." The next time my bank hassles me I'll tell them to honor that over-drawn check because sufficient funds are "constructively" in their possession. Yeah!

Another piece of the puzzle is that the delivery of the money took place on Monday, April 10, 1972. The final date for legal, secret contributions, April 6, fell on a Thursday and yet three full days passed before the money made that short trip between Fairfield, New Jersey, and 1701 Pennsylvania Avenue in Washington, D.C. Transportation was no problem. We not only had the Boeing, but we had a jet helicopter and half a dozen other twin-engine aircraft available. Also, Friday was a business day. CREEP offices were open. The answer has to be found in Stans' availability. Vesco's money was not about to be handed over to anyone except Stans or the The Big Enchilada himself, John Mitchell.

There were two reasons for this. One was to keep the knowledge of Vesco's contribution inside a very small circle of people. The other was to directly involve Mitchell and Stans with Vesco. The money would not leave Fairfield until either one or both of these men were on hand to take possession—after April 6. Just the way Vesco planned it.

To highlight Vesco's attitude toward his 200,000 dollars, we should take note that he left for Europe on Saturday evening, April 8, 1972, and didn't return until the 14th of April. Of course this also might have been part of the "game plan." He would be far removed from where Larry Richardson and Harry Sears were doing his dirty work with John Mitchell and Maurice Stans. The day after Vesco returned from Europe, Silver Phyllis went to California for Phase Three of her modification. This was when the "fun room" was installed. This section contained the much-touted discothèque and bar with its flight-stabilized barstools, beaded curtains, parquet dance floor, exotic lighting, quadraphonic stereo, strobe lights, black lights, and oversized beanbag loungers. It would be christened on the night of the 1972 Al Smith Memorial Dinner, to be held again at the Waldorf-Astoria Hotel in New York with Robert Vesco in black tie and within arm's reach of his buddy Richard Nixon.

May 16, 1972 0355Z JFK—NCE—BEY

The Port Authority station wagon sped across the ramp, made a buttonhook turn, and screeched to a stop at the foot of the steps leading to the main entrance of the Boeing. I was on the top landing, watching for Vesco's arrival. The approach speed of the station wagon had been strictly nonstandard. It looked like something out of a Kojak serial. For a second I thought something might be wrong. But only for a second. The doors of the station wagon popped open and Vesco and Dick Pistell practically fell out onto the ramp. They were starched. They weren't falling down drunk; they were loose and happy, and their gyroscopes weren't quite up to speed. Almost immediately two other people—both women—emerged from the station wagon. They appeared sober but they were giggly as hell. I had to wait until the four of them negotiated the steps before I got a good look at the women. They looked like a couple of stage extras from a second-rate production of Carmen. They wore flouncy dresses, the bosoms open almost to their belly buttons. One of them, in shiny black silk, sported a large fabric rose at the bottom of the vee. She looked like she had been shot in the stomach. They both had inky black hair and deep brown eyes. They weren't the prettiest things ever to come out of the shadows. Vesco had a silly grin on his face. His diction was mushy.

"All set for B'root, Ike?" he asked. He turned slightly to the girls. "That's in Leb'non."

"Goddamn right!" Pistell said. He made a flourish toward the two women. "Captain," he said, "give us a good smooth ride, if you will. We gotta lotta work to do and we don't want our sekaterries to get seasick—I mean, airsick." He giggled and poked Vesco in the ribs with his elbow. Vesco giggled.

"I'll fly low and slow, Dick," I said.

"Vunderful!" he said. He ushered the girls toward the rear of the Boeing, waited for Vesco to follow, and tagged on the end of the little parade waving his arms and shouting, "Vunderful! Vunderful!"

Dottie McCarty went back to serve drinks and get the names of our two passengers for the manifest. It turned out that they were sisters and that only one of them could speak any English. Just as I turned to tell the engineer to turn number three, I heard Pistell's booming voice.

"*Qué pasa*, baby?" he hollered. Fiesta time.

The new arrivals were totally unexpected. Vesco had called me at my home in Denville about six o'clock that evening to tell me he and Dick Pistell would leave for Beirut as soon as they could split from the Al Smith Memorial Dinner. I was to dead-head the Boeing from Newark to JFK where he and Pistell would board sometime before midnight.

I never found out where or when the two "sekaterries" were engaged. And I'm positive that Vesco and Pistell didn't tank up at the Memorial Dinner. Pistell is the kind of guy who would get itchy at such formal affairs and would duck out before the orating starts. I could just picture the two of them bouncing around the Upper East Side "employment agencies" conducting interviews.

About midnight Dottie served dinner and, later, drinks. About 2:00 A.M. Vesco told her to make up the beds.

One thing I will say for Robert Vesco is that most of the time he made an effort at decorum where Dottie was concerned, no matter what the appearance might be. At his instructions, she was to prepare two divans as single beds and a divan that opened into a double bed in the recently installed discothèque. The bed clothes were kept in a locker in that part of the airplane, which had not yet been modified. When Dottie went back to get them the two sisters had stripped down to their goose pimples. They seemed not the least bit flustered by Dottie's appearance. Dottie grabbed what she needed and beat a hasty retreat. Later, when Vesco called her back to serve drinks, the girls were clothed—each one wearing a set of Junior's Dr. Denton's. Vesco and Pistell had gotten out of their evening clothes. Pistell was in a robe and Vesco wore his velour play suit. After the last round of drinks Dottie drew the curtain between the main salon and the discothèque.

The next time that Dottie went aft was to awaken Vesco and his guests in time for breakfast before landing. That would be at Nice, France, for refueling. The two sisters were in the discothèque bed, naked, and Pistell and Vesco were in the single beds.

On night flights, Vesco would follow a set routine upon arriving. He would come forward to the lavatory, wash, and shave. Then he would stop at the galley where Dottie would give him a glass of juice and his Vitamin C and E tablets. On early morning takeoffs it would be a Bloody Mary with the vitamins. When Pat Vesco was not along on the flights there would sometimes be an added element. Vesco believed in the curative powers of penicillin and insisted that a supply of these pills be kept aboard at all times. He had asked Dottie to arrange for this but Dottie refused. So Norman LeBlanc became Vesco's supplier. Every once in a while, most often before early morning takeoffs in foreign countries, Vesco, with a sheepish smile, would ask Dottie for his penicillin pills. Of course with Pat Vesco along there was no need to take precautions against catching something dreadful.

Vesco followed his usual routine after Dottie woke him that morning before landing at Nice, except that he did ask Dottie for his penicillin. I got a good look at the sisters in broad daylight and wondered if Vesco had doubled up on his dosage. I wanted to advise him that he needed something a hell of a lot stronger like maybe against an attack of Bubonic Plague.

We dumped the sisters in Beirut. I never saw them again but that was not the last I heard of them. Nearly a year later, on March 21, 1973, to be precise, I was buttonholed at Beirut Airport by a good friend of mine who operated the ground handling agency that serviced the Boeing. He'd been on hand when we'd arrived with the two sisters. He was embarrassed. He told me that a few days after we had off-loaded the girls, they showed up at his office. They did not have to explain who they were. He recognized them. They were broke and without passports but they had a hell of a lot of luggage that they didn't have when they arrived. Very simply, they had not only spent the money that Vesco had given them, but they had cashed in the return air tickets he had provided them with as well, and had blown the money on goodies. My friend felt that he had an obligation to help the women and he bought them a couple of tickets to New York. To his surprise they showed up again a couple of days later. They had done the same thing with the tickets he'd paid for as they had done with the ones Vesco had bought them. This time my friend made certain that they got the hell out of Beirut. He personally put them aboard a New York-bound jet. I asked him how much it cost him. The bill came to over 2,000 dollars. I dropped the matter in Vesco's lap. He tossed it right back to me.

"Put it on your expense account," he told me. This pissed me off. I had to justify my expenses not to Vesco, but to Norman LeBlanc. I had been having problems with Norman over routine necessary expenses and I certainly could not list on my voucher "Vesco in-flight entertainment follow-up—dollars 2,000 plus." I paid my friend out of funds aboard the Boeing. To forestall any squabble I went to LeBlanc for his "guidance." I explained what the money was used for. He giggled.

"Hee Hee! That's funny, Ike," he said. "Uh—put it under 'fuel.' "

May 18, 1972 1410Z BEY—LHR—SAN

It was weird. The whole trip, beginning with the appearance of the two sisters at JFK, was punctuated by a series of strange events before we finally left Silver Phyllis at Newark.

I brought Vesco and Pistell up to London from Beirut and then continued up on to ATEL at Stansted where the Boeing would undergo a routine inspection.

On the flight from Beirut to London Vesco told me to arrange for an airplane to be available at Heathrow Airport. I told him that if he had other travel plans outside England I could postpone the aircraft inspection without difficulty. He was adamant.

"I want this airplane and the crew in England," he said. He was so insistent that the airplane remain in England that I thought back to the time in Toronto when he wanted me in the lobby of the Royal York Hotel in uniform for high visibility.

When Vesco and Pistell left the Boeing in London I asked Vesco where I should pick him up when the aircraft was ready—meaning either Stansted or Heathrow. Vesco must have been thinking of some other place.

"Either Paris or Amsterdam," he said. Then, "No! This airplane has got to stay in England. I'll get in touch with you."

I continued to Stansted and asked Dennis Dearlove to contact Vesco at his London Hotel about the airplane Vesco wanted. He said to forget about another airplane, that he would take care of it himself. It was not unusual for Vesco to make his own private travel arrangements. IOS, for example, had a number of aircraft available in Europe and it was a matter of a single phone call to have one dispatched to London for Vesco's use. I promptly forgot the matter.

On April 10, 1974, nine months after I had left Vesco and almost two years from the date I had dropped Vesco in London with Pistell, I received a phone call at my home in Denville from an attorney named von Stein, who was with the Securities and Exchange Commission. The Senate Watergate hearings had finished and the House Judiciary Sub-Committee hearings on whether or not to impeach Richard Nixon were in full swing.

Von Stein was interested in that May 18, 1972, flight from Beirut to London, and in Robert Vesco's movements until his departure from Stansted to Newark on May 21, 1972. He told me that an "informant," which he later modified to "newspaper informant," had learned of a meeting between Robert Vesco and President Nixon in Salzburg, Austria, on May 21, 1972. Nixon had been off on a trip to Moscow. Von Stein wanted to know if I could verify that Vesco had gone to Salzburg. I couldn't. After I dropped Vesco in London I had no knowledge of his movements for the next three days. Within hours after von Stein's call I began to hear from the news media. I was unable to give them a shred of useful information about a Nixon-Vesco meeting in Salzburg. I did learn, however, that the story of this supposed meeting came from Bernie Cornfeld shortly after he was released from St. Antoine prison in Geneva. He claimed that he was told by a senior secretary at IOS that Gil Straub had boasted to her that not only had the meeting taken place, but that he'd arranged it.

I don't know if Vesco went to Salzburg. He certainly could have. Salzburg is only an hour and a half from London by air. Vesco had arranged that he would call me at my motel near Stansted when his plans were fixed for our return to the United States. The call came about nine in the evening of May 20, 1972, the day before the alleged meeting. I couldn't tell whether Vesco was calling from someplace in England or someplace on the Continent. The direct-dialing system, which is just about universal in Europe, does away with the need for an operator. He told me that he would be ready to leave about 2:00 P.M. on the 21st. About fifteen minutes before his arrival at Stansted Dennis Dearlove of ATEL came out to the Boeing to let me know. And the way Vesco generally operated it was perfectly logical that he would leave London by private jet early in the morning on May 21st, fly to Salzburg, meet with the President and get back to England with time to spare before takeoff.

Vesco's usual method of transportation from London to Stansted was by helicopter. I cannot recall how he arrived at Stansted that day. It's possible that he came in by private jet. One of the reasons we used Stansted, although not very frequently, was because of the absence of heavy traffic there. I have a hazy recollection of some private jet landing about twenty minutes before Vesco's appearance. But I can't say for sure that he did not arrive by helicopter. If he had come directly from the Continent he would, of course, have had to clear British Customs. At Stansted that could be done very quickly under normal circumstances.

On the day I arrived there was another incident with British Customs, but because the fault lay completely with the British, it may even have accelerated Vesco's clearance. In any event Vesco arrived with Pistell and we departed Stansted for Newark precisely at 2:15 local time on the afternoon of May 21, 1972. The incident I refer to took place on the ground at Stansted immediately after landing.

The two items that most concerned British Customs were alcohol and tobacco. The usual procedure for transient aircraft landing at a British airport called for either securing all alcohol stores above the permissable amount under lock and key with Customs' seal on it while the aircraft is in the UK, or the removal of it to a Customs facility where it would be held under bond until departure. I preferred the former. I have lost too much good booze and tobacco either through carelessness or pilferage. It cost a great deal of money to install the theft-proof lockers aboard the Boeing and the Customs tab fittings for their seals. I had cleared Customs in London without difficulty, which meant that the seals were affixed to the lockers before I left London. I had complied fully with all known and existing regulations for transient aircraft in the UK.

Under international law regarding arriving aircraft, no one may board the aircraft without the Captain's specific permission until the aircraft has been "docked" according to prescribed procedures. These procedures vary from one aircraft type to another. On a Boeing the procedure is that the aircraft is directed to a predetermined position and stopped. The wheels are secured with blocks and a safety pin is inserted into the nose gear-retracting mechanism. As long as the aircraft is operating under its own power it is not secured or docked. The reason for these procedures is safety. Until the aircraft is secured, the Captain has the sole right of command. This is not a matter of vanity. As in the case of a ship's Captain it is a matter of law.

I had taxied off the runway and proceeded to the point on the ramp to which I had been directed by ground control, Stand 30. The taxi director on the ramp waved me to the exact spot he wanted the aircraft stopped. I waited for a signal that the wheel blocks had been put in place and ground power had been plugged in. I got the wheel-block signal but no ground power unit was immediately available. That meant I would have to keep number-three engine running to provide the electrical power necessary to carry out the shutdown procedure. Nor did I get a signal that the nose-gear pin had been inserted, which meant they did not have one. We would apparently have to wait until my engineer, Ron Dusse, went down and inserted the one that we carried on the flight deck. Ron left his seat, grabbed the pin, and started aft. Over the sound of the idling number-three engine I suddenly "felt" a thumping coming from somewhere behind me. There are noises that belong on an airplane and noises—even faint ones—that don't. This was one of those noises that doesn't belong. It could mean anything. I pointed at my first officer.

"You got it, Chuck," I told him. And jumped out of my seat. Just outside the flight-deck door I saw Ron in a shoving match with a big guy in a white shirt. He had little epaulets on his shoulders, but everybody in Europe wore some sort of uniform if they worked around an airport. Without his hat or my being able to see his blouse in order to identify the uniform, I had no way of knowing that he was a Waterguard, the British version of the Customs agent.

There were a lot of hijacking scares around the UK at the time. For all I knew this beefy clown could have been looking for a free ride to Algeria or someplace and a million pounds Sterling. He had slammed Ron, whom he outweighed by about forty pounds, against the bulkhead. Ron was a Marine Corps reserve major and could handle himself pretty well, but the surprise of the assault caught him off guard. Vito LaForgia, my second engineer, scooted from the flight deck ready to join in if necessary. But Vito wasn't much heavier than Ron and the guy in the white shirt was even bigger than I. There was a lot of shouting going on.

"Mate, I don't give a fuck what your bloody Captain said," the guy in the white shirt said. "I'm fuckin' well comin' aboard!" This was no time for observations. I moved in on that guy, grabbed him by the shirt front with both hands and slung him out onto the top step of the passenger-loading ramp.

A man I recognized as a Customs inspector because he was in full uniform was standing at the bottom of the steps. When the scuffle moved out of the airplane he mounted the steps two at a time. I had let go of the guy in the white shirt.

"You, mister," I shouted at him, "are interfering with the safe conduct of this aircraft during security routine and, if you don't get off these steps and down on the ramp where you belong, I'm going to place you under arrest." The uniformed officer had reached us but right then he did not interfere. The other guy came right back at me.

"I have the right to enter any aircraft at any time I

see fit without no permission from no bloody Captain." With that he barged back into the aircraft and stood just inside the door daring me to do something about it. I did. I placed him under formal arrest for an attempted act of international air piracy. I didn't have to lay a finger on him. Once I said the words to him it was a matter for higher authorities to decide. I turned to the man in uniform.

"You understand that I have placed this man under arrest" I asked him. He was very upset.

"I understand that, Captain," he said. He beckoned to his colleague. "Come out of the aircraft. Come out of the aircraft," he said. The guy in the shirt hesitated a moment, unsure of himself. But he decided to brazen it out.

"Not bloody likely," he said. "I'm placing him under arrest." And he pointed to me. I recognized that this was the crunch. Either I backed off or I made my point stick. Before I would take any drastic actions such as going back into the airplane, taking a pistol and handcuffs from the arms locker, and making a physical arrest, I would appeal to the man in uniform. But he was way ahead of me.

"Get off the airplane!" he commanded his colleague, "and be quick about it!" Shocked at the sharpness of the other's tone, the man in the white shirt stepped out of the airplane. The man in uniform indicated the ramp. "Wait down there," he said. The younger man did as he was told.

"He's still under arrest," I told the uniformed man.

"I understand that, Captain," he said. "May I come aboard your aircraft and talk with you in private?" I agreed.

Number three was still running. By this time the ground power unit had arrived. I sent Ron down to put the nose pin in and told Chuck to cut number three when he was ready. I escorted the uniformed Customs agent to Vesco's office.

He wanted me to forget the whole matter. I told him it was impossible. The safety of my crew and my aircraft had been threatened and my authority as Captain had been compromised not only with my crew but, in effect, with the British government. If I were to let the matter pass then any half-wit with an over-inflated sense of his own authority could do the same to any Captain of any aircraft. I intended to make an issue of it. I did agree to withdraw my arrest provided that he took the responsibility for reporting the incident to his superiors.

I filed an official report citing international law governing aircraft and the rights and the authority of an aircraft commander. It was a sticky situation. I could have carried this matter right to the Air Ministry. However, I was willing to let the matter end at Stansted if the Customs service at Stansted would issue an official, written apology for the misconduct of one of its subordinates. I got what I asked for. The British are fair. When they're wrong they are willing to admit it if given an opportunity to do so without losing face.

I left the frying pan in Stansted only to land in the fire at Newark.

May 21, 1972 1415Z SAN—EWR

I will never understand passengers—either the kind that fly in commercial aircraft or the kind that fly around in their own 707. There are professional smugglers who devise the most ingenious methods to sneak their contraband past the Customs agents of the world. Whatever it is they're smuggling is usually of great value and the penalties for getting caught are severe. They are willing to take the risk. And they get caught with great regularity. I don't know what it is that impels a man who can drop a fast five grand at a crap table to challenge the U.S. government over a lousy trinket that might cost him a few dollars in duty.

We landed at Newark at a little after 5:00 P.M. on May 21. Since I carried only two passengers, Vesco and Pistell, I didn't expect any delay whatsoever in clearing Customs and Immigration. Within minutes after the Boeing was secured, a Customs inspector and

Immigration agent came aboard. I knew them both. They hollered a hello to the flight deck as they passed and went into the rear of the aircraft. I paid no further attention to them as I went about my chores.

Maybe about ten minutes had passed. The Immigration agent had done his thing and gone. The Customs procedures usually took a little longer. I was surprised, then, when I felt a tap on my shoulder and turned to see the Customs inspector standing in the doorway to the flight deck, a grim look on his face.

"Captain Eisenhauer," he said, "I'd like to talk to you," and moved back toward the galley. I followed him. Beyond him I could see Vesco and Pistell standing together in the main salon. They looked worried and I wondered what the hell was going on.

"What's up?" I asked the inspector.

"Captain Eisenhauer, I'm placing one of your passengers under arrest," he said. "The one with the big nose and the skinny mustache." Ohmigod!

"You can't do that," I told him. "He's my bread and butter. He's the boss. You'll put me out of work."

"I have no choice, Captain," he said. "He offered me a bribe. I won't tolerate that. I have been in the service too long and I'm an honest man." He wasn't being pompous or self-righteous. He meant what he said. I succeeded in staying execution and persuaded the inspector to wait until I had a chance to get the details. I went back with him to where Vesco and Pistell, still looking worried, waited. I could see anger beginning to rise in Vesco and hoped to God he would keep his mouth shut. We all sat down and relaxed. I figured it would be pretty difficult to act too official sitting in one of those space-age seats in the Boeing. It did have a calming effect on everybody.

Pistell had bought something—and to this day I don't know what it was—in Beirut. He hadn't declared it and it was discovered by the inspector in his circuit of the interior of the Boeing. The inspector got angry, and rightly so, at this attempt to sneak something past him. Pistell admitted ownership and tried to double-talk the inspector into not confiscating the item. Vesco stuck his horn into the situation by trying to grease the inspector and that took the "rag offen the bush." I was able to convince the inspector that neither one of those clowns meant any harm. They both apologized to him. Pistell laid out $32.40 for his trinket and was given a receipt by the inspector. Customs Form 5104 No. 12461953. At that moment I didn't care if I never saw Vesco, Pistell, Customs agents, airports, or airplanes again.

June 17, 1972 2055Z EWR—LAS

Gil Straub got married. His bride was the former Barbara Rossner, who had been an executive secretary at IOS in Geneva. She had made many trips on the Boeing and was a lovely, charming woman.

They were married at a simple ceremony in New York City. Barbara's parents had come from Germany to attend the wedding. And this is where one of the good facets of Robert Vesco's many-sided personality showed. He turned the Boeing over to Gil and Barbara for their honeymoon flight to Las Vegas and the traditional wedding party was held in flight at 40,000 feet. Dottie McCarty, who had been given advance information by Vesco, mounted a tremendous and expensive effort to decorate the cabin in a manner to match the occasion. I wouldn't have believed that what she accomplished could be done to the interior of an airplane. It looked like a spring garden. There were flowers and greenery everywhere. I half expected to see the deck covered with sod. It was a happy trip, one of the most pleasant and free of trouble that I can remember. So, a pat on the head for big, bad Bobby.

June 21, 1972 1305Z NAS—PAP

I believe that Robert L. Vesco is the modern "man who would be king." A couple of times when he hunched behind my seat on the flight deck he would talk like a man who had a fantasy. This fantasy revolved around a place where he would be the Supreme Being. He hadn't located it yet but he knew generally where it ought to be: easily reached from any part of the Western world and in a subtropical zone. It would have the blessing of, or an understanding with, a strong permissive government that would permit and encourage him to establish an international free zone where every sort of commerce could be conducted without restriction or interference.

Vesco was not a bookish man. In fact he was a high-school dropout. He lacks finesse and culture but he has a breadth of vision, even if it is flawed, that makes your average corporate executive look like a lathe operator in a machine shop. Vesco's search for his commercial Shangri-La was almost an obsession. After the Geneva disaster he had said to me with fierce emphasis, "Goddamnit, Ike! I want my own fucking country." And he believed that he would get it.

I don't pay too much attention to my passengers unless there is reason to notice them. Either it's a new face I haven't seen before or it's an old one that means something big is on the burner. Howard Cerney was the old face that meant that something big was on the burner. Cerney is a small man who reminds me of a worried hummingbird.

The new face was a man Vesco introduced me to during flight, one Dr. Jean Claude Alexandre, whom I took to be a Haitian. Our destination was Port-au-Prince, Haiti. Before takeoff Vesco had only half jokingly told me to "stay the hell away from Cuba."

It was raining when we left Nassau and all my passengers, which included the entire Vesco family, Shirley Bailey, the newlyweds, Gil and Barba[illegible] a couple of friends of the Vesco children, [illegible] and subdued when they boarded. The moo[illegible] cabin brightened when we broke through the [illegible] into the brilliant sunlight.

At about the halfway point Vesco called me back [illegible] his office. He, Alexandre, and Cerney were gathered around a huge map, which was spread out on Vesco's desk. It was a map of Haiti and Santo Domingo and some of the surrounding islands. Alexandre placed his index finger on a long narrow island about thirty miles northwest of Port-au-Prince.

Gonave, the island indicated by Alexandre, is about forty miles long and ten miles wide. Looking at Haiti from a great altitude, or on a map, it has the appearance of a crab's claw that is about to close on the island of Gonave.

"I want to get a close look at that, Ike," Vesco said.

"How close?" I asked him.

"Close enough to get a good look at what I'm buying," he said and grinned. I looked at Alexandre, a little embarrassed at Vesco's bluntness. But he was grinning too. Cerney wasn't grinning. He was upset. And when he's upset he twitches—all over. He looked like a hummingbird with ticks and no place to scratch. I went back to the flight deck and told the crew that we were going to do a little crop-dusting with the Boeing. They were all for it.

"Just don't get the wings wet," Dottie commented.

I called Port-au-Prince approach control and advised them that I wanted to cancel my flight plan and fly VFR around Gonave for a while. They agreed and told me to call them back when I was ready to land.

My first pass around the island was at an altitude of 500 feet. Vesco came forward and said he wanted to go lower. I gave him what he wanted. I got so close to the tops of the waves that Chuck, my first officer, hollered at me, "Up periscope!" Vesco came forward again looking pleased. He told me to make one more circuit at the same altitude.

"That's it, Ike," he said. "That's my new country." He pointed to a mountain, 2500-foot Lapierre Peak, which rose impressively out of the lush green of the island. "That's where my summer home goes," Vesco said. "And I'll build the town right along that beach." He left me and went back to the cabin.

After the airplane had been secured, Vesco told me that he would be in Haiti for a couple of days at least.

"Why don't you take a look around Haiti for me, Ike, and tell me what you think?" he said. He took Alexandre by the arm. "Let's go buy that goddamn island," I heard him say. Howard Cerney prinked along behind him on his tiny feet.

Out of habit I ordered the Boeing fueled across the wings immediately. With Vesco, it was best to anticipate the unexpected. And more than once I have been called on to make a fast getaway.

I didn't know a great deal about Haiti but I had read about the repressive regime of the late "Papa Doc" Duvalier. I had heard enough about his private police force that was called the *Ton Ton Macoute* to be concerned about the safety of my crew. I had a general concern about my passengers but long experience had taught me that, while Vesco might have the connections to keep his retinue safe from harrassment, those connections did the *crew* damn little good. Cairo proved that. I warned the crew about the *Ton Ton*. They had heard about them too. There had been a motion picture some years earlier about Haiti with Richard Burton and Elizabeth Taylor, that was based on a novel by Graham Green, *The Comedians*. It painted a pretty frightening picture and, apart from the story line, it was authentic. Some of the crew had seen it and we talked about it.

We no sooner had cleared the terminal when the movie came to life. There were four *Ton Tons* lounging near a ratty-looking car parked behind the taxis I had hired to take us to the hotel.

"Hey, Mafia," Vito said, jerking his head in their direction.

"Don't even look at them," I said. I thought that maybe my imagination was working overtime. After all, Papa Doc was dead and the presidency had been taken over by his son who was called both "Baby Doc" or

"Baskethead," because of his round, oversized skull. Baby Doc was not even out of his teens when he inherited his father's office for life. From pictures I had seen of him, he looked like a fat, harmless, spoiled kid. There had been reports that he intended to run a less oppressive regime. But here were the *Ton Tons* who looked every bit as mean as their reputations.

It's easy to spot the *Ton Tons*. They are not a uniformed force in the military or police sense. But to use the term "plainclothes" or "secret" would be to misstate the case. The first thing you notice are the sunglasses. They are aviator's style and the lenses are mirrored. You never know where they're looking. Wherever we went we saw those glasses. They must have had a special deal with Foster-Grant. The other item that set them apart is they all wore Panama hats, a white-straw fedora that is made in Ecuador. About half of the *Ton Tons* we saw wore unpressed and grimy linen suits. The others wore sport shirts and slacks. They universally sported highly polished pointy-toed shoes—and every one of them carried at least one highly visible firearm.

They were there when we got to the hotel. After checking in I deliberately waited a short distance from the reception desk to see if any of them would come forward to check our registration cards. Two of them did.

I hired a car and a driver so that the crew and I could do some sight-seeing. We were followed everywhere. But the *Ton Tons* made no move to interfere with us. Since Vesco had said we'd be in Haiti for a few days, the first day's sight-seeing was devoted to touring the countryside outside Port-au-Prince to the east. The next day we planned to cover the city itself during the day, and the night life after dark. We never got the chance. Vesco awoke me at seven in the morning. His voice sounded angry over the telephone.

"How fast can we get out of here?' he asked me. I made some mental calculations.

"I can be ready to go at nine, Bob," I said.

"Good," he said, and hung up. He didn't even tell me where we were going.

The crew and I arrived at the airport a little after eight in two taxis. I wanted the taxis to go directly to the airplane to unload the crew gear. On our sightseeing trip through the countryside we had picked up some Haitian rum at an incredible price and some wood carvings and other souvenirs. It would have been a problem carting everything through the terminal and across the ramp. The *Ton Tons* again. I had told the driver to follow the dirt road past the terminal building and to go directly onto the ramp. There was no fence—just the road. Before we reached the ramp, the driver of my car jammed on the brakes and pointed off to his left. I looked and saw two *Ton Tons* approaching us. They were walking casually. I told the driver to keep going. He refused, pointed to the *Ton Tons*, and spewed out a stream of Haitian French. He wouldn't budge. He was scared to death of those *Ton Tons*. The *Ton Tons* came up to the cars and looked inside both of them. They spoke, in French, to my driver. The conversation lasted a couple of minutes. The driver suddenly turned off the engine, got out of the car, and indicated that the other car was to do the same. I wasn't about to argue the matter. Both cars emptied. We unloaded our gear and I paid the drivers. We had to carry everything to the Boeing anyway.

Normally I would not have gone directly to the airplane with the crew. They were competent and fully capable of getting the airplane ready to go without my presence. But, like Bombay, we were in strange and potentially volatile territory. I wanted to be sure that there were no *Ton Tons* hiding in the wheel wells or that somebody had not ice picked the tires. When I saw that everything was all right I went back to the terminal to wait for Vesco. I did not know our destination and he was obviously in a hurry. I could save time by finding out where he wanted to go before he got on the airplane and going directly to operations to file.

The Vesco party arrived in three Cadillac limousines at ten. They all had to go through the terminal as well as the departure routine for passengers. As soon as the limousines had pulled up in front of the terminal, about half a dozen *Ton Tons* materialized to gawk. This time they kept their distance. Vesco waited until everybody else had entered the terminal. He looked angry enough to bite through an iron spike. When we were alone I asked him what had happened.

"That black sonofabitch," he said. "All he's interested in is motorcycles and feeding his fat, fucking face!"

"Who?" I asked him.

"Baby Doç! Baskethead! Whatever the fuck they call him!" he said. "Imagine that, a shit-ass kid like that, president for life!" I looked around to see if the *Ton Tons* were close enough to overhear. This is one time when speaking French would have gotten Vesco and me in jail. Haitian jails would make St. Antoine Prison look like the Fontainebleu in Miami. I had to get him off the subject.

"Where're we going, Bob?" I asked him. I had enough fuel for 3,000 miles.

"Just out of this fucking place!" he said. He thought a moment. "Santo Domingo!" That was a little over a half hour away. Shit! I did some fast figuring. I was glad I hadn't tried to outguess Vesco. If I had, I would have been in worse shape than I was. I was glad I had not ordered any more fuel than I had. There would have been no way that I could have landed in Santo Domingo with all that weight. As it was, I barely made my landing weight.

We were on the ground in Santo Domingo for five hours and fifty minutes before we took off for Newark—enough time for Vesco to cool down a bit and collect his marbles.

We had left Dr. Jean Claude Alexandre in Haiti. For all I knew he was enjoying the ministrations of the *Ton Ton Macoute.*

Another country in the ditch.

In a little over a week, Vesco and Howard Cerney would go country shopping again with Dick Pistell as the broker.

June 29, 1972 1705Z NAS—SJO

Howard Franklin Cerney and Richard Chadwick Pistell! Wow! The eagle and the hummingbird.

When Cerney showed up, as I said, there was murky business afoot. With Pistell around, the earth would shake. With the two of them together I knew that Vesco was on the track of something big.

Our destination was San Jose, Costa Rica. This would be the first time Silver Phyllis would touch down in any mainland country in the Western hemisphere south of the Rio Grande.

Vesco and Pistell were in a jolly mood. Howard Cerney simply hovered and hummed. Pat Vesco was along. She was necessary for Vesco's good image. But she kept herself apart from the men.

When Vesco was in a good mood he ate. The flight to San Jose from Nassau would take about three hours and Vesco gorged himself practically every mile of the way. Dottie McCarty served up lashings of pepperoni pizza, chili dogs, roquefort burgers, fried chicken, steak tartare, Tab, Crown Royal, and Chivas Regal—twelve years old. He wouldn't touch dessert because he was conscious of the calories. I think Pistell could match Vesco bite for bite on the kind of stomach destroyers that Vesco ingested. But poor Howard Cerney. Dottie prepared something less corrosive for him.

San Jose was completely covered by clouds. The kind I call cumulus granitus because they envelop the mountaintops. I followed the Jeppesen approach plate to the letter. I had never been here before. I broke out of the clouds at about 2,000 feet on my final approach and saw directly ahead of me a fantastically beautiful sight. The city of San Jose lies smack in the center of Costa Rica, equidistant from the Caribbean and the Pacific. It is completely ringed by mountains and nestles at the end of a long valley. Even with the cloud cover it gave off a radiant green color.

The runway was not as long as I had hoped it would be and the elevation of the airport, approximately 4,000 feet above sea level, didn't leave much room for error. But Silver Phyllis eased herself gently and smoothly into her new country.

Even while taxiing in toward the terminal building I knew that horsepower was at work. It seemed as if there were as many Ticans waiting for us on the ramp as had come out to service the Boeing on that first landing at Geneva. But it was obvious that these people had been dispatched to attend to whoever got off the airplane—even if it was only one person. Where the Swiss had been contemptuous, these people were awestruck. I was flabbergasted. When the forward passenger door was opened a man almost as small as Howard Cerney but much younger stepped inside. He was accompanied by two aides. Pistell had come forward with Vesco even before the plane had stopped. He and the newcomer embraced fervently in the Latin-American manner. He introduced the man to me a little later as Marti Fegueres, the son of the president of Costa Rica. A Junior Nixon first class. Donald was only a nephew.

Marti was something of a dandy. He was slender and balding and wore a moderate-sized mustache. He was immaculately dressed in a conservative, expensive, American-style vested business suit. I was to learn later that he was something of a playboy and a business dunce. But he had plenty of clout in his homeland. He had been educated both in Costa Rica and the United States. In fact, his mother, Don Pepe Figueres' first wife, was an American. He spoke American English without a trace of accent except for the strong taint of New Yorkese. He peppered his conversation with the latest slang, which he updated during his frequent trips to New York. The way Pistell treated Marti Figueres, it was pretty obvious that the son of the president of Costa Rica was the key to turn the lock to open the gate to Vesco's Shangri-La.

Silver Phyllis would make many visits to Costa Rica over the next twelve months. She would carry a lot of important Costa Ricans back and forth between San

Jose, Nassau, the United States, and Europe. They would include not only Marti Figueres, but Gonzalo Facio, the Costa Rican foreign minister who was a partner in the country's most important law firm, Facio, Fournier, and Canas. Facio, considered about the best lawyer in Costa Rica, had been president of the Organization of American States for two years. Silver Phyllis also carried Figueres' wife, Sandra, and Facio's wife, Margarita, as well as other important Costa Rican businessmen and politicians.

Later that year, just before Christmas, Vesco released the crew to go home for the holidays. But it was impossible at that time of year for the crew and myself to get commerical air transportation out of Nassau. I was able to wangle some reservations out of Eastern from Ft. Lauderdale and since Vesco had his whole family in Nassau and would not need the Boeing until after Christmas, he had let me fly the crew to Ft. Lauderdale to catch their flights. I was not able to get reservations for everybody on the same day. I couldn't get out until the 23rd of December, two days after the rest of the crew had left for their homes. As usual, I notified Vesco where I could be reached, at the home of my old buddy and boss, Al Junker.

The day I was to leave I got a nervous-sounding call from Vesco.

"I hate to interrupt your holiday, Ike," he said, "but I want the airplane back in Nassau, now." I got mad.

"For Chrissakes, Bob, what for?" I said. "You told me your weren't going anywhere until after Christmas. Besides, I sent the crew home already."

"You read the papers!" he snapped back. "The SEC is on my back, and I don't want any government agents grabbing my airplane. From here on that airplane doesn't land in the United States again." He was out of his mind. We had a contract with Qualitron Aero for the final phase of modification to Silver Phyllis, which would include the gym, shower, steam bath, lavatory, dressing room, storage area, sauna bath, and which would also finish off items to complete the total modification. All the components had already been built and the money spent. After this Silver Phyllis would really be the Queen of the Skies. If we didn't show, Vesco would lose whatever money had already been advanced. He would also be liable for the additional costs spelled out in the contract and the job could not be done for at least a year—if at all. I told him all this. It stopped him.

The last thing in the world that would worry Vesco would be the loss of a couple of hundred thousand dollars. Since the airplane would be out of the country anyway he wouldn't worry about beating Qualitron for the additional money. But that airplane was Vesco's pride and joy. And it wasn't finished. And I think that's what made him change his mind.

"Okay, Ike," he said. "I'll take a chance. But as soon as the modification is finished, you get it to Nassau and it doesn't go back—ever!"

Vesco had mentioned the SEC and the possible seizure of the Boeing. But I had been hearing rumors from various mouths in the Vesco gang that the new ICC management, which now included Harry Sears, Larry Richardson, Elmer Sticco—the guy who sabotaged his own boss at ELS for Vesco—were ganging up to unload Vesco from his own company. On top of that, they wanted Vesco's Boeing. It was costing ICC too much money. I knew he was more worried about them than he was about the government.

Vesco's decision to base the Boeing at Nassau was the beginning of a dilemma that would plague me until the day I quit. It meant, for all practical purposes, that my new base of operations would be the Bahamas and not Newark. If I had a few days off I would have to commute to New Jersey and back to Nassau by commercial airline.

Heretofore, I could leave my job and be an hour away from my home in Denville. Two days off at Newark meant two days off. Two days off in Nassau meant, at best, twelve hours at home or two days off in Nassau. I decided that if Vesco really intended to keep the airplane out of the United States, I would go along for a while. Vesco's decision raised some technical problems. The maintenance facilities in Nassau were totally inadequate. Actually, they were non-existent for this type of aircraft. There were no spare parts. They had to be shipped from the United States. I carried a lot of key spare parts aboard the Boeing because of this. The situation was not unique to Nassau. It was the same at a lot of airports we operated in and out of.

Parts, which were replaced from my own stock, were never thrown away. They were kept on board until such time that they could be dropped off at a maintenance facility such as Eastern Air in Ft. Lauderdale for repair or rebuilding. In preparation for the Boeings' visit to Qualitron, the crew had cleaned out the airplane except for a lot of junk and spare parts that had accumulated over the past two years. It was the kind of stuff that could be compared to the useless dreck that gathers, somehow, in the glove compartments and trunks of cars. This was all packed in cardboard boxes to be taken off at a later date. A lot of it had been left by passengers aboard the aircraft. Each member of the crew, all facing the problem of being based in Nassau, had decided that the personal belongings which they kept on the airplane, would be taken off before Silver Phyllis went to Qualitron. The less clutter there was, the easier it would make things for everybody.

I flew from Ft. Lauderdale to Nassau, picked up Vesco's parents and Shirley Bailey, and went to Newark. All the cardboard boxes were placed in a storage room in our Newark Airport offices at Butler Aviation. They sat there for months.

On the few occasions that I got back to Newark, Lou Notte would remind me that I still had some junk in the storeroom. Sometimes I'd take a box home and stick it in the attic, and sometimes I would say the hell with it. On one of these trips back to Newark I was notified by Charlie Snell, manager of Butler Newark, that ICC had refused to pay the back rent due on the office facilities and storeroom and I would either have to pay for it or we would have to get the stuff out. That was an easy choice to make. I got my pickup truck, piled the rest of the shit from the storeroom into it and stuck it with the rest, under the eaves. Even if I had a mind to, I didn't have time to go through it. As far as I was concerned, there was nothing of importance in any of the boxes. The stuff I had considered important, aircraft records, crew records, manuals and such, I had carefully filed with detailed notations and indexing.

In October of 1973, October 30 to be exact, I was ordered by the Southern District of Florida of the United States Court to appear before a grand jury relative to an investigation of Robert Vesco, and to bring with me all records of flight plans, flight logs and passenger manifests for the Boeing from January 1, 1970, "to date." Fortunately, the grand jury was meeting at the U.S. Court House in Foley Square in New York City. I was to report at ten in the morning on November 1, which gave me less than two days to sort through a mountain of crap. I was to be called on many times to appear before investigative bodies since then, and as of this writing the end is still not in sight.

About a month after my latest appearance before a grand jury—in Detroit in November of 1975—I was rearranging my files to make it easier to find the stuff that I might still be asked to produce. I came across those boxes and decided that that was as good a time as any to see what the hell was in them.

As I expected, it was junk, ninety percent of which was destined for the garbage can. Whoever had packed the boxes had marked them IKE—PERSONAL. There was one item that did not belong to me. It was a thick loose-leaf binder covered in a blue fabric. When I opened it I saw that it was a memorandum prepared by a Michael Patrick Murray, Esq. and addressed to Howard Franklin Cerney, Esq. The subject covered "matters relating to potential foreign investment in Costa Rica." It had been prepared when Murray visited Costa Rica, having arrived there at 8:30 A.M. on June 14, 1972, and checking into the Hotel Europa in San Jose. This was exactly fifteen days before Vesco's first visit to Costa Rica.

The bulk of the memorandum is made up of attachments, fourteen of them, that summarize Costa Rican laws. They relate to "tax laws, effective since March 19, 1972, Costa Rican constitutional law, the banking system, currency-exchange controls, property and property rights, promotion of industry, and, significantly, the rights and duties of foreigners." The subjects of all the attachments are not listed. But they cover every single aspect of law relating to commerce and industry, domestic and foreign, in Costa Rica. The most interesting part of the memorandum is the summary of Michael Patrick Murray's impressions of Costa Rica and some of its prominent citizens, including don Pepe. On first reading it appears to be a flattering picture of Costa Rica, its people, and its customs. But it was obviously written as a background briefing on "the general social/political climate of the country" for Vesco's particular needs.

Mr. Murray, Esq., has a peculiar style. The "Esq." means that he is a lawyer. The "Esq." bothered me a bit until I asked somebody and was told that this is the way lawyers like to be addressed.

There are a few misspellings and strikeovers in the typewritten memo that lead me to believe that it was typed by Murray, Esq. himself, which would indicate one of two things: it was either written in haste or it had the highest degree of confidentiality.

I always believed that lawyers were a pretty noncommittal bunch. They generally avoid the kind of language or emphasis that can pin them down. In whatever they say or write there is always an escape hatch. But Murray's memo is shot through with underlinings, quotation marks, and parentheses that tell the reader to read between the lines. Mr. Murray, Esq. was telling Mr. Cerney, Esq., who would in turn tell Mr. Vesco, that Costa Rica was ready to be raped.

The first person Murray contacted for his report was Marti Figueres. He had lunch with him. He states that the lunch "gave me the opportunity to commence inquiry into the general social/political climate of the country." I had the chance to take the measure of Marti Figueres over a period of a year. Discussing the social/political climate of any country with Marti Figueres would be like discussing the geopolitical climate of the Soviet Union with Donald Nixon, Jr.

Murray comments in detail on Marti Figueres further on into the memo. Following are excerpts from the memo on Don Jose "Don Pepe" Figueres, the political situation in Costa Rica, Gonzalo Facio, foreign minister, and other matters:

On Don Pepe: "Popular with the people . . . ardent fighter of Communism . . . idealist of sorts, mainly honest but capable of maneuvers that smack of 'sharp' dealings, but only when the people will benefit. Democratic and capitalistic, he is center on the political structure and a little 'right' where 'commies' and 'socialists' are concerned."

There follows an aside about the American embassy ("two blocks from the Europa Hotel"). Mr. Murray either didn't bother about or was afraid to learn the correct spelling of the American ambassador's name. He gives it phonetically as either "a Mr. Plosher or Ploseur" whom, he says, "returned to the U.S. for President Nixon's re-election." He even strikes out on the spelling, also phonetic, of the name of the *chargé d'affaires*, whom he identifies as Mr. Rabinold, who wasn't there anyway. He mentioned another man, a Mr. Moon, with whose name I presume he had no trouble. It was the commercial attaché, a Mr. G. Beck whom Mr. Murray, Esq., found most helpful. He recommends a long talk with Mr. Beck by Cerney or whoever.

Mr. Murray seemed to have been hung up on political identities. But this might have been on instructions. He cites in his report an "incident" that occurred outside the U.S. embassy on May 16, 1972, which was mounted by "a handful of left-wing dissidents (including a couple of American 'hippie' types). Anti-American clichés were bandied about and some ink and paint splashed on the embassy. A crowd gathered, and before the police arrived (it took about thirty minutes) the people themselves took care of the situation." What were termed "right-wing" elements "charged in (some with sticks) and beat up on the dissidents. A couple of heads were cracked and by the time the 'police' arrived, the pro-American element had the whole thing resolved. The foreign minister (secretary of state), Mr. Facio, later sent over paint and workers and had the embassy repainted. Mr. Beck said it never looked so good (and whimsically suggests another 'incident' the next time the embassy needs painting)."

Murray goes on to state that a similar affair was "staged by rightist elements" at the Russian embassy and a couple of "Molotov cocktails and fireworks were thrown at the building. No serious damage, however, and it was viewed as a 'retaliation' for the American embassy matter." According to Murray, 85 per cent of the Costa Rican people are "highly favorable" to the United States and "all Latin American countries are moving slowly left *or* feeling *strong pressure* from the left while Costa Rica is strong *center* and the mood is decidedly anti-Communist and quite democratically bent."

Murray takes an amused view of Costa Rica's threatened invasion by Nicaragua in 1955. He cites the Costa Rican constitution of 1949, which abolished all military forces. The way he refers to the national police and "instant militia" would indicate that he believes that a military force does exist undercover in Costa Rica which, from what I have heard, is precisely the case. He pays some compliments to the literacy rate and the high standard of living in Costa Rica but goes on to state that, while "the government is stable," it is "fiscally in the hole (aren't they all?)."

His assessment of the political situation in Costa Rica seems naïve and he concentrated his attention on political opposition that, if in power, would be no threat "to foreign investors."

Mr. Murray indulges in gossip. He informs Mr. Cerney that Don Pepe is divorced, that his first wife was an American named Cobb from North Carolina who, at that time, lived in Alabama. Don Pepe's second wife is also an American, Murray states, of Danish parentage but "Don Jose's divorce and remarriage apparently did not harm his political career" in Roman Catholic Costa Rica.

Murray had a 2½-hour interview with Don Pepe on the evening of June 15, 1972. He comments on Don

Pepe's command of English as if Don Pepe was some sort of freak bush bunny. Without explicitly stating, he indicates that Don Pepe will be accommodating and that Don Pepe, whose party controlled the congress at that time, would get whatever he went after "every time."

Murray didn't think much of Marti, whom he describes as "of questionable business acumen. He nonetheless is well known and can open all the right doors. A natural charmer, he understands the natives and thinks 'American.' Can be a decided asset if handled right." Marti, who is married to Foreign Minister Facio's daughter, Sandra, "plays it straight at home, but like most Latin males to whom 'women's lib' is anathema, he implies he gets a little on the side outside of the country."

Murray is positively enthusiastic in the memo about Gonzalo Facio. After a number of compliments to Facio, Murray observes that "more 'arrangements' can be made through Facio than through anyone else—in or out of the government."

Murray's overall impression of Costa Rica is that it is a "lush, beautiful country many centuries old, but still *virgin* in a lot of ways. The standard of living is *high* by Latin American standards—*low* by North American."

There are a few more patronizing comments about the Ticans that sound like something out of a Colonial governor's report to Queen Victoria's foreign secretary. What is really interesting is a paragraph at the end of the report regarding the laws governing extradition from Costa Rica. What it says is not important since it simply notes that the law is in effect. And even though it is buried on the next-to-last page, it indicates one of the major concerns of Robert Vesco. Since that report was written, and since Robert Vesco has taken up more or less permanent residence in Costa Rica, a new extradition law was formulated that has been called the "Vesco" Law. It provides that the president of Costa Rica can stop any extradition on his own say-so, for any reason or for no reason, before it gets to the Costa Rican courts.

Michael Patrick Murray's final paragraph states that "the prospects of President Figueres' party being back in office in 1974 are excellent. They could be even better if Figueres could point to new industry and investment in Costa Rica. He and his party are ready and willing to cooperate 'to the fullest.' "

I wonder if the copy of the memorandum from Michael Patrick Murray, Esq. to Howard Franklin Cerney, Esq. is the one that put Vesco in such a jolly mood that day. For all his astuteness, Bobby Vesco occasionally did dumb things. One of them was to leave his copy of the report lying around loose where it could get lost.

14

July 11, 1972 1510Z AMS—FCO

Pistell was spastic with excitement. He waved his arms, clapped his hands, and slapped backs.

"Boy-oh-boy-oh-boy-oh-boy!" he kept saying. "Ike, baby, if this trip works out the way I think it's gonna, it will be worth ten of these fucking Boeings to Bobby—and a fucking bundle to yours truly." No wonder he was happy. He had come out to the airplane from Amsterdam ahead of Vesco. Now he was anxious for Vesco to arrive and kept going outside the airplane to the top of the step to look for him.

Silver Phyllis was parked quite a distance from the main passenger terminal at Schipol. Passengers were brought out to the airplane by bus. Pistell spotted them first. He came into the airplane grinning like an idiot.

"They're here!" he told me, "and so are the broads." Broads! When Vesco said we were going to Rome, he said nothing about broads.

Vesco came on board ahead of the women. He looked at me as if to say, "Who the hell owns this fucking airplane anyway?" I hadn't said a word—just smiled at him—and I got a good look at his defensiveness. Four women followed him aboard, all very attractive. I recognized one of them, a Pan Am passenger-service representative from London who had been Vesco's companion before, the one from the Yellow Submarine in Munich. I went about my business.

Dottie McCarty missed this particular flight because of illness and we had a new girl on the crew. Unfortunately she didn't have anywhere near the kind of capabilities for corporate aviation. She was competent all right, but as an airline stewardess. The minimum qualification for our type of work. She lacked the tact, imagination, and stamina that service on a corporate-aviation aircraft demands. I missed Dottie. We all missed Dottie, especially Vesco who had come to rely on her professionalism, discretion and unflappability.

About halfway to Rome—not even that—Pistell came up to the flight deck. His fuse was lit and he had a snickery look on his face.

"Hey, Ikey," he said, "we got a little thing going in the back. A kind of a practical joke we're setting up for some guys in Rome and we're practicing, so don't get upset." He giggled and left. I didn't give a damn what he did in the back as long as he didn't poke holes in the Boeing.

I didn't bother to discuss the matter with the crew. Fun and games in the back of the Boeing were nothing new. Standard operating procedure was for the crew to remain in the forward part of the aircraft unless specifically summoned by Vesco or ordered to go aft by me—except for the stewardess, who had free run of the airplane. And this is where that extra quality *not* required of airline stewardesses came into play. Dottie had it to the nth degree. Her replacement on this trip did not.

We had begun our descent about a hundred miles from Rome. I rang for the stewardess.

"Tell Mr. Vesco we'll be landing in twenty minutes," I said. She went back to the passenger cabin. I could have advised Vesco on the intercom system but loud speaker chitchat by the Captain is very irritating and is strictly airline jazz or Hollywood fill-in. On Silver Phyllis, loudspeaker announcements were saved for emergencies. It never occurred to me that this was one time I should have used it. Damn! I hadn't given all that much thought to what Pistell had told me earlier about this practical joke that was being planned. Hell, they might have been building a human pyramid back there. In any event, the stewardess came back to the flight deck all red-faced and fluttery only about twenty seconds after she had left.

"What's the matter with you?" I asked her. For a minute I thought somebody'd had a heart attack.

"Captain! They haven't got any clothes on back there," she said. "Nobody!"

"Sweet Jesus!" I said. Behind me, Vito the flight engineer began to whoop and giggle and make obscene noises. The first officer, on the other hand, was as serious as an FBI agent. I turned the aircraft over to him and got out of my seat to go back and take a look for myself. Vito cocked his thumb toward the stewardess.

"What have we got, the flying nun?" he said. "Hee-hee-hee!" I gave him a small rap on the top of the head and started back toward the passenger cabin.

I got as far as Vesco's office. I could see a portion of the discothèque. The only person I saw was Norman LeBlanc. He was balls naked, sitting in a yellow bean-bag chair. Norman looked funny with clothes on. In the buff he looked like a Chinese-souvenir Buddah. I almost burst out laughing. Instead, I made a quick one-eighty without breaking stride and went back toward the flight deck.

The stewardess had come back to the galley. A curtain closed off the galley area from the main salon and I drew it as I went forward. Even though the sight of Norman LeBlanc, whom most of us called "Giggles," had been hilarious, I kept a straight face.

"Did you say anything?" I asked the stewardess.

"Told them to fasten their seat belts," she said.

"Anybody answer you?" I asked her.

"Only Mr. Vesco," she said.

"What did he say?" I asked.

"Go away," she said. Right on, baby. I felt better. I told her—for her own good—to act as if she saw nothing.

"Play it cool," I said. "I don't want to have to get

you a ticket back to New Jersey." She knew what I meant. And, as I hoped, she regrouped.

At Fumincino Airport in Rome the ground controller directed me to the Pan Am cargo ramp, which set me to wondering since this was not standard procedure for passenger flights. A ground handling crew was standing by. There were also two little Italian police cars waiting on the ramp with their bubble-lights flashing.

Usually the flight engineer is the first to leave the airplane to do his thing with the nose pin. Then he gives me the signals that all is secure. Because the cops were obviously waiting for us I decided to be the first one out. I wanted to know what the hell was going on. As the main entrance door was swung open I came face to face with two Italian cops standing on the top step, right outside. One of them saluted me.

In dealing with officialdom outside the U.S. and England I found that my uniform had a very high intimidation quotient. And for this occasion, since I'd seen the police cars outside, I felt that full regalia was called for. As a matter of fact, there were times when I wished I had a college drum major's uniform along, including the baton and bear-skin busby. I was wearing my regulation uniform with the four gold stripes on the sleeve and a white Captain's hat with the scrambled eggs on the visor. Evidently the police were impressed.

"Scusa, Capitano," one of the cops said. He went on for a bit in a wierd mixture of Italian and broken English and I got the impression that he wanted me to stay where I was. I said, *"Sì,"* half a dozen times, which is what you say whether you understand or not. He knew he wasn't getting anywhere. "Ima no spika so good Inglese," he said, which was not exactly an earthshaking piece of information to me. My Italian was worse than his English. A Pan Am service rep, an Italian, horned in. With absolute confidence he screwed things up even worse except that he waved his arms with more fervor than the cops.

I called on Vito LaForgia, my flight engineer, to bail us all out. Vito waved his arms better than anybody. On top of that he spoke Italian *and* English. Everybody was happy except me. I still didn't know what was going on.

Vito sorted things out. The cops were escorting two people whom Vesco had come to Rome to meet. It was not, I learned, that they were important personages. The cops wanted to make goddamn certain that a) the visitors did not leave Italy; b) they took nothing aboard the airplane that would leave Italy; and c) they took nothing off the airplane into Italy. I was handed two passports. One was in the name of Edward Cellini, passport number C1376272, and the other was in the name of Robert Cellini, passport number A1436272. I didn't need to be told that these two cats were the famous Cellini brothers, Eddie and Dino, who had been tied in with the Mob in the United States and skipped out before they were deported. Both were experts in casino operations and Dino had been run out of England as an undesirable alien.

Vito told me that the reason the cops wanted me to hold the men's passports while they were on the Boeing was because I was being held personally responsible for them. I nodded I would do as they requested. One of the cops signaled to the police cars below.

All during this, Pistell, now fully clothed, was chafing at the bit. He wanted to come outside and join in all the arm-waving. I had trouble keeping him on board and out of sight. When the signal was given to allow the Cellini brothers to come on board, I told Pistell they were on their way and asked him to get back into the passenger cabin. He didn't move. I stood in the doorway at the top of the steps not only to keep Pistell inside but to keep the cops outside. All I needed was to have them stumble upon Pistell's skin party. We would have either all been arrested or we would have to call the Italian Army to get the cops out of the airplane.

The Cellini brothers came right out of Hollywood casting. Eddie appeared to be in his forties and Dino some years older. Their clothes were mobster classic, very classy, very expensive. I stepped aside to let them enter the airplane. I kept the cops at my back. I could hear Vito talking 2½ miles a minute and made a mental note to ask him what the hell he was saying. There was a lot of hugging and back-slapping among Pistell and the Cellinis. Then Pistell took them back to meet Vesco.

Vito was still talking. The cops looked nervous.

"What's happening?" I asked Vito.

"They want to go back with the Cellinis and see what the airplane looks like," Vito said. "But I'm talking them out of it." He had a little smile on his face that I had come to know and distrust. He was up to something. After a few minutes, the cops went down the steps to wait by the cars. They looked very disappointed.

"Okay, Vito," I said, "what the hell did you tell them?"

"I told them that Signore Vesco was a very big, very important American industrialist," Vito said. "They could see that from the kind of airplane he flew in. I told them that Vesco was (hee-hee) also a kind of unofficial representative of President Nixon." Vito was holding a piece of paper in his hand. He had shown it to the cops while he was handing out the snow job and had used it to prove his point. It was the very same "Notice" to my crew that I had written about Junior Nixon, advisor to Mr. Vesco, many months before, which had hung on the door to the flight deck under Vesco's orders to "leave it there."

"I hope for your sake, Vito," I said, "that neither one of those guys can read English."

"If they can't speak it, Ike," Vito came back, "how can they read it?" He held the letter up to me and ran his finger along the line which read ". . . Junior but as Mr. Nixon, nephew of the president."

"There's only two words that count," Vito said, "Nixon and president." It was a risky line of crap to use, but it worked. I left Vito on the top steps to stand guard and went back into the airplane.

I saw the Cellini brothers, followed by Pistell who was talking a mile a minute, in the passageway. The stewardess had backed into the galley alcove. Pistell drew aside the curtain to the main salon, describing its contents. The Cellinis were impressed. The curtain between the salon and Vesco's office had been drawn. The Cellini brothers stopped to admire. With a "Wait till you see *this*!" Pistell took two long strides and whipped aside the other curtain. I saw it before the Cellinis did. I caught a quick glimpse of Vesco, dressed. There was no sign of LeBlanc. One of the girls sat at Shirley Bailey's typewriter. Another sat in a chair holding a pad and pencil. Both were mother naked. The Cellinis went to the entrance to Vesco's office and nearly fell down laughing. That was Pistell's little joke. After the curtain was drawn there was a lot of hooting and hollering, and I heard one of the girls laughing. I drew the curtain to the main salon and told the stewardess to stay forward. If Vesco wanted anything from the galley, I decided, I'd let Vito handle it. He'd like that.

The Cellinis spent about two hours aboard the Boeing. Before they finished their business in Vesco's office, Pistell came out to have me alert the police to escort them away from the airplane. He was in a state of high excitement. He had his arms raised and his fists clenched like a quarterback who had just thrown a "bomb" for the winning touchdown.

"We're in, Ike—we are in," he said. What could I say?

"Do you know who those two guys are?" he asked me.

"Sure," I said, "Eddie and Dino Cellini." I told him that Numb-Nuts, Donald Nixon, Jr., had told me all about them in the casino at Paradise Island. "A couple of hoods."

"What does that pisshead know?" Pistell said. "Who gives a shit what they are? I'd rather do business with them than with a lot of pricks I know who are supposed to be upstanding citizens. Besides," he went on, "they're the ones you have to deal with. They control every card on every table, and every table and wheel in every casino in the world. There's no action anywhere without their say-so. They and Bobby just shook hands on a deal you can't imagine." I wasn't impressed. They were still a couple of hoods and that's what I told him. That didn't slow him down.

"C'mon, Ike," Pistell said, "We're talking about money, not people. Like I told you about the Boeings, that little business conference back there just paid for ten of them." At the going price for a Boeing, he was talking about a hundred million dollars. A lot of money. If the deal ever got past the handshake stage. As far as I was concerned, it was still just conversation.

Vesco escorted the Cellinis to the front of the airplane. The three of them looked pretty pleased with themselves. I had dispatched Vito to tell the policemen that the Cellinis were ready to leave. I took their passports from my pocket. Vesco introduced the Cellini brothers to me. We shook hands. They both had a good firm grip and their English was strictly Miami-New York American. And they looked me square in the eye. I have to admit that they impressed me as a couple of "stand-up guys." Eddie Cellini noticed the passports. He lifted my hand up to get a better look and showed them to his brother. For some reason they both got a big charge out of this. They laughed and carried on a rapid-fire dialogue in Italian.

"Hey, Captain," Dino said, "you tell those cops out there that we were good boys." The cops reached the top step. I handed over the passports. They stood aside respectfully to let Dino and Eddie Cellini go down to the car. That was the last I saw of the Cellinis. I never did learn if Pistell's boast about what the deal was worth ever came true.

Who Vesco invited aboard "his" Boeing was none of my business. Who he made his deals with was also none of my business. But I was not exactly overjoyed at the Cellini visit aboard the Silver Phyllis under the watchful eyes of a couple of Roman policemen. I don't know whether or not the Cellinis were ever convicted of anything. But they didn't earn their reputation by doing good works. It was pretty certain, from everything I'd heard, that they were associated with the notorious Meyer Lansky.

I thought back to the time in March when the Frenchman and my Lebanese friend came to my hotel room in Beirut with all that data from the Casino Leban, which Vesco was angling either to buy or buy into. I had heard from a number of sources that Lansky was a major partner in the Casino Leban.

As I said earlier, Vesco played his own hand—at least on the surface. But if he was dealing with the Cellinis—and Lansky—his associates would be people I wanted no part of. Although none of the crew nor I were any part of Vesco's schemes, some of the smell and dirt could rub off. The idea is not far-fetched. After I terminated my connection with Vesco, there were hints in some newspaper stories and suspicions among some prosecutors that the crew and I were somehow involved with some of the shadier activities Vesco was accused of.

Vesco and Pistell had waited at the entrance to the Boeing until the police cars carrying the Cellini brothers had departed. They were both still "high." Pistell slapped me on the shoulder.

"We're off on the road to Morocco," he kind of sang.

"Right on!" Vesco said. LeBlanc had come forward. Vesco noticed him. Gil Straub stood in the salon with one of the girls. She was wearing one of the lounge suits—one of Junior's. "Let's have a party!" Vesco said. Pistell stretched his arms out and herded everyone toward the back.

"Vunderful—vunderful!" he roared. He closed the curtain behind him.

July 11, 1972 1910Z FCO—RAB

Rome operations at Fumincino had warned me that my flight plan, Rome to Rabat, was dicey. They were unclear about details. The operations supervisor would only tell me that there had been an "incident" in Morocco the day before and that the government had imposed tight security. He wouldn't go so far as to say that martial law was in effect within the country but he advised that there might be a prohibition against inbound, noncommerical aircraft. This news did not elate me. It did not come under the heading of "Flying Can Be Fun."

I couldn't pry any further information from the supervisor, which made me believe that the "incident" was political in nature and, like a good bureaucrat, the supervisor was not about to commit himself in any way.

This kind of situation, an "incident" in an area as explosive as North Africa, has got to involve a shooting. I didn't have the time to make a lot of inquiries. Vesco was ready to roll. But I was not about to fly Silver Phyllis into the midst of a Moroccan "shoot-em-up." This was a decision for Vesco to make.

He was annoyed when I busted in on his party to tell him that we might not be allowed to land in Rabat or that, if we were, we might get shot at.

"We go to Rabat, Ike," he said. "If it was anything heavy, I'd know about it. Take my word for it, there won't be any trouble. We're expected." If "Chicken-of-the-Skies" wasn't worried, that was a stainless-steel guarantee as far as I was concerned.

Robert Lee Vesco was as right as rain. We were met at Sale Airport in Rabat by a whole covey of Moroccan big shots led by the Moroccan minister of foreign affairs, Ali Ben Hima. On the ramp there was a military honor guard complete with a band. In Ben Hima's party were a number of high-ranking military officers, one of whom was commanding general of the Moroccan air force.

For a minute I thought maybe I had misinterpreted ground-control instructions and was taxiing to the wrong spot on the ramp. But there, out in front of me, the taxi director was signaling to me as if he knew exactly what he was doing.

"Is this for us?" my first officer asked me.

"Beats me," I said. I wondered if somebody had made a mistake.

When the door was opened, a Moroccan air-force officer came aboard and asked to be taken to the aircraft commander, which was me. He spoke very precise English with a French accent. He saluted smartly. I got the impression that this was a very formal situation. I fell back on military protocol, which dictates that a salute is not necessary when one is uncovered—that is, without a hat on. He informed me that the foreign minister was ready to receive my passengers and asked if they were prepared to disembark. I said I would find out. He promptly did an about-face and left the flight deck. Uniform time again. Despite the fact that it was nine o'clock in the evening local time, the heat was oppressive. But anything to uphold the honor of my-country-tis-of-thee and my boss.

I instructed the entire crew to dress up and went back to inform Vesco, Pistell, Straub, LeBlanc, and the broads that there was a parade going on out on the ramp and I thought maybe it was for them. They knew. They were looking out the windows. Vesco looked a little bit concerned almost as if he were worried about whether all those soldiers were there to welcome him or to arrest him. He had been pretty confident back in Rome when he'd said that we were expected. But I don't think he anticipated this kind of reception.

Vesco was up to the situation. He straightened his tie, checked his fly, and strode with the assurance of a head of state toward the front of the aircraft. He was followed by Pistell, Straub, the four broads, and LeBlanc.

Maybe the welcoming committee was actually meant for somebody else and the Moroccans were too polite to embarrass all of us. Vesco was greeted with salutes and hearty handshakes all around. As most of the party plus the band and the honor guard disappeared, I marveled at what had happened. Robert Vesco spends two hours and change with a couple of hoods in Rome and is honored in Morocco with an official government reception headed up by the equivalent of our secretary of state.

Not everybody left. A guard of sorts was left around the airplane. We were parked directly in front of the "distinguished-visitors" terminal, an all-glass, modern, very attractive structure not far from the main terminal. A member of the official greeting party was a representative of Morocco's national airline, Royal Air Moroc. He had gone to the terminal with Ben Hima and Vesco but returned a short time later with a request. Would I be kind enough to allow visitors aboard the aircraft? The man was obviously curious about Silver Phyllis. So were a number of Moroccan air force honchos. He said that Mr. Vesco said it would be all right if I said it was all right. No argument. I gave the air force people and the man from Air Moroc the grand tour. Their reactions were predictable. Astonishment.

When that tour was over the Air Moroc man had another request. There was this flight from Cuba. A Russian flight. Would I extend the same courtesy to the crew of the Russian aircraft and their passengers? The U.S. was hostile to Cuba and that presented a sticky problem. I didn't believe that there were any CIA types lurking about to take pictures of whoever came on board the Boeing but, considering the situation, I had to rule out the Cubans.

About a quarter of an hour later I was informed that the Russian aircraft was on final approach. We had been asked to remain with the Boeing. We all went out to look. I had a professional curiosity. There wasn't a hell of a lot to see. Sale Airport is not exactly overwhelmed with traffic. Its lighting system is inadequate and the place is not surrounded by well-lighted communities to illuminate incoming aircraft. I had been hoping to get a good look at a Russian commercial jet liner. I had heard and read a lot about them. I was disappointed. All I could see were the aircraft's landing lights. The information I had was that Russian commercial jets were converted military aircraft and landed "hot." I half expected to see a drag chute pop out from the ass end to slow the landing roll. This particular aircraft was making a fuel stop, having come nonstop from Havana, which meant that in terms of fuel weight he was light. The runway at Rabat is almost 12,000 feet long—about two miles. And the Russian Captain used up just about every foot of it before he brought the airplane to a stop. Which told me something. Either the Russian aircraft was hotter than I was led to believe or that the Captain took a rather casual approach to getting his airplane on the ground. After I met him I was surprised that he was able to stop the airplane in that short a distance.

I had to wait until the Russian aircraft actually left the taxiway and pulled onto the relatively well-lighted ramp area. It was an Ilyushin-62, CCCP 86653, operated by Aeroflot, the official Russian-government airline. My first impression was that it was an ugly airplane.

Most aircraft-producing nations make an effort to design their commercial aircraft totally different from that of their military aircraft. But commercial or military, the airplanes have an integrity about them. Commercial aircraft look like commercial aircraft and the whole design is in harmony. The same is true of military aircraft. The IL-62 looked like it was built in somebody's backyard out of spare parts from a dozen different airplanes. The landing gear was high and spindly and looked as if it were too fragile to support the weight of the aircraft. But it did, so I have to believe it was structurally sound. The fuselage seemed to be too slender for any kind of passenger comfort unless the seats were arranged only two across. The engines were clustered around the tail and looked outsized. The IL-62 parked about 150 feet from us. Even its taxiing was erratic and bouncy. It kind of slurbed to a stop. I was astonished to see a long slender "bull pecker" telescope out from under the tail to the ground. The bull pecker had a pair of little bitty wheels on the end. Passenger doors were located both in the aft end of the airplane and farther forward. I found out immediately the reason for the bull pecker. The balance of the IL-62 was so critical that it was a toss-up either way as to which end, nose or tail, would dip with the shifting of passenger weight. If more than half the Cubans decided to exit the rear door the nose of the IL-62 would have been tilted up at a 45-degree angle—if it wasn't for the bull pecker.

The IL-62 has a capacity roughly that of the Boeing 707-300, configured for normal passenger-carrying—about 189. And if I hadn't known better, I would have thought half the population of Havana got off that Russian airplane.

The Russian crew, about a dozen people including a few Cuban stewardesses, were brought to the Boeing by the Air Moroc rep. The most impressive one of the bunch, or at least the one who stood out, was the Captain. He was a man in his middle fifties a little above average height and squarely built. He was in sharp contrast to what the appearance of a senior airline Captain has come to be. He looked like a slob, like anything but a flying man. His uniform was rumpled and seedy looking. He was expansive in his gestures, smiled a lot, and talked constantly—in Russian. The first officer, however, was stick neat. He was slender, tall, blond, and superior looking. And proved to be a thorough pain in my ass. The rest of the crew, including the stewardesses (Russian or Cuban), were nondescript. The women, especially, were about as interesting as a bunch of female hammer throwers.

I was prepared for a walk-through of the Boeing and maybe a short session on the flight deck. At the very beginning it had been agreed that I would have a chance to look over the IL-62. The last thing in the world I wanted to get involved in was a bragging contest with the Russians over which was the better society. The Russian Captain was a friendly bear of a man. I don't know what the standards for a senior Captain are in Russia. I have been pretty harsh in some of the things that I have said about American senior Captains. But from the brief chance I had to rate my Russian counterpart, and from the memory I had of that landing and the way he taxied in and stopped his airplane, I was developing a very negative attitude toward Russian civil aviation.

It soon became very obvious that what might have started out to be nothing more than a courtesy visit at the request of the Moroccans turned into the very kind of "can-you-top-this" exercise that I wanted to avoid. On top of that there were political overtones—Russian—that made me feel uncomfortable.

The Russian Captain of the IL-62 was a very likeable, openhanded kind of man. He didn't speak any English but his delight and his admiration for the Boeing was obvious. His first officer, on the other hand, was Mr. Obnoxious himself. He was deliberately unimpressed with the Boeing and all its parts. He was much younger than the Captain, I would guess by about twenty years. He seemed to hold the Captain in complete contempt, which is nothing new even in the West. I have seldom met a First Officer who did not have the confidence to do a better job than the Captain. I can understand that kind of rivalry. But there was another element about these men that had nothing to do with flying. It was of a political nature. The Russian first officer made it a point more than once to mention that he was a party member and that the Captain was not.

Whatever I showed him on the airplane he found some way to knock, but none of his criticisms were based on technological factors. He used phrases like "Yankee extravagance," "capitalistic redundancy," "bourgeois self-indulgence." The Boeing was an overdesigned and under utilized luxury for the ruling class. While the first officer was running off at the mouth, the Captain clambered around the flight deck like a little kid. He was delighted with everything he saw. He must have sensed—he probably knew damn well—that the first officer was busting my chops. And I guess he was glad that he could not speak English and therefore did not have to engage in a pissing contest over the relative merits of the Soviet and American technologies.

Before I lost my cool I decided to end the debate with the first officer by opening the crew bar. I wouldn't be flying for another day. I figured that the Russians followed the same rules about imbibing before flight and, in addition to an array of booze, I had had the stewardess lay out a good collection of soft drinks and juices. As host I invited the Russian Captain to help himself. He zapped right over the juices and soft drinks and picked up a bottle of Hennessy Five Star Cognac and measured out about a yard and a half of the stuff into a plastic tumbler. He dropped it into his stomach in one gulp. The rest of the crew followed suit, except for the first officer, who didn't touch a drop of the hard stuff. I couldn't believe it. I was told that Rabat was only a fuel stop for the Russians on their way to Moscow and that they would be taking off very shortly. The way they were going at the booze it looked as if they would be on the ground for a week. Just to be sure I asked the first officer when they were leaving. He looked at his watch and told me they would be leaving within the hour. Oh Jesus!

I did not want to be responsible—even remotely—for killing a Russian planeload of Cubans and the crew of the aircraft itself. Rather than shut down the bar abruptly, I suggested we "all go over to their place." Ivan the Terrible welcomed the idea. So we all trooped the hundred or so feet across the ramp to the IL-62. It was even uglier up close. It was high enough off the ground to be airborne even sitting on the ramp. From the top of the steps the ground looked as if it were three stories below.

My chief interest was the flight deck, the instrumentation, and the control system. The whole thing was pre-historic. The dials, clocks, and gauges looked as if they had come out of a foundry and were made for a Rocky Mountain sixteen-wheel locomotive. The control column was absolutely off the wall. Instead of having a single control wheel mounted on each side of the cockpit, there were two on each side. When I asked about this the first officer explained that the big wheel was used for takeoffs and landings since it provided more leverage, and the small wheel was used in cruise where control movement was very limited. The First Officer bragged that the Russians had no use for the sophisticated boosted control systems on Western aircraft. He made a fist.

"In Russia," he said, "we fly our airplanes." Just the way they did in 1928. Maybe. But what is saved in the Russian approach to aircraft control systems compared to American aircraft is lost in passenger comfort, crew fatigue, and safety margins. It's a matter of finesse vs. muscle.

Ivan the Terrible was not interested in inspections and professional chitchat. Several times he interrupted his first officer's glowing description of the IL-62. Finally he gave up and stomped off toward the galley. The first officer watched him go with a look of disgust on his face.

"He is too old for this job," he said. "He does not

have discipline and flies only because he enjoys it." He was running true to form for first officers. He went on.

"Very soon," he said, "I will take command and they will put him out to pasture." This was interesting to me in that he was really still pretty young and, by our standards, very inexperienced. He had already told me that he could claim more than 2500 hours' flying experience. That was total in all aircraft, including training. By American standards he was just a beginner—a short time out of flight school. It would be at least another ten years before he could even think about command of a transoceanic aircraft anywhere but in Russia. I felt it would be a wise idea on my part not to comment. I left the flight deck to join the Captain at the galley.

The Captain, with a broad grin on his face, welcomed me with a shout and held up a bottle of Russian brandy, although I didn't know what was in the bottle and had to ask the first officer. He poured out a healthy dollop for me and then one for himself and urged me to dump it down as he had in the Boeing. I did. Better the Russians should stick to vodka. But the Captain evidently felt about Russian brandy the way his first officer felt about Russian airplanes. He snapped off a few more shots for himself. So many that the first officer called him on it—or at least I think he did. He hollered at the Captain in Russian. Naturally I couldn't understand what was being said but there was no mistaking the outrage and anger in the Captain's response. I expected the first officer to shrivel up into a little heap of ash. The brief dustup took the edge off the party. The first officer was embarrassed and apologized for his Captain, which was an arrogance I didn't appreciate. But he went beyond this.

"But it is no matter," he said. "I will fly the leg to Moscow. He will go to sleep and snore all the way."

The cabin of the IL-62 was bulkheaded like a submarine. It was cramped and drab, and I was happy to leave.

I hope that airplane got to Moscow in good order. But with the Russian habit of keeping their air disasters secret, it's hard to say.

Before we left Rabat for Newark the following afternoon, I checked into the nature of the "incident" I had been warned about in Rome. From the reception we had gotten the night before there was not the slightest indication that anybody in Morocco was uptight about anything. A situation that could be serious enough to warrant "tight security" and a possible exclusion of incoming private aircraft would certainly have kept Morocco's foreign minister, its air force chief, and assorted military men in their offices and not out greeting a rich American con artist like Vesco.

It was not difficult to find out what I wanted to know. The papers were full of it. The official language was Arabic but French and Spanish are also spoken. I recognized some words in a headline in a French-language newspaper. I asked the hotel clerk what it was all about.

King Hassan II was returning from a trip to France in his Boeing 727 and was over his own country when a Moroccan air-force fighter plane fired a couple of shots across his bow, and a few more through the airplane. As yet there was very little information as to who was behind it or what happened to the attacking plane. I thought about the air force chief out on the ramp. He didn't seem too damn worried.

The four girls who were brought from Amsterdam were left at Rabat. LeBlanc assured me that they were not sold into white slavery but given first-class air tickets home.

Next stop was Newark, after which I brought Silver Phyllis to Burbank, California, where Steve Bragg and Associates, under subcontract to Qualitron, would install Vesco's private stateroom. It was Steve Bragg and Associates that built Vesco's mini-nightclub under subcontract to Qualitron during the previous phase. As usual it was a round-the-clock effort to get the work done. Bragg only had from July 17, 1972, to August 4, 1972, to do his job, for which twice the amount of time should have been scheduled. It was a race to the wire but Bragg finished the job on schedule. From now on, Vesco could rest his weary bones in solitary splendor and regal privacy.

15

September 10, 1972 2210Z EWR—LHR—SND

Al Junker thought I was kidding.

"I'm serious, Al," I told him. "Put your coffee cup down and come on up to the flight deck." I could see that he really wanted to handle Silver Phyllis. I knew why he was holding back. By his own admission, he had never been on the flight deck of a Boeing 707, and as a professional airman he didn't want to fool around with another guy's airplane. He must have thought I was just being polite.

"Hey, boss," I said, "stop playing hard-to-get." His wife Elaine gave him a nudge.

"Go on, Junker," she said, "you know you're dying to do it." He finally got up and came forward with me.

The Boeing was on auto-pilot and First Officer Dusse was in the right-hand seat. He turned and said "hi" to Al. Al waited for me to get into the left seat and Dusse to turn his seat over to him. I indicated my seat to Al.

"Take over, Captain," I said. He just didn't believe that I wanted him to sit in the aircraft commander's place. The position of aircraft commander is not just a matter of title or rank. It entails unique responsibility in that the aircraft commander makes the decisions that affect the lives not only of his passengers but also, too often, the lives of people on the ground or in other aircraft. An aircraft commander does not lightly turn over his role to anyone who is not a qualified crew member. I have done it only twice in my life, the first time to Al. The second time was to a member of the Spanish Royal Family.

I literally had to shove Al into the seat. It had quite an impact on him. He understood that it was not only a gesture of friendship on my part or the chance to share an experience. According to the protocol of the air (which grew out of the "law of the sea"), Al recognized that he was taking actual command of the Boeing. Whatever emotions he felt were put aside immediately. I could see the change in him. He immediately set about familiarizing himself with the cockpit. I was ignored. He talked with the first officer. I reached forward to Al's control wheel and disconnected the automatic pilot. Al looked down and then back at me with a slight frown, as if he would kick me in the wrist for daring to kibitz. Nobody touches anything without the aircraft commander's permission or direction. I flipped him a half-assed salute and left him. Al Junker was in charge.

Al came up from Ft. Lauderdale to Newark at my invitation. Ever since I left Bethlehem Steel I had stayed in touch with Al and saw him regularly a couple of times a year, especially after his retirement to Florida. This was not his first flight in the Boeing. During crew retraining in Florida and when the Boeing was in for inspection I would invite Al along, but only as an observer.

During World War II, Al, who had served with the RCAF before Pearl Harbor and switched over to the U.S. Navy, was stationed in England. Al had a great affection for England. Elaine, however, had never been there. Two weeks earlier I had visited with Al and Elaine in Ft. Lauderdale. I knew that we would be going to England and, with Vesco's permission, asked Al and Elaine to come along. Al was a guy who didn't accept favors easily. But he couldn't turn this one down.

With Al in the left seat I was able to go back to the cabin to catch up on some paperwork. Silver Phyllis was due for her final modification phase in one week, and I was able to go over the specs and drawings with Vesco in his office.

These airborne meetings with Vesco were usually of short duration. This conference lasted far beyond the time limit Vesco was used to. I did this deliberately. I wanted to get a reaction out of Vesco. He was always aware of what was happening aboard the Boeing, and my prolonged absence from the flight deck would have to make him uneasy. He finally looked up from the papers as if a light had gone on.

"Hey, Ike," he said, "who the hell is minding the store?"

"Al Junker," I told him. "But don't sweat it, Bob. Al is as good as they come." Vesco accepted that judgment. I took that as a vote of confidence in me.

I relieved Al after a couple of hours. He was exhilirated. But he wasn't the type to spill emotion all over the place.

"She's some machine," was all he said as I took over. After Al left the flight deck, Ron Dusse paid him the ultimate compliment.

"That man really knows his flying," he said. "He's as smooth as silk."

I had one more surprise for Al—Southend. Al and Elaine had planned to get off at Heathrow with the rest of my passengers. I was going to Southend for a routine inspection at ATEL. I couldn't let a chance like this—to show off a little for my old boss and teacher—slip by. I persuaded Al to come along without telling him what the runway situation at Southend was. He and Elaine could start their sightseeing in England from Southend instead of London. Besides, I was sure that Al would remember Southend as a wartime base. This time I had Al on the flight deck for the short trip and the landing.

Al didn't have to be told that landing at Southend in a Boeing was a piece of hard work and that there was no room for error. He had an eye that could measure a runway to the inch. If he was worried about that short runway, he didn't show it.

I did my number with Al watching every move and noting every call-out. This time I brought the Boeing to a stop in a shorter distance than my first landing at Southend. Al made no comments. He merely looked at me as if to say "you'll do." But I knew I had gotten to him.

Al and Elaine rejoined us a couple of days later for the return trip. It had been a great experience for both of them.

At Heathrow we added Marti Figueres and a British film producer, Enrique Carreras, to the passenger list back to Nassau. Carreras specialized in horror films and would later team up with Gil Straub in producing a real dog of a picture financed by Vesco and Straub, called *House of Horror*.

The Costa Rican business was developing rapidly. The day after we arrived at Nassau, Vesco went to San Jose with Marti Figueres and Dick Clay. Vesco was worried. He knew all about the investigation in the U.S. by the Securities and Exchange Commission. On the way to England, while we were going over Phase V modification plans, he had commented a number of times about "those bastards in Washington." He had a special hatred for Stanley Sporkin, at that time assistant director of the SEC's enforcement division, who was pressing the investigation. Vesco always referred to Sporkin as "that Jew bastard." I resented Vesco using me as a sounding board for his diatribes against people who annoyed him. The way he characterized people on a racial or ethnic basis irritated me. Any Jew who crossed him—Cornfeld, Sporkin, Schiowicz—was a "Jew bastard." His language was filled with words like "Guinea," "Frog," "Mick," "Spick." But it was for the Jews that he had the largest vocabulary. They were "Sheenies," "Heebs," or "Kikes."

Not only did I not want to hear this kind of garbage, but my relationship to him did not, in my book, entitle him to unload his prejudices and problems on me.

Vesco's comments about his problems with the SEC were not news. Almost everybody around him shot off their mouths constantly. Sometimes one of them would get me aside to pass on information I didn't want to hear in the first place. But most of it came to me during conversations conducted in my presence which I could not help but overhear.

I'm a realist about the role I filled as Vesco's chief pilot. Even a chief pilot can be made to feel like a piece of furniture or a pet cat. Vesco and his minions were no different than a lot of the wheeler-dealers I've carried around. They forget that flight crews are human.

Ralph Dodd had always been afflicted with the loose-lip syndrome. It seemed to me that his habit of dealing in gossip stemmed from the need to appear more important than he regarded himself. He told me that Vesco was using Harry Sears as his lever to pry cooperation out of Mitchell in stopping the SEC investigation.

On May 31, 1972, I had flown Sears and Vesco to Washington, only six weeks after the secret payoff to the Nixon campaign fund. It was on that date that Sears and Vesco were alleged to have met with G. Bradford Cook, General Counsel to the SEC. Dodd confirmed this.

There was a report that Vesco again met with Cook in Washington on June 27, 1972, along with Stanley Sporkin. I don't know if this meeting ever took place. I had brought Vesco and Gil Straub from London to Newark on June 24 and left Newark for Zurich, with Gil Straub as my only passenger, on June 26. I returned from Zurich to Nassau on June 27. After I had gotten to my hotel in Nassau, I received a call from Vesco that we would be leaving on June 29 on that first flight to Costa Rica with Pistell and Cerney. There was no way I could tell whether Vesco was calling from the family compound in Nassau or from Washington, D.C.

It was Dodd, again, who volunteered information that seems to substantiate the June 27 meeting at which Stanley Sporkin was alleged to have been present. That was a week later, after we returned to New Jersey from that first Costa Rican visit. Dodd was supposed to have broken with Vesco and ICC. The impression was that prior to the April 6, 1972 CREEP contribution, Vesco and Dodd had split and were wrangling over Dodd's severance pay. The truth is that the so-called resignation was an element in a Vesco game plan. Dodd, under instructions from Vesco, had allied himself—either by buying in or by special arrangement—with the investment house of Ross, Low, Bull & Co., 120 Broadway, New York City. Dodd was actually in a "training program" which would qualify him for a license as a securities broker,although Vesco was already hooked in with a Wall Street broker, Arthur Lipper III. Lipper had been aboard the Boeing a number of times, and it was obvious that he and Vesco disliked each other intensely despite their business associations. The game plan called for Dodd to function as Vesco's inside man at an established brokerage house such as Ross, Low, Bull. This would give Vesco a free-flow channel for whatever paper he wanted to move. So, except on the surface, my relationship with Dodd didn't change. I saw and spoke with him frequently at Fairfield after the "split."

Dodd told me that Vesco had "made a dumb move." Sporkin would not play ball. He was going ahead with the investigation. In fact, he was accelerating it. The way Dodd told it Vesco became incensed and swore that he would have Sporkin "taken care of." I gathered from Dodd's manner of telling me this that Vesco's threat implied physical harm, possibly death, to Sporkin. Dodd did not tell me to whom Vesco made the threat or whether he was present to hear it.

I would have dismissed Dodd's revelation as pure bullshit, except that more than once Vesco had angrily used the same kind of language against others. He has even used mobster phraseology, such as "I'll put a contract out on him."

This all might seem melodramatic, empty bravado. But I had only to remind myself of the gang of toughs with which Vesco surrounded himself, especially Vesco's head goon, a nasty looking piece of work known only as "The Major." The Major and his troops would have no doubts about what Vesco meant when he made these threats and each one of them had the balls and the know-how to carry them out to the limit. I got to know these guys very well in Costa Rica and actually taught them how to use the sophisticated weaponry that Vesco had. I myself was threatened directly by Vesco the day we parted company. On that day he meant what he said.

I constantly tried to maintain the same attitude towards Vesco and his dealings that I would for any other corporate entity I might have worked for. To a chief pilot, or any pilot, working in a corporate aviation set-up, how the company runs its business is immaterial so long as there is enough money to keep him employed. But there is always company gossip to spice up a conversation when nothing else is happening. In a way this is how it was with Vesco except that my involvement, unwilling though it was on my part, was a little closer to the bone. It was hard not to dwell on the kind of information, rumor, speculation and so forth, that came my way. What was especially disturbing was something like the Cellini business or Junior's blatherings about "the mob." It was too much to ignore. The picture that emerged was not a comforting one.

Vesco has been treated generally in the press and by book writers as a free wheeling, unscrupulous, international business freebooter. There have been allegations about ties to organized crime. But that aspect of Vesco's activities is treated almost as if it were something new to Vesco and were a way to garner even more wealth through mob "affiliations." What has not been commented on in any realistic way is Vesco's intention to control the kind of activity that has always been controlled by mobsters. No businessman, crooked or honest, "moves in" on the mob. Howard Hughes couldn't do it. You exist alongside the mob by agreement, you work for the mob—willingly or under duress—or you are part of the mob.

The conglomerate of casinos, hotels, airlines, and travel agencies that Vesco wanted to put together, along with his banking and brokerage network, is ideal for a currency laundromat, a dumping ground for "hot paper" and an underground railway for the movement of large amounts of cash and merchandise.

Almost everybody in the Vesco entourage believed absolutely that Vesco could buy or blackjack his way out of the SEC problem. Vesco believed this himself. But he was also a realist. He knew something could go wrong and was smart enough to recognize that he had to prepare a fall-back position.

September 16, 1972 0015Z SJO—MSY—EWR

"I'm going to fix that smart-ass Jew bastard Sporkin's wagon!" Vesco said. We were in his airborne office on the way to Newark from San Jose, again going over Phase V modification final plans. The only other passenger was a James Walker whom we were to drop at New Orleans, where we would also pick up Vesco's parents. The remark came out of the blue. Vesco was in a feisty mood. It came out as if he had devised the perfect plan and had to tell somebody. I didn't encourage him but he insisted on laying out the details. They shook the shit out of me.

"I'm going to dump ICC," he said. "I'm quitting." This was a real kick in the balls. If he quit ICC, there goes my job.

"Christ, Bob," I said, "that flushes me and the crew right down the drain. The company [ICC] will dump the whole aviation division and unload the Boeing." He laughed.

"Ikey," he said, "I wouldn't do a thing like that to you." I decided to be candid.

"Bullshit, Bob," I said. "I've seen you operate." There was a flash of anger. But he took it. And covered his anger with another laugh.

"It's just a smokescreen, Ike," he said. He was dead serious. I honestly believe he was hurt by my remark.

"I've got to get the SEC off my back. Once I'm officially out of ICC and Fairfield, Sporkin has nobody to squeeze. He's going to be taking a long walk on a short dock. Nothing will change." I wasn't too sure of that. The only thing that encouraged any optimism in me was the Boeing. I think Vesco would have sold his soul to keep it.

The Customs services of the world, it seems to me at times, is an international brotherhood. Screw one and you screw them all. Every international traveler knows about the big black book that contains the names of all those people who, for one reason or another, merit special attention. Vesco made the book and the Immigration "watch list."

There were enough government agencies interested in Vesco's comings and goings to warrant his inclusion in the book. But I think there is another category, which I fully expect I will fall into, after publication of this memoir, which I call "enemies of the service." It includes all those travelers who have in any way offended a Customs person anywhere in the world.

We landed at Moissant International Airport in New Orleans about 11:30 that night. Vesco, anticipating that he would be extended the usual courtesy of an on-board Customs and Immigration inspection, was clad in his velour lounging suit and slippers.

The Customs and Immigration people came aboard as expected. From that point on it was all downhill. The Customs inspector was in a lousy mood. The Immigration officer who accompanied him, a woman, seemed accomodating enough. But despite the fact that the two services were independent of each other, the Customs guy seemed to be running things. There are two things to remember. Customs cannot order anyone off an airplane—or a ship for that matter—unless an arrest is made for cause. Immigration does not search aircraft or ships unless they are looking for a person.

There were no preliminaries. The first thing the Customs Agent said was that "everybody" was required to leave the airplane and go into the terminal for clearance. It was not so much what he said as the way he said it that irritated me. I pointed out—something which Customs already knew, or should have known from advanced information I filed before leaving San Jose—that I had only two passengers aboard and a crew of six. One of my passengers was terminating in New Orleans and would follow standard procedures for arriving international passengers. I also told him that my remaining passenger was in transit to Newark and that two additional passengers would be boarding at New Orleans. Which was really none of his concern. I didn't see any reason why he had to empty the airplane. But there was no reasoning with the guy.

"Everybody into the terminal," he insisted. This was new to me. Apart from the fact that he was assuming an authority he didn't have, it was a departure from common practice, especially with regard to crew. Maybe I was feeling a little paranoiac. But it looked like a deliberate effort at harassment. I was ripping mad, but there was no point in starting a war with this guy. Even though I had legitimate cause for complaint. All this guy had to do—even if it was only a case of hurt feelings—was to holler for a demolition squad on the pretext of "a tip" and tear apart the interior of the Boeing. Government agencies seem to have—or think they do—complete license to wield their authority—often vague at best—to the limit. And, there is no recourse. The best you can expect is a flippant "Sorry about that."

I insisted—and made it stick—that one crew member would remain aboard to "assist" Customs in its "inspection." I didn't give a shit if the guy thought I was implying that he would develop sticky fingers. I went back and told Vesco what the situation was, expecting an explosion. He surprised me.

"Fuck 'em," he said. "Let 'em play their goddam games." He breezed out of the airplane, in his jammies and slippers, toward the terminal.

To reach the passenger holding area for international arrivals, it was necessary to pass through a glass maze in the terminal building. People who are waiting to greet arrivals could see passengers as they passed by. I spotted Momma and Poppa Vesco. Bobby waved at them as he passed them. Poppa shook his head in disbelief. Momma smiled proudly.

It may seem that I am continually beating the same drum—the Customs Service. The fact is that too often the behaviour of Customs Inspectors is indicative of the abuse of authority and function of too many government agencies in the United States. My most frequent encounters, because of the kind of work I did, were with Customs, Immigrations and aviation bureaucrats. But, especially over the last two years, I have butted heads with other government agencies and their functionaries. The New Orleans incident, by itself, was maddening enough. Who the hell do you complain to? As I've related in this book, it was neither the first nor the last—and it certainly wasn't the worst—incident in my experience. Once, coming into Newark, after a long flight and no sleep for twenty-four hours, the Boeing was boarded by a phalanx of Customs Officers, the demolition squad, and a drug sniffing dog. I had absolutely no warning. The only authority for the raid was an anonymous "tip" that—a telephone tip at that—drugs were being smuggled into the country aboard the Boeing. The sticking point was that I was well-known to the Customs supervisor who led the boarding party. I had to threaten him, citing government regulations to support my stance, with legal action if he persisted in his stated mission of ripping the guts out of the airplane. The matter was resolved strictly according to regulations and the airplane was generally unharmed. The point is that if I had not known the rules and regulations Silver Phyllis would have been ready for the scrap heap.

In the years since I left Vesco I have been hauled before grand juries, "invited" into the offices of prosecutors with the U.S. Attorney General's office and the Securities and Exchange Commission. I've been subpenaed on behalf of both pro and anti Vesco litigants. I have been visited by the FBI, IRS investigators, private detectives, and journalists. With damn few exceptions I have been treated—and this is true of a number of my crew members as well—as if I were a conspirator with Robert Vesco and his gang. The private detectives and the journalists, I could toss out on their ears. To openly defy a government stooge is to invite retaliation. I've seen too much of this type of official viciousness around the world. Government harrassment of citizens is something I associate with countries behind the Iron-Curtain or so politically primitive that they are still generations away from the kind of personal freedom that I've always believed was part and parcel of being an American. Now I'm not so sure that the "land of the free" exists. And the terrible part is that there is nobody around to holler "Stop!" and make it stick.

Vesco's plan to cut Sporkin off at the pass didn't work. Events proved that Sporkin, far from being discouraged or frustrated, bore down even harder.

September 17, 1972 1425Z EWR—GSW

Lou Notte handed me a shock. I was sitting in Jack Prewitt's office going over the bills from Silver Phyllis's last visit. ICC was a slow pay and Jack wanted my help in "expediting" payment by having me personally approve every invoice. Jack wanted everything cleared up before the final phase was completed.

The Boeing was sitting half in, half out of Qualitron's hangar at Greater Southwest Airport. Workmen were inside stripping out all the temporary furnishings and removing the floor panels and floor substructure of station 1220. This is where Vesco's mini-gym, dressing area, shower and tub, and the only airborne sauna—a five seater—on any airplane in the world were to be installed.

Lou interrupted us. He had a worried look on his face.

"We got a problem, Ike," he said, "a bad one. You'd better come and take a look." Lou was absolutely right.

The spongy floor panels were the problem. As I had mentioned earlier, while we worked our way aft during the successive phases of modification, the panels were replaced and necessary repairs made to make Silver Phyllis better than new. But what I saw under the spongy floor panels from station 1220 aft was enough to make me want to throw up. The entire aft end of the aircraft was a mass of corrosion. More than half of the underfloor structure, the cross supports and skin ties, were nothing but powder. The fore and aft skin stringers around the aft lavatory service panel were gone. The entire service panel was rotted from the inside to such a degree that it was a miracle Silver Phyllis didn't blow her whole ass out over the Atlantic as the result of a skin rupture. Christ almighty!

I didn't have time to dwell on what might have happened at any time under pressurization. What I faced, what Vesco faced, was a major rebuilding job that together with the already planned installation would take a minimum of six weeks and cost an additional 60,000 dollars. I called Vesco immediately and filled him in on all the gory details. He went bananas. I let him rant. He was entitled. I finally had to interrupt his screaming profanity.

"Bob, what do you want me to do about it?" I asked.

"What can you do about it?" he replied.

"We've got three alternatives, Bob," I said. "The first is we take care of the corrosion problem and put the airplane back in service. We can finish off the rest at a later date. The second is that we can do the whole job now. That will take about six weeks." I paused. He came back quickly.

"What's the third one?" he asked.

"Sell the airplane and get another one," I said. I waited for his answer. I waited a long time.

"No way!" he finally said. "We'll go with number one." He then launched into one of his patented tirades, chewing my ass out at a hundred-and-twenty bites a minute. He blamed me for the problem.

"Didn't you inspect that goddamn airplane when you bought it?" he yelled at me. "That's what I hired you for." I interrupted him.

"Now wait one goddamn minute, Bob," I yelled back. "In the first place, I didn't buy the goddamn airplane. You and Ralph did. You guys never consulted me. In the second place, Dodd is the one who arranged for the inspection. They could have handed him the annual report of the Florida Water Commission and he wouldn't know the goddamn difference. The only thing

Dodd knows about airplanes is how to get on and off without falling down the goddamn steps. And you sent him down to buy a goddamn Pan Am Boeing and hire personnel without any input from me. *That* was the job you hired me for. And to clean up the shit after guys like Dodd." It stopped him cold. He didn't say anything for a bit.

"Take it up with Ralph," he said finally. "I want that airplane in two weeks." Take it up with Ralph? He was supposed to have quit the company. That's when I learned another lesson in Vesco double-shuffle.

"Ralph quit," I reminded him. "How come I deal with Ralph?"

"It only looks that way," Vesco said. "Ralph is still in the picture. You deal with him and don't ask questions. You can still reach him at Fairfield." The only reason I would want to talk to Ralph was about the bills—the ones I had gone over with Jack Prewitt and the ones to cover the corrosion problem. There was no point in chewing Ralph's ass out over the foul-up with the inspection. He'd only start to whine and make excuses, and besides the damage was already done. The only satisfaction I got was in *telling* Ralph to pay the bills and not asking him. And getting his agreement without argument. Of course Dodd did not follow through on payment of the corrosion bills, which later became a part of an ICC/Fairfield hassle with Qualitron which almost lost the Boeing for Bob Vesco.

October 26, 1972 1400Z MAD—NAS

October was Spanish month in Vesco's schedule. The SEC situation had forced Vesco to re-align his ducks. The phony resignation from ICC hadn't fooled anyone. Vesco also realized that he was vulnerable because of his IOS caper. Howard Cerney and another New York attorney, Robert Foglia, served Vesco as legal hatchet men. If Cerney was a hummingbird, Foglia, in my book, was a spook. He was one of the lawyers in

Geneva when Vesco was trying to get sprung from St. Antoine Prison. In physical appearance he was a lot bigger than Cerney, but in manner he is "the man who isn't there."

The Spanish invasion began with a quick, probing thrust, on October 11, 1972. Vesco had with him his two jailbird buddies, Meissner and Strickler, and Marti Figueres. Oh yeah, Donald Nixon, Jr. was also on board. Out of Madrid we had two additional passengers, Frederic Weymar, an American and a carryover from IOS, and an English lawyer, Michael Rogers. Rogers was later accused of acting as courier, carrying "hot money" between countries and continents.

Vesco began to show the effects of his problems with the SEC. He had made a couple of appearances before it in Washington and had been subpenaed to appear before it again on October 18, 1972. It would be his final appearance. On the 17th of October I carried Vesco and Pistell from Nassau to Newark. Vesco was in a rotten mood. So rotten that even the irrespressible Pistell was subdued. I could see where Pistell's brand of hyperactive jollity could ossify your guts at the wrong time.

Vesco left the country for Madrid again, at seven o'clock in the evening of October 22, 1972. Lying on the table in the crew lounge were several newspapers, which carried on the front page an account of Vesco's SEC testimony, during which he took the Fifth Amendment. Unlike almost every executive I've ever flown, Vesco was not a newspaper reader. He not only hated the press with a passion but he really didn't give a rat's ass about what was happening around the world outside of his own concerns. When he saw the newspapers he angrily swiped them off the table onto the floor.

"Get rid of this shit," he snapped at Dottie, one of the few times he lost control of his tongue with Dottie. But he didn't apologize. He stormed back to the cabin followed by an embarrassed Pat, a hovering Howard Cerney, who didn't look at anybody, Marti Figueres and his wife Sandra, and two other passengers.

This Spanish visit was a short one. But a very busy one. It included an audience for Vesco with El Caudillo, Generalissimo Francisco Franco, the Spanish dictator, an event that Vesco later bragged about. He was moving up in the world. According to Junior Nixon there were also a number of high-level soirées, very formal, at which Vesco comported himself as if he were used to mingling with upper-crust society. Junior was afraid of Vesco even when Vesco was nowhere around, and he was very cautious not to say anything about "the boss" that could be construed as criticism. But the same was not true of Pat Vesco. His description of Vesco's obvious embarrassment at his wife's appearance and manners was so rough that I had to tell him to keep his mouth shut.

The last time I had seen Junior was in Nassau, where I left him after our return from the first visit to Spain. Thank God for small favors. Donald, financial advisor to Robert Vesco and nephew of the president, tried to create the impression that upon his return to Madrid he pulled the strings for Bobby.

Actually, Meissner and Strickler, the two smartest and most dependable of the Vesco money men, had stayed behind. So had Howard Cerney, and they had been joined by Gil Straub and Robert Foglia. With that kind of talent on the scene, it's probable that Nixon served as a "go-for."

When he called to tell me to get the airplane ready for a flight to Nassau, Vesco dropped the news that one of our passengers would be HRH Prince Gonzalo de Borbon y Dampierre, brother of Franco's choice to become the Spanish King, Juan Carlos. Vesco was firm that no word about the prince traveling on the Boeing should leak out. His name was not to be mentioned by any of the crew at any time and it would not appear on the passenger manifest until the very last second. I wish he had been as firm with his financial advisor, the butter-headed nephew of the president.

Take off was scheduled for ten o'clock on the morning of October 26, 1972. Destination, Nassau. I carried a full load of fuel.

The only job assigned to Junior Nixon that morning

was to honcho the baggage for our passengers from some point in Madrid, where it had all been gathered, to the airport and onto the Boeing. Oh yeah—he had one other job. That was to deliver into my hands the list of passengers.

It is a very simple matter, even when departing a country, to move baggage from a city out to an airport and have it loaded on an airplane. This would have required that Junior first locate the baggage, count the number of bags, find suitable transportation to the airport, arrange with porters to unload the baggage for passage through the terminal to the ramp, where it would then be transferred to ramp trucks which would move it up to the airplane. At this point it would be carefully stowed aboard the airplane under the supervision of a crew member and the alert, watchful eye of Donald Nixon, Jr., financial advisor to Robert Vesco and nephew of the president, who would make certain that the same number of bags went into the airplane that were loaded onto the trucks in the city. Following that, he would come up to the flight deck, hand me the passenger list, and advise me of the weight of the baggage, provided, of course, he weighed the baggage in the first place. It was not absolutely necessary for Donald Nixon, Jr. to weigh the baggage if it would interfere in any way with the swift dispatch of his duties. The crew had a practiced eye and could make a fairly accurate guess as to the tonnage.

Donald Nixon, Jr. arrived on the flight deck about the time I expected him, a little before ten. Breathlessly, he advised me that Vesco and his party were delayed and that takeoff would be pushed back to about noontime. This was not welcome news.

I had some refiguring to do. I had made some preliminary estimates on takeoff weight subject to final adjustments, when Junior told me how many passengers we would have and how much baggage. He handed me the passenger list. Twenty-two bodies at an average of 170 pounds each. Next was the baggage. Since I would be fuel critical at noontime, I wanted to see for myself how much we would be carrying.

"O.K., Don," I said, "let's go look at the baggage."

A stricken look came over his face. He whacked himself on the forehead with an open palm, almost smashing his sunglasses.

"Holy shit, Ike!" he said, "I forgot it." Mother of God! How do you forget what has to be—with twenty-two passengers—almost a ton of baggage, some of it belonging to a prince of the Spanish royal family. For the first and only time, I addressed Donald Nixon, Jr., financial advisor to Robert Vesco and nephew of the president, with a familiarity heretofore reserved for Vesco himself.

"You fucking idiot!"

I fired his ass off the airplane and told him to go get the fucking baggage, right fucking now, and get his fucking ass back to the airplane without further fucking delay. I should have locked him in one of the lavatories and sent one of the Spanish ramp sweepers.

The whole scene was witnessed by the crew—except that when Dottie got a look at my expression when I was told that Junior forgot the baggage, she beat it to the rear of the airplane correctly surmising that technical jargon indicating a high state of anxiety would assault her ears. After Junior departed I addressed myself to the weight problem caused by Vesco's change in departure time. I was smoking mad and the crew gave me a wide berth.

Airline passengers arrive at an airport, check in at the check-in counter, hand over their luggage and go to the boarding area to await the announcement of their flight departure. Usually within a reasonable time they board the aircraft and take their seats. On or near the scheduled time of departure the door is closed. A passenger who is late is out of luck. He doesn't go on the flight. Barring traffic, weather or other delays, the passengers begin their journey completely unaware and not really caring about all of the elements, all of the factors, that go into getting their flight off the ground on time or close to it. All of the same factors with the exception of a fixed departure time, governed my operation. However, although I was flying an airline-type aircraft, I did not have at my disposal the huge ground support echelon which relieves the Airline Captain of

90% of the over-all effort required to get the aircraft into the air.

I filed my original flight plan, Madrid to Nassau, at nine-thirty in the morning, based on the prevailing airport information on the active runway, temperature, and wind velocity predicted for my scheduled departure time. At that time my estimated ramp weight for this flight was 310,000 pounds. Since all the numbers indicated that I could have weighed as much as 314,000 pounds at the ramp, there was no problem. After I got the passenger list, and estimating the unarrived baggage, my weight would be 309,240 pounds, slightly less than my original estimate. This was good. But Vesco's change in takeoff time screwed me up—royally. A habit of his. Ground temperature, surface wind direction and velocity, runway length and its slope uphill or down, elevation of the airport above sea level, and in some cases the kind of tires on the wheels and the brakes, all determine the maximum weight allowable for every takeoff. Some of these factors can change without causing serious disruptions. All of them are figured for each takeoff. In scheduled operations, airplane A scheduled to depart at, say, ten o'clock in the morning would operate with one set of numbers. The same type of airplane departing the same airport two hours later would operate under a different set of numbers. For example, if the ground temperature is hotter the company will reduce the revenue load in some fashion—generally in the cargo area. In my case, I would have exactly the same weight elements at noontime as I did at ten o'clock in the morning. If the temperature rose, which it would, or the wind velocity and/or direction changed, which it could, I would be in trouble. I needed for example runway 15 at Madrid, which is 13,451 feet long. A wind shift of any significant degree would put me onto runway 19, which was 12,139 feet long—shorter by enough to make its use out of the question for this particular mission. No flight. Vesco would not tolerate any such thing.

The only recourse I had was to reduce weight by burning off fuel on the ground. It was a long way from Madrid to Nassau, close to ten hours flying time. I needed every ounce of juice in the tanks to give me a margin of safety. Another way to get rid of the excess weight, the fuel in my case, was by "defueling," that is, having the excess fuel pumped out of the aircraft tanks back into empty fuel trucks. This is a costly and time consuming operation. There are no refunds and you pay extra for the service. Burn-off was the answer. This would present an additional delay factor which could cause more problems. That is precisely what happened later in the day.

By noontime, there was no Vesco and no Junior. Scratch a noontime takeoff and recompute. But I couldn't do this until somebody showed up and gave me a new departure time, which set me to wondering about the president's nephew. I didn't have long to wonder. He showed up a little after twelve looking like a kid who had just totaled his old man's Cadillac. I was in no mood for any more horseshit—but I got it anyway.

"We got a problem, Ike," he said. I wanted to whack him on the forehead myself.

"Whaddya mean, we?" I asked him. He backed away. "What the hell's the matter now, Junior?"

"They won't release the baggage," he said. He dealt with a *lot* of "theys" between the city and the airport. This was a time for monumental forebearance.

"*Who* won't release the baggage?" I asked him.

"Customs," he said. Dottie again removed herself out of earshot.

"CUSTOMS?!" I murmured at the top of my lungs. "What in the name of weeping Jesus got Customs involved?" He backed up two more steps.

"I guess I did," he said.

"They want to see you," he said. "There's a car waiting on the ramp.

At that precise "point in time" I had a revelation that God placed Donald A. Nixon, Jr. on this earth to be the instrument of Murphy's Law.

I checked my watch. It was a quarter after twelve. I expected Vesco and his party to show any minute and I still had to pry loose their baggage, although I couldn't fathom any reason why Customs would have a hold on it. I needed to know how much time I had.

"What time is Vesco getting here?" I asked Dumbo. Again the stricken look.

"Uh—oh yeah—I almost forgot," he stammered. "He won't be here until two o'clock." I turned away and almost fell down the stairs in my anxiety to get away from him.

I was taken directly to the main terminal and up to the office of the airport director and found myself in the midst of a bunch of very angry Spaniards. A representative from almost every element of airport service was present—Customs, Immigration, airport police, operations, ramp service, passenger service. It wouldn't have surprised me to have seen a taxicab dispatcher or the restaurant manager there. Only the director spoke. His tone was not at all encouraging. His English was excellent. Without preamble he demanded that I produce in his office every certificate, document, manual, and record carried aboard Silver Phyllis, including the insurance policy. Apart from the fact that United States FAA regulation forbids the removal of some of the things he wanted from the airplane, there was no way in the world I could produce an insurance policy. This became a sticking point, because it was back in Fairfield, New Jersey. What had Junior done to incite these people into an absolutely unreasoning and unreasonable position?

The director ordered me to produce all of my own licenses and certificates and those of my first officer. I did this. Demand was heaped upon demand. The argument that outgoing passenger baggage was not subject to Customs inspection carried no weight. These people were angry and in a punishing frame of mind. There were trips back and forth to the Boeing. There were arguments. Finally there was the threat of arrest—mine. How the hell Vesco would explain *that* to his friend the prince was one of the panicked thoughts I had. The prince. Despite Vesco's warning, I was ready to invoke the prince to put a stop to what was happening. Fortunately I didn't have to. During the confrontation I had gotten a little stiff-necked, but I did not lose my temper and was careful to maintain an attitude of correctness. After all, these people undoubtedly had a legitimate beef. After a time everybody calmed down. Everybody was in agreement that the cause of the problem was Junior. He had come out with the baggage all right—a mountain of it. To make up for the original mistake, he tried to take a shortcut through the Customs area in the terminal that was reserved for inbound baggage. Naturally he was stopped and questioned, since he had sought no permissions from anybody. Immediately he pulled rank. And that's when the rhubarb hit the blower.

"What would you have done, Captain?" the director asked me.

"I would have arrested him," I said, "and then have called on the aircraft commander." This got a little laugh and the tension was broken. I apologized for Junior's behavior and accepted full responsibility. This satisfied everybody and I was free to return to the airplane.

When I got back to Silver Phyllis, Junior was forward in the crew lounge chit-chatting with the crew as if nothing had happened. I beckoned to him. Incredibly, he approached me with an expectant smile on his face. I was standing next to one of the forward lavatories. I opened the door nearest me and pointed my finger inside.

"Donald," I said, "this is your new office." He actually laughed as if it were all a huge joke.

By the time Vesco appeared about a quarter after one, I was already six tons over my allowable takeoff weight for the current conditions. And I was still hopping mad. To do the job he wanted me to do I needed his cooperation. Like an airline passenger he was interested only in results. Of all people he should have known better. I had explained to him often enough the elements that had to be considered in operating the Boeing. There were times when the "you can do it, Ike" response didn't wash. And this was one of them. I wasn't about to argue with him or lecture to him then. But I got a perverse kick when I informed him that because of his delay in arriving at the airport, my clearance for an ocean crossing to Nassau might be subject to an indefinite delay. If I could not get off the ground in fifteen minutes.

"So what's the problem?" he said. "I'm ready. Go!" I told him the problem about weight and the burn-off. I was lucky that a strong hot wind had developed which would reduce the amount of excess fuel I would have to get rid of. Even so, unless I wanted to punish the engines by running them at high power on the ground in this heat, which I would not do, it would take me at least a half hour to burn off what I needed to get down to takeoff weight. Vesco couldn't understand what the problem was. A half hour, fifteen minutes, what's the difference? The difference was this—our route from Madrid to Nassau would cut across the regular transoceanic routes. It would affect the traffic flow of aircraft on the normal routes and required careful coordination among the various controlling sectors to avoid interfering with other flights. My problem was twofold. If I didn't get airborne within the fifteen-minute time slot alotted to me, I would have to give up my clearance and wait until I could be fitted in with the flow of traffic. But I was too heavy to burn off the extra fuel within the fifteen-minute time period. Enter His Royal Highness.

Vesco had introduced us briefly upon boarding. He obviously had become aware that a problem existed when he saw Vesco and me in a huddle, with the engines running at low idle. He came forward.

"Captain, can I help?" he asked. I explained in basic, simple terms what was going on. He seemed to understand exactly what I was talking about. He heard me out.

"Captain," he asked when I had finished, "at what time would you like to take off?"

"Your Highness," I said, "I'll be ready to take off in thirty minutes."

"Captain, may I use your radio?" he asked. I handed him my mike and was about to show him how to use it. I didn't have to. I could see that this man had been in a cockpit before.

In an airplane a microphone must be held close to

the mouth, not a half a foot away, à la Hollywood, to avoid interfering with the profile. Even in a jet aircraft sitting on the ground with the engines running there is ambient noise. The usual procedure is to rest the microphone against the upper lip which helps to screen out much of the ambient noise, so that whatever is said into the microphone can be heard more distinctly at the other end. It is also necessary to speak clearly and to know the right words. The Prince knew the routine with a hand-held mike.

The Prince spoke in Spanish but I was able to get the gist of what he was about. Briefly, he secured for Robert Vesco's Boeing a "VIP priority one" clearance. This meant that we could take off at our convenience and all other flights within Spanish control would adjust to accomodate our flight path. This is what happens when Air Force One, or some other aircraft carrying a head of state or a high-ranking government official, travels. I hate to think what this did for Vesco's self-image.

Everything is relative. Back at Southend where I had control of everything, that 4600-foot runway wasn't all that short. At Madrid, even after burning off fuel, that 13,451-footer wasn't all that long. But Silver Phyllis started her takeoff run with all the confidence in the world.

Flying, especially takeoffs, is still a matter of feel. The dials and gauges are essential but they don't fly the airplane. A human being does. And with experience a pilot becomes so finely tuned to the sensations of flying, that he anticipates what the clocks will show. With the weight of Silver Phyllis there would be no rolling takeoff. I locked her brakes on the end of runway 15. I advanced the four power levers gradually until the gauges showed 80 percent of takeoff rpm on all four engines. Then I waited and listened. The engines had to sound right no matter what the dials told me. Nobody takes off a large four-engine jet all by himself. The Captain handles the controls, but he needs the eyes and the voices of his first officer and his engineer. Satisfied with the sounds of the engines and the look of the dials, I called for takeoff power on all four engines.

Again, the sound of the engines began to build and that big airplane began to tremble.

The natural element for an airplane is in the air. Like a hunt dog straining against the leash to get into the field, Silver Phyllis was straining against the brakes to start her run. At the instant that the Engineer confirmed that I had takeoff power on all four and my ears agreed, I released the brakes.

There was no sensation of acceleration at first. Silver Phyllis had to be slow coming out of the gate. Up where I sat, well ahead of the nosewheels, I could feel the bump each time the flat spot on the nose tires came around. This is normal. Nylon cord tires on your family car develop these flat spots when they are parked for a couple of hours. The little thump comes more rapidly as acceleration builds. Then there is the thump as the tires pass over the tar strips across the runway. These come closer together. The texture of the concrete becomes indistinct and it seems that we no longer approach the tar strips one at a time, but they begin to rush at us more and more rapidly. The next sensation is that of being pushed back against the seat as every molecule of that airplane begins to move across the earth faster and faster.

There is a point on every runway—for that airplane, at that weight, at that temperature, at that wind, at that field elevation, at that time of day—before which, if you must stop—you can and not run out of runway. Once past that point, there is no stop. The point is described as Vee-One. It is relative to an indicated air speed of the aircraft, which itself is relative to the weight of the aircraft and all the other elements involved. But there is also the feel—in the feet, in the hands, in the seat, and in the guts.

"Vee-One," my first officer called out. We were past that point, and Silver Phyllis moved still faster and faster toward another point on that runway at which I would "rotate," that is bring the control column back enough to lift the nosewheels from the restraint of the concrete and free Silver Phyllis to take to the air when she was ready. That point is called Vee-R.

"Vee-R!" I rotated and waited. And waited. And

waited. What was I waiting for? The sound that would tell me that Silver Phyllis was airborne, the thump, thump of the main gear struts extending. When I heard that sound, the end of the runway disappeared under the nose. That lazy bitch of a Boeing had dragged her ass over every inch of that goddamned strip of Castilian concrete. But I still love you, baby—wherever you are.

For a lot of reasons the flight back to Nassau was a memorable one for me. It was not that anything startling happened. In actuality, it was a quiet, easy flight. Maybe it was a result of a period of impacted hassles, what with Junior and the delay and the tight-ass takeoff, but shortly after reaching my cruising altitude I felt physically weary. I had nothing immediate to cope with. I felt a kind of emptiness and I remember thinking to myself, What do I need this crap for? What am I doing sitting in this little corner of this huge airplane with nothing to do and nothing to look at? I had never had the habit of mingling with my passengers, of going back among them with a fatherly smile on my face asking if they were enjoying their trip. This isn't the first time I felt like this. Usually I'd wait it out or have a sandwich or something and it would pass. But this time the feeling persisted. Ron Dusse made a couple of stabs at conversation but I just didn't feel like talking to anybody. I felt a little tight between the shoulders and got out of my seat to stretch. I found myself looking directly at Donald Nixon, Jr., who was in the crew lounge trying to impress Dottie. I couldn't hear what he was saying, but the pantomime he was going through told me that he was describing some marvelous adventure that never happened. The poor shit. I couldn't even feel mad at him any more. I looked beyond him and saw some of the guests lounging in the main salon. Vesco was talking with Prince Borbon using his hands a lot. They were both smiling. Jesus, I realized what a big airplane Silver Phyllis was. It was like a house party—a pleasant one—with people wandering around from room to room. Nobody got in each other's way. But after all, I thought, it's just a big aluminum envelope, and when it got down on the ground all of these people would go away and think of it only as a curiosity. I would have to wash its face and tuck it in bed and make sure it didn't have any aches or pains. I found myself wishing that I were in my own living room back in Denville deciding what I would do first, wash my truck or go fishing in the lake. I got back into my seat and stared down at the Atlantic ocean. I had the urge to dump the control column forward and drag Phyllis's brand new ass through the sea spray. But I've had that feeling before too. And as usual resisted it. Much later I recalled this prolonged feeling of being disconnected from everything and realized that I never even gave a thought to Vesco.

For the second time, Prince Gonzalo Borbon came to my rescue. He came forward to the entrance of the flight deck and I heard him ask my engineer to seek my permission for him to come on the flight deck. That impressed me. As Vesco's guest he didn't have to ask permission. Naturally, I was glad to welcome him.

We talked about the Boeing in general. He marveled at the flight deck and was full of compliments about the interior passenger area. I told him that I had been deeply involved in the technical work, but the cute little blonde chief stewardess, Dottie McCarty, was responsible for the décor of the back.

I sensed that there was more than polite conversation to his visit on the flight deck. There was something about the Prince that belied his title and position. He was a little above average height, well put together, and very good looking. His interest in the airplane was real and intent. It didn't occur to me that he wanted to get right up front on the controls. I had made an exception in Al Junker's case. But he was a professional pilot. I never extended the same courtesy to "Walter Mitty" passengers.

The prince placed each hand on the back of the pilot's seats and leaned forward for a close look at the instrument panel.

"Incredible," he said. "I have never had to deal with that many instruments." I felt he was sending me a signal.

"You fly, don't you, Your Highness?" I said.

"Yes, I do," he said. "But nothing like this. I have some airplanes. They're a hobby of mine." My ears perked up.

"What kind?" I asked him.

"I collect World War Two aircraft," he said. "Fighters, mostly. I've got most of the best ones, German, British, and American. They're all in mint condition—perfectly restored. And great fun to fly." He asked me if I had ever flown fighter aircraft, and he reacted enthusiastically when I told him that I had flown not only jet fighters but propeller fighters, like the Corsair, Wildcat, Hellcat, Bearcat, Tigercat, and so on. We talked about them for fifteen minutes. He told me he had always had an ambition to handle something as big as the Boeing. That was a cue if I ever heard one, and I was sore at myself for allowing him to have to go so far as to practically ask to sit behind the controls. I got out of my seat.

"Take over, Your Highness," I said. Like Al Junker, he was surprised. I think that he thought that any invitation to fly the airplane would mean the first officer's seat. But that didn't slow him down. He got into the seat in a hurry. Again like Al Junker, the first thing he did was to look around and see what was there. He didn't touch anything until he had a good idea. I signalled Ron Dusse that while the prince was technically in charge of the airplane, he was in charge of the prince. He got the message and gave the prince some solid instruction in flying a Boeing 707-300. Ron was not only up to dealing with a royal prince, but he was one hell of a good airman, for whom piloting was only one of several skills.

The prince flew the Boeing for almost two hours. He was profuse in his thanks to both Ron and me, and on his way back aft he congratulated Dottie on her decorating skills and taste.

I was on the ground in Nassau for about a day and a half. Vesco turned the airplane over to the prince and his party for a flight to JFK, where the prince would catch a flight back to Spain. As he was leaving the aircraft, he again thanked me for allowing him to fly the Boeing. He invited me to visit him in Spain and even to fly some of his aircraft. Not only do I believe the invitation to have been sincere, but one day I fully intend to take him up on it.

One of the passengers on the flight from Nassau was lawyer Foglia, and I felt a certain pride that a bond, the like of which Foglia, Vesco, Cerney, Straub, LeBlanc, and all the other schemers could never know, had grown between Prince Borbon and me. They were the screwers dealing with Spanish screwers. I had the feeling that the prince was being used by these people. Maybe it's my idealism. But I don't consider him one of them but one of mine.

At the end of October, Vesco flew to Newark from Nassau to deal with an insurrection at ICC. The new management, which included Larry Richardson, Frank Beatty, Harry Sears, and Elmer Sticco, the man who helped Vesco sandbag Sticco's old boss at ELS, were ganging up on Vesco with the intent of tossing him out of ICC on his ear. They were after a couple of things. Although Vesco was still a major stockholder and had ostensibly resigned all his offices with ICC, he still commanded a hefty annual fee as a consultant, a liberal expense account, and through Fairfield controlled the Boeing by the most ridiculous lease-back arrangement to have ever been fabricated. From Vesco's comments, it looked like a case of a bunch of sharpshooters trying to get out from under without losing their shirts. Vesco, their guru, was jammed up with the law in the form of the SEC. Vesco's resignation had not diminished the heat one bit. They could have run by getting out of ICC themselves but, as they saw it, it was Vesco the Feds wanted. The plan—unload Vesco and keep ICC. And they still have jobs, position, and prestige. It's ironic that one of the leaders of the pack of jackals was Sticco, the bald megaga bird, a bird whose head looks like a tail and whose tail looks like a head, which doesn't fly but sits on fences. And you never really know what side of the fence it's on. When I first met him in California the only thing that Sticco ever wore on his head was a hat. Sometime after that, when he came to ICC in New Jersey, he acquired himself a rug. He must have felt that it turned him into an eagle, from the way he carried on. But, in my book, he is still the California megaga bird.

The best that Vesco could manage was a stand-off. It was a victory of sorts because it gave him time to organize contingency plans, mainly involved with Costa Rica.

November 14, 1972 0955Z MAD—NAS—SJO

My next trip to Spain on November 14, 1972 was too brief to let me visit Prince Gonzalo de Borbon. It was mainly to pick up Strickler, Meissner, and Marti Figueres and haul them back, along with Vesco, to Costa Rica, with a fuel stop at Nassau. Don Nixon was along but this time he managed to stay out of trouble. Everybody carried his own bags.

Evidently things went well in Spain and the bar was open. Since it was early in the day, it was Bloody Mary sippy time and Dottie was kept busy serving up snacks. We were on the ground in Nassau for one hour and forty minutes. Everybody remained at the airport during the refueling except Vesco and Nixon. Vesco came back by himself and Junior followed not long after. He led a small caravan of station wagons out to the Boeing and supervised the unloading and transfer to the Boeing of a pretty good pile of boxes, cartons, and crates. This was not unusual. Especially on trips to San José. And it annoyed me. First of all, any assistance from me or one of my crew was rejected. Secondly, as Captain I didn't like anything to go in the cargo hold that I didn't know about. But when I expressed my complaint to Vesco I got a brush-off.

"Let Junior earn his keep, Ike," he would say. "That's what I hired him for."

The most serious aspect of the whole business was what invariably happened on the ground in San José. We usually parked directly across the ramp from the main passenger terminal at San José's Santa Maria Airport. In places like Costa Rica, the local airport has displaced the railroad station as a town "watching place." There was not that much traffic in and out of San José, and the number of watchers on the two terminal balconies far exceeded those who would logically be on hand to bid welcome or farewell to relatives. So there was always an audience on hand whenever Silver Phyllis arrived or departed. Actually, the audience grew in number as publicity about Vesco increased in the city.

Vesco had gone to great pains to present a proper image to the Costa Ricans. He wanted to appear as a benefactor, a family man, and an honest businessman. There was no way that he could be ignorant of the flagrant defiance of Costa Rican Customs every time we landed there.

Our parking space was about 300 yards from the Customs building and another 200 yards from the airport guard shack. Between them were a couple of small buildings and a chain-link fence with a gate, through which ran a rutted dirt road that wandered through a field and curved around to join the main airport service road for arriving and departing vehicles. The service road cut into the main highway to the city.

Whenever we arrived, whether or not Marti Figueres was aboard, a veritable fleet of cars and trucks would drive up and cluster around the airplane. They were all arranged for by Marti Figueres. Marti Figueres and Junior Nixon got along very well, and it seemed to me that Marti was even more blatant about flaunting his relationship to the presidency in his own country. I had been given to understand that the Customs regulations apply equally to everybody entering Costa Rica, in cluding the son of the president. Apparently Marti—and Vesco—believed otherwise. There was not even a pretense made at clearing the enormous volume of cargo and baggage we brought into that country. Not only Marti Figueres's employees, but airport personnel, loaded the trucks, which then headed directly for the gate, not even slowing down. Once through the gate they would follow the dirt road to the service road and onto the highway. They were never even challenged.

By contrast, the crew followed the rules scrupulously. We brought our bags and anything else we had into the terminal and through the Customs inspection area. More often than not, we would be waved straight through by pleasant, smiling Customs inspectors. The crew never had trouble with Costa Rican Customs.

Vesco's insolent disregard for Costa Rican laws eventually became something of a scandal, to the point that the presidential successor to Don Pepe, Daniel Oduber, sent Vesco a letter of mild rebuke and expressed the hope that Vesco's transgressions of the past would not continue. Sure.

After takeoff from Nassau on November 14, 1972, some heavy hitting went on in the discotheque, and by the time we got to San José a few of the passengers were feeling no pain. But Marti Figueres was legless.

The first indication that I got of any trouble aft was after most of my rubber-legged passengers had left the airplane. Dottie came forward and told me that Vesco was having trouble persuading Marti that he was home and really ought to get off the airplane.

After landing, Dottie had gone back to the cabin to help the passengers debark. She found Marti zonked out in a chair in the main salon, shoes off. She tried to wake him and got only a drunken grumble in reply. She asked Vesco's help. Vesco was half starched, and he thought it was the funniest thing in the world, although he did make a giggling, half-assed effort to rouse the sodden Marti. Marti did come part way out of his stupor, but he grabbed onto the arm of the chair and loudly insisted that he liked it where he was. Dottie thought I should go back and help. That's what I did.

I went back chipper as a beaver expecting no trouble. Vesco wasn't that drunk. He could really hold his liquor, but I could tell he had been slurping up the nectar of the gods by the fact that his bulb was lit. He always showed something of a rum blossom on the end of his horn when he juiced it up. He was in a hilarious mood as he tried to pick Marti out of the chair. There were two problems. Marti didn't want to get out of the chair and his seat belt was still fastened. I had to laugh. Marti's arms and legs were flailing like a guy fighting a swarm of bees. His eyes were glued shut but his mouth was working in a wild mixture of English and Spanish. I could understand only one word, "FOOK!"

He used it as a noun, verb, adjective, adverb, subject, predicate, and burp. To wit:

"Fook . . . mucho borracho! . . . fook you Vesco . . . Lemme the fook alone . . . (mumble, mumble) *. . . Goddamn fook . . . Go the fook away . . . Cheeeeeee! . . . Wha' the fook . . . Madre de Dios . . . Donde the fook estamos? . . . Hey! . . . Wha' the fook you doin? . . . Sangre de Christo! . . . Oh fook, I'm sick . . . Hey Vesco, you fook . . . You wanna get laid? . . . Oooooooh, fookie fookie . . . No fookie way . . .* (mumble, mumble, sniff, sniff) *. . . Fook you! Fook me! Fook the world! . . . Up your ass, gringo!*

I asked Bob if he needed any help. His voice had a slight slur.

"Take him out and leave him someplace safe," Vesco said. He giggled. "Put him in a locker in the terminal. But make sure you close the door tight so he won't fall out and break his goddamn neck."

Vesco wobbled toward the door and left me in charge. I unhooked Marti's seat belt. Then I picked up his shoes and jammed one in each of his coat pockets. I got him out of the chair. He was a wiry little bastard and he squirmed out of my grasp and ricocheted toward the back of the airplane. I chased him, caught up with him, and grabbed him by the ass of the pants and his shirt collar. He grabbed a hold of the beaded curtains that hung in the discotheque. I hauled and got him going in the other direction. Unfortunately so did the beaded curtains. They were all over the goddamn place. I slipped on a couple and wound up on my ass with Marti on top of me. He got up before I did, laughing like hell and FOOKING everything he could think of. He got his arms wrapped around one of the flight-stabilized barstools which were anchored to the floor before I could get my hands on him. I grabbed him by the ankles and pulled. It was like uprooting a tree with your bare hands. I was beginning to sweat. The trouble with handling a funny, spastic drunk like

Marti is that nothing stays still long enough to get a good grip on it. Besides, I was laughing so much I was weak. I finally fell on top of him like a wrestler and pried his arms from around the bar stool. I got him upright. And wrapped my arms around him pinning his arms to his side. He was wide-awake now. But he was wide-awake drunk and having a hell of a good time. I got his feet off the floor but his legs started going like he was treading water in a mill-race. I carried him, walking spraddle-legged into the main salon, where I finally got some help from my crew who were laughing their heads off. It took three of us to get Marti down to the ramp. There more help was waiting, including the driver of Marti's car who held open the door while we stuffed him inside. But he scrambled out again before we got the door closed. We grabbed him and stuffed him back inside again, and finally got the door slammed shut.

"Oh Jesus!" one of the crew said and vaulted the hood of the car just in time to stop Marti from getting out on the other side. I was looking for something to tie the goddamn doors shut. The driver ran over to where some men were standing and came back with a big guy who looked like he went well over 200 pounds. The driver spoke to the big guy in Spanish for a minute, then swung open the rear door of the car. The big guy dove in and fell on top of Marti. The driver slammed the door shut, jumped into the driver's seat, and was off like a shot.

16

December 4, 1972
1155Z EWR—IAD—NAS—IAD—EWR

I was beginning to feel as if I had been sentenced to spend the rest of my life on Silver Phyllis. In the past month the crew had been airborne for about 93 hours over 25 flights. Add to that pre- and post-flight servicing and paperwork time at the rate of four hours per flight, making a total of a hundred hours, and you find that the crew of Silver Phyllis worked more than double the time of airline flight crews. On top of that, as Director of Aviation, I put in over 125 additional hours. None of us had been home for more than three days total, less ground travel time, in the past month. When I was in the Newark area with Vesco, I chauffeured him around locally in the Jet Ranger helicopter. Conservatively speaking, I was averaging 80 hours a week. If I was in one spot for the whole time it would not have been so bad. A lot of people work 80 hours a week under pressure. But constant travel, especially east and west across time zones where you suffer from jet-lag syndrome, exerts a special kind of pressure and has a special kind of wearing effect. There is the constant, unexpected interruption of sleep, meals, relaxation.

I had gotten home to the house in Denville the night before at about eleven. I had a lot to think about. Vesco was up to his ass in trouble. The Securities and Exchange Commission had completed its investigation and announced that it had filed a complaint in Federal Court against Vesco and a host of his business associates and affiliated corporations. This was on November 28, 1972. We were in San José, Costa Rica. That trip had been sprung on me after I had landed from Newark. I was scheduled to take Vesco and a bunch of his Costa Rican contacts to Madrid. I had just checked into the Halcyon Balmoral Hotel when I got a message from Vesco to get back out to the airport and get ready for a fast trip to San José. It was typical Vesco. And it pissed me off for the moment. I was facing a ten-hour flight across the Atlantic the next day and the crew needed the rest. But what the hell, it was less than three hours to San José. The chances were that even if Vesco came back the following day the crew and I would get the rest we needed. Wrong.

We left Nassau at 8:30 that night. Aboard besides Vesco were Straub, Strickler, Dick Clay, Junior, a mysterious character named Alberto Abreu, and his wife Rosa. We had carried Abreu's wife on earlier flights with Marti Figueres' wife Sandra and Margarita de Facio, the wife of the Costa Rican foreign secretary. We also carried in the belly some more of Junior's "special cargo," consisting of a lot of unlabeled crates, cartons, and boxes.

Vesco was in a pretty good mood. There was no booze bust aboard as there had been the time I chased Marti all over the airplane. We landed in San José at 11:40 and there was the usual business with the cargo and Customs. I flopped into my bed at the Irazu Hotel about one o'clock in the morning and left word not to be disturbed—unless the call was from Robert Vesco. I should have known better.

The phone rang a little before seven. And sure enough it was Vesco. His voice was tight and he was very brief.

"Ike, we're going back to Nassau right away," he

said. "Have the airplane ready by nine." That was it. He hung up.

Vesco showed up at the airplane in a wild mood. He looked as if he hadn't gotten any sleep. He strode aboard the airplane ahead of everybody else, stopped near the flight deck long enough to tell me he wanted me back in his office right after takeoff, and went back to the main salon where he paced impatiently, waiting for the other passengers to come aboard. Strickler and the Abreus did not make the flight back, but we added one of Junior Nixon's playmates. The presence of Junior's "chick" on the airplane was just another indication of his lack of the simple smarts. Something was up. And it was serious. For Junior Nixon to have been more concerned about his sex life at that time could have been dangerous for him. Luckily, Vesco was so preoccupied with his problems that he didn't give a shit who was on the airplane.

Vesco laid it on me when I went back to see him. When I walked into Vesco's office, Junior, whom I had passed on my way through the crew lounge, followed me in. I didn't know it. Vesco looked up, red-eyed and furious.

"Get the fuck out of here!" he said. I thought he was talking to me.

"Sure, Bob," I heard behind me. I turned and saw Junior. Vesco indicated for me to sit down across from him—on the other side of his desk.

"That sonofabitchin' Jew bastard did it," he said. "He got me indicted." I knew he was talking about Sporkin. I kept my mouth shut. "I'm not going to Spain but you're making the flight anyway. Clay will call the shots. I want you back in Nassau as soon as possible but don't leave Madrid without Foglia. There are some other guys I want but they can follow commercial if they miss the flight. Foglia I need."

Vesco didn't waste any time in leaving the airplane at Nassau. In fact, I didn't even see him go. All I saw was his car pulling away. I was interested in an airplane, a Lear Jet N33TR, which was parked in my usual spot. I hadn't seen it at Nassau before. It was painted solid black, which was unusual. I asked one of the fuelers who owned the "Black Maria," and he told me it belonged to some guy from California named Richardson. The "TR" on the tail made sense. Tommy Richardson, a wheeler-dealer buddy of Vesco's from Los Angeles. I had met him at the Paradise Island casino and at Vesco's house. I would hear a lot more about that Learjet over the next couple of years.

When I checked into the hotel there was a message from Junior Nixon advising me that takeoff for the flight to Madrid had been advanced from eight o'clock the following morning to one a.m. I wasn't surprised considering the problems Vesco was having. I advised the crew and told them all to hit the rack immediately—and did so myself. I finally dropped off about four o'clock in the afternoon. I had left a call at the desk to ring all crew members at ten p.m.

I don't know how long the phone was ringing when I finally struggled out of my deep sleep to answer it. It was Junior. I looked at my watch. It was a little after six o'clock.

"Hi there, Capitan," I heard. "I have for you a hot flash from Numero Uno—zee passengaire leest for zee flight to zee Madrid."

"JUNIOR!" I hollered, "you dumb asshole! How many times have I told you never, NEVER, to wake me up in the middle of MY fucking night unless it is an absolute, real, fucking emergency? You can shove that list up your ass. Right now I don't give a shit WHO my passengers are. I don't need it until flight time. Now get out of my fucking hair and stay out of it!" I slammed the phone down onto the cradle. It took me an hour to get back to sleep.

I got back from Madrid at 7:40 on the morning of December 1, 1972 and did not leave Nassau again until six o'clock on the evening of December 3, 1972. I did not see Vesco during the layover in Nassau. But I did see N33TR in Nassau parked near the Hughes hangar.

Before I left the hotel at Nassau on the 3rd to fly Vesco's wife and kids to Newark, he called and told me that he would contact me at home around midnight about the schedule for the next day or two. I had the feeling he was playing it by ear.

His call came through almost on the mark. He was still angry. He told me that a package of papers would be delivered to the Boeing at Butler Newark at seven o'clock in the morning by a lawyer. I was to take personal charge of these papers. Then I was to proceed to Dulles International Airport where I would pick up two passengers at Page Airways promptly at eight o'clock in the morning. I would find out who they were when they got on the aircraft. Then I would leave immediately for Nassau. I finished making my phone calls to the crew and to Butler about 1:30 in the morning. I got some sleep and left the house at five a.m.

The lawyer—I never got his name—showed up promptly. He looked pretty haggard as if he had been up all night. He handed me a sealed manila envelope about an inch thick. And departed immediately.

I never even shut the engines down at Dulles. My passengers were waiting, and we were off the ground within fifteen minutes from the time we had taxied in to the Page terminal at Dulles.

We landed in Nassau at 9:10 a.m. I was out of my seat almost before the engines stopped turning. The passengers would still have to clear Customs which would not take a lot of time but more than I had to spare. I turned everything over to my first officer and left the airplane. I met the Customs inspector on the ramp and waved the envelope at him. He cleared me with a wave of his hand. He saw that I was in a hurry. I took a short cut to my rental car and arrived at Vesco's compound in little over twenty minutes.

It's always an adventure visiting Vesco. Even though I knew most of the guards by name, I'd had less trouble getting into a restricted military base. But Junior showed up to pass me through. Which didn't do much for my ego.

Vesco met me in the driveway. He grabbed the envelope from my hands.

"Go back to the airplane and hang loose," he said. "You'll be taking Pat and the kids home. Then you go home. I want the Boeing to stay in Newark. I want those bastards to think I'm in Boonton." Without another word he went back in the house. And I went back to the airport.

I didn't realize until I was back on the Boeing that I had not learned who my passengers were. I asked for the manifest and recognized both names. One was the former Secretary of Defense under Lyndon Johnson, Clark Clifford, and the other, also a former Defense Department big shot, was Paul Warnke. They were both Democrats and had the recent distinction of making John Dean's "Nixon's Enemies List." Then I realized that the 1972 Presidential election had completely passed me by.

It's a good thing his uncle didn't need Junior's vote. My records show that he was either on his houseboat at the Marina under the Paradise Island bridge or enjoying the sporting life at the casino.

Clifford and Warnke did not stay in Nassau very long. I dropped them at Dulles on the way to Newark. Nor did I ever see them again or hear that they had anything further to do with Vesco, if that's what they were in Nassau for.

I was told later on that Vesco felt that Nixon had betrayed him and had sworn vengeance. To this end he made contact with Clark Clifford and Paul Warnke, who at the time were practicing law in Washington, because as top-line Democrats they would leap at the chance to do Nixon dirt. He also wanted to use their influence with Congressional leaders. My guess is that they turned him down flat.

This time Vesco was true to his word. I didn't see him again until December 11. He called me from the house in Boonton on the 10th and set up a flight from Newark to Chicago, and then from Chicago to San José. I've often wondered how he got from Nassau to New Jersey. There was of course N33TR, the Learjet owned by his good buddy, Tommy Richardson. It is also interesting that there was another small jet available to Vesco. It was Sabreliner N44SB, part of the booty from the Butlers Bank takeover. Not only could this have gotten Vesco into Newark, but between the two airplanes he could have flitted up and down the east coast and all over the Caribbean.

The only companion that Vesco had on his Newark-to-Chicago-to-San José flights was Donald A. Nixon, Jr. He was also his only companion back to Nassau from San José. We were moving around so fast that there was no time for "cargo." On December 14, 1972, Vesco and Nixon were joined at Nassau by Eusebio Antonio "Tony" Morales, a former Ambassador from Panama to England. Morales, even though he was in his sixties, looked like a Hollywood version of a suave, international con man. Again, it was the rattlebrained Junior Nixon who gave me some of his pedigree. Morales, Junior said, had once been hooked up with "the Mob." And had been involved in a diplomatic scandal when it was discovered he was selling diplomatic posts to his friends.

The very last time that I brought Vesco into the United States on Silver Phyllis was on a flight from Nassau to Newark on December 19, 1972. Between that date and December 31, 1972, I made two additional trips between Newark and Nassau. On December 21, I flew to Nassau from Newark with twelve passengers—none of whom was Robert Vesco. The Boeing went immediately to Ft. Lauderdale and remained there until December 27, 1972. It was during that time that Vesco called me and told me he did not want the Boeing to operate into the U.S. any longer. It was also then that I reminded him of the contract for the final phase of modification. On December 27, I flew from Ft. Lauderdale, picked up Vesco's parents and Shirley Bailey, and flew them to Newark. On December 30, 1972, I flew the Boeing empty to Ft. Lauderdale, remained there overnight, and on the last day of the year flew empty to Nassau. On that same day, Robert Lee Vesco, his wife Pat, his four youngest children, and Donald A. Nixon, Jr. boarded the Boeing. They brought along a mountain of luggage as well as Don Nixon's inevitable crates and boxes. I flew them to San José, Costa Rica.

We landed at San José at 5:25 on New Year's Eve, 1972. I would be on the ground for one hour and twenty minutes and then leave for Greater Southwest, via Houston. Before he left the Boeing, Vesco had some instructions for me.

"Ike, we're coming up on a brand new year," he said, "and a brand new operation. From now on—no more records." Dottie was standing nearby. He turned to her. "That means no more passenger lists."

He wouldn't set foot on the Boeing again for nearly three months.

17

I was beginning to see cracks in Robert Lee Vesco's world. For the second year in a row I had "celebrated" New Year's Eve away from home. Maybe it was just my mood those first few days in January, 1973, but the quality of my professional life seemed to be changing. Suddenly the fun seemed to be slipping away. The last time I had spoken to Vesco, in San José a few hours before the end of the year, I sensed an anxiety about him that I had seen only once before. That was immediately after his release from St. Antoine Prison when he and I flew back together from Geneva to New York.

It wasn't only the "no more records" statement. I got the impression that he really didn't know where he was going. In addition to his troubles with the SEC, he was facing an insurrection at ICC by the very men who had helped him carry out his freebooting operations. One of the big bones of contention between Vesco and the ICC management was the Boeing. I knew that before too much longer, unless Vesco won, I would be a casualty. And there was nothing that I could do about it.

I wanted to stay with Silver Phyllis at Qualitron during the final phase of modification. Certainly it was important to supervise the installation of heavy components such as the mini-gym, the tub and shower, and the only airborne "sauna" in existance. Yet there was still another reason. This Boeing was unlike any other in existence. I had had more to do with the design and even the engineering than anyone else, and I wanted to be in on the finish. But I had other things to do.

Vesco still had transportation requirements that demanded a medium long-range aircraft while the Boeing was grounded. In December of 1972, he acquired by lease through Connex Press—a Bahamian shell company he inherited when he swallowed up Butlers Bank in Nassau—a Grumman Gulfstream Two which was owned by the Union Insurance Agency of Illinois. Union Insurance were trustees of The Central States, Southeast, and Southwest Area Pension Fund of the Teamsters Union. The head of Union Insurance was Allen Dorfman, who was convicted of misuse of Teamsters Union funds and was sentenced to prison. The lease agreement was signed by his wife Rose as a general partner.

This was not the first time that Vesco was involved with the Teamsters Union and the Dorfmans. In September, 1971, in a move that surprised me since he had only had the airplane a few months, he lent the Boeing and its crew to Dorfman to fly a bunch of Teamsters officials and friends from Chicago to San Diego for a golfing weekend at La Costa Country Club, not far from the then-California White House of Richard Nixon, San Clemente. La Costa, which includes a resort complex, was financed partially by Teamsters Union funds and one of the top men in the La Costa operation was Moe Dalitz, a top gun in Las Vegas, Nevada gambling, who is alleged to have connections with organized crime. La Costa, incidentally, was the site of Nixon's first excursion out of self-imposed exile in San Clemente after his resignation as President of the United States. He played golf with Frank Fitzsimmons, Teamsters Union president.

The Gulfstream Two, serial number 67 and registered as N711S, was originally owned by Frank Sinatra. Under the terms of the lease which would run for thirty-six months, Connex Press would be paying Dorfman 45,000 dollars a month, for a total of 1,620,000 dollars, for Vesco's traveling comfort. In addition to this enormous fee, the cost of operating and insuring this air craft would be borne by Connex Press.

N711S was delivered to Nassau on January 3, 1973. I left Qualitron for New York on January 2 for three days of retraining in Gulfstream II operation at Flight Safety, Inc., located at LaGuardia Airport. Following Flight Safety, my return to Qualitron was delayed even further while I ferried Vesco around. He was strangely uncommunicative. Once or twice he asked how the Boeing was coming along, and I assured him that the work was on schedule. But it was on a flight from Teterboro Airport in New Jersey to Washington that he threw me another curve and deepened my feeling of foreboding about my job and the future of my crew.

"I want the goddamn airplane out of there, out of the country, as fast as possible," he told me. "Things are getting sticky. I'm thinking seriously of loaning it to my friends in Argentina. That would keep the airplane on ice until the shit stops flying." I hated to think what Argentine crews would do to Silver Phyllis.

Qualitron would finish its work before the end of January. I finally got back to Greater Southwest on January 18, 1973. I spent several hours at Qualitron and was satisfied with the way things were going. There wasn't any hint of trouble during my session with Jack Prewitt. The first bomb fell at 4:45 that same afternoon. I got a call from Larry Richardson, who had been installed as President of ICC. He came on strong.

The substance of his call was that I was to take only his personal orders. He made it clear that he was the chief executive officer for ICC, and that *he* and the board of directors would control me from now on and I would answer to them. After Qualitron was finished, I was to fly the Boeing to Miami for inspection and then to Newark, at which time the crew and I would be terminated. ICC was closing down its aviation operation.

But it wasn't that easy. First of all, ICC still had a leasing agreement for the Boeing with Skyways. Secondly, there was Bob Vesco.

Richardson was feeling his oats. It was obvious that he had not thought the matter through. You don't simply dump an airplane like the Boeing onto the ramp at Newark airport the way you would turn in a rental car. We were the only legally qualified crew to operate that particular airplane, and regardless of ICC's desire to eliminate what they regarded as an unnecessary operation, until the proper disposition of the airplane was determined he would have to deal with us. I got on the phone to Vesco and gave him a rundown of my conversation with Larry Richardson.

"I don't give a shit what Larry told you," Vesco said. "I'm still calling the shots. It's my goddamn airplane. Get it finished and then I'll tell you what to do with it."

Silver Phyllis was ready on January 29, 1973, and I flew her on an acceptance test flight. I ordered the crew to load the aircraft and ready her to go back into service. On the following day I was to fly to Miami where the Boeing would be inspected by Pan American and she would be ready to face the world—complete. Then Qualitron dropped the second bomb. They would not release the airplane until their invoices were paid—in full.

Frankly, although it was a real shot in the guts to me, I didn't blame Qualitron. They were owed a quarter of a million dollars. They knew that the situation at ICC was scrambled. Their letters, telegrams, and phone calls to ICC management went unanswered. Until somebody whom they could count on responded or until the bills were actually paid, Silver Phyllis was going nowhere. This would be a long siege. I sent the crew back to New Jersey to wait things out. I stuck around for a few days to see what I could do to help. Sometime between Richardson's call to me on January 18 and my return to New Jersey on February 2, Larry Richardson resigned his post at ICC and Elmer Sticco took over as top banana, with Frank Beatty moving into the number-two slot.

On February 8, I got a memo from Beatty confirming the termination of the crew of the Boeing, effective February 15. Nothing had really changed. Vesco had yet to make his move.

It was obvious that there was something akin to panic at ICC. Richardson had bailed out and left the others to explain the mess to the SEC. Then I got a call from Dick Clay, who wanted me to sign an affidavit regarding some expense funds he had drawn for my use. There was no problem. It simply indicated to me that everybody was sniping at everybody else and it was "cover your ass time."

Vesco came back to New Jersey. If he was upset about the Boeing he didn't show it. On February 11, 1973, he asked me to come to his home in Boonton Township, New Jersey, which was just minutes away from where I lived in Denville. Junior Nixon was with Vesco. We sat around the kitchen table—just the three of us.

Vesco was in a very serious mood and filled with rage at "those disloyal bastards" at ICC. We talked about the Boeing and the crew. I was to meet with Frank Beatty and go through the termination procedures. Vesco told me to forget it. He made arrangements that would keep the crew working and intact. However, what was really on his mind was the future.

"I'm pulling out," he said. "I'm leaving the country for good." The announcement was greeted with enthusiasm by Junior. Vesco threw him a withering glance and Junior subsided. "I'm setting up shop in Costa Rica," he went on. "From now on we'll be operating in the Caribbean and Central and South America. They're breaking my balls here in the U.S. I don't have to stand for that kind of shit."

I didn't follow Vesco's orders to ignore Beatty. I wanted a clean break from ICC and I didn't want them to send the law after me. So I met with Frank Beatty on February 15, 1973, and gave him everything he had demanded—credit cards, expense and personnel records, and the request for payment of nominal termination allowance and unused vacation pay due. Beatty wasn't hostile to me. He was a Vesco creation but now

Sticco was his boss. He hadn't decided which way to jump when push came to shove. Beatty continued to work both sides of the street until sometime after I quit Vesco.

This was not yet the end of ICC for me.

Vesco followed through on his employment commitment for the crew and me. We met in Nassau to discuss his future aviation plans. Dick Clay and Norman LeBlanc were also at the meeting as were two pilots, Dorfman's and LeBlanc's. Both pilots were tied to the aircraft by contract. Although we would each be employed by different companies for the record, Vesco made it clear that I was still in charge and that when "we had the Boeing back," I would resume my duties as aircraft commander. I was satisfied.

On March 1, 1973, I had another meeting with Vesco at his Brace Ridge Road home in Nassau. He announced plans to visit Russia which shook me up. Vesco did not explain why he wanted to go behind the Iron Curtain. What he wanted from me were all the required navigation charts and documentation to accomplish the trip, which would generally follow the course of the Russian aircraft we had seen in Rabat. This was tricky business. Any American flag carrier seeking permission to both overfly Iron Curtain countries and to enter the Soviet Union would absolutely require the involvement of the United States State Department. In addition, I wanted to protect myself and the crew and therefore wanted to take the matter up with the FAA. Vesco vetoed this idea emphatically.

"I don't want anybody to know about this trip," he said. It was his contention—and it was a wrong one—that as we were operating out of Nassau we were immune from the FAA. I told him that since I had to get the charts from Jeppesen, there would be some record of my request, and it was entirely possible that somebody at Jeppesen could question this. I had no idea what the U.S. government required for flights to Russia, and until I did I was not about to agree to Vesco's plan. He sloughed off my concern about ordering the charts from Jeppesen.

"Gil Straub can get everything you need from Germany," he said. "He's already made the connection." I liked the whole idea less. Tentative departure date was set for April 7, 1973. I asked him what airplane we would be using.

"The Boeing," he said. "What else?"

When I left him, Vesco was still not convinced that I wouldn't make such a flight without being sure of the legalities. However, Vesco would get these brainstorms every once in a while. They would eventually wind up in the ditch. I wasn't particularly worried.

My last official dealings with ICC began on March 7, 1973, with a summons to Elmer Sticco's office at 200 Fairfield Road, Fairfield, New Jersey. This summons was not totally unexpected. There were still monies due me, and the crew and I believed that I was being called in to settle the matter. Instead, I came with a blackjack over my head. If I wanted to get paid anything and if my crew were to receive the money that they were due, I would have to sign a temporary employment agreement with ICC. The sole purpose of this agreement was to get the Boeing back to Newark from Qualitron at Greater Southwest Airport outside Ft. Worth. The major portion of what I was due would be withheld until I had accomplished the task. They agreed to cover my expenses and those of the crew and to settle with Qualitron. I signed it to get the crew paid. I had every intention of following through. But they kept forgetting about Vesco.

Over the next week I saw a lot of Vesco. I told him about the Sticco agreement. It didn't bother him. He already knew about it from Beatty. I didn't know what the hell was going on. He told me to go ahead and do what I had to do.

I went back to Qualitron on March 15. I showed the agreement I had with ICC to Jack Prewitt. I told him he could get in touch with me at the motel as soon as the bills were paid and the aircraft was released. Surprise! Surprise!

On March 16, Joel Grady flew into Dallas aboard American Airline flight 121, checked into the Villa Inn West, and called me on the phone. Joel Grady was president of Skyways Leasing Company, which owned the Boeing that was leased to ICC under a contract still in effect. When I met with Grady he laid in front of me a certified Skyways check in the full amount due Qualitron. Vesco had made his move.

"How long will it take to get the airplane out of here?" he asked.

"Two hours after Qualitron releases it," I told him. It was then early evening. I probably could have gotten out of Greater Southwest that same night. After all, all Qualitron wanted was to be paid. If I had requested it, Prewitt would have arranged for aircraft servicing so that we could take off that night. But there were some things about Grady's arrival that bothered me. First of all I had a legal authorization from ICC to deliver the plane to Newark which I could not do until ICC paid the bill. I pointed this out to Grady. Grady smirked. He said that if I waited for ICC to pay Qualitron or the crew and me, I would sit where I was until I grew roots out of my ass. Maybe so. But I still had a legal contract that prevented me from taking any other course of action. Grady asked to see my copy of the contract.

"I want to show you something, Ike," he said. That could mean only one thing, that he had already seen the contract. I dragged it out and handed it to him. His finger went immediately to paragraph one, which reads in part as follows: "Eisenhauer agrees to fly the aircraft at ICC's request and to provide the requisite FAA qualified flight crew personnel for all flights of the Aircraft which ICC deems necessary while the Aircraft is leased and under the control of ICC." The key words, he pointed out, were "leased" and "under the control of ICC." He told me flat out that Frank Beatty was responsible for their inclusion in the contract.

"Frank's on our side, Ike," he said. "He does what Bob tells him to do." He handed me back the contract. "ICC hasn't paid its bill yet to Skyways Leasing. They're a couple of months in arrears, and under the terms of the lease agreement I'm terminating the lease and taking possession of the Boeing. That contract you have with Sticco and ICC isn't worth a shit." That shut me up for awhile.

"What do I do next, Joel?" I asked.

The first order of business was to pay Qualitron and get the airplane released. I called Jack Prewitt at his home. I told him that Grady was with me and he had a certified check for the whole nine yards of the bill. He was tickled pink. I asked him if he could clear my crew with the guard so they could service the airplane that same night for an early morning takeoff. Jack agreed and said that he would be at the airplane at seven in the morning to accept the check. Grady was pleased.

"Great!" he said. "I want to be off the ground befor eight o'clock. That's very important."

"Why?" I asked him.

"Don't worry about it, Ike," he said.

"Bullshit! Joel," I told him, "I do worry about it. All I have is your word that everything is all right. I want to see a piece of paper, or at least know what the game is you guys are playing. Until I do, that airplane is staying right where it is." I had him by the shorts, and he knew it.

The story I got from Joel—with exhibits—was that a letter had been sent to Sticco citing ICC's default on lease payments and notifying him that Skyways was repossessing the Boeing. However, the timing demanded that the letter arrive at ICC on the same day that Skyways took the airplane back. This would allow ICC no time to take any action to block the move. But even here Grady was taking no chances. He wanted that plane airborne and on its way to Nassau before the mail was opened at ICC, which would be sometime around nine or nine-thirty in the morning. He would have preferred to have the airplane cross the east coast of Florida before the letter was laid on Sticco's desk. It was an incredible scheme and worthy of Vesco. Every aspect of it was confirmed to me in a memorandum that Grady had telephoned to Vesco in Nassau via LeBlanc's secretary, Wendy Kenyon, on March 14, 1973. A copy of the memo was inadvertantly included among my personal records aboard the Boeing. My grip on Grady's gonads got tighter.

I didn't trust Grady as far as I could spit against a strong wind. If I was going to fly that airplane to Nassau with my crew, I was going to get paid and they were going to get paid. In addition, I still had some heavy expenses while in Texas. I told Grady I wanted a contract to cover all of this plus any future flights to be made in the Boeing. He screamed and he squirmed, but I got what I wanted even though we both stayed up half the night to hammer it out. I was at Qualitron at six a.m. and used one of their typewriters to type up the handwritten (by both mine and Grady's hands) agreement. The airplane was ready. Jack Prewitt showed up at seven o'clock as promised and got his check. We departed GSW for Nassau at 7:25 a.m. and arrived at Nassau at 10:00 a.m., March 17, 1973.

There was a reason why Vesco acted when he did. He had an important trip coming up to North Africa and the Middle East. Grady told me about it on the flight to Nassau. We left the same night for Rabat, Morocco. Vesco got the plane not only out of the country—but far, far out of the country, while Elmer Sticco was still trying to figure out what had hit him. About an hour before landing at Rabat, Dottie came forward with a surprise for me. She had been preparing the standard general declaration required for entry to foreign countries.

"Guess who we've been flying all night," she said, and handed me the General Dec for my signature. My passengers were traveling with Costa Rican passports under assumed names. Vesco was traveling as Robert V. Sasek. Gil Straub was now Gilbert Straub Beatty. Dick Clay used the name R. C. Truesdale, and "Giggles" LeBlanc masqueraded as Norman MacDonald. Our itinerary took us to Agadir and Marrakech, Morocco, Tunis, and Beirut. We returned to Morocco via Tunis, but to Casablanca instead of Rabat. We picked up a passenger with the exotic sounding name of Dafir Laghzaoui.

Vesco made it seem that this man's presence had a more mysterious meaning than it probably had. He told me that it was vital that nobody know that the man was aboard the airplane. Then he compounded the situation by telling me that on our return to the Bahamas I was not to land at Nassau but at Rock Sound, a 7200-foot strip on one of the Bahamian out-islands. There, he and his passengers would board a chartered amphibian for an eighty-mile, low-level flight directly to the seaplane ramp on Paradise Island. The ramp is located close to the bridge, within walking distance of the casino. It is fairly well screened from general view by a stand of trees. The airplane could be taxied out of the water, up the ramp, and into a clearing where Vesco and his friends, especially his mysterious passenger, could land unobserved. At Rock Sound nobody knew Vesco by sight and the phony names and Costa Rican passports would arouse no suspicions. At Nassau however, where Vesco was a frequent transient, he could not get away with a phony passport.

Everything went according to plan as far as Rock Sound. After Vesco and the others departed for Paradise Island, I refiled and flew on into Nassau—empty.

The Bahamian Customs inspector at Nassau boarded the Boeing. I told him I had been on an interisland flight and showed him my Rock Sound clearance. There was nothing he could do and it bothered him. He left the airplane scratching his head. What I got a kick out of was the fact that there was a U.S. Customs agent down on the ramp waiting to learn what his Bahamian counterpart had found. Whoever in Casablanca had tipped U.S. Customs about Vesco's departure would have a hell of a time explaining what happened to the people he saw getting on the airplane. I never saw Dafir Laghzaoui again.

Even after I had worked out a contract with Grady in Texas, I did not feel entirely confident. Grady was a sharpshooter and I was determined not to get caught short with heavy bills and no money. Because of this I insisted that each Boeing flight be contracted for separately and that I be paid expense money and crew salaries before the completion of each leg of any flight. To prove to Grady that I meant what I said, I began to demand payment in-flight or threaten to return to the takeoff point. Even Vesco thought I was sticking it to Grady and he was right. But he didn't interfere. When the Boeing was not in use, the crew, which was under contract to me, serviced the Gulfstream II leased from Dorfman. Dottie McCarty crewed a flight to Teterboro, New Jersey and stayed in New Jersey for a couple of days to take care of personal business.

On March 25, 1973, Dottie went to Teterboro Airport to meet a G-II flight arriving from Nassau and to help the passengers, Pat Vesco and the children, once they were on the ground. It was a late arrival and it was dark. Dottie drove out onto the ramp when the G-II arrived. She saw a man in civilian clothes. She assumed that the man was there to greet somebody arriving on the Grumman. He certainly was. As soon as he learned Dottie's identity, he whipped out a subpena, striking Dottie on the shoulder with his hand and scaring the living lights out of her. She jumped into her car and locked the doors. It turned out that the man was a government attorney who had come to the airport with a pocketful of subpenas, which included the crew of the Grumman. There was one for me too. But I was in Nassau at the time and it was eventually accepted in my name by my attorney, Howard A. Singer of New York.

I had retained Howard for myself and the crew because of the regular harassment by various government agencies concerned with Robert Vesco. In addition, ICC had named me as a defendant in a suit they brought against Vesco and his gang. But that suit came later. In any event, both Dottie and I, as well as Lou Notte, were questioned by SEC attorneys and a grand jury about Vesco's activities with regards to the aircraft. There wasn't much I could tell them except the truth. They wanted all my records pertaining to my employment with any of Vesco's companies. I offered what I had, my own personal records. They wanted the official logs and passenger manifest for the Boeing. Which I did not have.

On March 31, 1973, I met with Vesco at the Bay Shore Marina in Nassau. He had asked me to retrieve from the Boeing the passenger manifest. This was before I was subpenaed. Grady had told me to turn over to him all aircraft logs and records, including the passenger manifest. Vesco's orders were to give him nothing. However, it turned out that Vesco was willing to give Grady the aircraft logs but only *copies* of those parts of the passenger manifest that he approved. I had brought the passenger manifest to Vesco at the marina and he examined certain pages and smiled. He handed it back to me.

"Stick it in the trunk of the car," he said. That was the last I saw of it until it turned up on a desk in the U.S. Attorney's office in Foley Square, New York a month later. On the 3rd of April, I turned over all other aircraft logs to Joel Grady and told him if he wanted the passenger manifest to get it from Vesco.

I heard no more about the Moscow trip. The April 7th departure date came and went. I made my appearance before the grand jury between flights in the Grumman. For some reason, Vesco did not want to use the Boeing. Again there was more talk of stashing the Boeing someplace in South America, probably Argentina. And when Vesco told me that we were going on an extended trip to South America I was certain that he had made up his mind. Departure date for the trip, which would include Argentina and Paraguay, was set for April 24, 1973. We were to leave for Buenos Aires sometime in the evening of the 24th.

The Boeing hadn't been flown in a month, having sat in the hot Bahamian sun that whole time. I therefore scheduled a test flight for four o'clock in the afternoon. Sometime during the flight, we began to talk about the fate of the Boeing and the possibility that she would be out of our tender, loving care very shortly—perhaps forever. I would never have believed that I could get personally attached to a flying machine. Maybe I was not the cold-hearted professional as thoroughly as I thought I was and was a victim of one of those "love affairs" that novelists write about. Anyway, I was hooked on Silver Phyllis and I wanted something really spectacular to remember her by. The landing at Southend was not quite it. So I rolled her—first one way, then the other—and brought her back to Nassau.

Vesco made no deals for Silver Phyllis. We made our swing through South America, landing at San José on April 28. The most memorable aspect of the flight was Vesco's impossible plan to fly Peron from Madrid to Buenos Aires nonstop.

Vesco had become a gun nut. I think it started in Beirut, sometime in 1972. I had bought a little 22-caliber, single-shot pen gun. I had been a gun enthusiast, myself, from boyhood. My father had been a gun collector and, under his tutelege, I came to understand and respect firearms and ultimately became a collector myself. I showed the pen gun to Vesco and he asked me for it. I gave it to him. Later, I bought him a 9mm automatic in Spain. He loved it. But I think that Vesco's fascination with guns was zeroed in on their menace. He wasn't exactly a cowboy, but he was fond of showing off his prowess with a pistol. After the South American trip we all took a day off and went to a ranch outside San José. There were three cars in the caravan which carried some of Vesco's business associates and friends. These "friends" were in reality Vesco's Costa Rican bodyguard. Their boss was the man whose only name to my knowledge was "The Major."

Vesco wanted to do some shooting. What surprised me was the weapon he intended to use. He carried the weapon in a molded plastic carrying case for tennis rackets. It was bright red and not unfamiliar. I had seen them on the Boeing, during cargo unloading at San José airport. They were part of Junior Nixon's sports equipment.

Vesco opened his case and revealed a brand new 9mm machine gun that he said was given to him by our passenger of the previous South American jaunt—the son-in-law of the President of Paraguay. I did not know the make. Vesco said it was the latest from the United States arsenal. It was equipped with a silencer.

Vesco, LeBlanc, Marti Figueres, and I took turns firing the weapon. Vesco of course was first. And looked like a guy with a runaway fire hose. He tried to put the entire clip through the barrel without stopping. The gun jumped up and away from him, and if he hadn't taken his finger off the trigger, he might have wiped out half of his own bodyguard. I showed him how to tickle off the rounds in short bursts. And he very quickly improved his performance. I did the same for LeBlanc and Marti. I think Vesco would have gotten rid of a couple of thousand rounds that day if he had had them with him.

The "weapons proving grounds" were in a fairly remote part of the *estancia,* several miles from any house. We had left the main road to take a dirt track that seemed to wander nowhere in particular. The driver of the lead car, LeBlanc, seemed to know where he was going. We stopped on the edge of a field that was impassable for the cars. We left the cars, Vesco carrying his tennis racket, until we came to a stream with a rather high bank. It was the bank that we used as a backstop for the shooting. I had thought that Vesco merely wanted to try out his new toy. I was jolted when I noticed that the Vesco bodyguard carried boxes and boxes of weapons of every description from the cars to the area where we fired the machine gun. These were followed by boxes of ammunition. There must have been a couple of dozen different weapons of various types and calibre, from 32-caliber automatics to 45s. In minutes the area sounded as if maneuvers were being held. Everybody was firing. The Costa Ricans were doing the loading. I wanted to remove myself several miles and get behind a large rock until they ran out of ammunition. My ears rang for the next couple of hours. These adult males, sophisticated in the business world, acted like a bunch of kids on the Fourth of July. Later on at the house I was inducted, with proper ceremony, into Vesco's recently organized "Club De Tiro Los Machos." And my membership card was signed by Norman (LeBlanc) MacDonald, acting President.

Vesco wasn't always that handy with a gun. In 1972, after I had given him his new Spanish automatic, he took it out behind his Boonton Township, New Jersey, estate to potshot at some bottles and cans. However he held the gun, the slide tore the webbing between his thumb and index finger of his shooting hand. It was a lesson he never forgot.

I made another visit to Foley Square on May 4. The

routine was the same. The proceedings didn't do much to elevate my opinion of government lawyers. For all their arrogance and the power of the Federal government behind them, they didn't seem able to find their asses with both hands. They were constantly fishing and looking for me to show them what direction to take.

On May 15, 1973, I took off from Nassau bound for Rabat, on what would be the last trip I would make in the Boeing with Robert Vesco. It was a memorable one.

In Rabat, Bob Vesco and his wife Pat left the Boeing for the city by themselves, as usual. Gil Straub took charge of the other passengers. Later on, I met Gil and the other passengers at the hotel. With them was a bevy of beautiful fräuleins who were flown down in a Learjet from Germany by Straub's arrangement. The Vescos were not with the party. Straub told me we would leave that afternoon for Nice to attend the Cannes Film Festival. I was surprised, therefore, when I was ready for departure and the Vescos had not shown up. This had never happened before. If Vesco intended to travel some other way he usually let me know. I was reluctant to leave without some idea of where Vesco was. I asked Straub about it. He said not to worry. I took off on schedule but I was uneasy.

Cannes was a wild scene, everything the press had painted it to be. We spent two days there. On May 18, Straub told me that we would be going to Athens. Still no sign of Vesco.

Our route to Athens would carry us directly over Rome. As we passed the northern tip of Corsica, Straub made an appearance on the flight deck.

"Ike, we have to land in Rome," he said.

"Gil, we can't land in Rome," I told him. "I need to give them advance notice. Shit, man, the only way I could ever get into Rome would be to declare an emergency."

"Goddamn it, Ike," he said, "this is an emergency. Bobby's going to meet us there. We have to pick him up." Sweet Christ almighty!

"Gil, why the hell didn't you tell me this in Nice?" I asked him.

"Security," was all he said. This puts me on the hook. Straub went back to the cabin leaving me to solve the problem. The crew couldn't help but hear the conversation and they waited to see what I was going to do. One thing was certain, I was not about to declare an emergency. But I would need a hell of a good reason to request permission to land in Rome. There was one other problem. There are two airports at Rome, Fumincino on the coast, and Ciampino outside town—Straub didn't tell me which one. I sent Dottie back to get the answer—Ciampino.

The only way that I could make the unscheduled landing at Rome without declaring an all-out emergency was to develop some kind of mechanical malfunction and ask Rome for permission to make a precautionary landing to inspect my aircraft. If handled with conviction, this could keep me out of a Roman jail. I decided that the malfunction would occur in the number-one engine. Now I had to psyche up my crew. I started with my F/O.

"Is number one still giving us trouble?" I asked him. He grinned and turned to the FEO.

"Is number one still giving us trouble?" he asked. The FEO stared at his panel for a bit then turned around and tapped me on the shoulder.

"Captain," he said, "something's wrong with number one."

"Thank you," I said. I contacted Rome and explained that I had an apparent malfunction in one of my engines, and I wanted to make a precautionary landing at Ciampino Airport. I got their O.K. to make the landing to have a look-see. Now we had to make it look real. I shut down number one so that there would be no telltale smoke on final approach and landed with three engines. I was directed to a spot in front of the tower. And wondered how in the name of Christ I could fake this one.

I had an idea. I had had so many hydraulic problems on Silver Phyllis over the years, that I had a collection of fractured "B" nuts and short pieces of hydraulic tubing in a large manila envelope. I took a couple of pieces at random and stuck them in my pocket. I grabbed a bunch of tools and told my F/O and FEO to roll up their sleeves, grab some tools, and follow me. I told the other two guys to strip the cowling off number one and go through a lot of motions without touching anything. We had collected a crowd of line personnel, crash crews, and mechanics. This had to look real good. The three of us poked around the engine for a bit, waved our arms and pretended we were discussing whatever went wrong.

I went to the belly of Silver Phyllis, took out an eight-foot piece of two-by-four and walked back to the engine. I gave the reverse cascades a couple of healthy raps with the two-by-four. Then I stuck the two-by-four up the tailpipe and banged on the thrust reverser clams as hard as I could. The noise was impressive. When I went back for the two-by-four I had also palmed one of the "B" nuts, a big one with a sizeable crack in it. I stuck my hands and head as far as I could into the engine and after a moment triumphantly "pulled out" the offending connector. A lot of heads bobbed up and down and for a moment I thought the Italians were going to applaud. The other guys and I examined the nut at great length and discussed it thoroughly. With pretended anger, I threw the nut away in the direction of the crowd. A mechanic pounced on it and the crowd gathered around him. Again, the heads bobbed.

I had killed about half an hour with this charade. Now, of course, I had to "repair" the engine. I went back to the cabin and grabbed hold of Straub.

"Where the hell is Bobby?" I asked him. "How much longer can I stall? If they send someone out to help me I can't refuse. If I accept the help, I'm up the spout." Straub shrugged his shoulders. He was getting worried.

"I don't know, Ike," he said. "He was supposed to be here."

I could still foozle around with the engine, and I realized I had another stalling tactic at hand. I had to pay airport landing fees. This is an absolute must. Even if you crash and burn there is always some sonofabitch who will show up with a charge sheet for landing fees, parking, and handling. Without the Captain present the engine couldn't be fixed. The landing fees gave me a perfect excuse to get into the terminal building and look for Vesco. If I played things right I could kill another hour. The big problem was that I was required to take off as soon as repairs were completed. I could only stall so long.

I got myself "lost" in the terminal. After twenty minutes or so of scouring the main passenger areas for Vesco without success, I finally "found" the airport office where I made a big show of paying the fees, complaining that I could not read the receipt. I got that adjusted and finally thanked everybody in sight, handshakes included, for their gracious Italian hospitality and help. Then I made certain that everybody understood that I had some very important phone calls to make before taking off. I went to a fairly remote wall phone and made a show of dialing. I argued for fifteen minutes with a dead telephone. Still no Vesco. Now I had to go back and "fix" the goddamn airplane before someone got suspicious. Before I did that I had to head off another problem. Because this was a precautionary landing and we were in transit to Athens, no Customs or Immigration official came out to the airplane. Therefore, nobody at the airport had any idea of how many passengers I had aboard. Technically, nobody should have left the aircraft. It would be very difficult to explain to the Italian authorities why two of my passengers—the Vescos—had violated the law. I had to find some insurance and I spotted him sitting in a station wagon observing the whole scene. He was a uniformed airport passenger service rep. Luckily, he could speak English. I invented a wild story on the spot. I told him that because of the delay caused by the unfortunate incident of engine failure, both my Chief Stewardess and I had exceeded the permissible "company" duty hours. The "company" had therefore dispatched a relief captain and chief stewardess who would be arriving momentarily. Would he be so kind as to expedite—without official encounters—their progress to the airplane? I secured an absolute guarantee of cooperation with the presentation of an American souvenir—a one-hundred-dollar bill.

The F/O and FEO were sweating dust. The crowd hadn't thinned much. I reached in my pocket and pulled out a nut similar to the one I had thrown to the crowd. I held it aloft so that everybody could see my good fortune. Both the guys looked as if they were ready to cheer. I stuck my head into the engine, told the engineer to poke the two-by-four up there with me and just kind of move it around. I told the F/O to keep an eye open for the Vescos. I must have been inside that engine for only a couple of minutes when I heard the F/O holler, "They're here!"

I came out of that engine faster than eagle shit. The FEO dropped the two-by-four. I could see Vesco and Pat racing across the ramp towards the Boeing. We had that engine buttoned up before they got to the steps. We gathered up tools and that two-by-four and carried the whole works into the cabin and slammed the door. I was filthy. So were the other two guys. Vesco stood inside the door huffing and puffing. Pat was ready to pass out. I just looked at Vesco.

"For Chrissakes, Bob," was all I said to him. He and Pat staggered back to the salon. They collapsed into seats.

Sometime while we were on the ground Straub had told me that there had never been any intention to go to Athens, and that we were heading back to Nassau via Casablanca. I made up a story for traffic control and got a change in destination from Athens to Casablanca because of "company" orders. I never did find out what Vesco was doing in Rome or how the hell he got there, or who was chasing him when he showed up at the airplane.

We got back to Nassau on May 18, 1973. The following morning I flew the Boeing to Ft. Lauderdale, prior to taking it to Pan Am in Miami for a routine inspection. I had to wait until the following day to confirm a maintenance time slot at Pan Am. Early on the morning of the 20th, Joel Grady called me from Nassau and told me to bring the airplane back, to forget the inspection. I started to argue with him. It would be stupid and dangerous to skip any inspections.

"Bob wants that fuckin' airplane back in Nassau

now" he said. I did as I was told. I parked the Boeing in its usual spot in front of Howard Hughes's hangar and locked it up. The Silver Phyllis would not take to the air again until I ferried it from Nassau to Miami on October 27, 1973 for the inspection it should have had in May. Ironically, Robert Vesco never got to use his sauna, tub, and shower, or his mini-gym.

The G-II became Vesco's primary airplane. He would comment on the Boeing when he would see it at the airport, but he never gave me a reason why he grounded it. It was during this period that Frank Beatty and Joel Grady, who had taken new offices for Fairfield General which Vesco still controlled, tried to involve me in a plot to sell the airplane out from under Vesco. Vesco got wind of the scheme. Beatty was in New Jersey, but Grady and I were in Nassau. Vesco called me into his BCB office with him and Norman LeBlanc for a showdown. Grady also showed up at the bank. He spent forty-five minutes alone with Vesco before I was called in.

Beatty and Grady had explained to me that what they were doing was designed to "protect" Robert Vesco. Reportedly, a large block of Fairfield General stock was owned by the Vesco children. The airplane represented the major asset of Fairfield General. If word got out that the airplane was being sold for over three million dollars, the value of the stock would appreciate considerably.

Frank Beatty, so he claimed, was fearful that Vesco's eldest son Danny, who was dabbling in the stock market, might buy up all the Fairfield General stock he could lay his hands on and thus show an enormous profit. He could be accused by the SEC—his father's enemy—of trading on inside information. Actually, if this were to happen, the vulnerable ones would be Grady and Beatty, since they would have to be the source of the inside information that Danny Vesco would be trading on.

Vesco was furious. He had never given Grady and Beatty any authority to negotiate the sale of the Boeing, something which Grady and Beatty had led me to believe was the case. I showed Vesco telexes from the two men which, in effect, forbade me to discuss the matter in any way with Vesco. Their intent to deceive me was clear as soon as I was confronted with the knowledge that they were acting on their own. Vesco knew all about the telexes.

"There is nothing that goes in or out of this island that I don't know about," he told me. He then said something about my obligation never to keep anything from him no matter what. Then he changed the subject.

This was the day after the incident at Teterboro when Pat Vesco was treated so roughly by Customs. Vesco wanted a full report and I told him what I remembered of the incident. What I didn't tell him was that after Pat Vesco had left for home, the Customs people called me aside to talk confidentially, out of earshot of the rest of my crew. I was asked if I would consider "bringing Vesco back to this country." The idea was ridiculous to me. It was not the first time the suggestion had been made. An SEC lawyer tried it on for size. I had actually forgotten about the Teterboro affair because the Pat Vesco incident had been so hairy. But Vesco, apparently knew more than I thought he would.

"Was anything said about bringing me back to the country?" he asked. And I knew immediately that he knew about what had happened after Pat left the airplane. I told him what went on and what was said. And I told him that I not only considered the proposal to be a frivolous one, but that he ought to realize that I would have no part in such an effort. Vesco wasn't satisfied.

"Ike, you should have told that guy that you wouldn't try anything like that, because you value your life," he said. I couldn't believe what I was hearing.

"What the hell does that mean, Bob?" I said.

"Exactly what I said," he said. "There are a lot of Costa Rican gorillas who would be very unhappy with you." He turned to LeBlanc. "Isn't that right, Norman?" LeBlanc giggled.

"Yeah, yeah, Bob," he said, "they wouldn't be very happy about it." I was getting goddam angry.

"Let's stop this shit," I said. "Save that for the flunkies."

"I'm not kidding," Vesco said. "There is no place you could hide." I tried to put a stop to this *macho* bullshit. But Vesco persisted. He was really worried about a kidnapping and believed that I was the only guy who could carry it off. I was ready to walk out when he finally dropped the matter.

He switched back to the business of the sale of the airplane. Then I knew what the sneaky bastard was up to. He was trying to box me in, to maneuver me into a position where I would be as vulnerable and malleable as the clowns around him, like Grady and Beatty and LeBlanc and Straub and Dodd. From his remarks about the sale at this point in the conversation and from something dropped by Grady before I came into the meeting, I saw that he not only knew about the sale "plot" from the very beginning, but had probably initiated the moves, using Grady and Beatty and me as a screen. As I said before, Vesco can be brilliant, but he can also do some very dumb things. Tipping his hand to me about his involvement in the sale was one of the dumb things. From this point on he wanted me to involve myself in the sale of the airplane, but I must keep the screen up around Vesco and pretend that I was acting against him. I couldn't wait to get out of the room and begin to put all this shit together.

What Grady had said to me was that the proceeds of the sale of the Boeing would be turned into British bank Certificates of Deposit and be stashed in a safety deposit box for Robert Lee Vesco. So much for protecting his children's interests.

The next day Vesco acted as though nothing had ever happened. I was still as mad as hell but in the back of my mind, because of the way he had acted, I wondered if maybe he wasn't beginning to lose some marbles. His manner and even his appearance had changed markedly over the past six or seven months. At one time he would listen to advice. Now he rejected it. I was beginning to not like the man.

There were still signs, however, that he might yet be willing to holler for help from capable people. He dispatched me to Washington to bring Edward Bennett Williams, one of the most capable lawyers in Washington, to his Nassau compound, along with his wife and children. I remember Williams as a dynamic-looking, likeable guy, although I later lost respect for him.

After the Williams visit I took Vesco to San José. As was his custom, he hopped into a car which then sped off toward the gate. As the car approached the guardhouse near the gate, the guard ran out waving his pistol and yelling to the driver of Vesco's car to stop. The car kept on going without slowing down. Frustrated, the guard ran to the airplane and stormed aboard screaming in Spanish and waving his gun. He pointed it directly at me and yelled something which I didn't understand. Instinctively, I grabbed for the gun. The guard wasn't a very big guy and my move surprised him. I ripped the gun from his hand and jammed the barrel into one of his nostrils. I was in a spasm of rage. The guard realized instantly what had happened. He turned gray and a look of utter terror came into his eyes. It was a couple of seconds before either of us moved. I backed off and saw that the guard had actually wet himself. I emptied the gun and threw the bullets out the door. I handed the useless weapon back to him and simply pointed. I was absolutely unable to talk, but he got the message and hightailed it out of there. Later, I felt sorry for the poor guy. His job probably conferred a great deal of status on him and he could no longer tolerate the insult of being ignored by the *Norte Americanos*.

Two days later, on June 4, 1973, I was arrested in the airport terminal building while filing my flight plan for the return trip to Nassau. To this day I don't know the circumstances that prompted it, whether it was the guard incident or Don Pepe's political opposition who wanted to embarrass him and his American protege, Vesco. The pretext for the arrest was that I had illegally purchased Costa Rican national treasures. Actually, I had bought curios in the open market place and paid a hefty price for them. There was no indication by anybody that the merchandise was anything but legitimately for sale. I even took the merchandise to the

Costa Rican National Museum for appraisal. Again, no problem. The people I bought the stuff from had asked an outlandish price. We haggled and I paid them exactly what we finally agreed upon. I've done this all over the world. Apparently in Costa Rica this honored custom is not observed. They hollered cop and the cops collared me. Fortunately, Marti Figueres was with me. He saw the whole thing as politically motivated. He made a call to his old man and the matter was straightened out within a half hour. But the taste lingered. Even Vesco's closeness to Don Pepe did not prevent the court from ordering Vesco to post a three-thousand-dollar bond for my release.

Right in the middle of this whole hassle, an earthquake—or at least a very violent tremor—shook the San José area. The terminal building at the airport trembled. Pictures and framed documents fell from the wall. Shelves emptied themselves onto the floor. Desks and chairs bounced around. The building emptied rapidly. Marti and I stayed put. The shock lasted only a few minutes. I left San José shortly after Vesco arrived. That was the last time I was in San José, Costa Rica.

A few days after my arrest in San José I had to return to my home in Denville to take care of some private business. In addition, I wanted to consult with my attorney, Howard Singer, not only on where I stood with the government, but also about the advisability of sticking with Vesco. If anybody could give me sound advice on the latter, it would be Howard Singer. He had been Vesco's chief counsel at ICC when I first started in 1968 and remained so until he left in 1970. We were very close friends. The day after I got home a parcel was delivered to the house. It was post marked Frankfurt, Germany and bore the imprint of Jeppesen & Co. When I opened it I almost went through the roof. It was obvious that it had already been opened, its contents examined and rewrapped—badly. It contained all the charts of all of Eastern Europe and the Iron Curtain countries including the Soviet Union. I was tempted to burn them in the fireplace. Instead, I flung them into a corner, intending to personally deliver them to Vesco along with a few well-chosen phrases.

I didn't get to meet with Howard until June 10, a Sunday, the day before I was to return to Nassau. We reviewed my situation. There wasn't much I could do about the government except to wait for its move. He had only two words to say about my difficulties with Vesco, "Get out!"

There was no flying that week. Vesco stuck close to home. I don't even think he went to his offices in the BCB. I had a feeling that something was stirring. The G-II and its crew were on standby alert.

On Friday, June 15, 1973, Vesco called and told me to come out to his house the next day at one o'clock in the afternoon. It had become routine for Junior Nixon to come out to the gate and pass me in. Junior hadn't changed much, but for some reason he was less of an irritant. The first thing Vesco touched on was his new boat. I was to fly his son, Tony, down to Antigua on Monday to meet the Captain and deliver cash. Tony Vesco was about fifteen at the time. Vesco hemmed and hawed a little. He wasn't used to making small talk, and I knew from experience that he was stalling. Waiting for something to happen that he expected to happen. He said something about Dottie and me signing some affidavits that would be useful to him and that he would explain what he meant after he got a call from his lawyer, Edward Bennett Williams. The call came. There were some hearty words and then Vesco mentioned that I was in the room. There's no doubt in my mind that the caller was Williams. Vesco said the name a couple of times. Then Vesco picked up a pencil and began to write rapidly on a pad. After a few minutes he assured Williams that "they will do it" and that "they're on my side." When he hung up, he asked me to come to his BCB office on Monday morning, June 18, 1973 to sign the affidavits just dictated to him over the phone by Edward Bennett Williams. Dottie and I were to sign these affidavits in the presence of a Bahamian notary and other witnesses. I told him I would show up with Dottie McCarty but I couldn't guarantee anything after that. He didn't like it.

The next day, Sunday, June 17, I got another call from Vesco. He wanted me to meet him at the Boeing just before dark. I showed up at the airplane by myself at about 8:30 that night. Vesco showed up with Junior Nixon a little after. I opened up the airplane and we went on board. Vesco asked me to break out a couple of flashlights. One for himself and one for Junior. I did. He asked me to wait up forward and told me that he had something that he wanted to discuss with me. Then he and Junior went aft and began to turn the interior of the Boeing inside out. At one point I heard Junior say earnestly, "But I saw it there in plain sight and it was there."

Until I heard Junior, I had no idea what they were looking for. Then I knew. It was a small-bore Italian automatic which I had given Vesco a couple of years before. It was his "dress gun." It could be carried unnoticed under a suit jacket or in a trouser pocket. I had found it several weeks earlier under circumstances that could have been very serious for me. We had landed in Nassau after an international flight. A Customs officer had come aboard and I accompanied him on his inspection rounds. For some reason I glanced down at the planter holding artificial flowers and ferns. Snuggled among them was the gun. How the Customs man missed it I'll never know. I was able to work it out of the planter and into my pocket while his back was to me. I was so angry at Vesco's stupidity that I decided to keep the gun. I still have it.

When the unsuccessful search was finished Vesco came forward with Junior.

"What are you looking for, Bob?" I asked him. He smiled.

"Uh—incriminating evidence." He told Nixon to get lost and Junior went down to the car to wait.

Vesco must really have been feeling the pressure or he was becoming paranoiac. There was this mysterious search immediately after the call from Williams, and now he trotted out another bizarre project. He told me that he needed to have handy an escape hatch in case "everything blew up." He wanted me to scout the out-islands and pick one that could not only be reached in under two hours in one of his "Cigarettes," an ocean-going, racing-class speedboat, but offer good cover and seclusion and be capable of accomodating an aircraft as big as the Boeing, or at least the G-II. I thought he had completely blown his mind. He left immediately. He sure as hell gave me something else to think about. There was not much I could do about his request until after the meeting on Monday the 18th in his BCB office and the flight to Antigua with Tony Vesco.

Dottie and I showed up promptly at 8:45 at the bank and were shown into a conference room where we found Vesco, Dick Clay, Wendy Kenyon, who was Norman LeBlanc's secretary and girlfriend, and Mr. Dana Wells, the Bahamian notary. Vesco got right to the point. He handed the typed copies of the affidavits dictated to him by Williams to Dottie and me and said, "Sign them." We both read our affidavits, and after we finished I read Dottie's. The substance was the same. If we signed these affidavits we would be swearing that Vesco was "in Nassau, Commonwealth of the Bahama Islands on March 30, 1972 and remained there without interruption until and including the entire business day of April 6th, 1972 [the last date for making unreported political contributions]. Mr. Vesco departed the Bahama Islands after the close of the banking business day on April 6, 1972, along with 22 other passengers." The affidavit also contained the paragraph that stated that "I have personal knowledge that Mr. Vesco was in Nassau, Commonwealth of the Bahama Islands, without interruption from March 30, 1972 until and including the entire business banking day of April 6, 1972. . . ."

Even without checking my own records these were documents that did not reflect the truth, and neither Dottie nor I would sign them. Vesco exploded.

"What the hell is wrong with them?" he yelled, directing his attention mainly at Dottie. I held up my hand.

"Stay cool, Bob," I said. "Let's you and I talk about this in private." He hesitated a moment and then took me into another, smaller conference room and slammed the door. We went at it. The first thing I told him is that we wouldn't even start negotiating this thing until Dottie was taken completely off the hook. The only two statements that I would permit her to put her name to were that one, at all times "pertinent hereto" she was employed as flight stewardess on the private aircraft used for all international travel by Mr. Robert L. Vesco, and two, the aircraft logs attached to my affidavit and "of this date" were prepared by her and were true and accurate. Vesco pissed and moaned and cursed and yelled but finally agreed. Then we got down to the business of my affidavit. He was asking me to swear to something that I knew to be neither true nor untrue, except for one significant date. First of all, on March 30, 1972, I dropped Vesco in Nassau and went to Miami, Florida and did not return to Nassau until April 4, 1972. I cannot swear that—even though I may have been in telephone contact with Vesco—that he either was or was not in Nassau. Even after returning to Nassau I could not testify from personal knowledge that he was or was not in Nassau, again even if I had telephone contact with him. Invariably, these telephone contacts were initiated by Vesco, and with the direct dialing system it would be impossible for whoever receives the call to know where it originated. As for April 6, 1972, my records show that Vesco was aboard the Boeing at two in the afternoon—with Howard Cerney—a full hour before what I believed to be the bank closing hour of three p.m. Even if the banks in Nassau do close to the public an hour earlier than they do, say, in New Jersey or New York, the phrase "business banking day" means five o'clock. I hit Vesco with all of this. His answer, boiled down, was that it didn't make any difference what the affidavit stated, that Williams had left me "18 outs." The ambiguous language was deliberate. Then he said he didn't give a shit what my records showed. The affidavit was prepared on the information contained in the official logs of the aircraft which he had in his possession and no further explanation was necessary.

He swore that the affidavits were for use before Costa Rican courts, that they would never appear in the United States. I didn't believe him. The April 6 date was too damn coincidental with the delivery of the 200,000 dollars destined for the Nixon campaign fund. Then Vesco took out the knuckle breaker. He reminded me that he had the power to put me and the crew out of work by hanging onto the Boeing and grounding it permanently. He brought up my heavy legal fees and hinted that, if I played ball, he would see to it that I wouldn't lose a dime to the lawyers. I considered the matter. It was slicing it pretty thin, I admit, but in the strictest sense, what I would swear to would be neither the truth nor the untruth. I signed. So did Dottie. An hour later I left for Antigua with Tony Vesco to see Vesco's new yacht.

It was a beauty. It was formerly named *"Romantica,"* but Vesco would christen the 137-foot aluminum-hulled, diesel-powered, shallow-draft, 200-ton vessel *Patricia III*. It was more luxurious than any other boat I had ever been on.

On June 20, I again flew to Antigua. This time with Robert Vesco. Again, he gave not the slightest hint that only two days before we had been snarling at each other over the affidavits. He was almost as excited about his yacht as he had been about the Boeing.

The next day, June 21, 1973, I had a twin-engine Piper Aztec flown over from Ft. Lauderdale for my island reconaissance of a suitable getaway location for Vesco. Vesco had made a big point about secrecy. Since I needed a copilot along, I took one of my crew that I trusted. I told him what I was looking for but not why I was looking for it. After about three hours of flying I spotted what looked to me like a runway, partially overgrown on the southwestern side of Andros Island, the largest out-island in the Bahamas. But also one of the least populated and least adaptable to tourist travel. I dropped down and circled the spot several times. It was easy to identify. It was an abandoned World War Two landing strip 5000 feet long and 200 feet wide, but enough to accommodate the Boeing or the G-II. I landed and got out to test the condition of the macadam that was laid right over hard-packed sandy clay. It could support the weight of a heavy aircraft, provided that the ground remained dry. The west end of the runway was less than half a mile from the closest feasible point where a boat could be safely beached. I found Vesco's "escape hatch." On a subsequent deadheading flight in the G-II, I tested the exact location of the strip, using the accuracy of the Inertial Navigation System on board, and found that the coordinates of the "escape hatch" to be precisely 24 minutes, 43.5 seconds north and 78 minutes, 08.0 seconds west.

Vesco released me for ten days and told me to go home and mow my lawn in New Jersey. He had some important things to discuss with me when I got back. He was very hazy about his plans for the future, but he assured me that I would play an important role in them.

"You've got some heavy thinking to do, Ike," he said, "and so have I. I've got to sort out who's with me and who's against me." He leaned back with his hands locked behind his head. "Dottie, for example," he said. "After that affidavit business, she's dead in my book." I wasn't going to go to war with him right then. I got up to leave. "We'll talk about it when you get back."

"Not about that, Bob," I said. "That's nonnegotiable. I'll see you on July 2." I walked out before he could answer me.

We had agreed that we would meet specifically to determine precisely where I stood after I had taken care of my personal affairs, and he had had a chance to analyze his own situation. My understanding was that we would meet in a business atmosphere to reach a clear-cut business arrangement. I did not want any more of the Grady, Beatty, LeBlanc type of horseshit.

Vesco contacted me by telephone two or three times during my absence from Nassau. He was having difficulties with the crew that came along with the Grumman. He hinted that he'd like me to come back to Nassau and bail him out. I refused for two reasons. First of all, I just could not spare the time, even though I could use the income, since at that moment I was not on anybody's payroll. The second was that with me out of the way, maybe Vesco would begin to appreciate the kind of service I had given him and could still provide—if the conditions were right.

I had a lot of time to think back home in Denville. Everything about Vesco had changed since November, 1968. I had had a lot of fun, improved my skills and capabilities greatly, expanded my range of professional experience. On those points I had no complaint. And the association with Vesco had been a generally rewarding one regardless of his business ethics and the accusations made against him. He could be infuriating and downright rotten at times. But he could be generous and disarming too.

Vesco was certainly a nonconformist. He was antiestablishment and anti-big government. He detested the bureaucrats and the Napoleonic nitwits who, using the authority of the government, brutalized the citizen. I couldn't agree with him more. But he was no Don Quixote. He was out to make a buck for Robert L. Vesco no matter what it cost somebody else.

I knew, before I left for Nassau on June 2, 1973, that I would have to make a decision whether to stay with Vesco or break clean. The way things looked to me then, I could see no future with this man.

I got back to Nassau about 9:30 at night on June 2 and called Vesco. He seemed glad to hear from me. He set up an appointment for me at 10:30 the following morning in his office at the Bahamas Commonwealth Bank. There wasn't much I could do to prepare for the meeting. I had a few complaints, a few unpaid bills, but it was Vesco who would determine the agenda. And he gave no hint of what precisely was on his mind.

I appeared in the BCB offices on schedule. No Vesco. I waited. At 11:20 I was told that he would be delayed until at least 12:30. I got mad. He might have been legitimately delayed but this looked like another example of Vesco chess. I was in no mood for games. I walked out without explanation. I left no word where I could be reached.

Vesco tracked me down at the Halcyon Balmoral Hotel where he reached me by phone. He couldn't understand why I hadn't waited. Or at least he pretended not to understand. I gave him a transparently phony excuse rather than get into a hassle with him. He understood my point and we set up another appointment for the following morning, July 4, 1973, at 9:30. This time he was only a half-hour late.

Vesco was in a confident, businesslike mood. After the treatment I had gotten the day before, I had been ready to take the first plane back to Newark. However, I decided to stick around and see what the man had to say. I still had an obligation to protect the interests of my crew, who were similarly in a non-pay status, still owed money for services rendered, and having no clear idea of their futures.

The first thing Vesco asked about were those goddamned Iron Curtain navigation charts. His mood changed instantly to anger when I told him I did not have them with me. He made a big thing of it and insisted on calling Shirley Bailey in Fairfield right then to have her send somebody to my house to retrieve them. This whole routine was a show. The maps could have been sent down by ordinary mail. What Vesco needed was an issue to put me on the defensive. He did it with everybody believing that it gave him the initial advantage.

With that out of the way he switched to the still live possibility of the sale of the Boeing. If the Boeing were sold, it would mean continued if somewhat shaky employment for the crew. But the major benefactor would be, as usual, Vesco. I was not interested at that moment in the sale of the Boeing. Once Vesco and I came to some sort of rational, business arrangement, negotiating the sale of the Boeing would be part of my regular services to Vesco.

Then he proposed a short-term solution to my problem—employment and income. I could be kept on a payroll as a consultant to Grady and Fairfield General until—and this almost knocked me over—"after the Mitchell-Stans trial." The Mitchell-Stans trial was then scheduled to begin in New York in September, 1973. After the trial was over, Vesco went on, he would make definite plans for the purchase of a Boeing 727, which would then be modified under my supervision and which I would then command. My head was spinning. It was now almost 11:30 and we still had to get to the point of our meeting—the future. It was obvious to me that he had no long-range plans. He wasn't thinking past the Mitchell-Stans trial. Its outcome was of critical concern to him. If he had been in the United States he probably would be sitting at the defendants' table along with Mitchell and Stans. All he was doing now was trying to keep me on the string. I wasn't interested.

"Bob, cut the bullshit," I said. "I'm not interested in becoming another Ralph Dodd or Frank Beatty, hanging around, living on handouts. If you don't have a real, professional assignment on a long-range basis for me, then let's break it off right now."

He didn't expect that. The issue was now smack on the table between us and he would have to deal with it.

"I need you, Ike," he said. "I've got plans, important plans, and you are an important part of them. I just can't give you details right this minute."

"I'm not asking for details, Bob," I said. "I want to know where I'll be a year, two years from now." He thought about this for a minute.

"With me, Ike," he said. "You'll be running your own airline. *Carte blanche*. That's a promise."

"Which one, Bob?" I asked him.

"Lacsa!" he said. Lacsa is the Costa Rican national airline. "Of course, you'll have to live in Costa Rica. But I'll make it well worth your while. You'll have your own staff. Liberal expense account. A house with a good piece of land and—if you want—a numbered account whenever you want." He looked like the godfather who just made me an offer I couldn't refuse. It sounded terrific. But then he blew it.

"You'll have to give up your American citizenship," he said. "Since your parents were both born in Canada, Norman can fix you up with Canadian citizenship. Or you can become a Costa Rican."

"No, Bob!" I said. "That's out. I don't give up my U.S. citizenship for anything or anybody." I was mad at him right then. I simply could not understand his lack of attachment to the United States. He was angry at the way he was being treated by U.S. authorities, and I guess he had a right to be. But his hostility was total.

"Bob," I said to him, "you're all fucked up. Why don't you fight those bastards in Washington? Come back with me. You know that I'll do every goddamn thing I can to help."

"No way, Ike, no way," he said. "Those bastards sold me out. They fucked me and they're going to keep on fucking me. They're no fucking good—everyone of them—from Nixon on down the line." He leaned across the desk. "You know what I have half a mind to do, Ike?" he said. "I have half a mind to put a fucking cannon on that boat of mine, anchor off Key Biscayne, and lob shells into that prick's living room!" Now I was sure he was going bonkers.

"I don't think we can get together, Bob," I said. "It's all over." He took out a Kool, lit it, took a long drag, leaned back in his chair, put his hands behind his head, and exhaled.

"Don't shit me, Ike," he said. "You need me. What are you going to do without me? Tell me what you want."

"No go, Bob," I said. "And that's final." He was getting angry.

"You're broke, Ike," he said. "How the hell are you going to get along?" I thought of something.

"Shit, Bob," I said, "I'm going to write a book about you. That'll make me more money than you could ever pay me. After all, who knows you better than I do?" He looked as though I had punched him in the belly. I had meant it as a joke but he took it seriously. He sat bolt upright and put his hands on the desk and clenched them. He was about as mad as I've ever seen him in my life.

"You do that, Ike," he said, "and you'll never live to spend the profits. I goddamn guarantee that."

"Is that a threat, Bob?" I asked him. He pointed his finger at me.

"It's a promise, Ike," he said. I didn't want it to end this way, the two of us glaring across the desk at each other. I laughed. It wasn't a forced laugh. I really thought the situation was funny.

"Now I'll make you a promise, Bob," I said. "You'll get the first copy—autographed." He hesitated a moment and then, as if he too wanted a friendlier parting, smiled. He stood up and stuck out his hand.

"It was a lot of fun, Ike," he said. "Whatever you do—good luck. And if you change your mind, you know how to reach me." We shook hands.

"I have no regrets, Bob," I said, "and no hard feelings. Stay loose, and give my best to the family." Then, I started for the door.

"Hey, Ike!" Vesco called. I stopped and turned. Vesco still stood at the desk. Again, he pointed his finger. "The book, Ike—don't do it."

I left the room.

Epilogue

I wasn't sure it would work. To my knowledge, nobody had ever gone into a foreign country and seized an airplane as big as a Boeing 707 to satisfy creditor's claims. But that was precisely what I had agreed to do.

On the morning of May 8, 1974, I left Newark Airport by helicopter for Kennedy with two former crew members, where we boarded a Pan American flight to Panama. We were all wearing our ICC uniforms and looked like a dead-heading crew, which was the way I wanted it.

The idea of repossessing Silver Phyllis had not originated with me. It had first been broached by an attorney whose firm had been appointed as receivers, when Fairfield General Corporation, a Vesco catchall corporation whose chief asset was the Boeing, was placed in "voluntary" bankruptcy.

The repossession was the price I would have to pay if I wanted to collect money owed to me for services rendered to Vesco corporations both before and after our split.

When I walked out of Vesco's office in the Bahamas Commonwealth Bank on July 4, 1973, the break was a clean one—and a final one, as far as I was concerned. Yet it was also a little like closing out a war or a marriage. There were still some bills to be paid and salary to be collected. And there was Silver Phyllis. In a suit initiated by ICC in the beginning of 1973, a Federal Court had forbidden Vesco, personally or through any of his shell corporations, from operating the Boeing, except for routine inspections and demonstrations for potential sale. Vesco had evaded the intent of the court order with a whole series of schemes that involved a host of shell corporations, with Norman LeBlanc in the catbird seat and a number of phantom buyers.

Even though I had split with Vesco and was technically out of a job, I was pretty sure that—for a period of time anyway—I would be called on whenever the Boeing had to be moved. It never occurred to me that Vesco would permit an unqualified crew to operate his pride and joy. I was right.

I was also right about another thing—that Vesco would not take my decision to leave his employ as final.

Joel M. Grady was president both of Fairfield General and Skyways Leasing. Skyways held title to the Boeing. Fairfield General, was the parent of Skyways Leasing. It was through Grady that Vesco carried out a campaign to keep me on the hook. The bait was the promise of a substantial commission, should the airplane be sold, and the command of a new airplane, a Boeing 727, with my old crew and without the necessity of renouncing my U.S. citizenship. I fell for it—for a while.

I agreed with Joel Grady to keep myself available at a weekly retainer, exclusively to move Silver Phyllis as required. For example, in September, 1973, I returned to Nassau to check out the Boeing and run up the engines. In October, I flew the airplane to Miami for a long overdue inspection. As an indication of how much the aircraft had deteriorated, I could not retract the landing gear and could get no indication of air speed on either side because both Pitot tubes were clogged with sand. And all along there was talk of selling the airplane.

Each of the flights or services I performed were contracted for separately. I had come to know and thoroughly distrust Joel Grady and insisted on payment in advance. But it didn't always work that way. And for that I have only Robert Vesco and myself to blame. I had not yet realized that I was being suckered.

In mid-September, 1973, during the routine check-out of the Boeing in Nassau, I was surprised by a call from Vesco. He wanted me to reconsider. He promised that "everything would be different" under a new set-up—the 727 business. But he could not move positively until the completion of the Mitchell-Stans trial. I did not understand the connection. I didn't make any promises except to agree to work along with Grady on a job-to-job basis.

The first inkling I got that I was getting screwed was when I brought the Boeing to Miami for inspection. Grady had told me that the inspection was a necessary step prior to a sale. He asked me to wait for payment until after the sale went through, at which time I would not only get paid along with my crew for services rendered, but would also receive a commission on the sale and would be paid a good price for the operational manuals for that particular 707 which I had developed. Against my better judgement I agreed to wait. I hung around Florida for more than a week. But no sale. Grady indicated to me that it was only a matter of working out some last minute details. Then he told me that Vesco had "changed the signals" and that a new buyer had come along and the deal was a better one. Grady wanted me to fly the airplane back to Nassau. The rat I had begun to smell was getting gamier.

Vesco was worried about ICC grabbing the Boeing. As long as it was on U.S. soil it was vulnerable. Since Skyways already owed me money, I could, if it came to that, slap a lien on the airplane, as long as it was in the U.S. In Nassau, I couldn't touch it. I told Grady that I would not fly the airplane to Nassau. I let him holler. I told him to get his act together and, when he was ready, to call me in Denville. He screamed and hollered, but when I told him that I had to go home because I had been subpenaed to testify at the Mitchell-Stans trial, he shut up.

I wasted nearly five hours in the U.S. Attorney's office in New York. There were a lot of questions which, to me, didn't lead anywhere. The trial was postponed, and the prosecution apparently agreed with my judgment since I was never called.

The final act in the Grady charade came in December of 1973. The negotiations that Grady had alluded to had gotten very complicated. All sorts of new people were coming on the scene. I began to get nervous. One of the most important provisions of the court order was that any buyer would have absolutely no connection with Vesco or any of his companies. A requirement for court approval of the sale stipulated that a letter be presented to the court by Skyways counsel attesting to the fact.

At first, after Grady had told me that Vesco had changed the signals for the sale of the Boeing, there were only hints that Vesco had no intention of getting rid of the Boeing completely. Before I left for my interrogation at the U.S. Attorney's office, Grady's hints were so strong that I began to worry that I might be involved in a conspiracy to violate a court order. That was when I decided to keep meticulous records of my dealings not only with Grady, but with all the parties involved in the so-called sale, including the attorneys for Skyways, Shanley and Fisher of Newark, New Jersey. I not only kept meticulous notes but recorded every telephone conversation with anybody involved in the scheme.

Briefly, this was the plan. An officer of Bahama World Airways would act as the middleman in the sale of the Boeing by Skyways Leasing to a British corporation called Salmavette, affiliated with a Panamanian shell controlled by Vesco, Air Inter-Sales. The money to pay for the Boeing would come from IOS funds in the Charter Bank in England which owned 80 percent of the Salmavette stock without voting power. The owner of the remaining 20 percent of the Salmavette stock, but holding 100 percent of the voting power, was Norman LeBlanc. The proceeds of the sale would be invested in British certificates of deposit in Robert Vesco's name. Grady admitted bluntly that on advice of his counsel, no letter would be presented to the court and that there was no way the court could trace Vesco's involvement with Salmavette or Air Inter-Sales. All of this meant that Vesco would not only again control the Boeing outright, but would actually receive the proceeds of the sale itself, a couple of million dollars. It got to the point that one of the senior partners at Shanley and Fisher, Grady's counsel for Skyways, suggested that there was no need for all the hokus-pokus. Vesco could simply provide the purchase funds with "laundered cash" and the lawyers would find a way to make it all work.

I confronted Grady. At first he denied that there was any hanky-panky. Then he finally admitted it, but assured me that "the lawyers would make everything legal"—barely.

No matter who was buying the airplane or selling it, nothing could be done while the airplane was in the United States. Grady wanted me to get my crew together and move Silver Phyllis to Nassau. I insisted that two conditions be met. One was that I be paid in advance. The other was that I would be legally free to move the Boeing from Florida to Nassau and that Judge Stewart, who issued the restraining order in the first place, would be notified that I was moving the airplane out of the country.

Grady assured me that his attorneys would take care of the second condition but, as to the first, he pleaded that Skyway's bank account was at zero. He promised me—and backed up his promise with an IOU that he signed personally and as president of Fairfield General and Skyways Leasing—that, within minutes after I landed in the Bahamas, I would be paid in full. Foolishly I agreed to go along with him.

There was no payoff in the Bahamas. Grady put me off with another promise that he would meet me at the Fairfield General offices in New Jersey in a couple of days. I didn't believe him, but there was nothing I could do. I went back to Denville realizing that I had been *had*. It was a hell of a way to wind up the year that Vesco had promised would be new and different. It was different all right. My domestic life was shattered. I was deeply in debt, held liable for countless expenses involved with the Boeing from fuel charges to car rentals. I was out of work.

Grady never showed up. The next kick in the face was when my attorney, Howard Singer, told me that Fairfield General had filed for voluntary bankruptcy. I contacted Joel Grady. I couldn't believe that even he would get that low. I reached him at the Balmoral Hotel in Nassau.

"Where do I stand, Joel?" I asked him.

"Sorry, Ike," he said, "that's the way the ball bounces."

"But, I've got your IOU," I reminded him.

"That and a token will get you on the subway," he said and laughed.

"You bastards owe me 37,000 dollars for openers!" I said.

"Tough shit, Charlie Brown," Grady responded. "Get in line with the rest of the creditors."

"Fuck you, Joel," I said. "I'm going to get in touch with Vesco."

"Don't waste your money, Ike," he said. "Bobby thinks you've already been paid enough. Who the hell do you think is running things?"

And that, Mr. Vesco, is why you lost your toy.

The voluntary bankruptcy was, like all of Vesco's moves, a gimmick. Whatever was in the Fairfield General or Skyways till, Vesco could afford to lose. He wanted the Boeing. And he had it. In 1973, ICC had filed suit against Vesco and a bunch of his associates. I was included among the associates. Howard Singer moved Federal Court to have me removed from the list of defendants and at the same time filed a counter-suit for the monies owed me. Again, it was Judge Stewart who was called to rule upon both matters. I was not only relieved from the list of defendants but Judge Stewart issued a finding in my favor for the monies owed up to a certain point, over 37,000 dollars. Unfortunately, the judge's order was more permissive than directive, and the attorneys appointed as receivers for the bankrupt Fairfield and Skyways elected to ignore the judge's order for payment. As far as I could learn at the time, there was a "gentlemen's agreement" between the receivers and the attorneys for ICC not to dispense any Fairfield or Skyways assets until all lawsuits, of which there seemed to be dozens, were settled. In my mind I had reached the absolute end of the Vesco Road. Except that, barring a miracle, I would be paying for the Vesco experience in hard cash for the next couple of years.

I could not stop thinking about Silver Phyllis. More than once I thought about going back to Nassau and taking the airplane back to the U.S. and keeping it there, until Grady or Vesco—or anybody—paid me what was due me. But it was a futile thought.

Both Fairfield and Skyways were incorporated in New Jersey, and when Grady's attorneys filed for bankruptcy, the judge who heard the case, Essex County Judge Irwin I. Kimmelman, appointed the Newark law firm of Benenson and McLaughlin as receivers. As in the case of estates, the first item of concern to lawyers appointed as receivers is to make goddamn sure that their fees are protected.

Sometime in February, 1974, I was contacted by Jay R. Benenson, Esq., a partner in Benenson and McLaughlin. As a former "executive" in Skyways Leasing and a fairly long-term employee in a variety of Vesco corporations, I might be of great assistance in helping to unravel the affairs of Fairfield General. Would I be willing to meet him at the Fairfield General offices at 167 Fairfield Road to search through the files, and very possibly locate physical assets which could be converted into cash to settle claims?

There would be no compensation, of course. But my cooperation would assure the "acceleration" of my claim against Fairfield. The implication was that if I did not cooperate, I would, as Grady suggested, be in line with the rest of the creditors. I cooperated.

I made three visits to the Fairfield offices without a hell of a lot of success. There was money in the bank—not much—but they knew about that. I helped them to locate a couple of small aircraft and other odds and ends of hardware. But considering the dollar amount of claims against Fairfield, the total was, to say the least, inadequate. But there was more than enough to satisfy my claims and I had court permission to collect. However, that didn't seem to cut much ice with the law firm of Benenson and McLaughlin.

It was Jay Benenson who first brought up the matter of repossession of the Boeing. He had mentioned the airplane a number of times and the desirability of getting physical possession of it. It became an obsession with him. Even though I had thought of the same thing myself, I had realized that there were too many practical hurdles to overcome. Like money. Like organization. Like a crew. Like aircraft deterioration. At first I didn't give Benenson's adventurous daydream any consideration. In fact, I was ready to write them all off as well.

On March 27, 1974, Jay Benenson called me into his Newark office to discuss something. I had half a mind to tell Benenson to go piss up a rope. I was sick of being jerked around and figured this would be just another one of those no-win sessions. Benenson surprised me. He wanted to talk about the Boeing. He wanted it in the United States at Newark Airport. There was the usual beating around the bush before he got to the point.

"What would it take to get the airplane?" he asked.

"Money," I told him.

"It can be done then," he said.

"With enough money, I can fly that airplane out of Nassau and park it right on the goddamn ramp out there," I said and pointed in the general direction of Newark Airport. He mulled this a while.

"I think I can get the court to award you 7500 dollars against your claim on a hardship basis," he said. His whole manner—even his appearance standing there in his expensive three-piece vested suit, thumbs hooked in the arm holes—irritated me. It was obvious to me, too, that he had already discussed the 7500 dollars with the judge. And that infuriated me. I already had a court order for a hell of a lot more than that. I resented Benenson's pompous "hardship" reference. I did not feel like a hardship case, although I could use the money. But that wasn't the point. I had that goddamn money coming for services rendered. I had Grady's IOU not only for services rendered, but for the highly technical manual I had developed for the operation of the Silver Phyllis.

"What the hell is the 7500 dollars for?" I asked.

"Why—to get the airplane," he said.

"Bullshit!" I said. "It will take a hell of a lot more than that." He called in his secretary, Lorraine, and told her to make notes of my conditions for repossessing Robert Vesco's airplane, which at that time was still in Nassau.

Benenson's main concern was that however I achieved the repossession, no laws of any kind would be broken. I couldn't find any fault with this reasoning. To that end he proposed to contact a Bahamian attorney to render an opinion. Which was stupid. Even if he could find a Bahamian lawyer who had not even the remotest connection with Vesco, it was a matter of certainty that Vesco would know immediately that someone was after his airplane. I suggested a Florida lawyer instead. As things turned out, I don't think Benenson followed my advice.

The essence of my conditions for going after the Boeing was payment of all my claims awarded by Judge Stewart in full, a separate fee for doing the job, and the receivers to pay all costs. In addition, I wanted a guarantee that if "complications" should develop, Benenson and McLaughlin would see to it that I had proper legal counsel whose costs would be borne by them, and that they would pay any fines or assessments. I also was to be held harmless for any and all future litigations from any source whatsoever. He wanted time to think about it. He then dictated to his secretary a memorandum which essentially agreed with my demands.

Even though the actual repossession was not carried out at Nassau but at Tocumen Airport in Panama many weeks later, the terms of our agreement did not change. It was even clearly understood that Judge Kimmelman would have full knowledge of what was planned and the costs involved before I ever left the United States. Even though Benenson insisted, I absolutely refused to disclose to him or to Kimmelman the exact details of the operation, once I worked them out. How I got the airplane out of Nassau would be my business alone. Benenson, McLaughlin, and Kimmelman all knew that the mission could be a dangerous one. There would be people, Vesco people, who wouldn't care about legalities. Guys who repossess cars can tell stories about being shot at and beaten up while carrying out their legal duties. Their best protection is to set their own procedures and timetable, and to do their job as quickly and as simply as possible. That's how I intended to handle this one. Benenson said he would discuss my demands with the court and get back to me.

Weeks went by without any further word from Benenson, and I figured that they had decided to let the matter drop. I didn't think about it much because I had other affairs to concern myself with. I had filed to run for county office and was up to my belly button getting ready for the primary election in June.

At the end of April, just about a month after my last contact with Benenson, I got an excited phone call from his partner John McLaughlin.

"We're ready to go, Ike," he said. "Come on in and let's talk." I wasn't too enthusiastic. My experience with Benenson had soured me and I had a severe case of political fever. But it wouldn't hurt to see what was rattling around inside their lawyer heads.

The first thing I had to do, of course, was to check on the status of the Boeing. Benenson's plan to seek out a Bahamian lawyer had bothered me. Sure enough, somebody had said something to somebody else. Silver Phyllis was no longer at Nassau. Nor was she at Freeport or Rock Sound. I actually enjoyed telling Benenson and McLaughlin that their bird had flown. Benenson especially was panic-stricken. He had built the repossession in his own mind as a vicarious adventure. He had said more than once that it would be "a feather in his cap" to get the Boeing back to the U.S.

"Can you find out where it is?" Benenson asked me.

"I probably can if you'll pay the phone bills," I told Benenson.

"Go ahead then," he said, "as quickly as possible."

It took me a couple of days and dozens of phone calls to various parts of the world. I located the Boeing at Tocumen International Airport in Panama and even found out how it got there. Whether because he learned of the repossession scheme or for some other reason, Vesco hired a Bahamian airlines crew (British) to fly the Boeing out of Nassau on a trip that took it to Buenos Aires, Caracas, and then to Panama. I learned also that this crew, which was not qualified to operate the Boeing, burned out an engine which had to be replaced in Caracas. It was this event that really helped me find Silver Phyllis. Joel Grady had to get an engine from Pan American in Miami and have it flown to Caracas. I had a lot of friends at Pan American in Miami who were more than willing to help me find Phyllis.

I reported back to Benenson and McLaughlin that I had found the Boeing. The news excited them and we agreed to meet on Monday, May 6, 1974 to set things in motion. I got their promise to keep their mouths shut about the plan to repossess the airplane. Surprise was the key to the whole operation.

I made no changes in my routine. I knew I would have to line up a crew but that would wait until the very last minute. I met with Benenson and McLaughlin in the library of their Newark law offices first thing Monday morning. The meeting was conducted with an air of secrecy and conspiracy. McLaughlin handed me a check for 10,000 dollars. I handed it right back to him.

"There are two things wrong with this check," I told him. "It isn't enough and it isn't cash." McLaughlin said that there would be no trouble converting the check to cash. But that was all the money the court would release. Benenson butted in.

"We gave you a check for 7500," he said. "With this additional 10,000 you should have more than enough."

"Wrong!" I told him. "Even if I still had all of the 7500, I still wouldn't have enough." I was ready to walk out. It seemed to me that Benenson considered the 7500 as something other than relief of my "hardship" status. If he meant that money to be used to get the airplane, he should have told me. The true nature of the 7500 later became a point of serious contention between us.

Since I had given my word that I would go after Silver Phyllis even if I had to bear part of the cost myself, I agreed to follow through. McLaughlin promised that once the Boeing was in the United States, he would deliver the balance of my claim by check to my attorney, Howard Singer. To satisfy legal requirements and to forestall any other party from seizing the airplane once it was inside the continental limits of the U.S., it was agreed that I would land the airplane in Florida where I, personally, on the basis of my legitimate claim, would secure a mechanic's lien against the airplane. A mechanic's lien takes precedence over every other type of lien. Upon arrival at Newark I would transfer my lien to Benenson and McLaughlin.

McLaughlin made arrangements to have the check converted to cash while I waited. In the interim we discussed some of the possible problems I might encounter. They would be far different in Panama than they would have been in Nassau. And there were *x* factors which nobody could predict. One of the *x* factors was Panama itself. Benenson, McLaughlin, and I had speculated on the reason for the Boeing being in Panama. It was my guess that Vesco deliberately chose Panama as a safe haven because of the friendship between the president of Panama and the president of Costa Rica. I ruled out Costa Rica as a safe haven because there was some student unrest and Vesco was one of the things the students were unrestful about.

The closer we got to zero hour, the more excited Benenson and McLaughlin became. Benenson especially was as high as a kite.

"I don't care what you have to do, Ike," he said. "Bring back that airplane." This was a perfect example of the old gag. "Let's you and me have a roast duck dinner. You bring the duck."

With the 10,000 cash and what I had left of the

7500, I was still short by at least 5000 dollars. I didn't have a lot of time to raise it. My first stop on the way home was to arrange a second mortgage on my home for the balance of the money I needed. My second stop was to go to my bank and withdraw what I had in my account. Then I went home and contacted the two men who would go along with me. We met that night, May 6, and the following day, May 7, 1974, to plan the operation in detail.

The airplane had been sitting in Panama for a month. Before that, it had been sitting at Nassau from the day I delivered it on December 28, 1973. In the interim it had been mishandled by an unqualified crew. The flight in October from Nassau to Miami for the inspection had given me a lesson in what can happen to a neglected Boeing 707. We tried to develop contingency plans for almost every conceivable circumstance from aircraft damage to in-flight failures of one and even two engines, and any systems that could affect our route. We computed various options of range capabilities based on limited fuel, adverse weather, and came up with a list of landing sites we guessed could be friendly to the United States.

We talked about booby traps, armed guards, and other dangers. Sitting in that comfortable house with those two friends of mine, I wondered if it was worth risking their lives and my own for money. I put it to them. They didn't back off. They wanted to go. I decided that we would leave for Panama the next morning, Wednesday, May 8, 1974. The only promise I made to Benenson and McLaughlin was that I would let them know when I got back.

I had set up in my mind various checkpoints which would tip me off to whether or not our security had broken down. The first of these was Customs and Immigration in Panama. If we were expected, that is where we'd find out about it.

We landed at Tocumen at about eight p.m. where we cleared Customs and Immigration without difficulty. We were inside. Now we had to do our thing and get back out. Our thing started immediately.

I sought out the Pan Am duty supervisor and introduced myself in as an authoritative manner as I could muster.

"Give me a status report on a Boeing out on the ramp—N99WT," I said (Silver Phyllis' tail number had been changed in anticipation of a sale).

"All I know is that it has been out there for many weeks," the man said.

"Who brought it in?" I asked.

"I'll have to look at the record," he said and left. When he came back he confirmed that Silver Phyllis had indeed been brought in by a Bahamas World Airways crew. He said that the airplane had been landed without clearance and that the crew had left on the next flight. They had left no word on why they had landed at Tocumen or when the plane would be picked up.

"That's why I'm here," I told him. "I'm flying this plane back to the United States." He shook his head.

"It is not so simple," he said. "The Boeing has been impounded by the Panamanian government for entering Panama illegally. You must clear the matter up with the sub-director of civil aviation, and you cannot do that before tomorrow morning." This was a real showstopper. I had actually believed that I could have handled the entire operation in a matter of a few hours and gotten off the ground before morning. The longer we stayed in Panama, the more people we had to deal with, the greater the chance of discovery.

My two partners looked sick and I guess I didn't look too happy myself. The duty supervisor suggested that he might be able to help. That sounded encouraging. Going through Panamanian bureaucratic channels could become a career in itself. We went into the supervisor's office where we could talk.

That the Boeing had landed without permission was bad enough, the supervisor told me. Such a violation of Panamanian sovereignty was sufficient to impound the aircraft. But not to give any explanation, to offer some face-saving excuse was an insult to Panama. I got the impression from the supervisor's attitude that the sub-director of civil aviation of the Republic of Panama was willing to let Silver Phyllis rot where she sat.

My first reaction was anger, although I made a strong effort not to let it show. I needed the help of the duty supervisor and I had no intention of giving him any excuse to get mad at me. He let me know that he knew the sub-director personally and was willing to make an effort to reach him by telephone that same night. This was unusual because, as in so many foreign countries, rank and position are rigidly observed, and in a case like this, it would be a violation of the class system for a duty supervisor to disturb the sub-director for purely official business.

The duty supervisor left a message at the home of the sub-director asking him to call back when he returned home regardless of the time. I was able to put the waiting time to good use. It was then eleven o'clock at night. I sent my two crew members out to check over the Boeing. They were accompanied by a Pan Am ground service crew that I borrowed from the duty supervisor. They returned an hour later and told me that Silver Phyllis looked fine from the outside. They could not check the interior because the underbelly entrance lock had been changed. But they confirmed my worst fears—that the fuel tanks were practically bone-dry.

I wasn't really concerned about gaining access to the airplane. I had installed locking devices on all the main entrance doors and escape hatches during modification. I was the only person who knew how to rig them and how to get around them if necessary. I would have liked to thoroughly inspect the interior and search for booby traps. But that would have required lighting up the aircraft, which at that time of night would certainly have drawn attention to us. Until I had squared things with the sub-director, I intended to keep a very low profile.

The sub-director's call came just after midnight. The duty supervisor explained the situation, and after he had finished his conversation told me that the sub-director would see me in his office in the morning. I tried to pin him down to a time. He could not be precise because of two conditions that the sub-director had imposed. The first was that I be accompanied by the duty supervisor to the sub-director's office in the middle of town. Since he was attending classes at the university, the sub-director would not be free until late morning. The second condition was that I write a letter of apology for the violation of Panamanian sovereignty. I was also required to explain in the letter the reason the Boeing entered Panama. The duty supervisor offered to help me compose the letter.

"The letter must be sincere," he said. "We are no different than anybody else. We are proud of our country and jealous of our reputation." He was not on a soap box. He was giving me practical advice. And maybe he was needling me a little bit about the attitude of North Americans toward their neighbors south of the Rio Grande. He found me a typewriter and office and guided me as I wrote the letter. "I know what is necessary to convince the sub-director of your sincerity."

The following is what I wrote Senor Miguel von Seidlitz at 1:30 in the morning of May 9, 1974:

Dear Director,

I offer you and your country my deepest apology for the serious mistake made by the Captain and crew who entered your country without regard for your laws and regulations. I had no knowledge of this act. I have come here many times as aircraft commander and have never violated your procedures or had any problems with your regulations. I respect the purpose of the laws of any country as you respect the laws of the country that I am licensed in. I do not know the reason the aircraft was brought here and left. I do not know why the Captain did not obey your requirements. As the director of aviation for the owner of the aircraft I must apologize and assure you that this will not happen again, and the Captain who did this act will not fly this aircraft again. May I have your permission to depart Panama and fly this aircraft to Pan American in Miami for maintenance and inspection? I will pay any costs you decide are necessary prior to departing. I look forward to seeing you again as my flight schedule allows and offer to act as your host if you fly to New York. I also work for the Civil Aviation as a pilot examiner for the Federal Aviation Administration.

Respectfully,
Captain A. L. Eisenhauer

We did not meet with the sub-director until about eleven o'clock on the morning of May 9, 1974. I was in a sweat. There wasn't a damn thing that could be done about getting the Boeing ready until this matter was settled. I had told my crew to stay out of sight, but in a place where they could see what was going on.

The session with Senor von Seidlitz went a hell of a lot more smoothly and quickly than I had expected. He was a pilot himself and that helped. He accepted my letter and my further explanations which were translated by the duty supervisor. He released the airplane to me. Just as we wound things up and I was getting ready to leave the sub-director's office, a call for me came through the secretary's phone. The guys were calling from the airport. This smelled like trouble. The plan was for *me* to call *them*. The news was not good.

They had observed a familiar airplane landing at Tocumen. It was Lear Jet N33TR, Tommy Richardson's airplane, the only one still in Vesco's stable. They recognized one of the passengers, Alberto Alvarez, a close associate of Vesco's and a former Panamanian diplomat who had been aboard Silver Phyllis many times. This could have sunk us. Fortunately, N33TR was making a passenger drop. Alvarez apparently had no interest in the Boeing, which seemed incredible. Especially since it was surrounded by a lot of ground support equipment and ground service crews. Alvarez was observed heading straight for the terminal, where he remained only a few minutes before climbing into a waiting limousine and speeding off toward Panama City. I told the guys that we were free to go. The only thing left was to fuel the airplane and pay the bills.

I hustled back to the airport with the duty supervisor. I couldn't get Alvarez out of my mind. His quick departure from the airport could have meant that he had seen the Boeing and the activity around it and would make his phone calls from the city. And I was worried about N33TR. I was certain I knew the crew, and that they would not miss what was happening around the Boeing. But the Lear jet had taken off by the time I reached the airport. I still couldn't be sure that the Lear jet crew was not then briefing Vesco in flight on what was happening on the ground at Tocumen. I threw everything into high gear. I paid all charges and levies which, while substantial enough, were a hell of a lot less than I could have been hit with if the Panamanians had been vindictive.

When I arrived at the Boeing, the fueling hoses were connected but not a drop would flow until I paid in advance for all the fuel I would need. I paid and they started pumping. I was about to board the Boeing when one of my crew pointed out to me a little guy in a cast-off uniform, with a forty-five strapped to his waist, looking dolefully in our direction. I grabbed a fueler who could speak English. I pointed at the little guy.

"Who the hell is that?" I asked him.

"He is the guard of the airplane," the fueler told me. The guy didn't look like much but the forty-five could more than make up for his lack of stature. I had to get rid of this man somehow. It was obvious to me that he was not the standard Vesco goon but that he was a local, hired on the spot. A number of airport administrative personnel had been drawn by curiosity out to where we were getting ready to depart. I enlisted one of them, a man with a good command of English and a fairly imposing appearance, to help me deal with the guard. I learned that he had been hired by one of the "officers" on the Boeing when it arrived. From his description, I knew who it was, a former crew member of mine, a flight engineer, who had elected to continue to work for Vesco. The guard had been promised ten U.S. dollars a day, an enormous sum by Panamanian standards. But he had not been paid a penny. He was torn between his anger at not receiving his salary and his sense of duty in keeping away from the airplane anybody except the man who hired him. My interpreter told me that the guard was confused by my presence since it was obvious to him that I was "somebody of importance." He had wanted to speak to me but was intimidated by my uniform. It was then a simple matter to remove the guard. I paid him his back pay, about 300 dollars, and gave him another hundred to perform a special task for me. I sent him into Panama City to retrieve a nonexistant rental car which, he was told, I had left somewhere near the University. The man expressed his gratitude and took off with dispatch.

I was getting itchy. The fuelers weren't pumping fast enough. And I was running out of money. If somebody else showed up with a bill, I couldn't pay it. The 400 dollars to the guard all but wiped me out. I checked the fuel gauges. I was still a couple of hundred gallons short of what I felt I needed. I decided to go with what I had.

"Pull the trucks and clear everybody away," I yelled to the ground service crews. "Plug in the start unit!" I shook hands all around and boarded the airplane.

The crew had already completed the pre-start checklist. Our initial inspection, as far as we could tell, had indicated that the engines had not been tampered with. But I couldn't be sure until we tried to start them. Now for the moment of truth. I had determined that I would take that Boeing off on *two* engines if necessary, provided, of course, the two operating engines were not on the same side. Such a takeoff would be dicey as hell, but I knew it could be done and so did the crew.

As soon as I hit the flight deck I hollered "turn three," dove into my seat, and buckled up.

"Pressure's up, turning three!" the engineer said. He sounded pretty cool.

"Fuel on three, ignition on three," I called out. "Fire in the hole—the bastard's lit!"

Woooosh! That's one engine!

Then two. Then three . . . four.

"All four going and checked normal," the engineer stated.

I felt a surge of relief and a rush of affection for

that pretty bitch, Silver Phyllis. In spite of our separation she still loved me too.

I got my clearance for Miami from Panama Ground Control, my taxi signal from the ramp, released the brakes and Phyllis started to move. I checked the brakes. They worked! I was certain I could get her off the ground, and when I got her back on the ground I could stop her. What would happen in-between was anybody's guess. But the gods were with us.

The first person aboard the airplane when I landed at Newark was Dottie McCarty. She had come out to warn me that the Butler Aviation passenger terminal was jammed with news-media people who would be brought out to the airplane in convoy as soon as the airplane was secured. One of my agreements with my "repossession" crew was that I would not reveal their identities since to do so would jeopardize their jobs. Dottie had arranged for a Butler station wagon to pick up my two buddies and whisk them out of sight before the press got to the Boeing.

The next couple of hours were bedlam. They started with the arrival of John McLaughlin and an Essex County, New Jersey, sheriff's officer who stood on the top step of the passenger loading ramp and, as if announcing great news to all the world, read the contents of the impoundment order of Judge Kimmelman. I then formally turned over my lien against the Boeing to McLaughlin. I had been informed by Howard Singer when I telephoned him from Fort Lauderdale that the promised check had been secured. Then I was smothered under a tidal wave of news people. I had landed at about 3:15 in the afternoon and finally broke loose from the press about six. They would have kept me longer but I had an important committment to fulfill. I was scheduled to address a Republican Party rally in my home county on behalf of my candidacy. The word of the repossession had not reached the people at the rally. Or maybe it had, and they regarded it as less important than how I planned to conduct myself if they should vote me into office.

Once more my life had undergone a radical change. I had become a public person and, to some extent, a notorious one. Within days of the repossession, Vesco let me know that he still had clout in Morris County, New Jersey, even though he was a couple of thousand miles away in Costa Rica. The bank which held the mortgage on my home—and still does—also held a note which was arranged for by Robert Lee Vesco after I bought my home. The note was a demand one, on which I paid the interest due at regular intervals. The note itself was not in default in any way. The bank, originally Trust Company National Bank of Morristown, New Jersey—later changed to American National Bank and Trust of New Jersey for a reason unknown to me—elected to file a collection suit for the total amount of the note, without advising me of its intent. The first indication I had that I was being sued for the note came exactly 14 days after I had returned from Panama with the Boeing. The news of the suit was broadcast over radio station WMTR in Morristown, New Jersey on the nine A.M. news.

The senior vice-president of the bank at the time the note was cast was Wilbert J. Snipes, an ICC board member, later indicted by the SEC. His bank was involved in the illegal contribution to the 1968 Nixon-Agnew campaign and identified as a vehicle in the transfer of IOS funds from the U.S. to offshore repositories controlled by Vesco. Coincidence?

I paid the note immediately, in full. But the issue was not the money. The public announcement by the bank was made at the height of my political campaign, and the manner in which it was made was obviously intended to embarrass me publically by branding me as a deadbeat. I lost the primary by a very slim margin. Chalk one up for Vesco.

The resultant publicity, much of it inaccurate and even hostile, took its toll of my career in aviation. On top of all this my personal physician, the flight surgeon who had been monitoring my physical well-being for almost twenty years, warned me that I was approaching a state of physical and psychical depletion. All my parts were in good order, but if I did not pull back and recharge myself I might burn myself out before my time.

Dr. Louis G. Kareha, head of the Abbington Clinic in Clark's Green, Pennsylvania and a certified FAA first-class medical examiner, has spent most of his medical career as an expert in the health problems of business executives and in aerospace medicine. During the Boeing years with Vesco, he had told me that I was running at too furious a pace. He knew that there was no way that I could let up and still do the job that was required of me. What he did was to suggest ways to help me cope with the pressure. There were no drugs or treatments but routines I could follow, involving diet, exercise, and rest cycles to minimize the effect of the most serious problem, jet-lag.

I took his second warning as seriously as I did his first. I withdrew to my lakeside home and, to a degree, shut myself off from the outside world. I welcomed the chance to get physically involved with my house and property. Gradually I felt my energies restoring themselves. The assault of the press tapered off to a trickle. And I began to look again for something to do.

A national magazine had been after me to "tell my story" of the repossession. The "caper", as a couple of newspapers called it, had struck the editors of the magazine as an exciting adventure. They promised me that they would print the story the way I told it and assigned a writer to work with me. The story was written and published, and was followed by a second story about Vesco's jailing in Geneva. The reaction of the editors and the public was gratifying. It started me thinking again about the book I had told Vesco I would write about us.

My anger with Vesco had subsided. The constant sessions with reporters, interrogators, and lawyers had shown me how ignorant not only they, but the public at large were about the phenomenon called Robert Lee Vesco. Whether I had any axes to grind was beside the point. Wherever I went people asked me about Vesco, the man. They could learn all they wanted to about his business and political activities by reading the papers. What fascinated them was the mystery of how he came out of obscurity and wheeled and dealed his way to enormous wealth—and to exile as a criminal fugitive.

I confided my plans to Howard Singer. If anybody knew Vesco, it was Howard. He had left NBC where he had been senior attorney to become general counsel to ICC and Robert Vesco. That was in 1967, when Vesco had just crossed the line that separates the small businessman from the corporate entrepreneur. Howard recalled that those early days were hectic, exciting, and productive. He was impressed with the brightness and eagerness of Vesco who also displayed a rare humility and who seemed to be fully aware of his own limitations. For over a year, Howard had almost daily contact with Vesco and not infrequently would spend as much as 12 hours a day in Vesco's company. In those days, Vesco showed, in Howard's words, "the hallmark of executive ability," the willingness to suggest and delegate. He was an avid reader of business and industrial books and publications. They were the source of Vesco's business knowledge. But Vesco began to change. He began to see himself as the sole authority. More and more he interfered in the minor functions of his business. Executives were at first discouraged from and then forbidden to make independent decisions. It was Howard's judgment that the turning point in Vesco's career came with the takeover of ELS. Overnight, his control of people expanded from a few hundred to more than 5000. And his corporate worth from less than 40,000,000 dollars to over 100,000,000. Vesco found himself suddenly at the center of a new universe, and he could not resist the temptations that supreme power offers. He became authoritative, distrustful, and dishonest. And that's when Howard A. Singer quit.

Howard encouraged me to go ahead with the book. Of all the people who had surrounded Vesco, he felt that I was the only one who could reveal the essential Robert Vesco.

During the planning stages, I was invited, through a third party, to have lunch with the only other man who had been part of the Vesco high command after the IOS takeover to have survived with his integrity intact, Marvin Hoffmann. Marvin had spanned both the Cornfeld and Vesco regimes at IOS. During Bernie's tenure,

Marvin had served as the IOS chief financial officer. He had seen what was happening to IOS and had tried to prevent the Vesco takeover since he felt it was neither necessary nor desireable. He stayed on after the Vesco takeover to use his abilities and influence to protect IOS shareholders. When it became obvious that he was fighting a losing battle and that he might very well be held accountable for later shenanigans, he resigned.

It was a pleasant lunch. Marvin Hoffmann had been a passenger on Silver Phyllis and we talked a lot about "the old days" like a couple of old warhorses. And like a couple of old warhorses we shared the common experience of combat in Vesco's army.

Marvin had been hurt by his IOS/Vesco experience. I knew exactly how he felt. Marvin was enthusiastic about the idea of a book and gave me a number of insights into the Vesco character that have proved useful.

The deeper I got into writing the book, the more aware I became of just how unusual the five years with Vesco had been. And I realized that I was embarking on a course that would force me to look at myself in a manner that demanded honesty and depth. Not many people are faced with putting their lives on paper. It is not easy. Truths have to be faced that have been buried and ignored for years. It struck me as ironic that it would be Robert Vesco who would serve as the medium for my self-evaluation. Without him this would never have happened. And it became very important to me to understand Robert Vesco so that I could understand myself.

Even now I don't know how successful I have been. The man still mystifies me. Howard Singer has said a number of times that Vesco could have achieved the power and wealth he has now—legally. It would have taken a little longer, but he would not now be a fugitive from justice, frightened for his life, worried about a kidnapping, and scared to death about going to jail.

Naturally, I have followed Vesco's career since I left him, mostly through the newspapers. Because of my various appearances before grand juries and government attorneys and the interest shown by the investigators for the Senate Permanent Subcommittee on

Investigations, headed by Senator Henry M. "Scoop" Jackson, I have been able to garner more of the substance that lies behind the headlines. And the more I have learned, the more I have been puzzled by Vesco's behavior.

Vesco has been charged with dealing in drugs and guns. Up to a point I can understand the gun business. It may seem farfetched, but in a country without an army the only protection Vesco could have is what he provided himself. He has his goon squad, a small band of well-trained mercenaries who, headed up by the "Major," would have no trouble with either the Costa Rican police force or what it calls its "instant citizen militia."

Vesco is alleged to have tried to smuggle 2000 machine guns into Costa Rica. He is also supposed to be trying to set up a machine gun manufacturing plant in Costa Rica. This would make it obvious that he has more than self-defense on his mind. Two possibilities come to mind—actually three. The first is that Vesco is preparing against a possible shift in political power in Costa Rica from right to left and plans to have the armament necessary to reverse the political trend. The second is that Vesco is somehow allied with the CIA as a presence in a country that occupies a position a lot closer to the Panama Canal than Communist Cuba. A political shift could pose a very strong threat to the Canal. Even the Senate Subcommittee does not dismiss this possibility, although they agree that Vesco, as an ally or agent, is not the most dependable or stable man the CIA could find. The third possibility involves Vesco's alleged connection to organized crime. A gun factory would fit very neatly into this proposition. Whether he is tied to the mob or not has never been proven. But his foray into gambling casino operation would have to bring him into some sort of mob partnership. It's been charged as well that mob money was heavily invested in IOS. The way Vesco played fast and loose with IOS funds, especially those which could not be claimed by their owners, could also be a source of trouble for Vesco from the mob.

But it is the drug angle that presents a new Vesco

mystery. A former informant for the U.S. Drug Enforcement Administration, Frank Peroff, has claimed that Vesco was involved in a heroin deal with a Canadian mobster to provide the financing for a major "buy," to the tune of more than a quarter of a million dollars. Even if Vesco were to quadruple his investment, the amount would still be a fraction of a fraction of what he swiped from IOS without the degradation of being a dope dealer. I don't know if Vesco is dealing dope or financing those who do. He's a pot smoker. He smoked it on Silver Phyllis, but if he's ever used anything else I never knew about it. I was ready to dismiss the allegations of drug dealing against Robert Vesco purely on the basis of logic and what I knew about the man. But I got a letter in the mail one day that not only made me wonder whether I was totally wrong in my assessment of Robert Vesco—and Donald Nixon Jr.—but damn near blew my mind with its implications and assertions.

The letter was accompanied by an enclosure, a statement under the letterhead of the Bureau of Narcotics and Dangerous Drugs of the U.S. Department of Justice. (Now the Drug Enforcement Administration.) This enclosure was dated April 4, 1973, and was signed by Richard L. Kobakoff, Staff Assistant, Strategic Intelligence Office. For reasons that will become very obvious, neither the content of enclosure nor of the letter will be quoted in full here, nor will the name of the writer of the letter be divulged. There is neither a heading, a date, nor signature on the letter, which was handwritten on lined loose-leaf paper. The letter was mailed on October 24, 1974, and bore a return address at a Pensacola, Florida, post-office box.

> "For obvious reasons my name will not appear on this letter and I'll describe my background only in general terms. I will be as specific as I can concerning one five-month period when I was an undercover pilot for certain individuals with major interests in Las Vegas and at the La Costa Health Spa in northern San Diego County. . . .
>
> "The period of time when our paths may have

crossed was between September, 1972—February, 1973. During this period I was a bodyguard and pilot for a man named I. O. Cauthen of San Marcos, California . . . I brought certain information concerning gold and narcotics smuggling to the attention of the FBI and the Bureau of Narcotics and Dangerous Drugs as it was then known. . . .

"Cauthen in concert with Carl Cohen (Howard Hughes' front man at the Sands in Las Vegas) and 'Moe' Daelitz [*sic*] were putting together a deal in which a Lear 25-C would be purchased by a phony company for the purpose of flying heroin across the Arizona-Mexico border.

"At this point the two words 'Rosemark' and 'Rosemont' entered into the planning. These words represent references to funds contained in the Union Bank of Switzerland and the Investment and Trade Exchange Central Bank in Zurich, Switzerland. Large amounts of money from underworld operations are funneled into these banks (casino skims, narcotics profits, prostitution income, etc.).

"These underworld figures claim to have loaned Hughes large amounts of these 'Rosemark' funds. The biggest loan was for his 707 buy for TWA in 1961. The money came out of Switzerland and was laundered through the Irving Trust Company.

"Puerto Rico and Santo Domingo appear to have been points for gold bullion pickups. Although I never was involved in any gold pickups, I heard it discussed on several occasions.

"During one flight, Donald Nixon was a passenger. My employers claim that their influence permeated the highest levels of the government."

The writer of the letter cited a few more "points of qualification" and then got down to the reason for the letter in the first place. What he proposed was a "repossession" of Robert Vesco. In the letter he was vague about who his "sponsors" were. He called me a couple of weeks after I got the letter. There was no telling from his voice whether he was for real or just a nut. He sounded serious. He made some references to people and events which convinced me that he was no weirdo acting out a "Walter Mitty" scenario.

His "people" were "government"—a group who, for reasons he did not go into, wanted Vesco back in the U.S. and were willing to mount a kidnap operation to achieve their goal. Because of my success in retrieving the Boeing under what he described as damn nigh impossible circumstances, I was tagged as the only guy capable of carrying out such an operation. I queried him on a final quote from his letter. I had no intention of going along with what I considered to be a highly dangerous and a totally illegal adventure. There is no lawyer in the world who could guarantee even a semblance of legality. My mysterious correspondent would not elaborate on the contents of the letter or give me any further details on the "operational plan" unless I agreed to meet with his people, which, from what I gathered, would mean that I agreed to cooperate.

> The quote:
>
> "Three contract CIA operatives are now in place in Central America. One in Guatemala City, one in Mexico City, and another in Panama. We have access to these people for support purposes and can get further help if needed in the way of weapons, maintenance, etc."

I told my mysterious friend that I really wasn't interested, and if he reads this book, I have a bit of advice for him: Don't play games—"It's a nice day for fishing." I also have a word of advice for Bob Vesco. Bob, if you hear anybody suggest that "It's a nice day for fishing," RUN LIKE HELL!

I haven't heard a word since the phone call from my friends who like to go fishing. Nor have I heard of any attempts to put the snatch on Bob Vesco. I know he's worried about it. He bought another big boat and armed it with heavy caliber automatic weapons. (*The Patricia III* was seized by the U.S. government.) According to the testimony of the former skipper of the craft, Vesco would take on the U.S. Navy, if need be, to avoid a return to the U.S. Incidently, the same skipper, Captain Jay Powell Cook, testified to the Jackson Subcommittee that he heard one of the Vesco children state that Robert Vesco intended to take care of me "in the Sicilian manner." He had, according to Cook, arranged for a contract on my life.

I don't believe that Robert Vesco would be that stupid. I can't believe, either—since I think I know the guy pretty well—that he is insensitive to the charges made against him. He has applied for Costa Rican citizenship which seems to indicate that he's written off the U.S.A. Apart from the effect the criminal charges against him here would have on his status there, he could kiss-off the flap about his alleged criminal actions. But apparently he is worried about his image, and maybe it's because of the kids.

In November of 1975, I was subpenaed to testify before a Detroit, Michigan secret grand jury looking into the drug traffic charges against Robert Vesco and Donald Nixon, Jr. There was nothing I could tell them. I had no knowledge of any such activities and I was not about to make any suppositions.

A couple of days after I got back to Denville, New Jersey, Danny Vesco, Vesco's eldest son, accosted me in the local post office. Surprisingly, his manner was cordial. He wanted to come to the house to talk. I had nothing against Danny and told him to come over that afternoon.

Danny is a nice kid and has elected not to join his father in exile. But that doesn't mean that he has broken with his father. On the contrary, he worries about him and wishes that "things were different." We talked about the past eight years and the good times we had. It was then that I learned just how Bob Vesco found out about the repossession of Silver Phyllis. When I landed at Newark on May 10, 1974, the airplane behind me had Danny Vesco aboard. He told me that he saw Silver Phyllis taxiing toward the Butler Aviation ramp and couldn't believe his eyes. He had just come from Costa Rica and knew of no plans of his father's to have the Boeing moved to Newark. And he knew it was Silver Phyllis. There was only one airplane like it in the world. In the terminal, even before he collected his luggage, he called his father and told him that he just saw the Boeing at Newark.

"Jesus Christ! Ike!" Danny told me his father said. "You really hurt him, Ike," Danny told me. "You really did."

But Danny's visit was not to tell me about how his father learned of the repossession. Vesco knew that I had just appeared before a Detroit secret grand jury and had given to his eldest son the job of learning from me what I said about the drug traffic charges against him.

"Danny, I said, "I told them nothing because I know nothing."

Danny seemed relieved. Then he esked me if I would be willing to sign a statement that stated that Robert Vesco had never smuggled drugs of any kind.

"Can't do it, Danny," I said. "I'll sign a statement, but only about what I know, which is that I have no knowledge of any drug activity by your father during the time I was employed by ICC as Director of Aviation and Captain of the Boeing. And that's as far as I will go." Danny accepted this reluctantly. He tried to get me to make a stronger, broader statement. He had a trade-off that he felt would convince me to see it his way—or rather his father's way. He told me that as a result of the repossession, I had been tried in Panama *in absentia* and convicted on a charge of international air piracy and had been sentenced to thirty months in prison. He also told me that the Panamanian government was even then pursuing extradition procedures with our State Department, and that if I cooperated in the matter of the statement, his father would use his influence to straighten things out with the Panamanians. That was the first I had ever heard of such an action by the Panamanian government. Shortly after the repossession, on May 16, 1974, I had paid a personal visit to the Consul General of Panama in New York, Aquilino Boyd, and explained fully the details, including the underlying reasons why I went after the airplane. At the time he seemed satisfied with my explanations and said nothing about any actions even being contemplated by his government. If there were any future problems they knew how to reach me. I put the whole thing down for another Vesco bluff and stood on my decision to sign the statement I had written.

I have heard nothing further on my so-called conviction, nor have I had any contact with Danny Vesco since.

It's not over yet. The Vesco hangover will last a long time and still promises a few aches and pains. I have no regrets. There are things that I have left out because of space or because they would add little more to the whole picture. I didn't tell about Bob Vesco breaking the bank at Paradise Island for a hundred grand, hootin' and hollerin' like a cowboy. And I forgot to mention how he wanted to impress the Spanish prince with a Vesco menu and had Lou Notte fly first-class from Newark to Madrid with over a hundred pounds of chopped beef, pepperoni, chili sauce, and hot dog and hamburger buns. Or how he hauled his entire executive corps to the Greenbriar in West Virginia for a physical checkup and refused to submit to one himself. Nor did I tell about the times I caught him reading books on self-improvement alone in his office in the sky.

Will Vesco ever come back to the U.S.? In his own words, "NO WAY!"

How rich is Robert Vesco? Very rich—in hard money. Forget his investments, his corporations, his condominiums. He could lose them overnight in a paper shuffle and he would still be rich. I don't know how much of the reported 224,000,000 siphoned out of IOS he got away with, but he told me once that he had a quarter of a billion dollars in gold. And that was when gold was still pegged at thirty-five dollars an ounce.

And still he's on the con. I had a report that Vesco had set up a gold shares dodge in Costa Rica. He was offering these shares to German investors for heavy money. There are 1800 gold mines in Costa Rica. Only three of them are producing, but even they are barely covering their cost of operation.

Robert Vesco is still a young man—in his early forties. If he's lucky, he still has a lot of road to travel. I don't dislike him. I wish him luck, but he's going to have a lot of time to live with himself.